UNEQUAL HEALTH

Racial disparities in health and life expectancy are public health problems that have existed since before the United States became a country and affect all American's lives. On average, Black Americans have poorer overall health than White Americans and receive lower quality healthcare. This volume presents research from a broad range of academic disciplines, personal narratives, and historical sources to explain the origins of anti-Black racism and describe specific ways in which it threatens both Black Americans' health and the quality of their medical care. Using their own research and public policy expertise, the authors analyze the critical roles of individual and systemic anti-Black racism in these racial health disparities and their consequence for all Americans. They also identify viable interventions that can reduce current racial health disparities. *Unequal Health* is invaluable to professionals who study health disparities and lay people who are concerned about them.

LOUIS A. PENNER, Ph.D. is Professor Emeritus of Oncology at Wayne State University, USA. His research focuses on the causes of racial health disparities. His research team was among the first to identify implicit racial bias as a source of racial healthcare disparities. He has published more than 190 scientific articles, books, and book chapters. He is a Past President of the Society for the Psychological Study of Social Issues; and Fellow of three professional societies. He has served on advisory committees for the National Cancer Institute and given lectures on health disparities to the American Cancer Society and other healthcare organizations.

JOHN F. DOVIDIO, Ph.D. is Carl Iver Hovland Professor of Psychology and Public Health Emeritus at Yale University, USA and Senior Scientist at Diversity Science, a company that translates the latest science to build diverse and inclusive organizations. He consults regularly on issues of diversity, equity, and inclusion in healthcare and in other areas. His research interests are in racism and implicit bias. He has published over 500 articles and chapters, and he has edited or authored over a dozen books. He has received numerous scholarly awards and has served in major leadership roles in several psychological organizations.

NAO HAGIWARA, Ph.D. is Professor of Public Health at the University of Virginia, USA. With training background in basic experimental social psychology, she grounds her applied health and healthcare disparities research in social psychology theories of stereotyping, prejudice, and discrimination. She has obtained multiple NIH grants on healthcare providers' implicit bias and published over 50 scientific articles and book chapters. Her recent work on provider implicit bias has appeared in flagship journals and scientific magazines, such as the Lancet and Scientific American.

BRIAN D. SMEDLEY, Ph.D. is an Equity Scholar at the Urban Institute, USA where he conducts research and policy analysis to address the impact of structural and institutional forms of racism on health. Previously, he held leadership positions at the American Psychological Association, National Collaborative for Health Equity, Joint Center for Political and Economic Studies, The Opportunity Agenda, and the Institute of Medicine (now National Academy of Medicine). Among his awards and distinctions, Dr. Smedley has been honored by the U.S. Congressional Black Caucus, American Public Health Association, American Psychological Association, and National Academy of Sciences. Both he and Dr. Dovidio were part of the Committee that produced the Institute of Medicine's landmark volume, "Unequal Treatment."

UNEQUAL HEALTH

*Anti-Black Racism and the Threat
to America's Health*

LOUIS A. PENNER

Wayne State University

JOHN F. DOVIDIO

Yale University and Diversity Science

NAO HAGIWARA

University of Virginia

BRIAN D. SMEDLEY

Urban Institute

CAMBRIDGE
UNIVERSITY PRESS

Shaftesbury Road, Cambridge CB2 8EA, United Kingdom

One Liberty Plaza, 20th Floor, New York, NY 10006, USA

477 Williamstown Road, Port Melbourne, VIC 3207, Australia

314–321, 3rd Floor, Plot 3, Splendor Forum, Jasola District Centre, New Delhi – 110025, India

103 Penang Road, #05–06/07, Visioncrest Commercial, Singapore 238467

Cambridge University Press is part of Cambridge University Press & Assessment, a department of the University of Cambridge.

We share the University's mission to contribute to society through the pursuit of education, learning and research at the highest international levels of excellence.

www.cambridge.org
Information on this title: www.cambridge.org/9781316519486

DOI: 10.1017/9781009023825

First published 2023

A catalogue record for this publication is available from the British Library.

A Cataloging-in-Publication data record for this book is available from the Library of Congress.

ISBN 978-1-316-51948-6 Hardback

Brian Smedley:
To my mother, Audrey, whose scholarship helped illuminate how the concept of race originated as an instrument of White supremacist ideology; to her grandchildren, Avery and David, who are building a new world of possibilities in their own ways; and to my wife, Carla, who inspires me daily. May we each bring our light together for a brighter future.

Endorsements

This book provides a timely and comprehensive analysis of America's most pressing societal dilemma – persistent, seemingly intractable racial health disparities. It is solution-focused, combining in-depth discussion of social determinants of health with a clear depiction of the inequities in the healthcare system. I highly recommend this book.

—Gail C. Christopher, National Collaborative for Health Equity, USA

For African Americans and for other Americans, it is difficult to witness the profound racial disparities in health and healthcare in our society and still trust the beneficence of this society. This book documents and explains those disparities as well as any book I've seen. But it also spells out plausible, feasible paths to remedy. Therein lies its major contribution: Against a backdrop of despair, it offers hope that, if taken up, can help renew our society. This book is a must read.

—Claude M. Steele, Stanford University, USA

Unequal Health succinctly synthesizes the root causes of health inequalities, backed by decades of health and healthcare evidence, practice, and the voices of racially and ethnically minoritized groups. This timely and well-written text does a phenomenal job of chronicling how we got here, where "here" is, and where we are going concerning the role of anti-Black racism in health and healthcare inequalities. After reading the first chapter, I knew this book would be one of the BEST evidence-based texts chronicling health inequities in our field. I found something interesting and insightful with the turn of each page.

—Daphne C. Watkins, University of Michigan, USA

Contents

Figures

Tables

Foreword

Black people are the least healthy population in America. This fact has been copiously documented for over a century. For the past quarter of a century, researchers have described reasons for this inequity. And for over a half century, policymakers have spent billions of dollars to reverse it and achieve health equity for Black people and all others. Yet, while some progress has been made, Black people overall still live sicker and die quicker than every other racial and ethnic group in America.

To be sure, we have made great strides toward improving overall health outcomes, and in some cases, we have also marginally improved health equity. For some cancers such as breast cancer, Black people now have lower incidence rates (though higher mortality rates) than White people. White adults have a higher rate of mental illness with accompanying substance use disorder (36 percent) than Black adults (28 percent). During the decade between 1999 and 2019, the gap between Black and White deaths due to cardiovascular disease narrowed. But, despite this progress, overall health outcomes continue to reflect egregious health and healthcare disparities between Black and other populations. Cardiovascular mortality in 2019 was 1.32 times higher for Black women than White women; it was 1.33 times higher for Black men than for White men. For the past century, Black infant mortality rates have been more than twice as high as the rates for White infants. Life expectancy at birth for Black people today is only 70.8 years compared to 76.4 years for White people, and this gap is wider today than it was at the turn of the twentieth century when life expectancy data were first collected in the United States.

Some racial health disparities are getting worse instead of better. Between 2016 and 2018, Black women suffered pregnancy-related death within one year of pregnancy at a rate of 41.4 per 100,000, outpacing this tragedy for American Indian and Alaskan Native women (26.5 per 100,000), White women (13.7 per 100,000), and Latinx women (11.2 per 100,000) women, and the gap is widening. In 2021, Black people had the largest share of diabetes diagnoses (16 percent). Death rates due to stroke among non-Hispanic Black adults aged 35 to 64 years in 2019 were 2.4 times that of their non-Hispanic White counterparts. Among people aged 13 and older living with a diagnosed HIV infection, Black people have the lowest suppression rate (61 percent), followed by American Indians and Alaskan Natives (63 percent), while White people had the highest rate (71 percent) during 2019. These disparities worsened significantly during the height of the COVID-19 pandemic when American Indians and Alaska Natives suffered the greatest age-adjusted risk of infection, hospitalization, and death from the coronavirus of any racial group followed by Black people.

Some would point to health behavior statistics to explain these disparities. Black people do not smoke more than White people, but they have much more difficulty quitting. Black people and Native Hawaiians have the highest rates of obesity (43 percent) as compared to American Indian (39 percent), Latinx (37 percent), and White (32 percent) adults. Some politicians and even a few medical professionals surprisingly still cling to long discredited biological and genetic explanations for health disparities. However, Drs. Louis Penner, John Dovidio, Nao Hagiwara, and Brian Smedley have written a definitive resource for understanding and addressing the true causes of the racial health disparities that Black people experience. These authors have compiled an impressive collection of empirical data, which they carefully and insightfully analyze in *Unequal Health: Anti-Black Racism and the Threat to America's Health* to present a courageous, comprehensive, and definitive explanation of why Black people have endured the worst overall health outcomes of any population groups for hundreds of years. In this book, four preeminent social science scholars make a powerfully persuasive case for their assertion that anti-Black racism best explains the persistent and pernicious harm to the basic human right to good health of Black Americans.

As others have, these researchers document socio-economic disparities that reflect systemic anti-Black racism and its effect on Black people's health. They also catalog laws and policies that have ensured a systemic deprivation of the neighborhood resources required for all humans to enjoy good health – decent education, fair earnings, well-built and maintained housing, clean air, fresh water, and healthy, affordable food. The authors document disparities in healthcare access and quality, and the dearth of Black physicians. But this research team goes further than treading the now familiar territory that describes racial health disparities and its causes.

In this book, the authors turn a research psychologist's lens on understanding health disparities to amplify and deepen our appreciation of how anti-Black racism is the underlying cause of the causes of health disparities that we have come to call the "social determinants of health." Many researchers have focused on unpacking this web of variables that comprise the "social determinants" of racial health disparities. Historians, epidemiologists, sociologists, philosophers, bioethicists, and hosts of physicians have reasoned that racial disparities in health status and outcomes derive from the interplay between complex social forces and health. More recently, Daniel Dawes in his book titled, *The Political Determinants of Health*, has taken the understanding of the social determinants a step further, providing an underlying framework of the political determinants of health to explain how governmental policies are a root cause that influences health outcomes. This present book penetrates the causes of the causes that we know as the political and social determinants of health. It explains the psychology of anti-Black racism that informs both individual and systemic social and political determinants of health.

Many have identified racism as a root cause of health disparities. Even the Centers for Disease Control identified racism as a public health threat in 2022. Moreover, once Professor Eduardo Bonilla-Silva challenged the prevailing notion that racism merely describes the objectionable prejudices of individual actors and advanced a structural understanding that racism is a *system* of institutionalized discrimination that directly informs the life chances of all in American society, the groundwork was laid to examine the health impacts of structural racism. In 2000, Dr. Camara Jones introduced a Theoretic Framework and a Gardener's Tale to do just that. Dr. Jones described three levels of racism: institutionalized, personally mediated, and internalized to understand the race-associated differences in health outcomes. And later in 2015, Drs. Jo Phelan and Bruce Link extended their ground-breaking fundamental cause theory, evaluating empirical data on race differences in health outcomes, risks, and resources to conclude that "racial inequalities in health endure primarily because racism is a fundamental cause of racial differences in socioeconomic status and socioeconomic status is a fundamental cause of health inequality." Finally, in 2017, Zinzi Bailey, Nancy Krieger, Madina Agénor, Jasmine Graves, Natalia Linos, and Mary Basset deftly integrated the conceptualization of structural racism into the medical and scientific literature to understand the ways in which racism contributes to poor health. After an exhaustive review of the literature, they concluded that "structural racism has had a substantial role in shaping the distribution of social determinants of health and the population health profile of the USA including persistent health inequities."

The current book, however, provides the first comprehensive and wide-reaching treatment of a specific and deadly form of racism – that is anti-

Black racism that turns its gaze on the Black body, mind, and spirit specifically. Anti-Black racism, these authors explain, is historically rooted in dehumanizing assertions that Black people were of a different species than White people, experienced different emotions than White people, and therefore were undeserving of social or political equality with White people. The machinery of an entire nation's legal, medical, educational, political, economic, and even religious institutions converged on systems built on assertions that Black people were more animal than human. These institutions were fueled by stereotypes and beliefs that quite literally confounded causes and effects to create an ideology of anti-Blackness.

The authors explain that anti-Black racist ideology is an elegant form of "getting it backwards." The authors begin with the premise that all humans seek to understand the information that comes to them in a complex world, and they seek to make sense quickly and efficiently as possible. Therefore, they use heuristics or "short-cuts" to interpret the evidence they see in the world around them. The problem is that they get it backwards where race is concerned. Anti-Black racism observes patterns of behavior and conditions that Black people are overrepresented in, and then ascribes the *impact* of the conditions as character traits of the people. The authors explain this as "confirmation bias." In other words, anti-Black racism turns the fact that slavery and chronic poverty have kept large segments of the Black population uneducated and underemployed into evidence that erroneously confirms that Black people are unintelligent and lazy. Drs. Penner, Dovidio, Hagiwara, and Smedley deftly trace the impact of this twisted thinking from slavery to modern day medicine to show how the underlying psychology of individualized anti-Black bias has been institutionalized in residential segregation, neighborhood deprivation, and the medical care industry itself throughout history. These authors also do a beautiful job of explaining the psychological stress of persistent racism as well as the neural processes that physiologically increase the risk of diabetes, cardiovascular disease, hypertension, and mental illness. The result is an elegant understanding both the science and the sociology of how anti-Black racism has been operationalized in the past, and why it persists to limit the quality and length of life for Black people in the United States today.

This book follows in the grand and pioneering tradition of the great African American scholar and activist, William Edward Burghardt Du Bois by focusing courageously on Black health in particular. They, like Du Bois, make no apology for their focus and recognize that though other health disparities are important, the problem of Black health disparities is uniquely deserving of study and solutions. Between 1896 and 1906, Du Bois published a set of sociological studies called "Studies of Negro Problems." These eleven reports were each accompanied by conferences held at Atlanta University and, according to Du Bois, were aimed at exhaustive studies of the human conditions of the physical, social, religious, and political life of the Negro Americans. Du Bois was the first intellectual to examine the social and environmental sources of health inequalities that characterized disparate morbidity. But most importantly, he labored to discredit the prevailing pseudo-scientific claims that dominated medical literature at the turn of the twentieth century, which asserted that the inequitable health outcomes between Black people and White people were due to the biological inferiority of Black people. Commentators described the groundbreaking studies as employing "the first significant scientific approach to the health problems and biological study of the Negro." In "The Health and Physique of the Negro American," Du Bois begins by citing the "new knowledge that has not yet reached the common schools" to refute unimportant anthropological notions and challenge false assertions that the physical size of the head and brain could be correlated with the intelligence and superiority of White people over Black people. Then, as now, Du Bois had to fight against the biologization of race, arguing in 1906 that the "so-called Negro races" had such "a great variety of human types and mixtures of blood representing at bottom a human variation, . . . and which has since intermingled with these races in all degrees of admixture so that today no absolute separating line can be drawn" (p. 18). He then catalogued a series of objections to arguments that the "Negro brain is smaller than the Caucasian."

> This Negro population, which began to reach the confines of the present United States in 1691, has increased until in 1900 in the continental United States it numbered 8,833,994 souls, or today, 1906, not less than 9,500,000. The first and usual assumption concerning this race is that it represents a pure Negro type. This is an error. Outside the question of what the pure Negro type is, the Negro-American represents a very wide and thorough blending of nearly all African people from north to south; and more than that, it is to a far larger extent than many realize, a blending of European and African blood. (Du Bois, p. 28)

Sadly, the authors of the present book must also begin their rigorous empiricism over 117 years later by similarly dismantling and discrediting the same fallacious claims of biological determinism. But they do so by soundly gathering the scientific evidence that explains the impact that even today has proponents who assert the inferiority of Black people as compared to White people that Du Bois faced down. But this book goes further – much further. It boldly and forthrightly calls out the insidiously pernicious doctrine of anti-Black racism as the underlying ideology that is responsible not only for the endurance that the biologization of race has enjoyed, but also to offer a bold and fresh set of insights into the causes, extent, and solutions to Black health disparities themselves. Drs. Penner, Dovidio, Hagiwara, and Smedley have turned their considerable expertise as four of the nation's foremost health disparity researchers to understand and attack what the great Du Bois called "the greatest group of social problems that has ever faced the nation" – the pervasive problem of Black people "dying before their time," living sicker, and dying quicker than White people all across America.

In his book, *The Philadelphia Negro*, Du Bois was the first researcher to explain that the housing, neighborhood, economic, and political drivers of disparate health outcome are, in turn, the drivers of excess morbidity and mortality among Black people as compared to their White counterparts. The genius of this work was to provide epidemiological data that correlated the living conditions and neighborhood variability of both Black patients and White patients with the death rates they suffered. The evidence was that Black mortality was higher than White mortality not because of race but because of the unsanitary slum conditions that led to patients – whether Black or White – dying disproportionately from consumption. The intriguing contribution of the present work is not the information that debunks the myth of biological race, but rather the refinement in our understanding of how the anti-Black racism that it spawned has seeped not only into laws and policies that endure to today but also into the academic and clinical settings of even the most enlightened scholars.

Du Bois was truly the first scholar to correlate social conditions with the inequitable health outcomes of Black Americans. As Professor Ruqaiijah Yearby makes clear, the concept that social conditions were the driving determinate of Black health originated with Dr. Du Bois. But although Du Bois' conceptual framework was first published in 1896, it was only when it was systematically applied to White patients by White scholars that Du Bois' method for interpreting disparate death rates through the variability of living and social conditions became broadly accepted. Sir Michael Marmot conducted two longitudinal studies of British civil servants between 1967 to 1977 (Whitehall I study) and between 1985 and 1988 (Whitehall II) to reveal a "steep inverse association between social class, as assessed by grade of employment, and mortality from a wide range of diseases," which he called the "social gradient." When Marmot reported that these "*social* determinants of health inequalities" could be changed by policy intervention, organizations such as the World Health Organization and others began to introduce the importance of developing health policy beyond the health sector in order to combat disparately poor population health. Marmot did not cite Du Bois.

Yet, Marmot's work quite literally disrupted all purely and erroneously medicalized understandings of health disparities and informed a new public health approach to tackling health disparities. This approach has guided public health experts such as Paula Lanzt, Richard Lichtenstein, Harold Pollack, and Alvin Tarlov, who quantified the estimated impact of social determinants and then called for corresponding health policy interventions aimed at eradicating health disparities to extend beyond the provision of medical care. They argued that health policy resources must improve the "socioeconomic conditions that give rise to health vulnerability in the first place." Meanwhile, scholars such as Margaret Whitehead and Paula Braveman importantly called for more precise understandings of health inequality and disparities linking them to groups who "persistently experienced social disadvantage or discrimination." And as noted earlier, Jo Phelan and Bruce Link concluded that racism itself is a fundamental cause of health inequality in the United States. They situated their analysis on Du Bois' foundational research on health and living conditions in Philadelphia. Phelan and Link constructed a model that explained that socioeconomic disparities alone could not account for racial differences in health outcomes, while systematic discrimination based on race operated independently of socioeconomic status, through multiple mechanisms such as access to power, social networks, and medical care to produce persistent health inequality.

Perhaps the most impactful contribution from the current excellent book will be the set of solutions for change that its authors present. By their admission, their proposals are bold and "immodest." Their boldness is, perhaps, one of the most important contributions of their work. Regrettably, these authors shrink back from calling for reparations to address the massive wealth gap between Blacks and Whites. But they do propose important, specific, and detailed reforms that can reduce the impact of implicit racial biases generally and in law enforcement. They urge equalizing school funding to remove the $23 billion gap that distinguishes the resources available to children in predominately Black districts from children in White school districts. They propose reducing the effects of anti-Black racism on housing segregation by investing in

Opportunity Zones, by providing Housing Choice Vouchers, enhancing the "Affirmatively Furthering Fair Housing" initiative, and emulating the success of the Moving-To-Opportunity lessons learned. The group forthrightly supports a Single Payer System to improve healthcare access, quality, and affordability while challenging healthcare providers to leverage their position as "anchor institutions," "upstream healthcare" delivery systems, and responsible and transparent data collection to shed light on disparate distribution of medical care services by race, ethnicity, and other metrics. In short, the authors recommend fundamental changes in the way that health care is delivered.

This book ends each chapter with a section called "Putting It All Together." In my view, that is exactly what Drs. Penner, Dovidio, Hagiwara, and Smedley have done. In *Unequal Health: Anti-Black Racism and the Threat to America's Health* they have put together a treatise on Black health disparities' origins, impacts, and cures to guide real and lasting change going forward.

Dayna Bowen Matthew, J.D.

Prologue

From the earliest days of the COVID-19 pandemic, headlines in the popular media regularly highlighted the disproportionate impact of the virus on Black Americans. Relative to White Americans, Black Americans were much more likely to be infected with, hospitalized for, and die from COVID-19. Some media outlets focused as much on this aspect of the COVID pandemic as they did on the pandemic itself. Most Americans were puzzled and surprised by this massive health disparity.

However, the issues that the media and the public were trying to understand were actually just the latest manifestations of racial inequities in health. Even as the health of all Americans has, on average, dramatically improved over the last 100 years (or at least until the pandemic), the size of racial health disparities in the incidence of certain diseases and the mortality rates associated with them have remained largely unchanged. For centuries, Black Americans have been much more likely than White Americans to contract most diseases, and they have been much more likely than White Americans to die from these same diseases. The core thesis of this book is that anti-Black racism plays a very significant role in these racial health disparities. That is, racism, which is a part of American culture, is the "culprit" in the very long story of racial health disparities in the United States. Anti-Black racism is an important cause of the economic and social conditions that lead to poorer health and shorter lives among Black Americans, and racism is also a major reason for the significantly poorer healthcare Black Americans receive relative to White Americans.

The kinds of health and healthcare disparities experienced by Black Americans occur for many other social groups. What members of these groups have in common with Black Americans is that they also are marginalized in some way. This can be because of their ethnicity, religion, country of origin, gender, sexual identity, or some other characteristic that engenders prejudice and discrimination similar to that experienced by Black people. Although the health needs of these other groups are no less important than those of Black Americans, we have chosen to focus on racial health and healthcare disparities of Black Americans because of their enormous scale and the extent to which they affect almost every aspect of life in contemporary American society.

The great number of Black Americans who, relative to White Americans, endure poorer health, lower quality healthcare, and the resultant greater mortality makes this a public health crisis that threatens the well-being of all Americans. But unlike most public health crises, it is not caused by a highly contagious virus, an environmental disaster, or some other "natural" process. There is a strong consensus among past and present leaders at the National Institutes of Health (NIH) and the Centers for Disease Control and Prevention (CDC), and even among the scientists who study the genetics and biology of health that anti-Black racism is a primary cause of racial health disparities. The fact that anti-Black racism is of sufficient magnitude to create widespread racial health and healthcare disparities in America directly contradicts the idea that the United States is a place where all people are treated fairly and have a basic right to good health. Racial disparities in health and healthcare are thus a grave social injustice that demands solutions.

In addition to the moral imperative, there are also significant practical reasons to address racial health disparities. The financial impact of racial health disparities on all Americans runs into hundreds of billions of dollars annually because of the expense of providing healthcare to people whose health is impaired by the effects of anti-Black racism and the costs of their lost contributions to the economy when they are too sick to work. The United States in the twenty-first century is a highly interdependent country, both economically and socially. Because of this, the health problems of one group, even a numerical minority, impacts every other group in contemporary America. Thus, solutions specifically designed to address health and healthcare disparities between Black Americans and White Americans will have cascading benefits for all Americans.

Why We Wrote This Book

The immediate impetus for writing this book was the dramatic and distressing racial disparities in the impact of the COVID-19 virus, especially during the first year of the pandemic. Although, of course, that is a topic we discuss throughout the book, this was never intended to be a book just about COVID-19-related health disparities. Rather, this book is intended to place the specific racial health disparities brought to public attention during the COVID-19 pandemic in the much broader context of anti-Black racism and the economic, social, and historical factors responsible for racial health disparities. In addition to describing the pervasive racial health disparities that exist today, we discuss the present and past *causes* of these disparities. We believe that we can use our professional training and experiences to inform readers about the various causes and consequences of poorer health among Black Americans and to offer insights about how to remediate these. Although we are all trained as psychologists, we present much more than just psychological explanations of racial health disparities. Our discussions of the causes and consequences of racial health disparities draw on the work of historians and contemporary research in medicine, political science, sociology, education, public health, and public policy. When we offer some potential solutions to this huge public health problem, we again draw from a variety of different academic disciplines and the work of both private and public institutions.

We believe the book will be valuable for professionals in a variety of different health-related fields, but the book is not directed only at them. We quite specifically wrote it so that it would be broadly accessible to a lay audience interested in the past, present, and future of race relations in the United States and their impact on health and healthcare in America. We draw on the research literature from many different academic and professional disciplines, but we also make extensive use of Black patients' first-person narratives, excerpts from newspaper articles and other media, and historical documents. We use all of these sources to place contemporary racial health disparities in the broader context of America's past treatment of Black people, the present-day status of race relations in the United States, and the fact that, as a nation, America has been unable to effectively address the causes and consequences of anti-Black racism. It is our belief that the book can make substantial contributions to solutions that constructively address racial disparities in health and healthcare.

When we began writing this book, we anticipated that it would mostly be about racial inequities in healthcare. Indeed, we do give particular emphasis to racial disparities in healthcare, which range from less access to healthcare for Black Americans than White Americans to the role of racial bias in lower quality medical care received by Black patients as compared to White patients. However, there are many more causes of racial disparities in the health of Black Americans compared to White Americans. Thus, in addition to our discussions of racial disparities in healthcare, we also consider the role of socioeconomic factors in people's health, how experiencing racial discrimination directly endangers the health of Black people, the negative health consequences of racially segregated neighborhoods for the health of the Black residents of these communities, and the historical legacy of both the formal and informal racism in American medicine that affects contemporary racial disparities in healthcare.

Of course, we are not the first social scientists to identify and write about racial health disparities. The eminent Black sociologist, W. E. B. Du Bois, documented such disparities over a century ago. We are also far from being alone in this enterprise today. Many scholars in the behavioral sciences, medicine, and public health are making major contributions to understanding the problems and proposing solutions. We acknowledge their work throughout the book. Our goal is to use their work and our own to present a comprehensive, multilevel examination of racial health disparities that draws upon medical research, a variety of other different academic disciplines, and day-to-day experiences recounted by Black Americans.

The information and insights we attempt to convey in this book may sometimes be discouraging because of the enormity of challenges, and the solutions we propose may arouse resistance by some. Nevertheless, knowledge is power, and this book is intended to empower and inspire readers to begin their personal and professional journeys to address unjust racial disparities in health and healthcare, and to promote social equity.

Who We Are

The four co-authors of this book share a common long-term interest in the broad causes and consequences of anti-Black racism and its more specific role in racial disparities in health and healthcare. However, we are diverse in our backgrounds, perspectives, experience, and expertise. Two of us identify as White, one as Black, and another as Asian (Japanese). Jack Dovidio, Nao Hagiwara, and Lou Penner all earned their Ph.D.s in social psychology; Brian Smedley's Ph.D. is in clinical psychology. Jack, Nao, and Lou began their careers as basic researchers and, over time, gravitated toward applied issues of health, with a special emphasis on the negative impact of individual racial bias on the health of Black Americans. In the course of his career, Brian has played a signficant role in shaping public policy regarding racial health and healthcare disparities, and he has held leadership positions in private and public institutions that address public policies related to health equity.

The personal and professional journeys that have brought us together around this topic are quite different but have intersected at various points. For example, a great deal of the current research on racial bias as a source of health and healthcare disparities can trace its origins to the publication of *Unequal Treatment: Confronting Racial and Ethnic Disparities in Health* by the then Institute of Medicine (IOM)[1] in 2003. Brian was the senior program officer at the IOM at that time and had primary responsibility for the coordination of the "Committee on Understanding and Eliminating Racial and Ethnic Disparities in Health Care." Jack was a member of the Committee. Brian also led the team that produced this seminal volume. Lou was a senior scientist in the Communication and Behavior Oncology Program of the Karmanos Cancer Institute, and he recruited Nao for a postdoctoral position in that program. Over the last 15 years, Lou, Jack, and Nao have co-authored multiple research papers on racial disparities in health and healthcare. These included some of the earliest reports on the effects of physician implicit racial bias in medical interactions. We had not formally collaborated with Brian before this book (other than Jack's and Brian's joint work on the IOM report), but Jack, Brian, and Lou have known each other for over 20 years, initially through joint projects with the Society of Psychological Studies for Social Issues and then through the IOM report.

Writing this book is an extension of our common professional interests in anti-Black racism and its consequences for racial health disparities. Our attempts to understand and reduce the effects of anti-Black racism is a thread that binds all of the authors of this book. However, there are different personal experiences that led each one of us to this collaborative effort. We share some of these with the readers.

John (Jack) Dovidio

I did not intend to study racial bias or racial disparities in health and healthcare. In fact, because I grew up in a segregated community as a White person I rarely thought about race or the impact of racism. But issues rooted in racism were all around me. I gradually became aware of these issues through experiences, beginning largely in college, with friends who were people of color. Slowly – way too slowly – I became aware of the profound, unjust impact of racism. This recognition fueled my academic interests, and it has sustained my work as a researcher in the study of bias for almost 50 years. But racial bias is not simply an academic issue; it is a pervasive societal problem.

[1] The Institute of Medicine (IOM) is now known as the National Academy of Medicine.

The more I came to understand the scope of the problem of racism in America through my experiences and research, the more uneasy I felt about only studying it as an academic researcher. When doors of opportunity were opened to engage in the hard, practical work of addressing racism – for example, by being on the IOM panel on racial and ethnic disparities in healthcare, and most recently through my work with Diversity Science (an organization that translates the latest research into practical and effective tools to create diverse, equitable, and inclusive institutions) – I knew that my path lay through that door. This book and the collaborations and friendships that led to this book have been the outcome of going through that door.

Nao Hagiwara

I came to the United States alone fresh out of high school, eager to study psychology. I went to a small, predominantly White college in the Appalachian Mountains in Kentucky. There, I experienced something I had never gone through in Japan because Japan is a racially/ethnically homogeneous society – discrimination. I was ignored while waiting in lines and made fun of because of my accented English. Although these were painful experiences, they fueled my motivation to study intergroup bias as a social psychologist. A turning point in my career came when I saw Lou's advertisement for a postdoc. When I applied to the position, I simply thought the training would help me expand my research skills and knowledge in social psychology. But, a few months into my training, a tragedy happened. My partner, Brian, suffered an injury to his spinal cord due to infection and became paralyzed. At the emergency room, it was concluded initially that his case was a psychiatric one, and they tried to discharge him while he was still unable to move. Two nurses came in, asked him if he was "this weak all the time," and told him that it was just all in his head, while he was begging them to stop trying to move his body to a wheel chair. The hospital staff's treatment of him changed 180° the next morning, however, with the MRI results showing a lesion to his spinal cord; everyone suddenly became kind toward him. My partner was able to escape from horrific medical mistreatment because his "minority status" was only temporary. But, I thought to myself: How about other people who have to deal with such mistreatment all the time? In that moment, eliminating disparities in health and healthcare became my personal passion.

Lou Penner

I grew up in the 1950s in an almost exclusively White neighborhood in the South Side of Chicago. It immediately abutted poor Black neighborhoods. One of my most salient memories from this time involved my mother. We were riding in a city bus through a very poor Black neighborhood. I looked around and asked her, "Why do *these people* live like this?" She replied something to the effect that it was because the Black residents had been forced to live in these neighborhoods and had not been given the advantages we had. I am honestly not sure how she developed this view. Perhaps it was because she and my father's parents had severely suffered from anti-Semitism in eastern Europe in the early twentieth century. Whatever the origins, my parents consistently conveyed to my brother, sister, and me a naïve sort of social justice and the idea that inequality and prejudice were simply wrong. This was a filter through which I processed the things I saw as I grew up, which included witnessing both violent and nonviolent kinds of anti-Black racism. This led to my activism in social justice causes, and becoming a social psychologist, interested in prejudice and discrimination. But it was only at a fairly late stage in my career that I moved to Detroit, Michigan, and the Karmanos Cancer Institute at Wayne State University. It was there that racial disparities in health and healthcare became the primary focus of my work, as part of the research program in communication and behavioral oncology created by my wife, Teri Albrecht. Jack and Nao have played critical roles in this and many other aspects of my career. This book is a culmination of personal and professional interests in addressing some of the great social injustices I have seen over my lifetime.

Brian Smedley

Growing up in Detroit in the 1960s, I was struck by how rapidly White families left our modest but comfortable neighborhood near Six Mile Road and Livernois. My earliest memories were of playing with a diverse group of kids in and around Bagley Elementary School; by the time I was in second grade, there was but one White child left in our school. Being from a family of activists and academics helped me understand what was happening – "block busting" and White flight, which we discuss in this book. We understood that racism was pervasive, and not a problem limited to individuals' attitudes. From those early experiences, I developed an interest in continuing the work that my family exposed me to. My mother, anthropologist Dr. Audrey Smedley, broke through barriers of racism and sexism to become a leading scholar on the origin of the idea of race, and my godfather, Dr. Charles Wright, established a museum of African American history in Detroit that bears his name today. These giants remain my inspiration today.

Acknowledgments

The authors thank Yale University for its financial support for the preparation of this book. We are also very grateful to Elena Abbott for her outstanding work in the editing of the initial chapter drafts, and to Conor Duffy for his assistance with locating the references. In addition, we express our appreciation for the help, guidance, and encouragement provided by Stephen Acerra, Rowan Groat, and Beth Sexton of Cambridge University Press throughout the process of bringing this book to press.

Introduction
An American Dilemma: Racial Disparities in Health – Past and Present

> The most difficult social problem in the matter of Negro health is the peculiar attitude of the nation toward the well-being of the race.
>
> Dr. W. E. B. Du Bois, 1899 [1]

Up until the late 1970s, Detroit, Michigan, was one of the great industrial American cities. It was the home of the "big three" American automakers (Ford, General Motors, and Chrysler) and many other businesses that supported the auto industry. Most of the residents (over 63 percent) were Black people.[1] Detroit had all the problems of any large American city, but the population was stable, and the city was "healthy." Then things changed dramatically. The city's population dwindled from about 1.2 million people in 1980 to just over 670,000 in 2019. About 75 percent of its current population are people who identify as Black [2]. The primary explanation of Detroit's population loss was that people (particularly wealthier White residents) were leaving the city because of their fear of crime and the movement of jobs, including a significant number initiated by the automakers, to other places. Because of this exodus, the city's tax base became smaller, the quality of the city's public services declined, and even more people left.

These explanations for Detroit's population decline are valid but incomplete. There is another critical reason why substantially fewer people lived in Detroit in 2019 than had lived there in the past. This other reason was identified by several physicians at Wayne State University (located in Detroit). These physicians were well aware of the health problems of Black Detroit residents and wondered whether health issues may have

---

[1] The terms "Black people" (or "Black Americans") and "White people" (or "White Americans") refer to whether a person's ancestors primarily came from Africa or Europe. We use "Black" rather than "African American" because it is a more accurate and inclusive term for the Black population of the United States. Black and White are capitalized on the basis of the cultural and identity markers that have been placed on the groups over time. As discussed later in this chapter, these words have no biological or genetic meaning.

played some part in the city's loss of population. To answer this question, they gathered 19 years of data on mortality rates (i.e., deaths per 100,000 people) in the Detroit area and compared them to mortality rates in the rest of the state. More specifically, they computed something called "excess mortality," which is the number of people who die before they would normally be expected to die (i.e., at age 75).

The results were striking. The physicians found that large numbers of older Black men living in Detroit were "dying before their time." For example, the excess mortality rate among men of ages 40 to 49 and living in Detroit was almost twice as great as was the excess mortality rate for men in the same age group, who lived in the rest of Michigan. The mortality rate for Detroit men aged 50 to 59 was 122 percent higher than for men in the same age group in the rest of Michigan. If older Black men living in Detroit had simply died at the same rate as men in the rest of the state, 1,600 more of them would have been alive for each year of the study. Across the 19 years of the study, concluded well before the COVID-19 pandemic, the total excess mortality among Black men living in Detroit was over 16,000 lives. The physicians estimated that about 33 percent of Detroit's population loss over the 19 years was due to these premature deaths and the fact that there was no influx of people to replace them. Detroit was losing population not simply because people were moving away. Actually, many people – predominantly Black men – were staying in Detroit and dying before their time [3].

The phenomenon of Black people "dying before their time" is not limited to Detroit. It is a national problem. National mortality rates during the first two years of the COVID-19 pandemic revealed that Black people were disproportionately affected by the virus and died at a rate much higher than White people. Although this racial disparity in deaths declined from the beginning of 2020 to late 2022, even then Black people were still almost twice as likely to die of COVID-19 as were White people [4].

Dr. Nancy Krieger, professor of social epidemiology at Harvard University, and her colleagues further illuminated the nature of these racial disparities by comparing mortality rates during the first year of the pandemic among White people and Black people of the same age. At all ages, the mortality rate was greater for Black, Indigenous, and Other People of Color (BIPOC) than for White people, but this disparity was the greatest among younger Black Americans than White Americans. By December 2020, the death rate among Black people under 55 was 7 times greater than the death rate among White people of the same age [5]. Almost 87,000 years of potential life were lost to COVID-19 among Black people under 55, compared to 61,000 years for White people. As in the pre-COVID study in Detroit, in 2020 Black people were much more likely than White people to "die before their time." These huge COVID-19-related health disparities were put in a historical context by Dr. Anthony Fauci, director of the National Institute of Allergies and Infectious Diseases. Dr. Fauci noted that "health disparities have always existed for the African American community. . . . But here again, with the (COVID) crisis, now it's shining a bright light on how unacceptable that is" [6].

In an interview for the television show, *60 Minutes*, Dr. David Williams, professor of public health at Harvard University and one of the leading authorities on racial health disparities, succinctly described the issue of excess mortality among Black Americans. He explained, "Imagine if every single day a jumbo jet loaded with 230 African Americans took off into the sky, reached a cruising altitude, and crashed to the ground killing all aboard . . . this is exactly the impact caused by racial health disparities in the United States" [7]. But, of course, this excess mortality is not due to plane crashes; it is because of the poor health of many Black Americans and inadequacies in the healthcare they receive. While we understand and acknowledge that many other racial and ethnic groups experience health disparities relative to White Americans, this book primarily focuses on the causes of many of the health and healthcare problems experienced by Black Americans. Where relevant, we also discuss health disparities that affect members of other BIPOC groups.[2]

Health Differences versus Health Disparities: An Important Distinction

The major causes of death in the United States are diseases, and the much higher mortality rates among Black Americans reflect the fact that a substantially larger percentage of Black Americans than White Americans suffer from the most common diseases. But, even when a Black person and a White person have the same disease, the Black person is much more likely to die from it. So, the simple and striking fact is that, on average, Black Americans are much less healthy than White Americans. There are two explanations of this fact. The first is that it represents a health

[2] The health disparities between Native Americans (Indigenous Peoples) and White Americans are about as great as the Black–White disparities. With respect to ethnicity, the disparities are smaller but still significant for Americans who identify as Hispanic. There are also substantial health problems among Americans whose ancestors came from many different countries in Asia.

difference – varying rates of deaths and illnesses between two groups because of some biological or genetic difference between them. The other is that it represents a health *disparity* – varying rates of deaths and illnesses between two groups that are the result of unfair economic, political, social, and psychological processes. The central thesis of this book is that much poorer health of Black Americans relative to White Americans represents a health disparity.

We believe that these racial health disparities are largely due to one insidious aspect of the current state of race relations in the United States – anti-Black racism – the idea that Black people are in some way different from and inferior to White people. Anti-Black racism also includes the notion of White supremacy, the belief that White people are superior and should control Black people. Anti-Black racism has a long history in the United States. The clearest example of it is the enslavement of Black people for about 250 years. There were, however, many social, cultural, and political forces that followed slavery that directly and intentionally disadvantaged Black Americans. Anti-Black racism is thus, an integral part of America's history, as well as of current race relations.[3]

Across this history, anti-Black racism has been responsible for laws, public and private policies, social customs, and individual beliefs and actions that directly or indirectly harm the health of Black Americans. These actions can be blatant, but often they are subtle. And it is not uncommon for people to engage in a racist action without consciously intending to do so. But whether blatant or subtle, conscious or nonconscious, anti-Black racism is dangerous because of the outcomes it produces.[4] Anti-Black racism provides the motivation to and justification for a host of actions that directly or indirectly oppress Black people, putting their health at substantial risk. As Dr. Rodney G. Hood, a former president of the National Medical Association, wrote, "the poor health of African Americans is not a biological act of nature or an accident but can be directly attributed to the institutions of slavery and racism – circumstances under which African Americans have continuously suffered from for nearly four centuries" [8]. We agree that the inability to equitably

---

[3] Two excellent books on the history of racism in the United States from the perspective of Black Americans are *How to Be an Antiracist* by Ibram X. Kendi and *How the Word Is Passed* by Clint Smith.

[4] The word "nonconscious" means that race-related thoughts, feelings, or actions may occur without a person being fully aware of them. The word, "unconscious" is often used to describe the same thing in the research literature. We discuss nonconscious aspects of anti-Black racism at length in Chapters 1 and 6.

treat Black Americans is an "original sin" that has plagued America for over 400 years, and its impact on the health of Black Americans continues to this day. This inequitable treatment is almost entirely based on a misunderstanding of what the term "race" really represents.

Race: A Biological Myth, a Social Reality

At the core of anti-Black racism is some variant of the myth that a person's apparent race reflects some important underlying biological attributes. For centuries, race has been used as a way to classify a person as being biologically Black or White. In fact, race is really a social construct that reflects how society identifies a person based on some easily observable physical characteristics, such as skin color, hair texture, and facial features. But, race has no biological or genetic foundation. People who are identified as Black or as White share over 99 percent of their genomes in common, and there is much more genetic variation within each group (that is, among people identified as Black and among people identified as White) than between them. Thus, there is almost a complete agreement among contemporary geneticists, biological scientists, and all major medical organizations that the notion of Black people and White people being from separate and distinct biological species or groups has no scientific merit.[5] For example, in 2020, the American Medical Association (AMA) issued the following statement: "[The] AMA confirms race as a social construct. Race is a socially constructed way of grouping people, based on skin color and other apparent physical differences" [9]. Indeed, today, scientists who study the genetic origins of disease do not even include race as part of their explanations because it has no scientific value.

This does not mean that the nature of an individual's genome is unimportant or that there is no variation in gene expression among humans with significant implications for their health. There are genetic diseases (e.g., cystic fibrosis, hemophilia, Huntington's disease, sickle cell disease, Tay-Sachs disease). Further, there are a few diseases that seem to be more common among people whose ancestors are from Africa: sickle cell disease and prostate cancer, for example. But there are similar kinds of differences in a few genetic diseases among all population groups, and

---

[5] Very accessible books that address this topic are: *Fatal Invention: How Science, Politics, and Big Business Re-create Race in the Twenty-First Century* by Dorothy E. Roberts, and *The Gene: An Intimate History* by Dr. Siddhartha Mukherjee.

genetic diseases are a minute fraction of the illnesses that kill Black people in the United States.

Further, socially constructed race is about much more than how a person is identified by a society; it is also about power within that society. Identifying a group of people as belonging to a race that is different from the majority provides the basis for assigning that group a lower social and economic status. As author Ta-Nehisi Coates explains, "race is the child of racism, not the father. And the process of naming 'the people' has never been a matter of genealogy or physiognomy so much as one of hierarchy" [10].[6]

This is especially true in North America. The early European settlers were not the first to use the terms, White and Black, to describe people. But among them, the words took on special significance as a way of describing those who had power and those who did not [11]. The concept of race became a rationale for the subjugation of Black people. As Alveda King, niece of Dr. Martin Luther King Jr., explained in 2019: "Racism springs from the lie that certain human beings are less than fully human. It's a self-centered falsehood that corrupts our minds into believing we are right to treat others as we would not want to be treated" [12]. Although it is the health of Black Americans that suffers the most because of anti-Black racism, all Americans pay a substantial price for racial health disparities.

The Cost of Racial Health Disparities

Research conducted in 2020 in Texas is an excellent case study of the economic impact of racial health disparities. In Texas such disparities created excess expenditures for healthcare amounting to $1.73 billion. In addition, the cost of productivity lost due to diseases was about $870 million, and the cost of lost contributions to the economy because of premature deaths was $10.3 billion. Across these three domains, the excess costs of Black–White racial disparities in health in just one state in one year were almost $13 billion [13].

Of course, Texas is a very large state with a conservative government and legislature. Thus, more may be spent overall for healthcare than smaller states, but proportionally less may be spent on healthcare for poor, minority patients than other states. But these estimates are in line with national estimates of the costs of health disparities. An article in the

---

[6] Coates' book, *Between the World and Me*, provides an insightful and personal discussion of race in America, which takes the form of a letter from a Black father to his son.

Harvard Business Review estimated that in 2015 the annual national costs of racial health disparities were $245 billion [14].[7] Dr. Paul Farmer, professor in the Department of Global Health and Social Medicine at Harvard Medical School and a long time advocate for healthcare equity, succinctly summarized this issue when he said that "it is very expensive to give mediocre medical care to poor or near-poor people living in a rich country" [15].

Not included in those estimates are the social, economic, and educational costs to the *individuals* who are the victims of racial disparities in healthcare. Serious medical problems almost invariably put a strain on personal and familial relationships. This may be especially true for women, who are much more likely to be abandoned by their partners after a serious medical problem [16]. For example, women with a brain tumor have ten times the risk of a divorce as do men with the same disease [17]. Serious diseases also very often prevent people from working and earning a living. This, in turn, prevents them or members of their families from obtaining an education that would increase their social and economic mobility. Thus, costs of healthcare disparities are intergenerational and grow, perhaps exponentially, over time.

Two Kinds of Anti-Black Racism

Social scientists and other scholars who study anti-Black racism usually talk about two different kinds of racism. They distinguish between racist thoughts and actions among individuals (*individual racism*) from racism that is embedded in the practices, policies, laws, and cultural values of a society (*systemic racism*). Both types of racism play critical roles in racial health disparities, but they do so in different ways.

Individual Racism

Individual racism involves negative thoughts (i.e., negative beliefs about Black people's personal and physical traits) and negative feelings (i.e., racial bias) toward Black people. These thoughts are usually called "stereotypes," a term first introduced in the 1920s by the famed journalist, Walter Lippmann. He described a stereotype as "a picture in our head" [18]. When applied to perceptions of social groups, a stereotype is the information people carry in their minds about the nature of people whom they

---

[7] The costs of the same kinds of disparities for the Hispanic population in Texas, which is somewhat larger than the Black population, was almost $14 billion.

believe share some characteristic in common. Together negative thoughts and feelings about Black people lead to unfair, discriminatory behaviors that harm individual Black people or Black people as a group. Many people thought that when Barack Obama was elected as president, America had become a "post-racial society" – that is, a place where a person's race no longer mattered. Indeed, some people claim, "When I meet a person, I just don't see their color or race." They describe themselves as being "colorblind."

There is, however, substantial research in social and cognitive psychology that disputes the accuracy of such claims. When people meet another person, they invariably see their race – immediately and automatically – and they use this information to categorize that person in certain ways. This process, known as "social categorization," forms the foundation for individual racism. Once people are identified as a member of a particular social group, stereotypes about them and feelings toward them are more or less automatically activated.

Individual racism greatly influences the actions that White people take toward Black people in a variety of ways. Substantial media attention has been given to one way it affects people's actions – when a White police officer badly mistreats or even kills a Black person who has been detained. However, the effects of individual racism are not confined to these dramatic and horrific examples of Black people being brutalized.

Individual racism also affects how White people make decisions about and act toward Black Americans in many different aspects of everyday life. This includes what businesses they patronize, what schools they send their children to, what political candidate they support, what movies or TV shows they watch, what friends they choose to have, and a host of other things in their day-to-day lives. In sum, individual racism in the form of anti-Black racism substantially determines how a White person or group of White people treat Black people.

Even more insidiously, individual racism can affect how a White person treats a Black person even when the White person does not want this to happen. For example, a White person who is racially biased against Black people may work hard not to show this bias, but their deeply held prejudice and negative stereotypes (sometimes held nonconsciously) often can "leak out" in actions that harm the Black person in some way. These behaviors could include unintentional "microaggressions" (e.g., expressing surprise at a Black person's expertise or professional status or checking your wallet when a Black person passes by). Microaggressions also occur in conversations with Black people in the form of behaviors that signal psychological discomfort, distancing, or lack of respect. Discomfort and distancing are manifested in making less eye contact, talking less, making more speech errors, maintaining greater physical distance, and adopting a closed body posture. Lack of regard can be seen in frequent interruptions and talk-overs, as well as looking away when a Black person speaks.

Irrespective of a person's intent to minimize their racist actions, individual racism can do great harm to the Black person who is its target. Often racist actions can have immediate material consequences, such as restricting someone's freedom or creating conditions that place them at a serious social, economic, and educational disadvantage. Further, as we discuss in Chapter 2, they can do great physical and psychological damage with direct implications for a person's health.

It may give us false comfort to think that individual racism is confined to a small number of Americans who, for a variety of reasons, espouse openly racist feelings. When we think of racists, the images that may come to mind are of armed "alt-right" White supremist groups marching in the streets, carrying flags with swastikas on them and yelling racial epitaphs. But the reality is that most Americans harbor, sometimes nonconsciously, thoughts and feelings that are racist to some degree.

Individual racism is woven into the fabric of most Americans' thoughts and feelings, but this is particularly so for White Americans. Racial biases develop early in life, at least by the time a child is age five and possibly as early as age three [19]. In a country where individual racism's long legacy has made a person's race such a critical aspect of who they are, race is and will probably always be a very important part of how individual White people think about Black people and their personal characteristics. (In the next chapter we discuss the historical events and higher-order mental processes that have made individual racism so pervasive in America today.)

Whether individual racism is conscious or nonconscious, intentional or unintentional, the consequences for Black Americans are similar – fewer economic and social opportunities and a raft of disadvantages. Individual racism, thus, tips the scales, such that Black people are disadvantaged, and White people are advantaged. For example, discrimination in hiring is one very important area in which Black people were historically disadvantaged. The Civil Rights Act of 1964 made it illegal to discriminate against Black people in hiring decisions, but researchers have studied whether the law actually eliminated this kind of individual racial discrimination.

One way to answer this question is to conduct something called an audit study. In an audit study, two résumés that are identical with regard to an applicant's professional qualifications are sent out to potential employers.

However, one version contains information that clearly suggests that one applicant is White, and the other version that the applicant is Black (e.g., giving them stereotypically White or Black names). This is done to eliminate the possibility that one could justify any racial differences in responses to an applicant on the basis of their actual qualifications. One analysis combined the results of 28 separate audit studies conducted between 1989 and 2017.[8] The researchers analyzed over 55,000 applications for over 22,000 jobs and found that White "applicants" received 36 percent more callbacks from the potential employers than did Black "applicants" [20]. Importantly, the size of this disparity did not change across the 28 years studied. Audit studies of racial discrimination in the renting and selling of housing show similar kinds of racial disparities. So, individual racism often persists even long after laws have been passed that prohibit it. It is also still present among healthcare professionals and creates racial disparities in the quality of healthcare patients receive. For example, over the last 15 or so years, almost every medical facility in the United States has implemented some kind of anti-bias training. Despite such programs, researchers find that physicians still consistently disparage their Black patients in the notes they make about their cases [21] (see Chapter 6).

Systemic Racism
Systemic racism encompasses a broad range of societal standards and cultural values, as well as formal practices, policies, and laws that systematically disadvantage Black Americans relative to White Americans. These practices can occur in large and small institutions in both the public and private sectors (which is sometimes termed "institutional racism"). It represents a social, economic, political, and legal system that essentially legitimizes racism and inequity by making it a "normal" part of everyday life. The fact that this kind of racism permeates all essential facets of Black American's lives has led some researchers to characterize it as "atmospheric racism" [22]. Its effects can be seen in the vast racial disparities in the income and wealth of Black Americans versus White Americans, and a similar kind of disparity in political power. These things, along with a host of other consequences of systemic racism, endanger the health of Black Americans.

[8] This kind of study is called a meta-analysis. The results of many different studies are statistically combined to produce an estimate of the consistency and strength of some finding or relationship between two variables. Meta-analyses are widely used in studies of racial health disparities.

Historically, the most obvious and dramatic example of systemic racism in the United States was the legalization of slavery. The notion that enslaved people had no legal rights and could be "owned" by another person was written into laws at all three levels of government (i.e., local, state, and federal) and reinforced by numerous court decisions, including those made by the US Supreme Court before slavery was finally ended by the 13th Amendment. However, formal laws and informal customs and practices have resulted in the continued social dominance of White Americans over Black Americans.

For example, after the Civil War ended, as part of a desire to resolve some of the enormous racial inequities of slavery, the US Congress passed the Reconstruction Act of 1867. It established a list of things southern states needed to do to be readmitted to the Union. These involved endorsing the constitutional amendments that gave Black residents of these states the same set of political and economic rights as the White residents. Federal troops were sent into many of these states to ensure that promised changes were translated into actual changes in the economic and political structure of states in the former Confederacy. These efforts should have given formerly enslaved Black people more political power and control, as well as many more personal rights, but there was massive political resistance to the Reconstruction Act and the political, economic, and social rights it gave to Black Americans. Thus, Reconstruction was short-lived; it ended 10 years after Congress had enacted it.

Shortly after Reconstruction ended, all the states that had been part of the Confederacy passed a number of laws that collectively came be known as "Jim Crow" laws [23]. Similar laws were later enacted by some states outside the former Confederacy. These laws legalized racial segregation and ensured that the legal and social status of Black residents remained significantly lower than that of White residents.[9] Many states incorporated biology, such as the "one-drop rule," into their Jim Crow laws. These laws proclaimed that a person with any Black ancestry (just one drop of "Black blood") was legally Black. That is, if it could be found that even a very distant ancestor of a person was Black, then that person was also Black. Some examples of Jim Crow laws were that Black people could not own property, vote, or serve on juries; they had to attend segregated

---

[9] Laws that specifically target Black people or other groups and deprive them of certain rights and privileges are examples of "structural racism." They often provide a legal basis for certain aspects of systemic racism. Because these laws place Black people and many other groups at a fundamental disadvantage, their impact continues long after the laws are repealed.

schools that received substantially fewer resources than White schools in the same area; they could not live in certain neighborhoods, shop in certain stores, or use the same public facilities as White people; and if they could find medical care, it was segregated and far inferior to the medical care available to White people. The overall consequence of Jim Crow laws was described by the psychologist Dr. John Dollard, who extensively studied their effects in the 1930s by going to southern towns. He concluded that "the Negro must haul down his social expectations and resign himself to relative immobility" [24]. The Jim Crow laws rendered the Black people who lived under them virtually powerless.

These racist laws covered every aspect of a Black person's life. For example, in Alabama it was unlawful "for a negro and white person to play together or in company with each other at any game of pool or billiards." They even reached into people's bedrooms in the form of anti-miscegenation laws, which made it illegal for people identified as Black and as White to marry or have any sort of sexual relations. As another example, in Florida, the anti-miscegenation law read, "All marriages between a white person and a negro, or between a white person and a person of negro descent to the fourth generation inclusive, are hereby forever prohibited."[10]

And, there were many Jim Crow laws that even tried to control what people said or wrote about the rights of Black Americans. The state of Mississippi actually banned people from promoting equality between its Black residents and White residents: "Promotion of Equality–Any person...who shall be guilty of printing, publishing, or circulating printed, typewritten or written matter urging or presenting for public acceptance or general information, arguments or suggestions in favor of social equality or of intermarriage between whites and negroes, shall be guilty of a misde-meanor and subject to fine or not exceeding five hundred (500.00) dollars or imprisonment not exceeding six (6) months or both" [25]. And, of course, Jim Crow laws rigidly segregated medical care in the southern United States until 1964. Because of this, there was little adequate medical care for Black people in these states.

---

[10] It was not until 1967 that the US Supreme Court ruled that the right to an interracial marriage was protected by the "Equal Protection and Due Process" clauses of the 14th Amendment to the US Constitution. It made the same ruling about same-sex marriage in 2015. In 2022, the US Congress passed the "Respect for Marriage Act," which guaranteed the legal validity of both interracial and same-sex marriages. They did this after the Court ruled that the same clauses in the 14th Amendment did not guarantee a woman's right to an abortion.

Systemic racism has been used to maintain White dominance throughout the US history. It has caused harm to every racial or ethnic minority group in the United States. From the sixteenth to the nineteenth century, large numbers of Indigenous Peoples were enslaved in the American Southwest [26]. In addition, laws that restricted a host of their rights resulted in enormous damage to the lives and traditions of Indigenous Peoples that affect them to this day. Their land was taken, they were forced to move from their original homeland to distant locations, denied basic rights of self-governance, and their children were forced to attend residential schools, where the curricula deprived them from knowing about their cultural heritage [27]. A visit to most contemporary "Indian" reservations will show the long-lasting and devastating effects of the racism directed at them. ("Indian" is the term used by the Federal Agency responsible for these reservations.) At one time, people of Chinese ancestry who had lived in America for many decades were denied the right to become US citizens because they were not considered to be "White." During World War II, laws were passed that put over 100,000 people of Japanese descent, the majority of whom were US citizens, in internment camps [28]. Many states still have anti-immigration laws that almost exclusively target Hispanic immigrants. ("Hispanic" is a U. S. government demographic designation. Some individuals prefer "Latino/a" or "Latinx" in place of Hispanic.)

Racism in the Civil Rights Era
It was not until the 1950s and 1960s that actions in the courts and Congress began to dismantle some of the laws that were part of systemic racism. For example, in 1954, the Supreme Court ruled that segregating people by race in "separate but equal" public schools (and other facilities) was unconstitutional. In 1964, Congress passed the Civil Rights Act that, in addition to prohibiting racial discrimination in employment, banned racial discrimination in restaurants, hotels, and public facilities, such as bathrooms and service stations. But, there was an important qualifier to this law. The law only applied to entities that engaged in interstate commerce or received federal funds. This left plenty of room for racial exclusion to continue. Private medical facilities that did not receive funds from the US government continued to exclude Black patients for several more years.

Because of the 1964 Civil Rights Act and subsequent acts passed in 1968 and 1988 that prohibited racial discrimination in housing and numerous court decisions upholding these laws, there are no longer any statutes in the United States that *explicitly* target the rights of people of color. But, the spirit of the structural or legal part of systemic racism is not gone. In the 2020s, laws were passed in several states that were clearly intended to restrict the voting rights of Black and other minority voters. Once again, there were laws on the books that were intended to deprive Black Americans of their basic rights.

One major problem in addressing contemporary systemic racism and its consequences for the health of Black Americans is that it is not as blatant and obvious today as it was in the past. Further, it is so ingrained in American society that it may not stand out. As Kareem Abdul-Jabbar, an author and Hall of Fame basketball player, noted, "Racism in America is like dust in the air. It seems invisible – until you let the sun in. Then you see it's everywhere" [29]. But not everyone sees it. As a result, a substantial portion of White Americans think of racism primarily as a relic of the past, when laws formally restricted the freedom of Black people in almost every aspect of their lives. Indeed, a large number of politicians and their followers have vigorously disputed the notion that systemic racism is real and still a major social problem. They want, for example, to ban classes that taught about racism as it existed in the past and exists today. As of 2023, a total of twenty-three states have passed or are in the process of passing laws that would at least severely restrict the way public schools teach students about racism and/or the history of racism in the United States.

Thus, systemic racism is just as real as it was in our past, but it is often cloaked in socially acceptable forms that do not appear to systematically disadvantage Black people until we pull the curtain back a bit. We offer a few recent examples. The National Football League (NFL) provides us with a clear instance of systemic racism in a large organization. It involves how retired players are compensated for the brain injuries they suffered while they were playing. In 2013, the NFL signed a $1 billion settlement to compensate players who had suffered brain trauma during their careers in professional football. To determine the level of brain trauma that merited compensation, the NFL used a supposedly race-neutral, "objective" criterion of the amount of decline in a player's cognitive functioning. But, this objective criterion was different for Black and for White ex-players. The NFL justified this by using a practice called "race norming." Race norming simply means that separate norms or averages for performance on some tests are created for Black people and White people; in race norming, an individual's score is only compared to other people of the same race. This was originally done on tests of things such as job skills or intellectual ability because it was believed that socioeconomic hardships or bias in the test itself could put Black test-takers at an unfair disadvantage. Race norming would correct this.

Even critics agreed that this norming in that context was a well-intentioned idea. But, the NFL used it in a way that made it more difficult for Black, relative to White, ex-football players to receive compensation for their injuries. The criteria for cognitive decline were based on a player's current level of cognitive function compared to cognitive functioning for someone with mild or moderate dementia. But, this left open the question of mild or moderate dementia among which group of people? The NFL used different norms for dementia in Black people and White people, with the assumption that all Black people with dementia would show a substantially lower level of cognitive functioning to be classified as having dementia compared to White people. This virtually assured that the difference between an ex-player's level of cognitive functioning and the norm for their race would be much smaller for Black than White ex-players. As a result, the percentage of Black ex-players' claims that were denied by the NFL was much higher than the percentage for White ex-players. In 2022, after numerous legal challenges, the NFL finally agreed that there was no scientific basis for using such race-based norms and said that it would stop this way of deciding who was eligible for compensation [30]. (We do not know, however, if this agreement will compensate the families of Black ex-players who died of brain injuries before it was reached.) This case illustrates how large institutions may engage in practices that are presented as "fair" and "free of racial bias" but, in fact, are grossly unfair in their consequences for Black people.

Systemic racism also pervades health and healthcare in the United States, but sometimes it is quite subtle and not obviously racist. Consider how a community might decide where to put vaccination centers for COVID-19. In 2020, a National Public Radio (NPR) investigation revealed that, in Dallas, Texas, there were three times as many COVID testing sites in the neighborhoods where the residents were predominantly wealthy and White than in the neighborhoods where the residents were predominantly poor and Black [31]. As the result of this disparity in testing, it appeared that the COVID-19 problem was greater in the wealthy White neighborhoods than in the poor Black neighborhoods, which would very reasonably influence where resources were placed to fight the virus, especially the distribution of vaccines.

While one cannot totally discount some intentionally racist actions being responsible for this kind of health disparity, the NPR investigation concluded that there is no evidence that any city official had intentionally decided to put fewer testing sites in certain neighborhoods because the residents were Black. Rather, the immediate causes were disparities in socioeconomic status (usually called SES) between the neighborhoods. Usually, wealthy White people can demand and support many more medical services than can poor Black people. Thus, facilities housing these services in the rich, predominantly White neighborhoods quickly became COVID testing sites. As a consequence, there were many more places to test for the coronavirus and thus more reported cases of infections.

However, the situation in Dallas begs the question of *why* the disparity in wealth and power existed in the first place. It is not much of a stretch to tie these things back to the Jim Crow laws that existed in Texas up until 60 years ago and to the institution of slavery in this region before that. So, again, we see that one of the particularly insidious aspects of systemic racism is that there is often no obvious "villain" directly responsible for some current social injustice.

"To the Full Extent of the Law": Individual and Systemic Racism Intertwined
Although individual and systemic racism are conceptually distinct concepts, in practice, they often operate in consort. One example is the enforcement of laws regarding the questioning and detention of private citizens. The US Constitution says that law enforcement officers can only detain a person if they have reason to believe the person has or is about to commit a crime. But, all 50 states have had some version of stop and frisk laws that permit a police officer to stop and frisk a person without stating a reason. For many of the laws, all that is needed to do this is "reasonable suspicion," which can be based on the person *looking* suspicious to a police officer. These laws as originally proposed appeared to be a race-neutral way to reduce crime. But, the racial disparities in the actual enforcement of these laws are glaring. Between 2004 and 2012 in New York City, 4.4 million people were detained under this law. Although the Black and Latinx residents of New York City comprised slightly over half of the city's population, they comprised 83 percent of the people stopped [32]. Because of successful legal challenges to the stop and frisk law in New York City, the number of these actions by the police declined dramatically. By 2017, it was only a fraction of what it had been earlier, but 90 percent of the people stopped were still Black residents of New York City. These patterns are replicated in most other major American cities, such as Boston and Chicago [33, 34].

A multitude of other studies show the impact of a person's race on how they are treated by the police [35]. Consider traffic stops. Black drivers are more likely to be stopped than White drivers, but the biggest difference occurs during the daytime when a driver's race can be easily identified; this difference largely disappears at night when it is more difficult to identify the race of a driver [36]. In Florida, Black drivers are twice as likely as White drivers to be pulled over for seat belt violations. In one large Florida city, Black citizens were three times more likely to get tickets for jaywalking. Black suspects stopped by the police are three times more likely to be searched. This occurs even though police are more likely to find drugs on White than Black suspects. Finally, although there is no racial difference in marijuana usage, in 2018, Black people were four times more likely to be arrested for possession of marijuana.

While some of these examples of individual and systemic racism have not directly involved health disparities, they serve to illustrate the pervasive and oppressive nature of both kinds of racism in the United States. Understanding both kinds of racism is critical to an understanding of the large racial disparities in health that exist today.

Racial Health Disparities Today: A Massive Racial Injustice

In this book, we specifically focus on the disparities between the health of groups of people in America who are socially assigned the racial designation of "Black" and people who are socially assigned the racial designation of "White." Thus, we talk about disparities between these two quite large groups, and we use statistics that provide information on *average* disparities in the current frequency (or "incidence") of some disease or the rate at which people die. But, neither Black Americans nor White Americans are a homogenous group; we acknowledge that there is enormous variability among people within either of these groups.

There is a widespread acknowledgment that White Americans represent a "melting pot" of family backgrounds, but it is less widely acknowledged that there is comparable heterogeneity among Americans who are identified as Black. Some Black Americans are the descendants of the enslaved people brought to America centuries ago; others are much more recent immigrants from different countries. These differences are not only in their nativity, heritage, and family histories but also in their particular circumstances, personal experiences, and a variety of other important ways. Thus, when we discuss some racial health disparity, we are not suggesting that all Black Americans are basically the same or are more homogenous than White Americans. To do so would be an echo of past and present racist tropes about Black Americans being indistinguishable. But, despite this substantial variability, Black Americans do share the same racial designation and the lived experiences associated with this designation. Consequently, as a group, they may experience social, economic, and political circumstances and interpersonal experiences that are different from White Americans as a group. These differences cause racial health disparities [37].

It is generally acknowledged by the Centers for Disease Control and Prevention (CDC) and other government health agencies that racial disparities in health represent a massive public health problem. It exacts an enormous physical, emotional, and social toll on all Americans, but especially Black Americans. Moreover, racial health disparities differ from other public health problems, such as salmonella in the food supply or the outbreak of certain diseases after some natural disaster pollutes the water supply. Unlike these other problems, racial health disparities are a racial injustice that threatens the fundamental right of a healthy and long life for a significant portion of the US population – Black Americans. We label it as a racial injustice because it is caused by anti-Black racism. To be more precise, anti-Black racism leads to three characteristics of modern America that endanger the health of Black Americans. They are (1) widespread racial discrimination that causes physiological and psychological responses that threaten a person's health; (2) racial housing segregation that creates neighborhoods whose residents are predominantly economically disadvantaged Black people; these neighborhoods are under-resourced in terms of the housing and economic opportunities, have a lower quality of life for the residents, and contain numerous threats to the residents' health, including substantial difficulties in the access to and quality of healthcare; and (3) great inequities in the quality of healthcare that is available to and used by Black patients and White patients that create threats to the health of Black people who require medical care.

Healthcare in Black and White

Perhaps the most clearly identifiable examples of racial health disparities are the ways in which Black patients are treated when they seek healthcare. Thus, we begin by presenting some of the experiences of Black people seeking healthcare. Our first informant is Voncile Brown Miller, a Black longtime resident of Detroit, Michigan. She has a long history of involvement in healthcare disparities as a social activist and later as part of a research team that studies racial disparities in the treatment of Black patients and White patients with cancer. But, she has also encountered some of these disparities firsthand.

In a 2016 interview with a local magazine, she described one of her first experiences with such disparities. In 2008, her brother was hit by a car and was taken to an emergency room. Ms. Miller was there to meet him. The attending physician did not give her brother anything for his pain and did not even bother to clean the wound. Ms. Miller asked the physician why, and the physician replied, "Well, um, he's so drunk right now that he wouldn't even know I'll be doing this." She told the physician that she "worked on health disparities and this is something we address, and I just need to let you know that this is what I am seeing right now. I need you to do your best ... you can give him a stitch that won't even show a scar. That's what I want you to do." The physician apologized and said that he had been having a "bad day." Ms. Miller doubts that such things would have happened this way had her brother been White. But, this was not the last disturbing encounter with the healthcare system that she had.

In another interview we conducted with her, Ms. Miller told us a different but equally chilling story about a relative who needed heart surgery. The relative was a middle-aged married Black woman. Her primary care physician brought in a prominent heart surgeon to perform the needed surgery. When the surgeon looked at the woman's medical history, he saw that many years earlier she had been an intravenous drug user, a problem she had long since overcome. But, the surgeon told her that he was not going to do the surgery because she had brought her heart problem on herself. He said that he "didn't want to waste his talent" on someone like her. Her physician pleaded with the surgeon to reconsider, and the surgeon reluctantly agreed to perform the operation. However, in the pre-operative consultation, he told the patient, "OK, I'm going to do this, but *you* better not mess this up." The surgery was a success, but the woman's family has never been able to forget the degrading way the surgeon had treated her.

Of course, we do not know for sure whether the uncaring attitude of the emergency room physician in the first example or the surgeon's atrocious behavior in the second one was solely because their patients were Black people. It is possible these physicians would have behaved in the same way even if the patient was White. But, other stories of Black patients' encounters with the healthcare system can make the role of racism in medical treatment clearer.

One of these stories requires that we talk about two racial stereotypes that exist among many healthcare providers. The first is that Black people feel less pain than White people. This is a myth that most likely has its origins in old racist theories about innate biological differences between Black people and White people that has permeated American medicine for at least 400 years. It was often used by slaveholders as a justification for the physical abuse they inflicted on enslaved Black people. Despite there being no scientific basis for this belief, it persists in modern medicine. As recently as 2016, a group of researchers at the University of Virginia found that about half of the medical students in their study believed that Black people had a greater tolerance for pain than do White people [38].

The second commonly held stereotype among healthcare providers is that Black patients are much more likely to abuse narcotic pain killers than White patients. Thus, healthcare providers generally are less likely to prescribe these drugs to Black patients than White patients; this is true even when the Black patients are children [39]. These two racial stereotypes came together to dramatically affect the life of Lisa Craig [40].

Ms. Craig is a middle-aged Black woman who suffers from sickle cell disease. Sickle cell disease is much more common among Black Americans than White Americans. It is caused by a mutation in a single gene that results in a person's blood cells being shaped like a sickle rather than being round. This makes it more difficult for the sickle cell to carry blood through the body, and this causes severe chronic pain. Over the years, Ms. Craig's attempts to find relief from her debilitating pain have exposed her to both of the racist stereotypes.

On numerous occasions Ms. Craig has gone to emergency rooms because her pain has become unbearable. When she arrives, however, she is very often told that her pain cannot really be that bad, and she is sent home without any pain killers. Why would the emergency room staff do that? There are no objective ways to measure pain. Thus, the only information a staff member has is what a patient tells them, and they have to evaluate that information. In Ms. Craig's case, it appears they believed that the pain or at least the discomfort it was causing was much less than Ms. Craig said it was. It seems quite possible that the emergency room staff relied, perhaps even nonconsciously, on the racial stereotype about Black people's greater tolerance for pain.

Ms. Craig had never abused narcotic pain killers but, when the opioid crisis hit, the second racial stereotype seemed to have kicked in.[11] Her physicians became suspicious of her many requests for pain killers and

---

[11] The opioid crisis began in the 1990s when, with the considerable support and encouragement of large pharmaceutical companies, many physicians began to seriously over-prescribe narcotic opioid

usually denied them. As one physician said to Ms. Craig, "So really I don't have any justification why you should have pain"; he refused to provide any narcotic pain killers. He justified his actions by saying he might be "red-flagged" and asked by authorities to justify prescribing these drugs, when he only had Ms. Craig's report to go on. This is a remarkable statement because, as we just noted, there is really no way to assess a patient's pain other than the patient's self-report. But, he claimed to be worried that drug enforcement officials might think that he was just helping an addict get some drugs. Ms. Craig replied, "You don't under-stand [my pain] because you don't have the disease. And, you're not one that they look at and go, 'Oh she's just exaggerating her pain,' when I want to saw my own freaking legs off." Her pain from sickle cell disease has never been effectively treated.

These kinds of stories serve to illustrate the types of medical inequities many Black patients and their families continue to confront. But, they are only part of the much broader problem of racial health disparities.

A Portrait of Health in Americas: Separate and Unequal

The system for gathering statistics on the overall health of Americans is pretty simple and straightforward. Health departments in cities, counties, or other geographic areas gather data on the incidence of diseases and mortality from the local healthcare systems and other sources (e.g., county coroners) in their areas. They compile these data and send to "reporting jurisdictions" who collate these data and send them on to the CDC. The CDC collects these various reports and provides weekly summaries of the incidences of "morbidity" (i.e., diseases) and "mortality" (i.e., deaths) and annual summaries of these and various other aspects of Americans' health. The National Vital Statistics Center of the CDC has been keeping such health records since 1915. It and other similar public health records document the significant health disparities between Black Americans and White Americans for at least the last 100 years.

The most direct way to illustrate the extent of these health disparities between Black Americans and White Americans is to use the data in these health reports to compute ratios that reflect these disparities. One such

---

pain killers to their patients. In many instances, there was no medical reason for giving a patient these drugs, but many physicians and especially the companies became very rich from the illicit provision of them to basically any patient who requested them. As a result, many people died of opioid overdoses. An excellent book on this is *Dopesick: Dealers, Doctors, and the Drug Company That Addicted America* by Beth Macy.

ratio compares the "incidence rate" of an outcome (or condition or disease) for the two groups. An incidence rate represents the number of people per some number (e.g., 100,000) who have a certain disease at some specified point in time (e.g., the number of people per 100,000 who had a COVID-19 infection in 2022). The disparity ratio is usually computed by dividing the rate for Black Americans by the rate for White Americans. A ratio of 1.0 would indicate that the health problem occurs at the same rate for Black Americans compared to White Americans. A ratio of 2.0 would show that the condition occurs much more frequently for Black Americans – specifically, it occurs twice as often for Black Americans compared to White Americans. The same kind of ratio can also be computed for mortality rates – the number of people per 100,000 who die from any cause within some specified period of time. We use these ratios as we discuss contemporary health disparities.

Specific Health Disparities
The United States has a higher infant mortality rate (the number of children born during a specific year who die before they reach the age of one) than 33 other industrialized countries. Embedded in this disturbing statistic are large racial health disparities [41, 42]. From the moment they are born, Black children are at a greater risk of dying than White children. Their mortality rate is over twice as high. This disparity exists for neonates (less than 28 days) and for babies between the ages of 28 days after birth and one year. Remarkably, although health statistics show that infant mortality rates have declined quite dramatically in the last 100 years, this disparity in mortality rates (2.0) is actually the same as it was 1915. This disparity is actually greater than was the disparity in infant mortality rates that existed between Black women who were enslaved and White women over 160 years ago (1.6). Currently, Black mothers are also twice as likely as White mothers to have a "stillbirth," a fetus dying while still in the womb.

The risks during childbirth are not only greater for Black children than for White children but also for their birthing parents. In 2020, Black women were about three times more likely to die during childbirth than were White women [43]. This likely contributes to the fact that the United States has a higher maternal mortality rate than 11 other of the most developed countries [44].

The role of long-term exposure to systemic racism in these disparities is suggested by another study. Dr. Tiffany Green, professor of population health sciences and obstetrics and gynecology at the University of

Wisconsin–Madison, and Dr. Tod Hamilton, professor of sociology at Princeton University, compared infant mortality rates for Black women born in the United States with Black women who were recent immigrants to the country [45]. The infant mortality rate was 1.5 times greater among the native-born Black women. This disparity was greatest among the women who had the lowest levels of education. It may reflect the cumulative effects of being disadvantaged in the United States.

Disparities in how long White people and Black people live on average represent another example of racial health disparities. But, because of the COVID-19 pandemic and a sudden increase in mortality rates, a discussion of past and present racial disparities in Americans' life expectancies and mortality rates becomes a bit more complicated. Before 2020, the health trends for all Americans across the years were quite constant. If one wanted to compare disparities in Black Americans' and White Americans' life expectancies from, say, 1900 to "now," it really did not make much difference if they used data from 2017, 2018, or 2019 as "now." But, in 2020, there was a quantum shift in life expectancy and mortality rates from these previous years. The CDC data from 2020 showed that the trend of 100 years of longer life expectancies and lower morality rates for all Americans abruptly stopped in 2020. So, we separately discuss racial disparities before 2020 and what we know about these disparities that year and after.[12]

Before 2020 (the first full year of the COVID-19 pandemic), the average American's life expectancy at the time of birth was almost twice as long as it was in 1900. This reflects the improvements in medical care and the development of new drugs to treat many diseases that occurred during this time period. Racial disparities in life expectancy have also declined dramatically from the early twentieth century, when Black Americans' life expectancy was almost 15 years less than the life expectancy for White Americans. The disparity has significantly closed over the years, but it has never gone away. In 2018, Black Americans' life expectancy at birth was still about 3.5 years less than that of White Americans. This disparity was a bit more for men (4.2 years) than for women (2.8 years). Also, the size of the disparity became somewhat smaller as people get older. For example, at age 65, the racial disparity in life expectancy was 1.6 years for men and just less than one year for women [46].

---

[12] The CDC's final reports on the nation's health usually present data from one to two years before the date of the report. Throughout the book, we discuss the most recent data we can locate. Usually this is for 2020 or 2021.

COVID-19 reduced the life expectancies of all Americans over the first two years of the pandemic. The COVID-19 pandemic also significantly increased the racial disparities in life expectancies. From 2019 to 2021, the overall average life expectancy for White Americans declined by slightly more than one year. Among Black Americans, the average life expectancy was about 4.0 years shorter, and Black people's life expectancy was the lowest it had been since 2000. Most public health officials believe this increased racial disparity in life expectancy will continue well after 2021 [47].

Closely related to disparities in life expectancies are disparities in mortality rates. The mortality rate is the number of people per 100,000 in the United States who die in a given year from any cause. The vast majority of deaths in the United States are due to diseases. Before the pandemic, the annual mortality rate in the United States due to diseases was roughly half of what it was in 1950. But, of course, our interest is in racial health disparities. Despite the dramatic decline in the mortality rates for both Black Americans and White Americans, disparities in the mortality rate between them have not changed much over time. The racial disparity ratio in mortality 70 years ago was 1.22 (or 22 percent higher for Black Americans than for White Americans). In 2019, the year before the pandemic, the disparity ratio was about 1.20, a trivial decline from 70 years earlier. The racial disparity ratio in mortality was greatest among Black Americans and White Americans between 35 and 49 years of age (1.41 or 40 percent higher for Black Americans than for White Americans). So, again, we see that there are more years of potential life lost among Black Americans than White Americans [48]. Data for the first 11 months of 2020, the first year of the COVID-19 pandemic, indicated that the overall increase in mortality rates across all races and ethnicities was about 16 percent. The racial disparity in mortality rates increased from the previous year to 1.33 – the mortality rate among Black Americans was 33 percent higher than among White Americans [49].

Disease and Mortality
Looking for historical trends in disparities in the incidence of diseases other than COVID-19 is also difficult, but for different reasons than life expectancy or mortality rates. The kinds of diseases that killed people in the past are very different from those of the present. Seventy years ago, before the existence of flu vaccines and the widespread usage (perhaps over-usage) of antibiotics, influenza and pneumonia were among the four

leading causes of people's death. Today, they are not even among the top eight.

Heart disease, cancer, cardiovascular diseases (e.g., strokes), diabetes, and asthma are among the most common causes of death in the United States today. Black Americans are more likely than White Americans to die from all of these diseases. The disparity in mortality rates ranges from 1.10 for cancer to about 3.0 for asthma [50]. The only two main exceptions to this pattern of health disparities are with respiratory diseases (i.e., diseases of the lungs) and Alzheimer's disease; White Americans are more likely to die than Black Americans from these diseases. The complete data on the direct effects of COVID-19 on mortality rates will likely not be available before this book is published. But, as noted earlier, from the beginning of the pandemic until August 2022, twice as many Black Americans had died from COVID-19 infections as did White Americans [51].

Are these kinds of disparities in mortality primarily because Black Americans are more likely to have these life-threatening diseases than White Americans? Data on racial disparities in cancer incidence rates versus mortality rates suggest that this usually is not the reason. Cancer is the second leading disease-related cause of death in the United States, ranking just behind heart disease. It is expected that about 600,000 Americans will die from cancer each year [52]. There is no single type of cancer. Rather, cancers are presently classified by the part of the body they primarily attack, such as pancreatic cancer, prostate cancer, or lung cancer. One of the most common cancers is breast cancer. It is, by far, the leading cause of cancer-related deaths among women in the United States.

The incidence rate for breast cancer among Black women is actually slightly lower than among White women, although that gap appears to have narrowed in recent years. Our interest here, however, is in how these racial disparities in incidence rates compare to racial disparities in mortality rates from breast cancer. According to the 2022 report from the American Cancer Society, despite the lower incidence rate, the mortality rate among Black women is almost 40 percent higher than the mortality rate among White women (28 deaths per 100,00 versus 20 deaths per 100,000) [52]. That is, even though Black women are less likely than White women to develop breast cancer, they are much more likely than White women to die from it. The disparities in mortality rates also far exceed the difference in incidence rates for other diseases that are major causes of mortality (e.g., strokes, diabetes, and asthma). This kind of disparity exists for heart disease, too, but it is a much smaller disparity compared to these other diseases [53, 54].

Explanations for Racial Disparities in Health

We have described *what* the problem is – widespread racial health disparities between Black Americans and White Americans that have persisted
across the history of the country. Our core thesis is that anti-Black racism
creates the conditions that lead to these disparities. But, other explanations
have been offered as well.

Socioeconomic Disparities and Health

One explanation of racial health disparities that enjoys considerable support in lay and academic circles proposes that racial health disparities are
primarily due to racial disparities in socioeconomic status (SES) rather
than individual or systemic anti-Black racism.[13]

To be sure, SES, and especially income, is strongly associated with a
person's health: The higher a person's SES, the healthier the individual
tends to be. The average SES of Black Americans is substantially lower
than that of White Americans. The median annual family income for
Black Americans is about $30,000 less than that for White Americans; the
average net worth of a Black family is about 10 percent of what it is for a
White family (about $17,000 versus $170,000) [55]. The average level of
educational achievement is also lower for Black Americans than for White
Americans [56]. For example, the percentage of Black Americans who
complete high school is about 10 percent less than for White Americans.

At first glance, disparities in SES present themselves as a reasonable
alternative to anti-Black racism as an explanation of racial health disparities. One strategy to test this idea and separate SES from race as a cause of
health disparities is to statistically divide people into different levels of SES.
Then, the health of Black people and White people within the same level
of SES is compared. The logic of such comparisons is this: If a racial health
disparity disappears when one compares the health of Black people and
White people who are equal in their SES, then SES rather than anti-Black
racism, per se, provides a better explanation of that racial health disparity.
But, if the health disparity is still present, people's racial identity plays a
significant role in it.

Studies that examine racial disparities while statistically controlling for
SES generally find that the magnitude of racial health disparities within a
given level of SES becomes smaller; however, racial health disparities still

[13] A person's SES is generally based on three factors: their income, the highest level of education they
completed, and the status of their occupation.

remain. Also, there are some health disparities that do not get smaller even after controlling for SES. Thus, there is something causing racial health disparities beyond a person's SES. We can see evidence of this in what Americans tell us about their health. In their annual assessments of Americans' health, governmental agencies, like the CDC, conduct interviews with a randomly selected number of US households. Among the questions they ask is, "Would you say your health is excellent, good, or fair, or poor?" We are going to focus on the "fair or poor" category. In the CDC's report, "Health United States 2020-2021" (the most recent report available at the time this book was being written), about 10 percent of the Americans interviewed answered that their health was only fair or poor [48]. People's SES clearly affected how they felt about their health. Whereas 25 percent of the people whose annual income fell below the federal poverty level said their health was fair or poor; only five percent of people whose income was 400 percent greater than this level gave this response. Race had a similar effect; whereas about 16 percent of Black Americans said they were in fair or poor health, only about 10 percent of White Americans gave this answer.

But, our interest here, again, is in disparities between the responses of Black people and White people who earned roughly the same amount of money. These are presented in Figure I.1. It shows the percentage of Black people and White people at different levels of family annual income who reported their health was only "fair or poor." Black people whose income was between 100 percent and 199 percent of the poverty level were slightly less likely to report their health was fair or poor than White people at this income level. However, at all the other income levels Black people reported poorer health than White people. For people whose annual income was below the poverty level (far left side of the figure), the percentage was about 28 percent for Black people versus about 24 percent for White people – a racial *disparity* of 16 percent. But, now look at the far-right side of the figure; it shows the racial disparity in self-reports of health among people whose income was at least 400 times greater than those at the poverty level. The percentage of Black people who reported poor or fair health was 7.5 percent, much smaller than for poorer Black people, but it was almost one and a half times high as the 5.0 percent for the White people at this same income level. The racial disparity in people's reports about their health was much greater among the wealthiest people than among the poorest people.

More evidence that being well-off financially not only fails to eliminate but also can magnify racial disparities in health comes from a study with

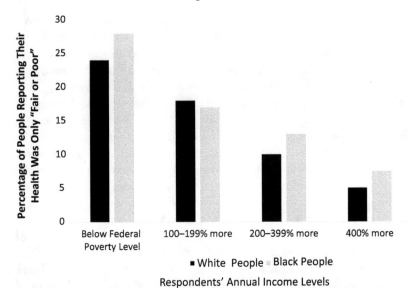

Figure I.1   Income and health status: The percentage of Black people and White people at four annual income levels who report their health to be only "fair or poor." For both groups, higher income is associated with better health status, but substantial racial health disparities remain even at the highest income levels.

Source: CDC Health United States 2020-2021 www.cdc.gov/nchs/data/hus/2020-2021/Hstat.pdf

some atypical participants. This study compared the health of a sample of very high-income Black Americans and White Americans. These were people who made over $175,000 per year, or about three times what the typical American makes. In a survey, they were asked whether they had been diagnosed by a physician as having hypertension (i.e., high blood pressure), diabetes, or high cholesterol, and about their overall physical and mental health. The high-income Black people were much more likely than the high-income White people to report that they had all three diseases and to describe their overall health as poor [57]. Thus, even among people who have the financial means to get the best health insurance and health-care, there is still evidence of the pervasive disparities in the health of Black Americans and White Americans.

Another component of SES that has been theorized to impact people's health is education. And, like overall SES, educational level predicts certain health-related outcomes. One example of this is infant mortality rates. The better educated a mother is, the less likely her infant will die during the first year after birth. This may suggest that education serves as a "protector" against losing an infant in the first year of life. This is, in part, because more educated mothers may start prenatal care earlier and engage in fewer behaviors that would jeopardize the health of the fetus (smoking, for example) than less educated mothers. But, there is also a racial health disparity hiding in this relationship.

In the same study we presented earlier, Dr. Tiffany Green and Dr. Tod Hamilton used data from the National Center for Health Statistics to also look at the impact of education on infant mortality among children who survived more than 28 days after birth (post-neonatal) [40]. They examined data from 13 million Black mothers and White mothers. Among White mothers, their level of education had a strong impact on infant mortality; the mortality rate per live 100,000 births for White mothers who did not complete high school was almost five times as great as among White mothers who had a college degree. There was also an association between education and infant mortality among Black mothers, but it was not nearly as strong. The disparity ratio for infant mortality between the least and most educated Black mothers was less than three, or about half of what it was for White mothers. Perhaps most strikingly, the infant mortality among Black mothers with a college degree was greater than among White mothers who did not finish high school. In sum, a mother's education is a much weaker "protector" of Black infants than of White infants. The conclusion from this and other studies is that higher SES often does not produce the same health-protective benefits for Black Americans as it does for White Americans.

Still, it is true that the studies that statistically equate SES of Black people and White people do show a reduction in health disparities; SES disparities thus cannot be ignored in discussions of racial health disparities. But, studies that statistically equate Black people and White people on things like income must be put in context. A study that statistically places Black people and White people at the same SES levels has created an artificial world that does not exist. As already discussed, in the real world, Black Americans' SES is substantially lower than the SES of White Americans. So, dismissing racial health disparities as simply due to the effects of SES disparities is really ignoring the harsh realities of how the racial SES disparities that actually exist create substantial health disparities.

Further, attributing some portion of racial health disparities to disparities in the components of SES misses a larger point. Racial disparities in economic status, educational level, and occupational status did not just happen. Anti-Black racism created and then sustained these large societal inequities. To be sure, many of the formal and legal barriers to social and economic mobility for Black Americans that once existed are gone. But, their legacies and contemporary individual and systemic racism still lead to substantial economic challenges for Black Americans. We discuss this legacy of past racism in more detail in Chapter 3. In sum, SES is one consequence of anti-Black racism that serves as a proximal cause of racial health disparities. This book reviews this and the other pathways from anti-Black racism to racial health disparities.

Putting It All Together

The dramatic racial disparities in infection and morality rates over the course of the COVID-19 pandemic are really only the latest chapter in a very long story of large racial disparities in the health of Americans. Poorer health among Black people (and many other racial/ethnic minorities) predates the founding of the United States and, despite the dramatic improvements in the health of all Americans over the least century, this racial health disparity is still glaringly present.

For far too long a time, the most influential explanation of the disparities in the health of Black people versus White people posited that Black people are more likely to get sick and to die simply because of inherited biological and genetic defects. That is, the Black "race" was inferior to the White "race." We acknowledge that there, of course, are biological and genetic causes of health problems. However, race is a social construct used to identify groups of people and has no biological foundation or meaning. The actual genetic differences between people identified as Black or White are miniscule. Like all intergroup disparities that place minorities at disadvantage, health disparities are primarily due to political, economic, and social factors.

It would be far beyond foolish to propose a simple, unitary cause for all racial health disparities, but the evidence for individual and systemic racism as two of the most powerful causes is overwhelming. Anti-Black racism offers a far better explanation of why Black Americans are so much less healthy than White Americans than any pseudo-scientific genetic explanations or overly simplistic ones based solely on SES disparities between Black Americans and White Americans. Our task in this book is to present the empirical evidence that supports our position and describe the different ways in which anti-Black racism endangers the health of Black Americans.

What Lies Ahead: An Overview of the Chapters That Follow

In the remaining seven chapters in this book, we describe the current state of scientific knowledge and theories relevant to racial disparities in health and healthcare. In Chapter 1, we discuss the reasons for the persistent presence of anti-Black racism. The first part of discussion is about the historical roots of racism within the United States and its impact on current social and economic racial inequities and the content of many of today's racial stereotypes. The chapter then considers how the intellectual capabilities of human beings make it quite likely that they will develop negative thoughts and feelings about people who look, think, or act differently from them. Later chapters show that anti-Black thoughts, feelings, and actions are directly and indirectly responsible for the pervasive and substantial racial disparities in health and healthcare.

In Chapter 2, we describe the deleterious health effects of exposure to racial discrimination. We discuss the pervasive nature of racial discrimination in the United States and the extent to which it intrudes on the day-to-day lives of Black Americans. We then present evidence of a causal link between experiencing racial discrimination and the health problems experienced by many Black Americans. In this causal process, consistent exposure to racial discrimination produces high levels of chronic stress in Black people in the United States. This stress, in turn, has physical and psychological effects that put Black people at dramatically increased risk for a wide variety of diseases and even premature mortality.

In Chapter 3, we consider the health consequences of residential racial segregation. We first examine the ways in which systemic racism produced public and private policies and practices that dictated where Black Americans could and could not live. Usually, the places where they could live were undesirable locations with few natural resources and isolated from surrounding communities. Then, we discuss the current health dangers contained in these neighborhoods. They range from high levels of environmental toxins to the inadequate amount of healthcare available in many of America's under-resourced, Black neighborhoods.

In Chapter 4, we review the long and shameful history of anti-Black racism in the practice of medicine in the United States. This includes the formal and informal policies that greatly restricted Black people's access to medical care and the horrific medical experiments conducted on Black people as subjects through coercion and/or deception. Other policies enacted by professional organizations greatly reduced the number of Black people in healthcare professions. This racist past in medicine continues to affect how non-Black physicians and their Black patients feel about and act toward one another.[14]

In Chapter 5, we discuss contemporary racial disparities in the quality of healthcare received by Black patients and White patients. Chapter 5 concerns the way healthcare is financed and structured in the United States, which causes large racial disparities in the quality of healthcare patients receive. Because healthcare in America is not a single-payer system that covers the medical expenses of all citizens, the quality of healthcare provided to Black Americans is directly affected by the broad political, economic, and social inequities created by systemic racism. Systemic racism within the healthcare system also creates policies and practices that further disadvantage Black patients. These include educational and institutional practices that result in a dearth of Black physicians and the widespread use of supposedly race-neutral diagnostic algorithms that, in fact, disadvantage Black patients.

In Chapter 6, we first document the pervasive disparities in the medical treatments received by Black patients and White patients who have the same diseases. Then, we discuss how race relations in the United States and the race-related thoughts, feelings, and actions of healthcare professionals and their patients may contribute to these kinds of racial disparities in healthcare. The discussion includes the impact of racial bias among non-Black physicians on how they interact with their Black patients and the patients' responses to this. In addition, we consider how past and present racial disparities in healthcare create mistrust among Black patients, with implications for the kind of healthcare they receive.

In Chapter 7, we present a number of interventions that might significantly reduce racial health disparities. These proposals largely parallel the causes of the disparities presented in the earlier chapters. Some of them involve significant changes and innovations in broad public policies that could reduce the breadth and depth of some racial disparities. Others focus on specific changes directed at the healthcare system and healthcare

---

[14] We use the term "non-Black" to describe physicians who do not identify as Black or African American because a significant minority of the physicians in the United States may be Asian (especially South Asia) or Middle Eastern. Thus far, research has not found that such racial and ethnic differences among non-Black physicians produce differences in how they treat their Black patients or how the patients react to them. However, it is possible that subsequent research could identify such differences.

professionals that could eventually mitigate differences in the quality of care that Black Americans and White Americans receive. We harbor no illusions about the potential difficulties of implementing the changes we propose. Nevertheless, there is a moral imperative that we try to address these unfair and pernicious racial health disparities.

REFERENCES

1. Du Bois, W. E. B. (1899). *The Philadelphia Negro: A social study*. University of Pennsylvania Press.
2. Aguilar, L. (2020, May 21). Detroit population continues to decline, according to census estimate. *Bridge Michigan*. www.bridgemi.com/urban-affairs/detroit-population-continues-decline-according-census-estimate
3. Smitherman, H. C., Jr., Kallenbachm L., & Aranha, A. N. F. (2020). *Dying before their time III: 19-Year (1999–2017) comparative analysis of excess mortality in Detroit*. Commissioned by Detroit Area Agency on Aging. www.docdroid .com/w7ygRoO/dying-before-their-time-iii-daaa-2020-final-pdf#page=13
4. Hill, L. & Artiga, S. (2022, August 22). *COVID-19 cases and deaths by race/ethnicity: Current data and changes over time*. Kaiser Family Foundation. www .kff.org/coronavirus-covid-19/issue-brief/covid-19-cases-and-deaths-by-race-ethnicity-current-data-and-changes-over-time/
5. Bassett, M. T., Chen, J. T., & Krieger, N. (2020). Variation in racial/ethnic disparities in COVID-19 mortality by age in the United States: A cross-sectional study. *PLoS Medicine, 17*(10), e1003402. https://doi.org/10.1371/journal.pmed.1003402
6. Lahut, J. (2020, April 7). Fauci says the coronavirus is "shining a bright light" on "unacceptable" health disparities for African Americans. *Business Insider*. www.businessinsider.com/fauci-covid-19-shows-unacceptable-disparities-for-african-americans-2020-4
7. Whitaker, B. (2021, April 18). Racism's corrosive impact on the health of Black Americans. *CBS News*. www.cbsnews.com/news/60-minutes-disease-black-americans-covid-19-2021-04-18/
8 Hood, R. G. (2001). The "slave health deficit": The case for reparations to bring health parity to African Americans. *Journal of the National Medical Association, 93*(1), 1–5. https://pubmed.ncbi.nlm.nih.gov/12653374
9. American Medical Association. (2020). *The AMA's strategic plan to embed racial justice and advance health equity*. www.ama-assn.org/about/leadership/ama-s-strategic-plan-embed-racial-justice-and-advance-health-equity
10. Coates, T. -N. (2015). *Between the world and me*. One World.
11. Roediger, D. R. (n.d.) Historical foundations of race. *National Museum of African American History & Culture, Smithsonian*. https://nmaahc.si.edu/learn/talking-about-race/topics/historical-foundations-race
12. The Pastor's Workshop. (n.d.). *Sermon quotes on race*. https://thepastorsworkshop.com/sermon-quotes-on-race/

13. Turner, A. L., Laveist, T. A., Richard, P., & Gaskin, D. J. (2020). Economic impacts of health disparities in Texas 2020: An update in the time of COVID-19. *Altarum*. www.episcopalhealth.org/wp-content/uploads/2021/01/Econ-Impacts-of-Health-Disparities-Texas-2020-FINAL-002.pdf

14. Ayanian, J. Z. (2015, October 1). The costs of racial disparities in health care. *Harvard Business Review*. https://hbr.org/2015/10/the-costs-of-racial-disparities-in-health-care

15. Farmer, P. (2013, June 5). Investigating the root causes of the global health crisis: Paul Farmer on the TED Book, The upstream doctors. TEDBlog. https://blog.ted.com/investigating-the-root-causes-of-the-global-health-crisis-paul-farmer-on-the-upstream-doctors/

16. Glantz, M. J., Chamberlain, M. C.Liu, Q., Hsief, C.-C., Edwards, K. R., Van Horn, A., & Recht, L. (2009). Gender disparity in the rate of partner abandonment in patients with serious medical illness. *Cancer, 115*(22), 5237–5242. https://doi.org/10.1002/cncr.24577

17. Carlson, R. H. (2001). Study: Women with brain tumors have 10 times rate of divorce as men with brain tumors. *Oncology Times, 23*(8), 63. https://journals.lww.com/oncology-times/Fulltext/2001/08000/Study__Women_with_Brain_Tumors_Have_10_Times_Rate.24.aspx

18. Lippmann, W. (1922). The world inside and outside and the pictures in our head. In W. Lippmann (Ed.), *Public Opinion* (pp. 3–32). Macmillan Press. https://doi.org/10.1037/14847-001

19. Over, H., Eggleston, A., Bell, J., & Dunham, Y. (2018). Young children seek out biased information about social groups. *Developmental Science, 21*(3), e12580. https://doi.org/10.1111/desc.12580

20. Quillian, L., Pager, D., Hexel, O., & Midtbøen, A. H. (2017). Meta-analysis of field experiments shows no change in racial discrimination in hiring over time. *Proceedings of the National Academy of Sciences, 114*(41), 10870–10875. https://doi.org/10.1073/pnas.1706255114

21. Sun, M., Oliwa, T., Peek, M. E., & Tung, E. L. (2022). Negative patient descriptors: Documenting racial bias in the electronic health record. *Health Affairs, 41*(2), 203–211. https://doi.org/10.1377/hlthaff.2021.01423

22. Desai, M. U., Guy, K., Brown, M., Thompson, D., Manning, R., Johnson, S., Davidson, L., & Bellamy, C. (2023). "That was a state of depression by itself dealing with society": Atmospheric racism, mental health, and the Black and African American faith community. *American Journal of Community Psychology*. https://doi.org/10.1002/ajcp.12654

23. History.com Editors. (2021, March 26). *Jim Crow Laws*. History.com www.history.com/topics/early-20th-century-us/jim-crow-laws

24. Wilkerson, I. (2010). *The warmth of other suns: The epic story of America's great migration*. Vintage Press.

25. Jim Crow Museum of Racist Memorabilia. *Examples of Jim Crow Laws - Oct. 1960 – Civil Rights*. Ferris State University. www.ferris.edu/htmls/news/jimcrow/links/misclink/examples.htm

26. Romero, S. (2018, January 28). Indian slavery once thrived in New Mexico. Latinos are finding family ties to it. *New York Times.* www.nytimes.com/2018/01/28/us/indian-slaves-genizaros.html?hp&action=click&pgtype=Homepage&clickSource=story-heading&module=second-column-region&region=top-news&WT.nav=top-news

27. Black, S. S. (2008, December 1). *American Indian tribes and structural racism.* Poverty & Race Research Action Council. www.prrac.org/american-indian-tribes-and-structural-racism/

28. Office of the Historian, Foreign Service Institute, United States Department of State. Chinese Immigration and the Chinese Exclusion Acts. https://history.state.gov/milestones/1866-1898/chinese-immigration

29. Abdul-Jabbar, K. (2020, May 30). Op-Ed: Don't understand the protests? What you're seeing is people pushed to the edge. *Los Angeles Times.* www.latimes.com/opinion/story/2020-05-30/dont-understand-the-protests-what-youre-seeing-is-people-pushed-to-the-edge

30. *New York Times.* (2022, August, 12). *More Black former N.F.L. players eligible for concussion payouts.* www.nytimes.com/2022/08/12/sports/football/nfl-concussion-settlement-race.html

31. McMinn, S., Carlsen, A., Jaspers, B., Talbot, R., & Adeline, S. (2020, May 27). In large Texas cities, access to coronavirus testing may depend on where you live. *National Public Radio.* www.npr.org/sections/health-shots/2020/05/27/862215848/across-texas-black-and-hispanic-neighborhoods-have-fewer-coronavirus-testing-sit

32. The Editorial Board. (2013, August 12). Racial discrimination in stop-and-frisk. *New York Times.* www.nytimes.com/2013/08/13/opinion/racial-discrimination-in-stop-and-frisk.html

33. ACLU Massachusetts. (n.d.). *Enduring racist stop and frisk.* www.aclum.org/en/ending-racist-stop-and-frisk

34. Stolper, H. J., J. (2018, April 16). The enduring discriminatory practice of stop & frisk. *Community Service Society.* www.cssny.org/news/entry/stop-and-frisk

35. Balko, R. (2020, June 10). There's overwhelming evidence that the criminal justice system is racist: Here's proof. *Washington Post.* www.washingtonpost.com/graphics/2020/opinionss/systemicracism-police-evidence-criminal-justicesystem

36. Racial and Identity Profiling Identity Board. (2021). *Annual report.* https://oag.ca.gov/sites/all/files/agweb/pdfs/ripa/ripa-board-reportt-202.pdf

37. Griffith, D. M. (2019, September 13). *What racism is and is not.* www.vanderbilt.edu/crmh/What_racism_is_and_is_not.pdf

38. Hoffman, K. M., Trawalter, S., Axt, J. R., & Oliver, M. N. (2016). Racial bias in pain assessment and treatment recommendations, and false beliefs about biological differences between blacks and whites. *Proceedings of the National Academy of Sciences, 113*(16), 4296–4301. https://doi.org/10.1073/pnas.1516047113

39. Chen, I., Kurz, J., Pasanen, M., Faselis, C., Panda, M., Staton, L. J., O'Roke, J., Menon, M., Genao, I., Wood, J., Mechaber, A. J., Rosenberg, E, Carey, T., Calleson, D., & Cykert, S. (2005). Racial differences in opioid use for

chronic nonmalignant pain. *Journal of General Internal Medicine, 20(7)*, 593–598. https://doi.org/10.1111/j.1525-1497.2005.0106.x

40. Eligon, J. (2021, May 30). 'On that edge of fear': One woman's struggle with sickle cell pain. *New York Times.* www.nytimes.com/2021/05/30/us/sickle-cell-black-women.html

41. Central Intelligence Agency. (n.d.). *Country comparisons: Infant mortality rate.* www.cia.gov/the-world-factbook/field/infant-mortality-rate/country-comparison

42. Artiga, S., Pham, O., Orgera, K., & Ranji, U. (2020). Racial disparities in maternal and infant health: An overview. *Issue Brief. Kaiser Family Foundation.* www.kff.org/report-section/racial-disparities-in-maternal-and-infant-health-an-overview-issue-brief/

43. Hoyert, D. (2022, February) Maternal mortality rates in the United States 2020. *Health E-Stats.* www.cdc.gov/nchs/data/hestat/maternal-mortality/2020/E-stat-Maternal-Mortality-Rates-2022.pdf

44. Melillo, G. (2020, December 3). US ranks worst in maternal care, mortality compared with 10 other developed nations. *The American Journal of Managed Care.* www.ajmc.com/view/us-ranks-worst-in-maternal-care-mortality-compared-with-10-other-developed-nations

45. Green, T., & Hamilton, T. G. (2019). Maternal educational attainment and infant mortality in the United States: Does the gradient vary by race/ethnicity and nativity? *Demographic Research, 41(25)*, 713–752. www.jstor.org/stable/26850665

46. Aria, E., Tejada-Vera, B., Kochanek, K. D., & Ahmad, F. B. (2022, August). Provisional life expectancy estimates. *Vital Statistics Rapid Release* www.cdc.gov/nchs/data/vsrr/vsrr023.pdf

47. Scholey, J., Aburto, J. M., Kashnitsky, I., Kniffka, M. S., Zhang, L., Jaadia, H., Dowd, J. B., & Kashyap, R. et al. (2022). Life expectancy changes since COVID-19, *Nature Human Behavior 6*, 1649–1659. https://doi.org/10.1038/s41562-022-01450-3

48. National Center for Health Statistics. (2021). *Health, United States, 2019.* https://www.cdc.gov/nchs/data/hus/hus19-508.pdf

49. Ahmad, F. B., Cisewski, J. A., Miniño, A., & Anderson, R. N. (2021). Provisional mortality data - United States, 2020. *Morbidity and Mortality Weekly Report, 70(14)*, 519–522. https://doi.org/10.15585/mmwr.mm7014e1

50. Asthma and Allergy Foundation of America. (n.d.). *Asthma disparities in America.* www.aafa.org/asthma-disparities-burden-on-minorities.aspx

51. Centers for Disease Control and Prevention. (n.d.). Risk for covid-19 infection, hospitalization, and death by race/ethnicity. www.cdc.gov/coronavirus/2019-ncov/covid-data/investigations-discovery/hospitalization-death-by-race-ethnicity.html

52. Giaquinto, A., Sung, H., Miller, K. D., Kramer, J. L., Newman, L. A., Minihan, A., Jemal, A., & Siegel, R. L. (2022). Breast cancer statistics, *CA: A Cancer Journal for Clinicians* (electronic preprint in advance of publication) (72) 524–541. https://pubmed.ncbi.nlm.nih.gov/36190501/

53. Kaiser Family Foundation. (n.d.). *Number of diabetes deaths per 100,000 population by race/ethnicity.* www.kff.org/other/state-indicator/diabetes-death-rate-by-raceethnicity/?currentTimeframe=0&selectedRows=doctor%22wrapups%22:%

7B%22united-states%22:%7B%7D%7D%7D&sortModel=%7B%22colId%
22:%22Location%22,%22sort%22:%22asc%22%7D

54. National Institutes of Health. (2016, June 21). *Racial disparities in stroke incidence and death.* www.nih.gov/news-events/nih-research-matters/racial-disparities-stroke-incidence-death

55. Shiro, A. G., Pulliam, C., Sabelhus, J. S., & Smith, E. (2022, June 29). Stuck on the Ladder: Intragenerational wealth mobility in the United States. Brookings. www.brookings.edu/research/stuck-on-the-ladder-intragenerational-wealth-mobil ity-in-the-united-states/

56. Statista. (n.d.). *Percentage of educational attainment in the United States in 2018, by ethnicity.* www.statista.com/statistics/184264/educational-attainment-by-enthnicity/

57. Wilson, K. B., Thorpe, R. J., & LaVeist, T. A. (2017). Dollar for dollar: Racial and ethnic inequalities in health and health-related outcomes among persons with very high income. *Preventive Medicine, 96*(3), 149–153. https://doi.org/10.1016/j.ypmed.2016.08.038

CHAPTER I

The Past Is Prologue
The Roots of Anti-Black Racism

History doesn't repeat itself, but it rhymes.
—Mark Twain, date unknown

In December 2019, the *New York Times* published the "1619 Project," which was created and coordinated by the journalist Nikole Hannah-Jones. The title of this project and the accompanying podcast refer to the date that enslaved Black Africans were first brought to North America. The 1619 Project explored various historical aspects of racism in America through narrative essays, poetry, and photography. It addressed American history from the date enslaved Black people were first brought to North America (1619) to Hurricane Katrina and featured contributions from a wide range of respected professors, writers, and artists. The project's core argument is that the United States is steeped in racism from its very founding to today. Nikole Hannah-Jones won the 2020 Pulitzer Prize for Commentary for her introductory essay.[1] Although the project included a panel of respected historians to fact-check the work, some of its more critical arguments, such as the idea that the Revolutionary War was fought in part to preserve the institution of slavery, became the object of criticism and debate among some historians [1].

The later edition modified this characterization of the Revolutionary War and did other things such as expressing more nuance in the discussion of Abraham Lincoln's views on race. However, the most heated and vocal criticism did not come from academics. It came from conservative media outlets and then from politicians. Indeed, in July 2020 Senator Tom Cotton of Arkansas introduced a bill in the US Senate that would prohibit schools from receiving federal funds for teaching about the 1619 Project. In a statement that accompanied the bill, Senator Cotton wrote, "The *New*

---

[1] The revised version of the original 1619 Project, *The 1619 Project: A New Origin Story*, published in 2021, also assigned specific dates to the events described in the book and broadened the discussion of slavery to include other parts of the Americas.

York Times' 1619 Project is a racially divisive, revisionist account of history that denies the principles of freedom and equality on which our nation was founded" [2].

Such reactions to the 1619 Project and similar efforts have led legislators in at least twenty-three states to propose or pass laws that would either prohibit or severely restrict teaching about racism or "Critical Race Theory" in public schools [3]. Critical race theory is actually a 40-year-old academic and legal concept that emphasizes that racism is not confined to individual bias but is also embedded in economic, political, and social systems in America. It has been applied in various forms, and there is no specific critical race theory curriculum or lesson plan of which we are aware, but there are educational materials available that are related to the 1619 Project. It appears that the core issue is really about whether public schools should teach *anything* about past or present racism. Advocacy groups who oppose teaching about racism (e.g., Moms for America) argue that such material is psychologically harmful and disturbing to children. However, to many, this opposition appears to be primarily concerned with hiding a critical part of America's past and present from White children.

The fact is that most White people (and Black people as well) find talking about race and racism in America uncomfortable and difficult [4]. Yet it is important to have these conversations. Understanding the origins of anti-Black racism in the United States and the reasons for its persistence in America over the past 400 years is essential to understanding current racial health disparities. Anti-Black racism is not an idea held by just a few "bad apples" on the political extremes. America is a much more open and egalitarian country than it once was, but anti-Black racism exists across a very wide spectrum of people and institutions. These various forms of racist thoughts and actions seriously disadvantage Black Americans and endanger their health.

What explains the persistence of anti-Black racism in America today? There are two partially interlocking explanations. The first is historical. It involves both the ideas that many influential European scientists and philosophers had about the nature of race and racial differences among human beings, which was known as "scientific racism," and the historical events that were unique to the United States – the most significant of these being slavery. Thus, thoughts and actions that occurred hundreds of years ago have had a direct and powerful influence on the creation of contemporary negative racial stereotypes, which play a critical role in anti-Black racism and health disparities in the United States today.

The second explanation of enduring anti-Black racism, covered later in this chapter, involves two processes that enabled early human beings to successfully evolve in a very dangerous world. The first was the sophisticated ways that humans are able to organize and make sense of the things they encounter in the world around them, including the actions of other people and the groups to which they belong. The second was the ability to form enduring social groups, which provided their members with protection and a stable source of food and other resources that they needed. These keys to evolutionary success led to the ways the typical human being thinks about and acts toward the people around them. However, these same processes provide foundations for the development of anti-Black racism.

The Historical Roots of Racial Beliefs

Theories about the inherent personal deficiencies of people from Africa certainly did not begin with the large-scale arrival of White Europeans in North America and the subsequent importation of enslaved Black Africans. For example, Greek philosophers such as Aristotle, Plato, and Socrates expressed ideas about the differences between citizens of Greece and people from Africa and stereotyped the people from these regions. Some writers claim that during the time of these philosophers, most Greeks believed that slavery was part of the natural order of things and that Africans were biologically different from and inferior to them. One such writer, Dr. Benjamin Issac, professor of ancient history at Tel Aviv University, has argued that these ideas provided the philosophical basis for what came to be known as scientific racism [5].

The "Natural" Order of Things: Scientific Racism

The core concept of scientific racism is the idea that people whose immediate family origins are in Africa are biologically distinct from and inherently inferior to those people whose immediate origins are in Europe. Today, we know that the core idea underlying scientific racism has no foundation in scientific fact. As discussed in the Introduction, race is a social construct that concerns how a person is identified by society, and any genetic differences between people identified as Black and as White are miniscule – much less than the genetic differences within each group. Nonetheless, scientific racism was widely accepted among intellectuals, physicians, and scientists in Europe and the United States for a long time.

The Basic Tenets of Scientific Racism: Terribly Wrong but Enduring

A particularly important figure in the history of scientific racism was a Roman physician who lived in the second and third centuries AD, Galen of Pergamon. Galen was the most famous physician in the Roman Empire [6]. He strongly believed he could "document" the physiological inferiority of people who would now be described as Black in comparison to people whom we would now classify as White [7]. Galen's ideas about the causes of diseases and racial differences persisted in medicine for millennia after his death. In his book on the 1918 flu pandemic, historian Dr. John Barry, professor at the Tulane University School of Public Health and Tropical Medicine, writes that if Galen had somehow been transported to the late nineteenth century, he would have been relatively familiar and comfortable with how medicine was being practiced. Galen's beliefs about the essential inferiority of Black people had an enduring and substantial influence on the practice of medicine [8].

The belief that there were different species (or races) among humans gained widespread acceptance outside of medicine largely because of the work of Carl Linnaeus, an eighteenth-century Swedish botanist. Linnaeus is known as the father of modern taxonomy, which is the classification of living organisms. He devoted his life to categorizing all of the different kinds of living organisms, both plants and animals. In his system of classification, Linnaeus represented all living things as part of a tree with a common trunk but with very separate branches that represented biological differences between and within all plants and animals (species). When it came to the separate branches (or "species") for humans, Linnaeus arranged them in order from best to worst. On the top branch were people of European ancestry, who were "smart, inventive, and ruled by law." On the lowest branch were people of African ancestry, who were "sluggish, crafty, slow, careless, covered by grease, ruled by caprice" [8, pp. 29–30]. Linnaeus' ideas about the distinct and immutable differences between Black people and White people – and indeed most of his other ideas – were quite wrong in a host of respects. Nonetheless, theories of scientific racism such as his were widely accepted among the intelligentsia of the eighteenth century.[2]

---

[2] A very interesting discussion of the things that Linnaeus (and later Darwin) got wrong about the organization of plants and animals can be found in David Quammen's book, *The Tangled Tree: A Radical New History of Life*. Sonia Shah also examines the errors in Linnaeus' thinking and its lasting impact on scientists and lay people's beliefs about environmental dangers in her book, *The Next Great Migration: The Beauty and Terror of Life on the Move*. Science writer Angela Saini provides an overview of past and present race science in her book, *Superior: The Return of Race Science*.

Eighteenth-century intellectuals generally believed in the innate inferiority of Black people. The English philosopher David Hume, for example, wrote, "I am apt to suspect the negroes ... to be naturally inferior to Whites." The French philosopher Voltaire also believed that people from Africa and people from Europe were two separate species [9, 10]. Ideas like this influenced the founders of the American republic. Thomas Jefferson, for example, stated that "all men are created equal," but his writings contained the belief that Black people were inherently inferior to White people. Although Jefferson did later write tracts in which he opposed slavery, he never freed his hundreds of slaves.

Scientific racism also flourished during the second half of the nineteenth century in America, and the idea that Black people and White people were likely separate species proliferated. This was largely due to the writings and activities of Dr. Louis Agassiz. Agassiz was a Swiss-born biologist and geologist, who later became a physician and emigrated to the United States in 1847. Agassiz became a distinguished professor at Harvard and a very significant person in the US scientific community. He founded the National Academy of Science and was a rector of the Smithsonian Institute [11]. His major significant scientific contributions were actually in geology, but today he is best known for his ideas about race. In 1867, Agassiz formally proposed the theory of polygenism – that Black people and White people were genetically distinct and different kinds of humans. He also speculated, as Linnaeus had proposed, that they were even a separate species. In part, these views may have been due to the fact that he was repulsed by the appearance of Black people. In a letter to his mother in Switzerland shortly after his first encounter with Black servants at a hotel, he wrote that "it is impossible for me to repress the feeling that they are not of the same blood as us" [11].

Agassiz was not alone in his beliefs. He was joined by another very prominent American scientist of the same era, Dr. Samuel George Morton. Morton was a strong believer in craniology, the idea that the size of a person's skull reflected their intelligence. He conducted numerous measurements of the skulls of Black people and White people and concluded that Black people's skulls were inherently smaller than those of White people [12]. There is substantial evidence that his methods were flawed and that he interpreted his findings in a biased way that supported his polygenist views. Moreover, there is no correlation between the size of a person's skull and the individual's intelligence [13].

Together Agassiz and Morton did much more than simply argue for the existence of separate races; they vigorously denigrated people of color.

Morton stated that "Ethiopians [i.e., Black people] . . . represent the lowest grade of humanity" [12]. Agassiz, meanwhile, argued that because of their genetic inferiority, Black people should not be allowed to intermingle with White people and that being enslaved was an appropriate place for them in society.

The freeing of millions of Black people with the end of the Civil War actually exacerbated attempts to prove their inferiority. One of the most influential arguments that Black Americans were biologically different from and inferior to White Americans came from a massive study funded by a coalition between the United States War Department and the United States Sanitary Commission, a private organization whose original mission was to provide "comfort and support" to Union soldiers.[3] It was by far the largest study ever conducted of the physical characteristics of people classified either as Black or as White. Over 15,000 Black and White (and Native American) Union soldiers willingly or unwillingly participated in a study of their physical attributes. The study's leaders believed that they would find large physical differences in the bodies of Black soldiers and White soldiers, which would show that Black people are intellectually and morally inferior to White people [14].

This study was flawed in a multitude of respects. For example, the study coordinators made racial classifications of people by simply looking at them. They classified almost all of the Black soldiers as "full blooded Blacks." But it is likely that most of the Black soldiers had White ancestors [15]. Many of the Black soldiers (and some of the White soldiers as well) refused to participate or disrobe, producing biased samples for their measurements. The physical measurements the study collected were often inaccurate because many of the people who took them were untrained and did not know how to use the measurement instruments, so they often guessed at the actual measurement. Perhaps most importantly, many of the characteristics they measured, including the angle of lines from the ear to the nose and skull size, were based on the erroneous idea that such measurements reflected intelligence. These assumptions came from earlier ideas that were part of scientific racism and without any scientific merit. Also, there was little consideration of the role that a person's life experience might play in certain physical characteristics. For example, the measurements of lung capacity and chest size showed racial differences, but today

---

[3] An excellent account of how the commission's primary mission changed from providing medical care to Union troops to proving the racial inferiority of Black people can be found in *Maladies of Empire: How Colonialism, Slavery, and War Transformed Medicine* by Jim Downs.

such differences are usually attributed to the debilitating effects of life as an enslaved person and the hardships that free Black people faced, as well.

The study, published in 1869, found racial differences in cranial measurements, which were quickly interpreted by the study leaders as showing that Black people and White people were biologically distinct and that Black people were inherently inferior to White people. In fact, the conclusions from the study were more or less preordained. For example, well before the study began, the secretary of the United States Sanitary Commission, Frederick Law Olmsted, wrote that nature distinguished the "negro class of the South with distinctive form and color that were marks not only of 'historical' but also mental and moral peculiarities" [16].

Nonetheless, the findings of this study were influential because the study claimed to provide "hard data" to document differences between the races. It was labeled a "truly scientific work" by the head of the Commission that initiated and oversaw it. In reality, it reflected a significant effort in the scientific and medical communities to reveal a "natural law" underpinning the notion of a racial hierarchy. The Civil War historian, Dr. John Haller, professor of history at Southern Illinois University, described this and other similar studies of the time as the making of a "racial ideology" [17].

Some of the ideas contained in the study's final report have shown remarkable resilience and can be found in racist stereotypes that still exist today. For example, one conclusion from this report was that Black people were biologically closer to apes than to other humans. About 150 years later, a government official from West Virginia denigrated First Lady Michelle Obama as an "ape in heels" [18]. Similarly, after *Fox News* reported that Barack and Michelle Obama's daughter, Malia, had been admitted to Harvard, the comment page associated with the report had to be disabled because it was flooded with comments that called Malia an "ape" or a "monkey" [19]. In the 1990s, one Los Angeles police officer referred to the beating of Black suspects as "monkey slapping time," and described a Black family they had to visit as "Gorillas in the Mist." It was also common among Los Angeles police to report incidents in which a Black person died as "NHI" – no humans involved [20].

Significantly, this stereotype is not confined to a few bigots. Dr. Phillip Atiba Goff, professor of African American Studies and Psychology at Yale University, Dr. Jennifer Eberhardt, professor of psychology at Stanford University, and several of their colleagues found a widespread tendency among White participants in their experiments to automatically associate Black people with gorillas or other kinds of apes [20].

The ideas contained in scientific racism thus created many of the derogatory and demeaning characterizations of Black people that have survived long after scientific racism became thoroughly discredited in the scientific and medical communities. These characterizations, in turn, caused the social and economic conditions that directly contribute to health problems among Black Americans. In addition, although the primary motivation for the enslavement of Black people in North America was financial (i.e., it provided free labor), the pervasive scientific racism that existed for centuries in Europe and the Americas helped slaveholders rationalize slavery and maintain it for about 250 years.

Beliefs about Black Americans: The Impact of Slavery

The existence of slavery in North America for about 250 years played a particularly critical role in the content of systemic and individual racism throughout our nation's history, including present times. Slavery formally established a model for the unequal distribution of power and economic resources based on a person's assigned race and was critical to shaping a broad social structure that did and still does significantly disadvantage Black Americans and their health: that is, systemic racism. The institution of slavery and its legacies have also been powerful forces in creating the specific content of many negative racist beliefs.

Slavery existed in some form around the world long before enslaved Africans were brought to North America. What made slavery in what became the United States somewhat different was that the enslaved individuals were almost exclusively defined by their perceived race or ethnicity. Not all slaves in America were Black. For example, Indigenous Peoples were also held as slaves. Nor were all slaveholders White. Indigenous Peoples and even some Black Americans owned slaves. However, in the main, slaves were Black people whose ancestors came from Africa, and those who enslaved them were White people whose ancestors came from Europe.

American slavery was also somewhat unique in terms of slaveholders' rights. In some other countries, the children of enslaved people were not automatically condemned to slavery. In the United States, however, state legislatures passed laws that said the status of all children "born in this country" was derived from "the conditions of the mother" [21]. Thus, if the mother was a slave, so was the child, and they both belonged to the mother's enslaver. This meant that slavery was essentially "inherited" in much the same manner as some physical characteristics are. Moreover, while some slaves could buy their freedom with money or certain other services, whether or not a slave would be freed was solely determined by the slaveholder in the vast majority of the cases.

The realities of slavery and its horrors and brutality are a matter of historical fact and a critical part of American history that cannot be hidden by ill-founded attempts to rewrite our national heritage. However, we are not historians and will not attempt to describe the history of slavery in the United States.[4] Rather, our discussion of slavery in the United States focuses on the role it played in shaping the way White people view Black people in the United States today. Slavery resulted in pervasive negative beliefs about enslaved Black people among slaveholders and their families. One reason for this was that slaveholders needed to justify their enslavement of other human beings.

The Power of Rationalization: The Justification of Slavery
To be sure, there were probably many slave traders and slaveholders so motivated by the economic gains derived from slavery that any personal conflicts about the morality of this enterprise simply never came to mind. Indeed, some simply rejected the moral implications altogether. The author of a pro-slavery article published in the *Washington Telegraph* in 1836 wrote: "[W]e ... deny that slavery is sinful or inexpedient...We deny that it is wrong in the abstract. We assert that it is the natural condition of man; that there ever has been, and there ever will be slavery; and ... we insist that the slavery of the southern States is the best regulation of slavery, whether we take into consideration the interests of the master or of the slave, that has ever been devised" [22].

However, many White slaveholders were quite aware of the moral conflict of owning slaves. As Dr. Ibram X. Kendi, professor of humanities at Boston University, argued in *Stamped from the Beginning*, such slaveholders felt a need to reconcile the basic tenets of their Christian faith with their enslavement of other human beings [21]. Many years of research and theory in social psychology provides at least a partial explanation of how slaveholders squared their behavior with their moral beliefs. Stanford Psychology Professor Dr. Leon Festinger, who first coined the phrase "cognitive dissonance," showed that most humans cannot comfortably live with an inconsistency between their thoughts and actions. They must

---

[4] There are numerous books that provide excellent and accessible historical accounts of the causes and consequences of slavery in America. Among them are: *Many Thousands Are Gone* by Ira Berlin, *Soul by Soul* by Walter Johnson, and *The Half Has Never Been Told* by Edward Baptist.

change one of them. In most instances, people change or modify their thoughts rather than their actual behaviors, because it requires much less immediate personal effort or, in the case of slavery, would cost much less. Slaveholders were not prepared to pay the financial cost of freeing their slaves; rather, they were going to rationalize enslaving them. Their justifications played a direct and important role in shaping how they viewed the people they considered their property.

A Theological Basis: God's Plan
One of the slaveholders' primary justifications was that slavery was part of God's plan and biblically sanctioned. This idea was based, in part, on an interpretation of the biblical story of Noah and his son, Ham. The story in the Hebrew Bible is that Ham saw Noah drunk and naked and, because of this, Noah cursed Ham's son, Canaan and his descendants to remain slaves forever [23]. The passages describing this event do not explain why Noah issued this curse or why he chose Ham's son Canaan. The Hebrew Bible also does not make any mention of Ham's race, but that the idea he was Black has a long history. (At least one biblical scholar, Dr. David Goldenberg, posits that misreadings of the original Hebrew text led to the mistaken idea that the Hebrew word for "Ham" meant black.) [24]. While the association between being Black and being a slave did not originate with White southerners, they seized on it as a biblical justification for the idea that slavery was ordained by God.

Slaveholders also used passages from the New Testament to justify slavery. One of these came from Paul, a disciple of Jesus. According to Christian tradition, while he was in prison, Paul wrote a letter to early Christians living in what is today Turkey. In one part of the letter Paul said, "Servants be obedient to them that are your masters, as unto Christ" [25]. This was interpreted by slaveholders as requiring slaves to do the bidding of their masters. Most White southerners were deeply religious, and such sentiments were often strongly supported by most southern ministers and churches, which split from many northern churches over the issue of slavery. According to Bishop Stephen Elliot of Georgia, slavery was the "key to the greatness of southern life and civilization" [26].

Biblical justifications of slavery even made it to speeches in the US Senate. For example, in 1850, Senator Jefferson Davis (who later became President of the Confederacy) stood on the floor of the US Senate and proclaimed that slavery "was established by decree of Almighty God . . . it is sanctioned in the Bible, in both Testaments, from Genesis to Revelation . . . it has existed in all ages, has been found among the people of the highest civilization, and in nations of the highest proficiency in the arts" [27].

Most of the people who opposed slavery, the abolitionists, were also deeply religious. To them such interpretations of biblical passages and God's will were hardly Christian at all. One of the most eloquent and famous abolitionists was the former slave, Frederick Douglass. He was a prominent advocate for the rights of Black Americans in the nineteenth century. He was also a devout Christian and wrote, "Between the Christianity of this land and Christianity of Christ, I recognize the widest possible difference – so wide as to receive one as good and pure and holy is of necessity to reject the other as bad, corrupt and wicked" [28].[5]

The "Positive Good" Thesis

Yet another kind of rationalization was that slavery was actually good for enslaved people. Perhaps the strongest and most eloquent person to argue that slavery was inherently good was John C. Calhoun. He was himself a slaveholder and a powerful figure in state and national politics. Calhoun was a US senator and a vice president in two different administrations. In 1837 he wrote, "I take higher ground. I hold that in the present state of civilization, where two races of different origin, and distinguished by color, and other physical differences, as well as intellectual, are brought together, the relation now existing in the slaveholding States between the two, is, instead of an evil, a good – a positive good" [29]. Such arguments included the racial stereotype that if freed, slaves would not be able to take care of themselves.

Similar ideas were reinforced in findings from other sources, such as the US census conducted at the time. The census of 1840 reported that freed Black people were 11 times more likely to be "insane or an idiot" than were Black slaves, implying that being free endangered the mental well-being of Black people [30]. This is almost certainly a politically motivated falsehood; findings from censuses of the time were often distorted to support the institution of slavery.

Getting It Backward: Confusing the Effects of Slavery with Their Causes

Among all the rationalizations used to justify slavery, there is one that seems to stand out as having the most impact on contemporary racist

---

[5] Biographies of Fredrick Douglass (e.g., *Fredrick Douglass: Prophet of Freedom* by David W. Blight) provide vivid pictures of what slavery was like and the political and social climate in America during and after the Civil War, especially the nature of the abolitionist movement.

attitudes and beliefs. This explanation was that because of their personal characteristics, Black people *deserved* to be enslaved. To understand this, we first should get some sense of what the experience of being an enslaved person must have been like. Historical descriptions of the living conditions of enslaved people and statistics about their health are important and informative, but they cannot really convey the full horrors of slavery. Indeed, it is probably impossible for anyone today to truly understand and appreciate what it was like to be an enslaved Black person.

However, there are first-person historical narratives that vividly describe the horrors of slavery. Thomas A. Jones was born in 1806. He spent the first 43 years of his life as a slave, but he escaped in 1849 and became a prominent spokesperson for the anti-slavery movement [31]. Jones was basically illiterate, but sometime in the 1850s his story was told in a book titled, *The Experience of Thomas H. Jones, Who was a Slave for 43 Years*. These excerpts from his book give us some idea of what life was like on slave plantations.

> I was born a slave. My recollections of early life are associated with poverty, suffering and shame. I was made to feel, in my boyhood's first experience, that I was inferior and degraded, and that I must pass through life in a dependent and suffering condition. The experience of 43 years, which were passed by me in slavery, was one of dark fears and darker realities. . . The supply of food given out to the slaves was one peck of corn a week, or some equivalent, [coarse bread] and nothing besides. . . Many of the slaves were so hungry after their excessive toil that they were compelled to steal food in addition to this allowance.

> During the planting and harvesting season . . . men and women were called out at three o'clock in the morning and worked on the plantation til it was dark at night, . . . Parents would often have to work for their children at home after each day's protracted toil, till the middle of the night and then snatch a few hours' sleep to get the strength for the heavy burdens of the next day. . . Little boys and girls too, worked and cried toting brush to the fires, husking the corn, . . . and running errands for the master and mistress and their three sons . . . and constantly receiving from them scoldings and beatings as their reward.

> One of the earliest scenes of painful memory associated with my opening years of suffering is connected with a severe whipping which my master inflicted on my sister Sarah. He tied her up, having compelled her to strip herself entirely naked, in the smoke house, and gave her a terrible whipping – at least so it seemed to my young heart, as I heard her scream, and stood by my mother, who was wringing her hands in an agony of grief, at the cruelties which her tender child was enduring.

Slaveholders forced enslaved people to act and live in ways that made them look less than human or at least certainly not the kind of human being who fit the norms of the White slaveholders and members of their families. Further, most of the slaveholders accepted some version of scientific racism and one or more justifications of slavery we presented earlier. These two things led them to develop certain beliefs about Black people. Some of these beliefs were factual – enslaved people were almost invariably uneducated and quite poor, for example. However, observing the behaviors of enslaved people on a daily basis also affected the ways that slaveholders thought about the reasons why the people they had enslaved were uneducated and poor, as well as many other similar characteristics. In contemporary terms, the slaveholders developed stereotypes about the Black people they had enslaved. Recall that a stereotype is the information people carry in their minds about the nature of people whom they believe share some characteristic in common. Stereotypes lead people to strongly link some set of common personal traits to membership in a specific social group that is easily identified by by things such as the color of their skin, their gender, or their ethnicity. The stereotype that most slaveholders held was that the Black people they had enslaved were sub-humans who should be controlled by White people.

There was nothing about slavery that was "natural," nor could slavery be explained by some innate characteristics of human beings. However, making strong inferences about the innate characteristics of a group of people is a natural part of how humans think about the world around them. When people (especially those in Western societies) see members of some clearly defined social group acting in a similar way and/or typically occupying a similar role in society (e.g., menial laborer), they are strongly inclined to ignore the situation that may have caused these behaviors or forced people into some role in society. Instead, they are inclined to attribute what they see to some innate or inherent characteristic of members of that group. (The theories that specifically explain these human tendencies are called "the fundamental attribution error" and "role theory." They are discussed in detail in the second half of this chapter.)

Although stereotype formation is a general human tendency, formation of negative stereotypes about Black enslaved people was especially likely among slaveholders. They were highly motivated to hold stereotypes that helped them to rationalize away the inhumanity of enslaving another human being. As we have already said, there was nothing natural or innate about enslaving another human being.

An American Tradition Continues: Perpetuating Racial Stereotypes

Slavery formally ended after the Civil War, but great social, economic, and political inequities continued; anti-Black racism was undiminished; and negative racial stereotypes remained part of American society. Part of the reason for this is that most Black Americans lived in the South and for them life actually changed relatively little after they were freed. The severe race-based "Jim Crow" laws enacted in the 1870s created social and economic conditions for freed Black people that were almost as abominable as those that had existed when they were enslaved. Racial segregation continued, and the economic and social conditions of Black Americans for the most part remained far below that of most White Americans.

In Chapter 4, we discuss how these racist laws directly affected the healthcare received by Black Americans. Here we discuss how these racist laws served to reinforce old racial stereotypes and create new ones. To begin, as was the case with slavery, living under these conditions likely produced many behaviors among Black people that resulted in more negative stereotyping of them. For example, Black people who were, in fact, usually forced into conditions of poverty, homelessness, and unemployment were often disparaged as being "lazy" and "dirty" rather than being recognized as victims of inequitable opportunity and resources. That is, once again the thought processes described earlier led White people to attribute the behaviors observed among Black people to inherent negative traits of that group. Such stereotypes had real implications for how White Americans of the time viewed the many problems of Black Americans, including their health problems.

Dr. W. E. B. Du Bois, who conducted the most thorough and systematic analyses of racial health disparities across several US cities in the late nineteenth century, found the incidence rates for diseases such as pneumonia and "consumption" (i.e., tuberculosis) were about three times greater among Black residents than among White residents [32]. Popular thought placed the blame for these disparities on the personal characteristics of Black Americans. "The mortality of Negroes in and near large towns still continues to be very great," stated an 1866 article in the *New York Times*. "The smallpox rages among them ... dirt, debauchery, [and] idleness are the major causes of this inordinate mortality." Some newspapers in both the North and the South even predicted the extinction of Black people by the twentieth century [33].

By contrast, Du Bois forcefully and eloquently (and correctly) argued that the causes of these racial health disparities were not biological but were the result of the racist society that most Black Americans had to endure. "Broadly speaking, the Negroes as a class dwell in the most unhealthy parts of the city and in the worst houses of those parts." He continued that, "The most difficult social problem in the matter of Negro health is the peculiar attitude of the nation toward the well-being of the race . . .. There have. . . been few other cases in the history of civilized peoples where human suffering has been viewed with such peculiar indifference" [34]. The negative health effects of contemporary segregated and under-resourced neighborhoods are discussed in Chapter 3.

Racial Stereotyping in the Northern United States

Although slavery had ended in northern states by the beginning of the nineteenth century, anti-Black racism did not, and negative racial stereotypes were widespread before and after the end of the Civil War. They did not differ much from those that existed in the southern states [35]. For example, in 1933 Dr. Daniel Katz, professor of psychology at Princeton University, and Dr. Kenneth Braly, professor of psychology at the University of Minnesota, asked Princeton undergraduates about their perceptions of various racial and ethnic groups in the United States. Students were asked to indicate what "traits" were more characteristic "of African Americans than other people." Black Americans were seen as more superstitious by 84 percent of the respondents, lazy by 75 percent, ignorant by 38 percent, and stupid by 22 percent [36].

One reason for the wide acceptance of these views of Black people is that stereotypes are a cultural phenomenon. Once established, they are transmitted in the ways people are socialized to view the world and are conveyed in conversation and popular media – historically, newspapers and books. Historians have documented the pervasive racism in the popular media of the late nineteenth and early twentieth centuries. According to Dr. Brian Behknen and Dr. Gregory Smithers, professors of history at the University of Iowa and Virginia Commonwealth University, respectively, "novels, advertisements, movies, children's cartoons, that were so saturated with racist references and representations of Native Americans, African-Americans, Asian-Americans and Latinos that racism in its many ugly forms became completely embedded in how most Americans saw the world around them" [37]. Themes related to racist stereotypes were widely featured in vaudeville and later the movies.

The early part of the twentieth century also saw the emergence of widespread attempts to sanitize slavery and offer justifications for the way Black people were treated in the southern states (and perhaps in the northern states as well). One example of this was a movie released in 1915, *The Birth of a Nation*. It contained an unfiltered and crude justification of Jim Crow laws and of the oppression of Black Americans; it was extremely popular throughout the United States. It portrayed freed Black people as bloodthirsty criminals and savages, intent on sexually assaulting any White woman they encountered. In the movie, Black people were defeated, and the purity of White southern womanhood was maintained by heroic members of the Ku Klux Klan. It was shown on the White House lawn and praised by President Woodrow Wilson. "It's like writing history with lightening," he said, and added, "My only regret is that it is all so terribly true" [38]. Most historians believe that *The Birth of a Nation* and the other aspects of this broad-based campaign to denigrate Black Americans had a substantial impact on racial attitudes and stereotypes throughout the United States.

In the northern states, animus toward Black people further increased as the result of enormous demographic changes in America brought about by what is known as the "Great Migration" of Black Americans. The migration began in the early twentieth century because of the extremely difficult conditions faced by Black people living in the American South. The poverty that southern Black Americans experienced was grinding. Most Black people worked in agriculture, and many of them were sharecroppers, who often wound up at the end of the growing season owing to the White landowners more in rent for their homes and the tools they used than they had earned [39]. Of course, there were the severe restrictions on the basic rights of the Black people who lived in the South, such as not being allowed to vote or to own certain kinds of property. Further, there were considerable dangers for Black Americans, especially Black men. They were lynched by White people for the most minor of supposed transgressions. For example, in 1919 in Georgia, a Black soldier returning from World War I was lynched simply because he refused to take off his uniform [40]. It is estimated that at least 4,000 Black people were lynched in the southern states between about 1880 and the end of World War II.

Underlying all these hardships was the fact that in the view of most Black southerners there was little, if any, hope that things would ever change. So, seeking to escape the difficulty of living in the American

South, millions of Black people began to move north.[6] Beginning in the 1920s and continuing for the next 50 years, about 6 million Black Americans left their homes in the South and moved northward, primarily to large urban centers in the Midwest and East. As a result, cities such as Detroit and Chicago, which had been almost exclusively White at the beginning of the twentieth century, saw an incredible rise in the number of Black residents. In Detroit, the increase was over 500 percent, and Chicago experienced about a 150 percent increase.

The Black migrants were not welcomed with open arms, as racist stereotypes and antipathy toward Black people were already firmly entrenched in northern cities. There were race riots in Chicago in response to the influx of Black people, which resulted in the deaths of 38 Black people and demolition of about 1,000 Black homes. Black people were not allowed to live in White neighborhoods, which produced the racial residential segregation that still characterizes most modern urban centers [41].

Further, as was also the case for many European immigrants arriving in the United States during this period, the arrival of large numbers of Black people was perceived as a very serious threat to the economic and political status of the White American majority. They were seen as competitors for jobs, especially when jobs became scarce because of the Great Depression of the 1930s. As we discuss more fully later in this chapter, intergroup competition for the same scare resources creates intergroup conflict. As documented by Isabel Wilkerson, this conflict led to actions that directly disadvantaged Black job applicants. Many companies simply refused to hire Black workers. For example, one company in Milwaukee told Black people to stop applying for jobs with them because the company "never did and didn't intend to hire Negroes" [41]. But even these kinds of job discrimination did not eliminate economic competition between Black people and White people, which became even worse when the Great Depression began in the 1930s.

The racist residential and occupational restrictions they faced in northern cities often forced Black residents into the worst neighborhoods and into the most menial jobs. The over-representation of Black Americans in densely crowded poor neighborhoods and low status jobs created negative racial stereotypes via the psychological mechanisms we have already

---

[6] In her Pulitzer Prize–winning book, *The Warmth of Other Suns: The Epic Story of America's Great Migration*, journalist Isabel Wilkerson provides a comprehensive description of the migration and the lives of the people who took part in it.

discussed. These negative stereotypes were not held by just a few avidly racist people; instead, they were widely shared by northern cities' White residents. In many respects, these stereotypes became part of the shared culture in large northern American cities.

This historical analysis tells us much about why anti-Black racism is part of America's history and how it became part of the fabric of American society. However, historical events are only part of the reason why anti-Black thoughts and feelings are still so pervasive in the United States. To fully understand anti-Black racism in the United States and its persistence across time and places, it is necessary to also consider how people think about the world around them and how they typically react to members of another social group that is in some way different from them. The origins of how we think about other people are rooted in our evolutionary past and provide fertile ground for racial bias to develop, spread, and thrive in today's world.

Human Thought and Motivation: The Psychological Roots of Racial Bias

The human beings who evolved successfully did so because of two things. The first of these was developing the kind of intellectual abilities that enabled early groups of humans to efficiently solve survival-related problems. Although other primates are capable of higher-order thinking, humans' much greater intellectual abilities make us unique from them. The other thing that we discuss in detail later in the chapter was the ability to form stable social groups, which provided safety and needed resources. Racial differences in appearance between people or groups initially played no role in either of these key aspects of the success of the human species. Early humans typically did not travel far enough to encounter people who looked different from them. Thus, racism per se is not an evolved, inherent part of human nature. Nevertheless, evolutionary forces did shape humans' current intellectual abilities in ways that created a foundation for racist thoughts and feelings to eventually become common [42]. They are unintended by-products of what human beings needed to do to be evolutionarily success-ful – that is, to live long enough to produce healthy offspring.

Higher-Order Thinking and Its Flaws

One critical intellectual ability or kind of higher-order thinking that early humans possessed was the power to see patterns in the environment around them, which enabled humans to better understand their surround-ings. If people can understand their environment, they can predict and substantially control and shape their futures. For example, any group's future survival depends directly on having reasonably reliable sources of food. Thus, early humans observed and learned the migratory patterns and habits of certain animals, which made it easier to hunt them. A bit later in their evolutionary and social development, humans used their ability to see seasonal patterns to learn how to plant crops in order to avoid the uncertainty of getting their food only from hunting. The development of agriculture is a signal event in human history.

Of course, humans can also detect patterns in the behavior of other people. These patterns may form the basis for expectations about how these people will behave. This may have been very useful for identifying friends and enemies as humans were evolving, but these processes can also lead to some form of stereotyping about other people. The typical human tendency to develop beliefs about the enduring characteristics of things in the world around them can devolve into hateful racial stereotypes about Black people that are at the core of many racial biases today.

Social psychologists have developed explanations of how and why people stereotype other people, especially those who are different from them. One of them was proposed in 1977 by Dr. Lee Ross, professor of psychology at Stanford University. His theory begins with the widely accepted premise that humans have a basic need to understand and make sense of the world around them. However, when people try to understand why others behave the way they do, they often make systematic errors. Specifically, they overestimate the extent to which a behavior is determined by an individual's personality or character, and underestimate the role of the person's situation in causing the behavior. Ross called this the "fun-damental attribution error" because, although the strength of its effects does differ across cultures, it is a more or less automatic tendency that occurs in a host of different situations [43]. This process applies not only to how people perceive a particular individual but also to how they come to see groups.

Another theory that explains the formation of negative stereotypes is "role theory," an idea first advanced by sociologists in the 1930s. Role theory begins with the premise that a very important determinant of how people act is the role they have taken on or been assigned in society (e.g., mother, teacher, blue collar worker, corporate executive). The behaviors associated with a given role are reinforced and maintained by social norms and people's personal expectations. Dr. Alice Eagly, professor of psychology at Northwestern University, and Dr. Anne Koenig, professor of psychology at the University of San Diego, have applied role theory to the development of stereotypes [44]. Their research shows that when members of an identifiable social group are likely to take up certain occupational roles, this causes other people to assume that the behaviors they observe are enduring personal characteristics of members of that group. In other words, social and occupational roles cause people to develop group stereotypes – beliefs about the characteristics of the typical member of some social group that occupies a certain role in society (e.g., unskilled occupations).

These processes can also occur when people are trying to understand some societal event they have read about, and it can lead individuals to form a racial stereotype. For example, consider high school dropout rates among Black students. Most Black students finish high school but, historically, the dropout rate is much higher among Black students than White students [45]. A person-oriented attribution for this is that Black students care less about their education or perhaps might not have the intellectual capacity to finish high school. In fact, however, there are much more complex explanations for dropping out of high school. Many students are "pulled" out of high school for a host of reasons like financial worries, out-of-school employment, family needs, or family changes such as marriage or having a child [46]. Deborah Feldman, an expert on the reasons behind high school dropout rates, interviewed 50 young people who dropped out of high school. She found that many high school dropouts come from poor families and confront academic challenges without any support from their schools or their families [47]. In sum, dropping out of high school is a complex social and educational phenomenon with multiple causes often involving the particular social and economic situations that a student faces. But, for a White person looking at the racial differences in dropout rates, it makes the world simpler and more predictable to attribute this phenomenon to the personal attributes of Black high school students rather than these situational factors. Critically, this can occur in the absence of any *conscious* racial bias.

Although these theories describe a more or less "neutral" human process of forming ideas about a social group, the ways people think about the actions of members of social groups are also often significantly shaped by their own needs, concerns, and goals. That is, this can be a *motivated* process. In many instances, people may be personally motivated to ascribe negative characteristics to certain groups different from their own, and reluctant to ascribe positive characteristics. For example, they may see the bad things these other people do as part of their nature, and good things as an exception to the rule or just luck [48]. Obviously, existing animus toward Black people makes it much more likely that a person will make this specific kind of attributional error. Similarly, racially biased individuals may be motivated to pay more attention to people in roles that confirm their racially biased stereotypes than to people in roles that would refute these stereotypes.

Thinking Efficiently (But Not Always Correctly)

Another aspect of higher-order thinking that has greatly benefitted humans' survival is the ability to quickly and efficiently take in new information about the world around them. We store that information in a way that makes it quickly accessible to guide our thoughts, feelings, and actions as we encounter new and often complex situations. When this stored information involves a person's social world it is called a "social cognition." Social cognitions are made up of the way we think about others and come to understand our social world. And today many of these cognitions are about a person's or group's race. Understanding how social cognitions operate is therefore crucial for understanding racial bias.

Thinking Fast, Thinking Slow

Throughout human history, people have regularly confronted two kinds of problems in their daily lives. There are those that require fast, almost automatic responses, and those that require slower and more thoughtful processes. Humans developed two different cognitive systems to address each kind of problem [49].[7]

The fast-thinking system uses long-term, stable, and well-established knowledge that people can access automatically and nonconsciously when one of their sensory systems detects something noteworthy in their environment (e.g., a car suddenly stopping in front of them). It produces very rapid responses without much thought (e.g., immediately hitting the brakes). The fast-thinking system was very valuable to our ancestors when they confronted an immediate danger. The fast-thinking system is not, however, reserved to responding to immediate physical threats. Today,

---

[7] A very clear and accessible description of the two systems of thinking can be found in *Thinking Fast and Slow* by Nobel laureate Daniel Kahneman, professor of psychology at Princeton University. Author Malcolm Gladwell also has a best-selling book about the fast-thinking systems, *Blink: The Power of Thinking without Thinking*.

fast-thinking can make the world an easier place to address a host of different problems because we do not have to stop and consciously consider every action we take.[8]

The slow-thinking system is activated when people have the time and motivation to reflect on their decisions and potential actions, or when life becomes a little more complex and presents us with situations or problems that might be more difficult to solve. A quick or automatic response to complex issues may not solve the problem and can often make it worse. When confronted with more complex problems, people consciously try to retrieve past memories and experiences that may help them solve the problem and to explore different solutions; these are both processes that take some time.

These two thinking systems operate in parallel, which has served humans very well. We would not have survived had they not. However, the way the fast-thinking and slow-thinking systems operate is critical to understanding the nature and dynamics of anti-Black racism in the United States today because they also lead to different kinds of racial bias.

Implicit and Explicit Racial Biases

In a highly influential research article about racial prejudice, Dr. Patricia Devine, professor of psychology at the University of Wisconsin, wrote that much of the research on prejudice, discrimination, and responses to diversity focused only on people's conscious attitudes and beliefs – what they tell us they were feeling, and their reasons why they do something (i.e., slow thinking) [50]. These are called explicit biases – positions that people consciously endorse and express. Dr. Devine argued, however, that explicit bias is not the whole story of racial prejudice. To fully understand the nature of prejudice, she suggested that scientists must also study nonconscious or implicit bias, which is composed of feelings and thoughts that are automatically and very quickly activated when people are exposed to a member of a social group different from their own and for which they already have developed a bias. Implicit stereotypes and attitudes represent thoughts and feelings about some target group that are part of a person's culture, to which they are constantly exposed. As people become socialized into their culture, such beliefs and feelings become so ingrained that they

---

[8] The fast-thinking system can also produce many faulty judgments. For more about these kinds of errors in everyday life, see Michael Lewis, *The Undoing Project: A Friendship That Changed Our Minds*, which chronicles Kahneman's and his longtime collaborator Dr. Amos Tversky's research on these kinds of errors.

create strong and automatically activated associations between specific groups and the characteristics culturally attributed to the group. Further, stereotypes of this nature are so well-learned that people are often unaware that they are using them [51]. In other words, they are part of the nonconscious racially biased thought processes discussed in the Introduction chapter. Even as America has moved toward a more egalitarian and less racist society, these nonconscious racial biases are very resistant to change.

For example, a White person who is striving to be more egalitarian in their beliefs might consciously try to substitute positive thoughts for negative thoughts when they interact with Black people. But the person's more or less automatic implicit stereotypes and attitudes are so well-learned that they may still remain. These implicit biases can affect people's feelings, thoughts, and actions toward a Black person whom they encounter, despite their conscious efforts to be egalitarian [51]. As we discuss in some detail in Chapter 6, physicians' implicit racial attitudes affect how they communicate with their Black patients.

Researchers have developed a number of different ways to measure the implicit and nonconscious attitudes and stereotypes, which people may not know they possess or cannot verbally express. The basic principle behind many of these techniques is that a person more quickly processes or responds to ideas or concepts that are strongly associated in their mind than to those that are not. The most commonly used test to assess implicit attitudes based on this principle is the Implicit Association Test (IAT) [52].[9]

In the IAT, people are seated in front of a computer screen and shown pictures of a Black person or White person that are accompanied by words in the corners of the screen. They are asked to make very quick decisions about whether the words that appear with the picture are positive or negative. If people have an automatically activated bias favoring White people over Black people, they will be quicker in responding to pictures of White people that are paired with positive words and also quicker to respond when the pictures of Black people are paired with negative words. Because these responses occur in a split-second, they are very difficult to control. While explicit attitudes often vary across people who differ in socioeconomic status, educational achievement, and region of the country

---

[9] The Implicit Association Test is also used to measure a host of other kinds of implicit responses to things like a person's gender, or certain occupations, or different political systems. Readers interested in anonymously taking the IAT can go to Project Implicit website: https://implicit.harvard.edu/.

where they live, these kinds of differences do not usually occur in implicit attitudes.

There are scientific concerns about the actual importance and nature of implicit attitudes and stereotypes, however. Some social psychologists have argued that they are not nearly as important as explicit attitudes and may not even exist.[10] However, many years of our own research on implicit convinces *us* that they do, indeed, reliably predict actions and are critical to the understanding of racism and other aspects of contemporary society. Implicit racial prejudice predicted, for example, whether someone would vote for Barack Obama or John McCain in the 2008 presidential election more accurately than explicit racial prejudice did [53].

The simple fact is that implicit biases play a significant role in contemporary race relations. They reflect the reality that while we live in a society that strongly endorses the principle of equality, most people have been exposed to the kinds of racist feelings and thoughts that have existed historically in our country and are embedded in its culture. In the middle of the twentieth century, in response to the civil rights movement and changes in social norms, many White people began to recognize that racial and ethnic prejudices were wrong, and they began trying to change or actively suppress such feelings. As a result, overt expressions of racial prejudice and stereotypes began to dramatically decline. For example, a study that compared racial stereotypes in the 1990s to those found by Daniel Katz and Kenneth Braly in 1933 revealed that the percentage of White people who associated negative characteristics with Black people had decreased substantially by the mid-1990s: None of the White people in the study described Black as "superstitious" (down from 84 percent), 45 percent described them as "lazy" (down from 75 percent), 14 percent described them as "ignorant" (down from 38 percent), and 11 percent characterized them as "stupid" (down from 22 percent) [54].

Implicit racial biases, however, have not declined to the same degree. Although data from over four million people who took the IAT between 2006 and 2017 show that implicit bias declined by about 17 percent, it is still quite common for White Americans to have high levels of implicit racial bias [55]. The result of this is that, today, many White people are well-intentioned and sincerely value an egalitarian society at the explicit

---

[10] Interested readers can find articles in psychological journals that challenge the IAT. One of them is "You can't assess the forest, if you can't access the trees: Psychometric challenges to measuring implicit bias in crowds" by Hart Blanton and James Jaccard. It appears in *Psychological Inquiry*, 2017, Volume 28, Number 4, pp. 249–257.

level, but they still have non-egalitarian thoughts and feelings at the implicit level. This does not mean that they are hypocrites or secret racists. People can genuinely hold both kinds of beliefs in their two separate cognitive systems.

Dr. Samuel Gaertner, professor of psychological and brain sciences at the University of Delaware, and, one of the co-authors of this book, JFD, have used the term "aversive racist" to describe such people – at a conscious, explicit level they do not feel antipathy toward Black people and actually find racist thoughts and feelings highly aversive. At the implicit level, however, they still harbor negative thoughts and feelings about Black people. Another name for this phenomenon is "prejudice of the well-intentioned" [56, 57].

The fact that White Americans may view a minority group positively at an explicit level but harbor bias that is implicit and often nonconscious is currently at the heart of much intergroup bias. This pattern of differing explicit and implicit racial attitudes affects many professional and social interactions between people of different races, but it does so subtly. For example, in one experiment conducted on how aversive racism operates, White participants were presented with an applicant for a job who was White or Black. They were asked how strongly they would recommend the candidate for the position. Different participants in this experiment also received different kinds of information about the applicants' qualifications. For some, the job candidate's credentials were impeccable (the person was clearly qualified for the job); for other candidates, they were mixed (the person was arguably qualified but perhaps not). The White participants did not discriminate against the Black applicant when both the Black candidate and the White candidate had obviously outstanding qualifications; in fact, they recommended the Black applicant slightly more strongly than the White applicant. However, when the case was not clear – when the applicant's qualifications were mixed – the White participants gave the White candidate the benefit of the doubt, recommending him more fre-quently and strongly than the Black candidate. In addition, participants in this condition of the experiment appeared to emphasize the strongest qualities of the White applicant and the weakest aspects of the Black applicant as being most relevant to success in the position. In other words, they discriminated against the Black applicant who had the same qualifica-tions, but only when they could justify it on the basis of some factor other than race (e.g., the Black candidate's lack of experience) [58].

What role does implicit bias play in this process? Decisions that are made consciously and with considerable reflection can override implicit biases, especially when the consequences of the actions are clear and there are strong social norms against such actions. This is the situation when a candidate – a Black applicant or a White job applicant – has impeccably strong credentials. Arbitrarily discriminating against either one would publicly violate a social norm of fairness. However, when a decision is not clear, as when a candidate's credentials are mixed, people's implicit or automatic feelings – things they cannot verbalize or may not be fully aware of – tend to guide their behavior. Although implicit bias was not actually measured in this study, a number of subsequent studies have measured the relative impact of explicit and implicit biases in situations where people's qualifications are ambiguous or there are no clear social norms as to how a White person should treat a Black person. Across these many studies, it has been found that aversive racists think and act more negatively toward Black people than their explicit attitudes would suggest.

People who have explicitly egalitarian attitudes but who harbor negative implicit bias may verbally express positive feelings but display nonverbal behaviors that contradict what they say. This mixed message creates uncertainty, and so subtle bias can be even more difficult than overt bias for minority group members to cope with psychologically. For example, in a study conducted by Dr. Jessica Salvatore, professor of psychiatry at Rutgers University, and Dr. J. Nicole Shelton, professor of psychology at Princeton University, Black students and White students were exposed to either ambiguously or blatantly prejudiced hiring recommendations. Then the White students and Black students were given a cognitively demanding task to perform. Whereas the White students experienced the greatest cognitive impairment after they were presented with blatant prejudice, the Black students showed more impairment after exposure to the more ambiguous prejudice [59]. Black people exposed to a case of blatant discrimination did find it stressful, but exposure to subtle discrimination is particularly challenging because of the effort they have to devote to determine whether and how bias was occurring. Moreover, when people continue to question why they were treated in a particular way, this rumination is damaging to people's mental health, leaving them particularly vulnerable to anxiety and depression.

Several studies have shown that Black people can accurately detect implicit racial bias and aversive racism when they interact with White people and that they react negatively to the person displaying these subtle biases [60]. Discrimination that is expressed subtly undermines Black people's trust of White people, who appear to be saying one thing but may be acting in a very different way. At the risk of being redundant, we point out we are including this somewhat academic discussion of explicit and implicit bias because of the critical role they play in racial health and healthcare disparities. For example, in Chapter 6 we discuss how explicit and implicit racial bias affects medical interactions between Black patients and non-Black physicians.

Simplifying Rules: Making the Complicated (Seem) Simple
Embedded in the fast-thinking and slow-thinking systems are ways to effectively deal with the incredibly complex world around us. People simply do not have the intellectual capacity to take in and consolidate all of the information that comes to them. Instead, we have ways to use our existing social cognitions to understand and organize the new things we encounter in the world around us. For example, most people have some perceptions of what neighborhoods in the city where they live are more or less dangerous. They know that there are exceptions to this perception and that it may not be totally accurate, but they still feel it useful as they plan travel around the city. These perceptions provide an efficient way to guide our behavior regarding these neighborhoods (e.g., to avoid them). In this respect, humans are "cognitive misers" – they use mental shortcuts, based on what they already know, to limit the effort they would spend processing new information, while maximizing their belief that they understand the world around them. This enables people to believe they are better prepared for new situations, and, in most instances, this actually does help.

Individuals' need to feel that they can predict and ultimately control the world around them is responsible for another way of trying to simplify that world. People pay attention to and seek out information that confirms what they expect, and they pay much less attention to information that is inconsistent with their expectations. That is, people have a *confirmatory bias*. Although it was not until the mid-to-late twentieth century that psychologists conducted formal experiments on the confirmation bias, at the beginning of the seventeenth century Sir Francis Bacon observed, "The human understanding when it has once adopted an opinion (either as being the received opinion or as being agreeable to itself) draws all things else to support and agree with it" [61].

We all engage in the confirmation bias to a greater or lesser extent. Relating this to intergroup relations, if we already have beliefs about a person's or group's typical attributes, we will – often without conscious intention – give more attention to behaviors that are consistent with these existing beliefs about the group (i.e., stereotypes) than those that are not. This has special significance in racial stereotyping because it can affect how

White people actually see Black people. For example, research reveals that people who see young Black men as threatening are more likely to also perceive their bodies as taller and heavier than comparable young White men of the same height and weight [62]. These findings may partially explain why police are usually more likely to use force with Black suspects than White suspects [63].

Again, the confirmation bias is a natural way humans process information, but when it comes to explanations of situations involving Black people, some people will try especially hard to look for information that confirms the idea that something bad about Black people caused a certain outcome. One instance of this was how people with a certain political agenda used the information that George Floyd had used recreational drugs to claim that it was these drugs rather than the actions of the police officer who sat on his neck for 40 minutes that caused his death. For example, some national figures, such as Tucker Carlson of Fox News, actually claimed that George Floyd in fact died of a fentanyl overdose [64].[11] (There is absolutely no evidence that this politically motivated explanation of Mr. Floyd's death is actually true.)

The Rest of the Story: Forming Social Groups

The second element that enabled early humans to survive in hostile and dangerous environments – the ability to form social groups that protected individual members and obtained the resources they needed – provides further understanding of the origins and continued presence of anti-Black racism. By living in groups in which people share responsibilities and coordinate activities, humans could accomplish much more than they could individually. As social life became more complex, the more successful and efficient societies were those organized by group hierarchies – with certain groups at the top and other groups far below in the pecking order. This made the groups better coordinated and more able to deal with the survival challenges they inevitably confronted, such as finding food and defeating rival groups. But group hierarchies also create social inequities. People at the top of their group hierarchy make the rules of the society. To quote a line from *Animal Farm*, George Orwell's classic fable about animals who took over a farm and formed a social group, "All pigs are equal, but some are more equal than others."

---

[11] More recently the performer "Ye" (nee Kanye West) has made the same fallacious claim about the cause of Mr. Floyd's death.

A main consequence of living in social groups is that we are typically inclined to view people in terms of their group membership, and we further identify them in terms of whether someone is a member of our own group or of another group. Again, initially none of this had anything to do with *racial* animus or conflict. As already noted, in the very long history of humans, racial conflict is a very, very recent event, mainly because early humans did not interact with people who looked much different from them.

However, at least by medieval times, people were traveling far enough to encounter other people who looked different from them. Specific inter-group conflicts, economic concerns, and social customs caused people to specify which personal attributes marked someone as an in-group or an out-group member. Very early in the history of Europe, skin color (which became presumed biological race) became a very important quality used to mark a person's group membership, and this was especially true among the Europeans who immigrated to North America.

Race became a critical element in another kind of mental shortcut people use, which we discussed earlier. Race became a societally significant marker for social categorization. When we see others, we do not see them only as individuals but also as members of groups who share similar qualities. As with other mental shortcuts, people engage in social catego-rization because there is just too much information to process and com-prehend at any one time. People need to simplify their social world in order to understand it.

Perceiving Us and Them: Social Categorization

Social categorization makes people feel that they understand the world better because once they categorize a person into a group (e.g., "low socioeconomic status" or "Black"), they see that person as like other members of the same group. Thus, applying what they believe about the group in general creates a feeling that they know more about the person than they actually do.

Seeing a person as a member of a social category allows people to organize the information they have about groups of people in their social world and use it to attribute certain characteristics to an individual member of that group. This is called "top-down" perceptions. That is, people fill in gaps about what they know about a particular person with information about what they think people in that group are generally like. Moreover, as with the attributional biases that we considered earlier, people see the common qualities of the group as the core attributes of people with that group. This leads to statements like, "Oh, they did that because that's the way *those* people are!"

Once we view a person in terms of group membership, we automatically also determine whether that person is a member of our own group or of another group. We view our own group (the in-group) as a community of people who are like us, who depend on each other, and who are good and trustworthy. Our group makes us feel like we belong and gives us a sense of security.

There are profound effects that occur when people see other people in terms of being in-group or out-group members [65]: some of these are

- Members of a group other than one's own (an "out- group") are seen as very similar to each other (this is called the "out-group homogeneity effect")
- Differences between in-group and out-group members are exaggerated
- People feel closer to in-group members
- Out-group members are perceived as less human
- The lives of in-group members are seen as more valuable than those of out-group members
- People think more deeply and in a more detailed fashion about in-group members
- In-group members are seen as sharing attitudes while out-group members are believed to have contrasting attitudes
- People want to approach in-group members but avoid out-group members
- People anticipate out-group members to be biased against them
- In-group members are valued more when they are biased against the out-group
- In-group members are more helpful, cooperative, and generous with each other

People do see differences among individual members of their in-group, but they are much less likely to differentiate among members of the out-group. There is nothing intentional about this catergorization process; it is simply due to the fact that humans are inherently social animals.

In the United States, a person's race is an especially powerful determinant of how we socially categorize others, and consequently how we perceive those in our in-group and those in an out-group. This is because, as we have documented, race has been one of the most socially significant ways to classify people throughout US history. Indeed, as also mentioned in the Introduction, for a long time in the United States a Black person was formally *defined* as an individual who has "one drop of Black blood in their family heritage. But this is because of the particular history of the United States: Using ancestors as part of racial classification is nowhere near as relevant in many other societies across the world. For example, although Brazil also has a long history of enslaving Black people and many of the same problems with anti-Black racism as the United States, Brazilians rarely consider a person's ancestry in identifying their race, and the Brazilian government has never asked about a person's "race" in their national census [66]. In the United States, race has been formally included in national censuses since 1790. So, while social categorization is a normal human process, historical and contemporary political, economic, and social factors affect the things that people pay attention to for classifying people into groups, and in the United States race is a powerful determinant of the social category in which a person is placed. A person's race therefore typically determines whether they are part of "us" or part of "them."

Classifying people into groups affects the way people feel about individual members of a group and the group as a whole. It also brings to mind a mental picture of what members of that group are like. These are the stereotypes or beliefs about a group's common characteristics. As is true with all forms of social cognition, stereotypes are not only formed about minority racial groups. Any social group defined by some observable characteristic can and usually will be stereotyped. However, stereotypes become particularly relevant to anti-Black racism when these group generalizations negatively and unfairly devalue people, and they generate emotional reactions like disgust and fear. The belief that all members of a group have specific negative qualities leads to individual and systemic discrimination that motivates segregation and restricts that group's social and economic opportunities.

What Is Should Be: System Justification

Yet another general human tendency is, because they think favorably about the groups to which they belong, they are inclined to justify or defend their own group's beliefs and actions. Moreover, people not only want to hold favorable attitudes about themselves and their own groups, but also they want to hold favorable attitudes about the overarching social order. To hold these favorable attitudes, they engage in system justification [67].

Consequently, people engage in a range of efforts to maintain and reinforce the current social structure – particularly when they are members of socially dominant groups. We presented a clear example of this at the beginning of this chapter when we discussed some politicians' negative reactions to the 1619 Project and other efforts intended to make people aware of the pervasive racism and racial discrimination in America's past. While it is quite possible that some politicians oppose teaching about racism in America to gain the support of potential voters who are opposed to such curriculum, system justification may be at play as well. They do not want schools teaching about events in American history such as slavery because they believe these teachings will challenge the prevailing view of the United States as a kind, benevolent place that has always treated all of its citizens equally.

Yale historian Dr. David Blight has argued that a desire to defend the American system is, in fact, why so many school systems are reluctant to teach about past racism. "The biggest obstacle to teaching slavery effectively in America," he states, "is the deep, abiding American need to conceive of and understand our history as 'progress,' as the story of a people and a nation that always sought the improvement of mankind, the advancement of liberty and justice, the broadening of pursuits of happiness for all" [67].

People tend to be committed to the systems guiding their society and, thus, when they encounter information that challenges the fairness (and, ultimately, the stability) of their society, they tend to invoke system-justifying ideologies that rationalize this unfairness. In the case of systemic racism and widespread social and economic inequities, these are justified by widespread beliefs like, "People can succeed if only they work hard enough" (i.e., meritocracy and the "American Dream"), or "People get what they deserve" (i.e., the belief in a just and fair world) [68]. People may therefore seek to explain the current racial social and economic disparities not as the result of systemic racism but rather caused by something that Black people themselves are personally responsible for (e.g., lack of initiative, not being interested in getting an education, a lack of family values). This justification enables them to see their social world, and thus themselves, as fair and just. To be sure, anti-Black racism increases the tendency to do this. However, even people who are not active and aggressive racists will attempt to defend the system of which they are a part. In fact, there is evidence that some members of traditionally oppressed racial and ethnic groups may also engage in system justification, even when the system is blatantly unjust because most people have a fundamental need for order, understanding, and control [68]. System justification can make social inequities appear logical and sensible, and therefore system-justifying ideologies can be used to explain why some social group is socially and economically disadvantaged relative to other groups. In other words, system justification can support systemic racism.

Sometimes particularly dramatic and well-publicized instances of a social injustice can cause people to challenge the system to which they belong. Such things are, however, frequently short-lived. For example, in the wake of the murder of George Floyd in 2020 there was an increase in support among White Americans for Black organizations that challenge systemic racism in America. This change in attitudes was, though, quite transitory. One year after Mr. Floyd's murder by a Minneapolis police officer in the summer of 2020, the level of support for Black Lives Matter was 37 percent, exactly what it had been before George Floyd was murdered. Further, the percentage of people who *opposed* the movement in July 2021 was actually about twice as high as it was immediately after Floyd's murder [69]. There was also a dramatic rebound in trust of law enforcement. In the month after George Floyd's death, 56 percent of Americans expressed trust in law enforcement; one year later 69 percent said they trusted law enforcement. The rise in trust of law enforcement almost perfectly paralleled the decline in support for the Black Lives Matter movement [63].

Motivated Bias: The Role of Threat

From the time humans first organized themselves into social groups there was competition and the threat of harm between different social groups. This affected not only a group's strategies about how to deal with the competition and threats from another group; it affected their thoughts about the other group as well. How members of a group think about, feel about, and act toward another group and its members strongly depend on whether they see the actions of the other group as beneficial or harmful to their own group. Seeing other groups as competitors arouses bias, leads people to discriminate, and often produces open conflict. In addition, people tend to create or change the content of their beliefs about individual members of the threatening group. That is, they form stereotypes about a competitive or threatening group that tend to derogate and dehumanize members of the other group. This can be seen even among groups of people who are members of the same racial group and similar in a number of other ways.

For example, in a classic experiment on how competition can create conflict between different groups, twenty-two 12-year-old boys attending summer camp were randomly assigned to two separate groups. Initially, the members of each group were unaware of the other group's existence. Midway through the first week, the boys in each group got to know one another. The mere fact that another group existed made each group of boys develop their own sense of in-group identity. One group named itself the Eagles, and the other group called itself the Rattlers, and they quickly became territorial, saying things like "our diamond" and "our swimming hole."

During the second week of the experiment, the researchers brought the two groups together. The boys were not only surprised to see the other group but also suspicious and concerned. Hostile rumors emerged. By the end of the second week, each group insisted that it wanted to challenge the other group in competitive games. The experimenters satisfied the boys' wishes. They had the groups compete against each other in a number of athletic activities such as tug-of-war, with the winning group receiving prizes. The groups quickly developed stereotypes and engaged in prejudiced behavior. Group members regularly exchanged verbal insults ("ladies first") and engaged in name-calling ("sissies," "stinkers," "pigs," "bums," "cheaters," and "communists"). These exchanges soon escalated into physical conflict. There was genuine hostility between these groups. Each group conducted raids on the other's cabins that resulted in the destruction and theft of property. The boys carried sticks, baseball bats, and socks filled with rocks as weapons. Intergroup conflict began to spiral. Even when they were not in direct competition, the boys showed animosity toward each other. In the dining hall, some of the Eagles protested that they did not want to eat in the same place as Rattlers. Conflict became more and more intense. Fistfights broke out, and food and garbage fights frequently erupted. This bias and conflict were only alleviated after the two groups of boys were placed in a situation where it was necessary to cooperate to achieve a mutually desired goal [70].

We have already discussed how the interracial competition for certain kinds of jobs that emerged in large northern cities when large numbers of Black people moved into them affected race relations in these cities. This was especially true for unskilled, menial jobs, which unskilled White workers had all to themselves until the Great Migration. The competition changed a good number of White people's beliefs about Black people and led to anti-Black thoughts and actions. This resulted in many physical confrontations between Black people and White people in northern cities such as Detroit, Michigan, in the early part of the twentieth century [71].

Perceived competition and threat have fueled racial and ethnic conflict in the past, and this problem continues to today. The effects of perceived threat among White Americans can be seen in the increase in their feeling that "reverse racism" is somehow negatively affecting their lives. Indeed, researchers at Tufts University have found a disturbing historical trend over the last 60 years in the feelings of White Americans about the social and economic gains Black Americans have made [72].

Most White Americans generally believe that in recent years there has been dramatic decline in the level of anti-Black bias, accompanied by a parallel increase in anti-White bias. That is, they believe that Black Americans' social and economic gains have been largely achieved at the expense of White Americans. Racism is seen as kind of "zero sum game," in which a gain for one side automatically means a loss for the other. In this case, there is a perception among many White Americans that as anti-Black racism declines, anti-White racism increases. This perspective is especially strong among people who identify themselves as politically conservative. The actual facts, of course, refute such perceptions: There is no evidence that Black Americans have done better at some cost to White Americans. However, the widespread perception of so-called reverse discrimination creates a backlash against attempts made by many social programs and presents yet another major barrier to reducing the racial inequities that exist in America today.

Contemporary Anti-Black Racism

All of the historical events and intellectual processes we have discussed play significant roles in the level of anti-Black racism in twenty-first-century America. Although nationwide polls have demonstrated significant overall reductions in expressions of negative attitudes and negative stereotypes of Black Americans by White Americans over the last 50 to 75 years, explicit anti-Black racism still exists, and in a very virulent form among portions of US society. The Southern Poverty Law Center, which has followed the activities of extremist groups for many years, determined that there are over 700 organized hate groups operating in the United States today [73]. These groups are more common in the South than elsewhere but are present in at least 47 different states. Negative feelings toward people of color are not confined to the political extremes, however. Racial stereotypes are still very common among White Americans in general. For example, in 2019, a survey by the Pew Research Center found that more than 50 percent of the non-Black respondents thought that a lack of effort among Black Americans was a reason for the racial inequities that exist in America [74].

Besides asking people directly about their own racial attitudes, researchers also find it valuable to understand how people perceive race and race relations in America more generally. Such questions in recent national polls reveal large differences as a function of respondents' race. White people and Black people see the world in quite divergent ways. For example, only 5 percent of White Americans overall believed that being Black hurts a person's ability to get ahead, but 52 percent of Black Americans believe this to be true [74]. Meanwhile, Black people are far more likely than White people to identify racial discrimination as a major obstacle for Black people in America (84 versus 54 percent). And perhaps most tellingly, whereas only 8 percent of Black respondents to the poll felt that racial equality has been achieved in America, almost 40 percent of White Americans believe this is true.

The feelings that Black Americans and White Americans have about one another and the nature of contemporary American society affect every aspect of their lives. In the remainder of the book, we focus on one incredibly important social problem that is directly tied to racial attitudes in the United States – pervasive racial disparities in the quality of health and healthcare between Black Americans and White Americans.

Putting It All Together

Anti-Black racism is an integral part of our nation's history that persists despite enormous time and effort spent to eradicate racial bias. Certainly, the vicious and overt manifestations of racism that were common during slavery and the Jim Crow era have diminished substantially, but anti-Black racism persists and does great damage to all Americans. It is particularly harmful to the health of Black Americans.

We separated our explanations of the persistence and pervasiveness of anti-Black racism into the effects of certain historical events and the way in which humans naturally think about the world around them. However, in reality, these two explanations are intertwined. Scientific racism and slavery both played enormous roles in past racial injustices and provided a legacy for many present ones, including social and economic inequities and anti-Black thoughts and feelings among many Americans. However, the ways humans think about their social world and process social information have also significantly contributed to the justification of these inequities and the development of the racial biases that exist today.

People are not born as racists. Racism is not part of human nature, but the things we have discussed make racial animus an integral part of the social fabric of America. This makes the solutions to widespread contemporary racial inequities much more difficult, but (writ large) does not mean solutions are impossible. Before we consider some of these solutions, we turn to the role of anti-Black racism in those inequities that directly affect the health of Black Americans and should be of concern to all Americans.

REFERENCES

1. Onion, R. (2021, November 16). *The New 1619 Project.* https://slate.com/news-and-politics/2021/11/1619-project-book-review-whats-changed-from-the-original-magazine-issue.html
2. Cohen, S. (2020, July 23). Defund teaching about slavery? Sen. Tom Cotton proposes legislation attacking The 1619 Project. *Forbes.* www.forbes.com/sites/sethcohen/2020/07/23/tom-cotton-proposes-legislation-attacking-the-1619-project/?sh=5b598f66c3c0
3. World Population Review. (2023). States that have banned critical race theory. https://worldpopulationreview.com/state-rankings/states-that-have-banned-critical-race-theory
4. Trawalter, S., Richeson, J. A., & Shelton, J. N. (2009). Predicting behavior during social interactions: A stress and coping model. *Personality and Social Psychology Review, 13*(4), 243–268. https://groups.psych.northwestern.edu/spcl/documents/PSPR09.pdf
5. Issac, B. (2013). *The invention of racism in classical antiquity.* Princeton University Press. https://doi.org/10.1515/9781400849567
6. BBC History. (n.d.). Galen (c.130 AD–c.210 AD). www.bbc.co.uk/history/historic_figures/galen.shtml
7 Byrd, W. M., & Clayton, L. A. (2003). Racial and ethnic disparities in healthcare: A background and history. In B. D. Smedley, A. Y. Stith, & A. R. Nelson (Eds.), *Unequal treatment: Confronting racial and ethnic disparities in health care* (pp. 455–527). National Academies Press.
8. Roberts, D. (2011). *Fatal invention: How science, politics, and big business re-create race in the twenty-first century.* New Press.
9. David Hume, "Part I, Essay XXI: Of National Characters." In *The Philosophical Works of David Hume, Including all the Essays, and Exhibiting the More Important Alterations and Corrections in the Successive Editions Published by the Author: Essays, Moral, Political, and Literary* (Vol. 3, pp. 217–236; 228–229). Edinburgh/Boston, 1854. https://medium.com/@christopherrichardwadedettling/modern-european-right-david-hume-and-the-negro-as-an-inferior-human-race-f6916ee41a66
10. Voltaire on Racial Differences. *Bartleby Research.* www.bartleby.com/essay/Voltaire-On-Racial-Differences-FJTX3YW5DDT

11. Menand, L. (2001). Morton, Agassiz, and the origins of scientific racism in the United States. *The Journal of Blacks in Higher Education, 34*, 110–113. https://doi.org/10.2307/3134139
12. Mitchell, P. W. (2018). The fault in his seeds: Lost notes to the case of bias in Samuel George Morton's cranial race science. *PLoS Biology, 16*(10), e2007008. https://doi.org/10.1371/journal.pbio.2007008
13. Deutsches Primatenzentrum (DPZ)/German Primate Center. (2020, September 25). Primate brain size does not predict their intelligence. *ScienceDaily.* www.sciencedaily.com/releases/2020/09/200925113353.htm
14. Schwalm, L. A. (2018). A body of "truly scientific work": The U.S. Sanitary Commission and the elaboration of race in the Civil War era. *Journal of the Civil War Era, 8*(4), 647–676. www.jstor.org/stable/26520990
15. Byrd, W. M., & Clayton, L. A. (2012). *An American health dilemma: A medical history of African Americans and the problem of race – Beginnings to 1900.* Routledge.
16. Library of Congress. (n.d.). *Frederick Law Olmsted Papers.* www.loc.gov/collections/frederick-law-olmsted-papers/
17. Haller, J. S. (1970). Civil War anthropometry: The making of a racial ideology. *Civil War History, 16*(4), 309–324. https://doi.org/10.1353/cwh.1970.0065
18. Narayan, C. (2016, December 14). Official who called Michelle Obama "ape in heels" gets job back. *CNN.* www.cnn.com/2016/12/13/us/official-racist-post-return-trnd/index.html
19. Fox News readers bash Obama's daughter with racial slurs, "Ape," "Monkey." (2016, May 3). *DiversityInc.* www.diversityinc.com/malia-obama-fox-news/
20. Goff, P. A., Eberhardt, J. L., Williams, M. J., & Jackson, M. C. (2008). Not yet human: Implicit knowledge, historical dehumanization, and contemporary consequences. *Journal of Personality and Social Psychology, 94*(2), 292–306. https://doi.org/10.1037/0022-3514.94.2.292
21. Kendi, I. X. (2016). *Stamped from the beginning: The definitive history of racist ideas in America.* Bold Type Books.
22. Garrison, L. (1835, August 29). Refuge of oppression. *Washington Telegraph.* www.newspapers.com/clip/43028602/a-pro-slavery-piece/
23. *Genesis 9:20–27.* King James Version.
24 Goldenberg, D. M. (2003). *The curse of Ham: Race and slavery in early Judaism, Christianity and Islam.* Princeton University Press.
25. *The Bible. King James Version. (Ephesians 6:5–7).*
26 Mounger, D. M. (1975). History as interpreted by Stephen Elliott. *Historical Magazine of the Protestant Episcopal Church, 44*(3), 285–317. www.jstor.org/stable/42974673
27. Davis, J. (1850, February 14). Speech of Mr. Davis of Mississippi, on the subject of slavery in the territories. *The Portal to Texas History.* https://texashistory.unt.edu/ark:/67531/metapth497836/
28. Douglass, F. (1845). *Narrative of the life of Frederick Douglass, an American slave.* Anti-Slavery Office. https://docsouth.unc.edu/neh/douglass/menu.html

29. Calhoun, J. (1837, February 6). *John Calhoun: Slavery a positive good.* University of Missouri, St. Louis. www.umsl.edu/~virtualstl/phase2/1850/events/perspectives/documents/calhoun02.html

30. Washington, H. A. (2006). *Medical apartheid: The dark history of medical experimentation on Black Americans from colonial times to the present.* Doubleday Books.

31. Documenting the American South. (n.d.). *The experience of Thomas H. Jones, who was a slave for forty-three years.* https://docsouth.unc.edu/fpn/jones/summary.html

32. Du Bois, W. E. B. (1906). The health and physique of the Negro American. Report of a social study made under the direction of Atlanta University, together with the Proceedings of the Eleventh Conference for the Study of the Negro Problems, Held at Atlanta University, on May the 29th, 1906. Atlanta University Press. www.ncbi.nlm.nih.gov/pmc/articles/PMC1449799/

33. Downs, J. (2012). *Sick from freedom: African-American illness and suffering during the Civil War and Reconstruction.* Oxford University Press.

34. Du Bois, W. E. B. (1899). *The Philadelphia Negro: A social study.* University of Pennsylvania Press. https://repository.wellesley.edu/object/wellesley30494

35. Lemons, J. S. (1977). Black stereotypes as reflected in popular culture, 1880–1920. *American Quarterly, 29*(1), 102–116. www.jstor.org/stable/2712263

36. Katz, D., & Braly, K. (1933). Racial stereotypes of one hundred college students. *Journal of Abnormal and Social Psychology, 28*(3), 280–290. https://doi.org/10.1037/h0074049

37. Smithers, G., & Behnken, B. D. (2015). *Racism in American popular media: From Aunt Jemima to the Frito Bandito.* Praeger.

38. Benbow, M. E. (2010). Birth of a quotation: Woodrow Wilson and "Like Writing History with Lightning." *The Journal of the Gilded Age and Progressive Era, 9*(4), 509–533. www.jstor.org/stable/20799409

39. History.com Editors. (2019, June 7). Sharecropping. *History.com.* www.history.com/topics/black-history/sharecropping

40. Army uniform cost soldier his life. (1919, April 5). *Chicago Defender.* www.nypl.org/research/collections/articles-databases/chicago-defender-1905-1975

41. Wilkerson, I. (2020). *The warmth of other suns: The epic story of America's great migration.* Penguin UK.

42. Cosmides, L., Tooby, J., & Kurzban, R. (2003). Perceptions of race. *Trends in Cognitive Sciences, 7*(4), 173–179. https://doi.org/10.1016/S1364-6613(03)00057-3

43. Ross, L. (1977). The intuitive psychologist and his shortcomings: Distortions in the attribution process. In L. Berkowitz (Ed.), *Advances in experimental social psychology* (Vol. 10, pp. 173–220). Academic Press. https://doi.org/https://doi.org/10.1016/S0065-2601(08)60357-3

44. Koenig, A. M., & Eagly, A. H. (2019). Typical roles and intergroup relations shape stereotypes: How understanding social structure clarifies the origins of stereotype content. *Social Psychology Quarterly, 82*(2), 205–230. https://doi.org/10.1177/0190272519850766

45. The racial gap in four-year high school graduation rates (2021, April 5), *The Journal of Blacks in Higher Education*. www.jbhe.com/2020/03/the-racial-gap-in-four-year-high-school-graduation-rates/

46. Doll, J. J., Eslami, Z., & Walters, L. (2013). Understanding why students drop out of high school, according to their own reports: Are they pushed or pulled, or do they fall out? A comparative analysis of seven nationally representative studies. *SAGE Open*, *3*(4), 2158244013503834. https://doi.org/10.1177/2158244013503834

47. Long, C. (2017, December 19). Some of the surprising reasons why students drop out of school. *National Education Association*. www.nea.org/advocating-for-change/new-from-nea/some-surprising-reasons-why-students-drop-out-school

48. APA Dictionary of Psychology. https://dictionary.apa.org/ultimate-attribution-error

49. Smith, E. R., & DeCoster, J. (2000). Dual-Process models in social and cognitive psychology: Conceptual integration and links to underlying memory systems. *Personality and Social Psychology Review*, *4*(2), 108–131. https://doi.org/10.1207/S15327957PSPR0402_01

50. Devine, P. G. (1989). Stereotypes and prejudice: Their automatic and controlled components. *Journal of Personality and Social Psychology*, *56*(1), 5–18. https://doi.org/10.1037/0022-3514.56.1.5

51. Greenwald, A. G., & Lai, C. K. (2020). Implicit social cognition. *Annual Review of Psychology*, *71*, 419–445. https://doi.org/10.1146/annurev-psych-010419-050837

52. Greenwald, A., Brendl, M., Cai, H., Cvencek, D., Dovidio, J. F., Friese, M., Hahn, A., Hehman, E., Hofmann, W., Hughes, S., Hussey, I., Jordan, C., Jost, J., Kirby, T. A., Lai, C., Lang, J., Lindgren, K., Maison, D., Ostafin, B., Rae, J. R., Ratliff, K., Smith, C., Spruyt, A., & Wiers, R. (2022). The Implicit Association Test at age 20: What is known and what is not known about implicit bias. *Behavior Research Methods*, *54*, 1161–1180. https://doi.org/10.31234/osf.io/bf97c

53. Greenwald, A. G., Smith, C. T., Sriram, N., Bar-Anan, Y., & Nosek, B. A. (2009). Implicit race attitudes predicted vote in the 2008 U.S. Presidential election. *Analyses of Social Issues and Public Policy*, *9*(1), 241–253. https://doi.org/10.1111/j.1530-2415.2009.01195.x

54. Devine, P. G., & Elliot, A. J. (1995). Are racial stereotypes really fading? The Princeton trilogy revisited. *Personality and Social Psychology Bulletin*, *21*(11), 1139–1150. https://doi.org/10.1177/01461672952111002

55. Charlesworth, T. E. S., & Banaji, M. R. (2019, August 14). Research: How Americans' biases are changing (or not) over time. *Harvard Business Review* https://hbr.org/2019/08/research-on-many-issues-americans-biases-are-decreasing

56. Dovidio, J. F., Gaertner, S. L., & Pearson, A. R. (2017). Aversive racism and contemporary bias. In C. G. Sibley & F. K. Barlow (Eds.), *The Cambridge handbook of the psychology of prejudice* (pp. 267–294). Cambridge University Press. https://doi.org/10.1017/9781316161579.012

57. Gaertner, S. L., & Dovidio, J. F. (1981). Racism among the well-intentioned. In E. Clausen & J. Bermingham (Eds.), *Pluralism, racism, and public policy: The search for equality* (pp. 208–222). G. K. Hall.

58. Dovidio, J. F., & Gaertner, S. L. (2000). Aversive racism and selection decisions: 1989 and 1999. *Psychological Science, 11*(4), 315–319. https://doi .org/10.1111/1467-9280.00262

59. Salvatore, J., & Shelton, J. N. (2007). Cognitive costs of exposure to racial prejudice. *Psychological Science, 18*(9), 810–815. https://doi.org/10.1111/j .1467-9280.2007.01984.x

60. Dovidio, J. F., Kawakami, K., & Gaertner, S. L. (2002). Implicit and explicit prejudice and interracial interaction. *Journal of Personality and Social Psychology, 82*(1), 62–68. https://doi.org/10.1037/0022-3514.82.1 .6261.

61. Bacon, F. (1620). *Novum organum.* https://oll.libertyfund.org/title/bacon-novum-organum

62. Wilson, J. P., Hugenberg, K., & Rule, N. O. (2017). Racial bias in judgments of physical size and formidability: From size to threat. *Journal of Personality and Social Psychology, 113*(1), 59–80. https://doi.org/10.1037/pspi0000092

63. Ross, C. T., Winterhalder, B., & McElreath, R. (2020). Racial disparities in police use of deadly force against unarmed individuals persist after appropriately benchmarking shooting data on violent crime rates. *Social Psychological and Personality Science, 12*(3), 323–332. https://doi.org/10.1177/ 1948550620916071

64. Vaillancourt, W. (2022, August 3). Tucker Carlson: Convicted murderer Derek Chauvin didn't murder George Floyd. *Daily Beast.* www .thedailybeast.com/tucker-carlson-says-convicted-murderer-derek-chauvin-didnt-murder-george-floyd

65. Kawakami, K., Amodio, D. M., & Hugenberg, K. (2017). Intergroup perception and cognition: An integrative framework for understanding the causes and consequences of social categorization. In J. M. Olson (Ed.), *Advances in experimental social psychology* (Vol. 55, pp. 1–80). Academic Press. https://doi.org/https://doi.org/10.1016/bs.aesp.2016.10.001

66. Nobles, M. (2000). History counts: A comparative analysis of racial/color categorization in US and Brazilian censuses. *American Journal of Public Health, 90*(11), 1738–1745. https://doi.org/10.2105/ajph.90.11.1738

67. Southern Poverty Law Center. (2018, January 31). Teaching hard history: American slavery. www.splcenter.org/sites/default/files/tt_hard_history_amer ican_slavery.pdf

68. Jost, J. T., Gaucher, D., & Stern, C. (2015). "The world isn't fair": A system justification perspective on social stratification and inequality. In M. Mikulincer, P. R. Shaver, J. F. Dovidio, & J. A. Simpson (Eds.), *APA handbook of personality and social psychology,* Vol. 2, Group processes. (pp. 371–340). American Psychological Association. https://doi.org/10.1037/14342-012

69. Civiqs. (2021). Black Lives Matter: Registered voters. https://civiqs.com/ results/black_lives_matter?uncertainty=true&annotations=true&zoomIn=true

70. Sherif, M., Harvey, O. J., White, B. J., Hood, W. R., & Sherif, C. W. (1961). *Intergroup conflict and cooperation: The Robbers cave experiment.* University of Oklahoma Book Exchange. www.jstor.org/stable/4148836

71. Detroit Historical Society. (n.d.). Race riot of 1943. *Encyclopedia of Detroit.* https://detroithistorical.org/learn/encyclopedia-of-detroit/race-riot-1943

72. Rasmussen, R., Levari, D. E., Akhtar, M., Crittle, C. S., Gastely, M., Pagan, J., Brennan, A., Cashman, D., Wulff, A. N., Norton, M. I., Sommers, S. R., & Urry, H. L. (2022). White (but not Black) Americans continue to see racism as a zero-sum game; White conservatives (but not moderates or liberals) see themselves as losing. *Perspectives for Psychological Science, 17*(6), 1800–1810. https://journals.sagepub.com/doi/abs/10.1177/17456916221082111

73. Morrison, A. (2022, March 9). Number of hate groups declined in 2021, but Proud Boys chapters surging say SPLC. *PBS News Hour.* www.pbs.org/news hour/nation/number-of-hate-groups-declined-in-2021-but-proud-boys-chap ters-surging-says-splc

74. Horowitz, J. M., Brown, A., & Cox, K. (2019, April 9). *Race in America 2019.* Pew Research Center. www.pewresearch.org/social-trends/2019/04/09/ race-in-america-2019/

CHAPTER 2

A Threat to the Common Good
Racism and the Health of Black Americans

What we know is this: racism is a serious public health threat that directly affects the well-being of millions of Americans. As a result, it affects the health of our entire nation.

Rochelle Walensky, MD, Director of the Center for Disease Control and Prevention April 8, 2021 [1]

Michelle Thomas is a single Black mother living in Atlanta, where she raises her six children. In a 2021 interview with Bill Whitaker for the CBS News show, *60 Minutes*, she talked about the persistence of racism's stressors and the damage it has done to her family: "You see the Confederate flag being flown. You see people driving by are calling you the N-word. And you're just walking down the street. I don't know any other race that actually says they have to have a talk with their kids about how to handle yourself when you're in the street or how to handle yourself around a police officer or how to handle yourself when you go shopping in a store. Make sure your hands are not in your pocket."

Indeed, Ms. Thomas' greatest fears for her children were realized one night when her teenage son with autism, Jerome, was stopped by a police officer while walking home because he supposedly fit the profile of a robbery suspect. He was handcuffed and briefly held in custody, even though, as Ms. Thomas told the interviewer, "If you talk to him for a little while you would know for a fact that my son had autism." Her son was eventually released but was deeply shaken. He asked his mother whether he had done something wrong. Ms. Thomas recounts the exchange that followed his question: "[I said] No baby. You did nothing wrong. It's just your skin. [And he said], 'Well, you think this is gonna happen to me again?' And – you know, I had to say...'Yes. Nine–nine times out of ten this is gonna happen to you plenty of times in your lifetime'" [2].

Almost everyone would agree that experiencing racial discrimination of the kind described by Ms. Thomas in this *60 Minutes* interview is humiliating and psychologically painful. The question here, however, is whether being the victim of racial discrimination can actually make a person physically ill? Over the course of our professional careers, we have encountered considerable skepticism when we have argued that it can. As a former colleague once said, "Sure racial discrimination is bad, but what does it have to do with health?" The answer is, "an awful lot," and thankfully this opinion is now widely shared among the scientists who study racial health disparities. This chapter presents what health researchers have learned about the impact of experiencing racial discrimination on the health of Black Americans.

Racial Discrimination: "Nowhere To Run, Nowhere To Hide" [3]

The vast majority of White Americans perceive society as fair and just, and a significant number of them also believe that anti-Black racism is largely a "thing of the past." While they acknowledge the injustice of individual, well-publicized occurrences of blatantly racist actions (e.g., the murder of Black people, such as Breonna Taylor), these are seen as rare exceptions to how Black people are treated in the United States. White Americans see society as fundamentally fair and equitable. One reason why White people generally have this view is that, because of the traditional opportunities that White people have had in the United States, White Americans' personal experiences are largely fair ones, in which people tend to get what they deserve. Dr. James Jones, professor of psychological and brain sciences at the University of Delaware, has described this perspective as the "universal context of fairness" [4].

In addition, a large portion of White Americans has very limited interpersonal contact with Black Americans, and thus they may not witness or recognize the harm that racial discrimination does to them. Most Americans live in highly segregated neighborhoods. The average White American lives in a neighborhood where about 6 percent of their neighbors are Black Americans [5]. Therefore, in the United States, Black people and White people are very unlikely to interact with one another or share common experiences.

For Black Americans, however, discrimination is a significant part of their lives. For example, over 80 percent of Black Americans believe that they are treated less fairly than White Americans in hiring, pay, and promotions [6]. Dr. Jones refers to this view of everyday bias as the "universal context of racism." From the perspective of Black Americans, racism provides a readily available explanation that ties together how they have been treated across time, locations, and interactions with various people. As Michelle Obama, the former First Lady, explained, "It just goes on, and on, and on. Race and racism is a reality that so many of us grow up learning to just deal with" [7].

The reality of racial discrimination pervades Black Americans' lives. In her brilliant book, *Caste*, author Isabel Wilkerson argues that race creates a lower "caste" (a rigid, generally agreed upon assignment to a certain social position in society) in the United States from which Black people cannot really escape. Race, she suggests, "is what we can see, the physical traits that have been given arbitrary meaning and become shorthand for who a person is" [8]. The quote from Ms. Obama is only one of the numerous examples supporting Wilkerson's argument that Black people's objective social status is often much less important than the color of their skin.

We can find yet another example from an altercation that occurred in an upscale hotel in New York City in 2020. A 14-year-old Black teenage boy was sitting near the exit of the hotel where he and his father, a Grammy-winning musician, Keyon Harrold, had been staying. Like any ordinary teenager, he was looking at his smartphone while waiting for his father. Out of nowhere, Miya Ponsetto, a 22-year-old White woman, approached the boy, incorrectly claiming that the phone was hers and demanding that he return it.

The boy, shocked and confused, moved toward the hotel exit, but Ms. Ponsetto assaulted him. She grabbed and scratched him, and then later tackled him. The boy's father loudly defended his son and had the presence of mind to record the incident. In his recording you can hear Ponsetto screaming, "I'm not going to let him walk away with my phone." Meanwhile the hotel staff began reviewing their security footage to see if, indeed, the teenager had stolen the phone, but none of them intervened to protect him.

The incident ended when an Uber driver entered the hotel to return Ms. Ponsetto's phone, which she had left in his car. She did not apologize to the boy or his father before they left the hotel. In a later interview, she was asked whether she had stopped any other people leaving the hotel. She responded, "[well] not everyone, just the people that . . . I just wanted to do my part."

This incident was video recorded and garnered considerable national attention and the media sought to interview the boy's parents. The boy's mother told one interviewer that her son had asked, "Why me, mom?" She said that giving him an answer "just hurt," and that "the toughest answer a [Black] parent has to give a child [is] unfortunately that it was probably because you are Black" [9].

A few years before the altercation in the hotel, the home of professional basketball superstar and very successful entrepreneur LeBron James was vandalized, with the "N-Word" sprayed on the front gate. In the aftermath of this episode, James expressed pretty much the same feelings as the boy's mother: "No matter how much money you have, no matter how famous you are, no matter how many people admire you, being Black in America is tough and we got a long way to go for us as a society and for us as African Americans until we feel equal in America" [10].

Black Americans' Experiences with Racism

Among Black Americans, there is nothing unusual about the experience of being the target of racial discrimination. Ninety-two percent of the Black people who responded to a 2017 national survey said that pervasive racial discrimination still exists in the United States. The most commonly reported acts of anti-Black discrimination were interpersonal incidents, which included people acting afraid of them (40 percent), receiving racial slurs (51 percent), and people making insensitive or offensive racial comments or negative assumptions about them (both 52 percent) [11, 12]. In a survey conducted in 2019, about 60 percent of the Black respondents reported they had personally been treated unfairly in the past 12 months. The kinds of discrimination described involved difficulties in a wide range of situations and circumstances, including experiences at work, finding employment, interacting with the police, and finding housing (all reported by 50 percent of the respondents or higher), as well as in college applications and healthcare (over 30 percent each). These data very likely underestimate the number of Black Americans who have had such experiences, however. Research shows that when Black people respond to surveys that ask about their experiences, they are often reluctant to admit they personally have been the target of racial discrimination [13].

In addition to these nonviolent kinds of racial discrimination, there are, of course, violent acts as well. The clearest and most dramatic example of violent racial discrimination is a hate crime. The 2020 US Department of Justice report states that there were over 8,000 hate crimes in the United States. The majority (64.8 percent) involved a person who was targeted because of their race or ethnicity. Of these, about two-thirds had a Black victim. This is a very disturbing statistic but, in fact, the report probably represents a substantial underestimation of the actual number of hate crimes in the United States [14]. A hate crime is only officially a hate crime when it is identified as such by a law enforcement agency and a state official reports it to the FBI. In many instances, labeling something as a hate crime involves a subjective judgment as to whether racial hatred was the reason for the crime. It seems likely that, because of personal biases and political pressure, many police departments and state officials are reluctant to do so. In 2018 and 2019, for example, the state of Alabama reported zero hate crimes. Organizations that are concerned with hate crimes, like the Anti-Defamation League, describe these figures as "highly implausible" [15].

The rate of fatal shootings of Black people by the police is about two and a half times the rate of fatal shootings of White people [16]. In a 2022 national survey, about 70 percent of the Black respondents said they were afraid or very afraid of being killed by the police. Only about 10 percent of the White respondents expressed such fears [17]. In other surveys, 30 percent of Black men reported they had been the victim of police violence. However, violence toward Black Americans is not confined to their interactions with the police. Almost half of the Black people interviewed said, without naming a specific source, that at some time in the past they felt that their life was in danger because of their race. Forty-two percent reported that they or a family member had actually experienced some sort of racial violence [18, 19].[1] Motivated by fears of police violence, many Black parents, particularly those of sons, have something called "The Talk" with their children. "The Talk" is about what young Black men should do and not do so they can avoid being a victim of racial violence when they encounter police officers. In one interview, Kenya Young, executive producer of National Public Radio's (NPR) *Morning Edition*, recalled her interactions with her children: "I remember the kids asking to go to the park and the laundry list of what I had to tell them: 'Don't wear your hood. Don't put your hands in your pocket. If you get stopped, don't run. Put your hands up. Don't make a lot of moves. Tell them your mother works for NPR.' I mean, it just went on and on. There are stages of the talk as they start to get older. One is you just don't want them to draw attention to themselves enough for someone to call on them or get stopped. Then, there's the stage of what you do if you do get caught" [20].

---

[1] In 2020 and 2021, there was a dramatic increase in violent crimes, generally, and in Black and other minority communities, in particular. Interpersonal violence within Black communities is yet another significant social and health problem, which almost certainly has its roots in the effects of systemic racism. However, the number of deaths due to this kind of violence, while tragic, is far less than the number of deaths due to diseases. https://everytownresearch.org/report/gun-violence-and-covid-19-in-2020-a-year-of-colliding-crises

Thus, among Black Americans there is the "universal context of racism" that Dr. Jones proposed [4]. One consequence of this perspective is the need to constantly anticipate episodes of bias and prepare the various courses of action that are required to navigate a world in which Black Americans may encounter racism around any corner. It is a world that is unpredictable, unfair, and highly stressful.

Violent and deadly acts toward people of color have stained the history of America for hundreds of years. The physical mistreatment of enslaved Black people for about 250 years in North America is but one aspect of this story. From the early- to mid-twentieth century, groups of White citizens often banded together to conduct organized violent assaults on Black communities in their cities. Such attacks occurred in Tulsa, Oklahoma; St. Louis, Missouri; Chicago, Illinois; Detroit, Michigan; and many other American cities. These attacks not only destroyed Black-owned homes and businesses, they also killed hundreds of Black Americans. There is also a long history of uncounted and unrecorded racially motivated murders and assaults of Black people in both the American South and North.

Black Americans' knowledge about the history of virulent and lethal anti-Black racism in the United States reflects what Dr. David Williams, professor of public health at Harvard University, calls a "historical trauma." This kind of trauma has an impact on the health of Black Americans. Indeed, a Black person does not actually have to be the direct target of racial violence to be greatly affected by it. When, in 2020, the murders of unarmed Black people by both the police and various racial bigots were shown on news programs and widely shared in social media, Black Americans experienced an increase in psychological distress. For example, the levels of anxiety and depression among Black Americans increased substantially following the viral exposure of the video showing the murder of George Floyd by former Minneapolis police officer, Derek Chauvin [21]. This did not occur for White Americans. It seems safe to say that these feelings continued and perhaps became even stronger in 2022 with a new spate of police killings of unarmed Black people and Brown people.

The psychological impact of well-publicized violent and nonviolent discrimination against Black Americans is eloquently captured in an op-ed written by Dr. Robert M. Sellers, a Black man who is a professor of psychology at the University of Michigan. After several widely publicized acts of racial discrimination, Dr. Sellers wrote:

> This morning, I woke up very tired. Not your normal tired. I woke up with a kind of tired that can only be found on the other side of loss, anger, frustration, sadness, and despair. This morning, I woke up in a state in

which African Americans make up roughly 13 percent of the population but comprise 31 percent of the people with COVID-19 and 40 percent of the people dying from COVID-19. I woke up in a country where a White woman can not only accuse an African American man of threatening her because he is simply asking her to obey the law in a public space, but she can actually weaponize the police for her own aims simply by repeatedly referring to him as being African American.[2]

Professor Sellers concluded that, as a Black American, he had a responsibility to the next generation to try to change America for the better. But, he acknowledged, he is still "tired of this shit" [22].

Everyday Racism: A Persistent Stressor

The physical consequences of violent acts of racism are obvious, but the psychological damage caused by both direct and indirect experiences with racial discrimination can be severe and have real implications for a person's health. In 2018, a group of researchers from different universities wanted to learn about what Black Americans saw as the sources of their health problems. They conducted a series of focus groups with Black people in the American southwest. Their collective answers are best represented by the answer of a 40-year-old Black woman from Tucson, Arizona: "There's the stress of being Black in America that nobody's writing about," she said, "or being a minority in America that nobody's writing about – of being a certain minority in America. And, you know, I'm not one to-to blame anybody or play the race card, but in my life experience, it's just a part of reality" [23].

This respondent was far from alone in her feelings. In a 2020 survey conducted by the American Psychological Association, nearly half of the Black people surveyed reported that being discriminated against is a significant stressor [24]. This percentage was higher than for any other racial or ethnic group in the United States. Again, this stress can come from their own personal experiences of discrimination, observing other Black people experiencing discrimination, or anticipating that one will become the victim of discrimination. This may result in heightened vigilance for acts of discrimination – that is, increased attention to the

---

[2] The incident Professor Sellers was referring to at the end of this passage happened in 2020 in Central Park in New York City, where a Black man simply asked a White woman to leash her dog and she called the police, claiming that he was threatening her.

environment in anticipation that one will directly experience racial discrimination, which is yet another kind of stressor [25].

One analogy that has been used in recent years to describe the cumulative stress that results from individual acts of anti-Black discrimination is that of being bitten or stung by mosquitos [26]. Being stung by one mosquito (i.e., experiencing a single, minor instance of racial discrimination) is certainly annoying and uncomfortable, but it might not be a source of major distress. Nevertheless, if one is stung by multiple mosquitos every single day, mosquitos quickly become more than just annoying. Over time, they will take a serious toll on a person because they cannot be stopped. As the frequency of experiences with racial discrimination increases, so does stress and the incidence of a wide range of diseases. These supposedly minor instances of racial discrimination are often called racial microaggressions. Microaggressions are very subtle expressions of racial bias. They involve objectively "small" things a person might say or do when they are interacting with a Black person. A microaggression could involve showing obvious surprise that a Black person knows some fact or disregarding what that person has to say in discussions of some topic. This could include certain facial expressions or physically turning away when a Black person is speaking [27]. Most microaggressions are unintentional, but that does not eliminate their "sting." In addition to their immediate consequences, microaggressions have a significant cumulative negative impact on a Black person. That is, just as an infestation of mosquitos can do some substantial harm to a person, a large number of racial microaggressions can also do substantial harm to a Black person.

Whether racial discrimination is personally experienced or observed, intentional and blatant or unintentional and subtle, its physiological impact on the health of Black Americans is profound. As Dr. Aletha Maybank, the chief equity officer and group vice president of the American Medical Association, explained in a 2020 podcast for the association, "Sustained exposure to racism in all of its forms increases our stress hormones such as cortisol, which causes havoc in our physical bodies and while we know that [race is] a social construct and has no biological or genetic basis, racism can actually, literally change the patterns of how genes are expressed" [28].

Sounding the Alarm: Physiological and Psychological Responses to Stress

One of the best descriptions of what happens when people are stressed comes from Dr. Steven Porges, professor at the Kinsey Traumatic Stress

Research Consortium at Indiana University: "Even though we may not always be aware of danger on a cognitive level, on a neurophysiological level, our body has already started a sequence of neural processes that would facilitate adaptive defense behaviors such as fight, flight, or freeze" [29].

People's physiological reactions to stress have their origins in how our very distant ancestors reacted to physical threats, such as potential attacks by a dangerous animal or maybe from a hostile member of another tribe. When this happened, someone who was the target of these attacks needed to *very quickly* move toward (fight) or away from (flight) the source of danger. Our ancestors who were best able to do this were most likely to survive and pass their genes on to subsequent generations. Through the process of natural selection, rapid and automatic physiological responses to threat became an integral part of the human repertoire.

Initially, these threats were primarily physical. But, because humans are intelligent and social animals, the way they lived changed. Over time it became more likely that they lived in socially complex communities. In such communities, the sources of stress included social threats, such as rejection, exclusion, or loss of status. However, evolutionary changes in physiological responses are quite slow. Thus, today, humans' physiological responses to social threats are basically the same as their ancient ancestors' adaptive responses to the physical threats that confronted them hundreds of millennia ago. These reactions involve getting our bodies ready to engage in some physical action without much thinking.

Physiological Responses to Threat
This process of responding to threat, like almost everything else we do, begins in the brain – specifically in a part of the brain called the *amygdala*. The amygdala initiates the fight-or-flight response. The amygdala actually performs several different functions, but it is primarily known for its role in the emotions we feel. The activation of the amygdala triggers the onset of strong negative emotions, such as fear, anxiety, and anger. At the same time, the amygdala's activity also diminishes a person's ability to think more objectively and rationally about the situation at hand by inhibiting higher-order mental processes in the brain. Confronting a serious physical danger is a time for action not for sitting around and pondering various ways you might counter the threat. Note how primitive the amygdala's functions are. Some neuroscientists talk about the amygdala as "hijacking" the higher-order, more thoughtful functions in the brain [30].

When the amygdala is activated, it immediately sends a distress signal to another brain structure, the *hypothalamus*. The hypothalamus is an important part of the brain because it is responsible for controlling all the basic bodily functions a person needs for survival, such as breathing, body temperature, blood pressure, and heart rate. The hypothalamus controls these by activating certain hormones, which are chemical messengers secreted by our glands (e.g., pituitary, adrenal) directly into our blood. These hormones affect a multitude of bodily functions and processes. The primary goal of these hormones, however, is to do things that will allow the body to reestablish a "steady and stable state." Doing this is known as achieving *homeostasis*, which is vital to all organisms' survival. Homeostasis is a self-regulatory process that normally occurs more or less easily and automatically. Our bodies are constantly trying to establish homeostasis, and most times when we are upset, we simply "calm down" physiologically and psychologically. When confronted with an external stressor, a big part of getting the body back to this stable state requires actually dealing with the stressor either by effectively eliminating it or fleeing from it. That is, the person needs to engage in physical activities that are going to require strength and effort, and this often makes restoring homeostasis more difficult.

To provide humans with the physical resources needed to confront the threat, the hypothalamus activates two systems. The first is called the *sympathetic–adrenal–medullary (SAM) axis*. It serves to get a person moving in response to threat by causing the adrenal gland to instantly secrete catecholamines, or "stress hormones," into the blood stream [31]. Epinephrine and norepinephrine are two of the better-known catecholamines that are involved in responses to threat. They serve to mobilize a person. To engage in almost any physical action, a person is going to need an ample amount of oxygen moving into their body. These hormones increase heart rate and constrict blood vessels, which pushes more blood to the muscles and organs and increases the intake of oxygen. This is why people sometimes report that their heart is "pounding" when they are in danger. Epinephrine and norepinephrine also increase blood sugar levels, which give the body more energy to engage in actions that reduce the threat.

Following the initial surge of these hormones, the hypothalamus activates the second system – the *hypothalamic–pituitary–adrenal (HPA) axis*. The most important thing about the HPA axis is that it helps a person to continue to engage in the fight-or-flight response until they successfully cope with the threat or successfully escape from it. One way in which the

HPA axis does this is by releasing another important stress hormone – cortisol. Cortisol further facilitates the secretions of glucose (or blood sugars) and fats into the bloodstream, supplying energy to all parts of the body. The primary function of cortisol in the fight-and-flight response is therefore to help the body replenish energy stores that are going to be depleted in responding to some stressor. This enables the person to remain active until the threat stops (e.g., the dangerous animal is killed). Once the threat is removed, secretion of cortisol is reduced, and the body attempts to restore homeostasis or stability, which humans (and all other mammals) need to do to continue to thrive. They cannot be in a constant state of physiological arousal and be healthy. The process of trying to return the body to homeostasis by adjusting physiological and hormonal activities is called *allostasis*.

Psychological Stress: Threat That Just Won't Go Away and Allostatic Overload
In 1936, Dr. Hans Selye, an endrocrinologist, developed the first general theory of humans' responses to stress. He proposed that the real problem with the flight-or-fight response is that while it can very effectively protect us from physical danger, it can interfere with our functioning in the modern world, where the threats are often more subtle and psychological in nature.

Most physical threats, such as a large dog growling and baring its teeth at you, are acute. They only last for a limited amount of time. When an acute physical threat is over, the person usually begins to return to homeostasis fairly quickly, and the person's functioning returns to a normal steady state. Psychological stress, however, is often a chronic condition, and trying to get back to homeostasis can be a big challenge. This is often the case for the stress caused by racial discrimination, a chronic psychological stressor that just does not go away.

The chronic experience of personal threats, such as discrimination, pushes people from a state of just being "stressed" to a state of being "stressed out." When a person must continuously cope with stress, it is like forgetting to turn off some appliance after you have used it. Eventually the device will be damaged, and over time it stops working altogether because the motor "burns out." In the case of continuing psychological stress, the body keeps secreting the so-called stress hormones, including cortisol. Normally, a person's cortisol level fluctuates with the events of the day, usually starting high in the morning and declining over the course of the day. But in the face of the continuing psychological stress caused by racial discrimination, an individual's cortisol level stays relatively high – which makes the person's motor run high – so high that if this level is maintained, damage will occur. If a person cannot terminate or at least tamp down the hormones associated with the fight-or-flight stress response, the physiological stress responses can become toxic and damage the body [32].

The specific bodily process that causes this is called *allostatic load*. Allostatic load, or maybe more appropriately allostatic *over*load, is created when the body tries to achieve homeostasis but cannot because the stress a person experiences never goes away. It is one of the major keys to the dangerous associations among racial discrimination, stress, and health. It is the villain in the story of how experiencing racial discrimination makes Black people sick or even die. Although the name implies that it is a single thing, in actuality the term allostatic load is a catch-all for the wide variety of physiological responses to chronic stress. These responses are the immediate and downstream effects of the release of the stress hormones, such as epinephrine, norepinephrine, and cortisol, into a person's body. These hormones can be detected in samples of a person's blood, saliva, or urine. The effects of continuing allostatic overload manifest themselves in a wide variety of serious ways, including susceptibility to very large number of diseases and even premature death [32].[3]

Allostatic load in response to prolonged stress is not, of course, unique to Black Americans. All humans react to prolonged adverse events by experiencing stress followed by an increased allostatic load. This response is an essential part of being a human being and common to people across the world irrespective of the culture in which they were raised. However – and this is critical – because Black Americans are, on average, so much more likely to be actually exposed to persistent and pervasive racial discrimination and also have to worry about future racial discrimination more than White Americans, their stress levels will be higher, last longer, and be more difficult to resolve [33]. Thus, the allostatic load that results from unresolved stress is likely to be higher among Black Americans than White Americans. Once again, Dr. David Williams provides a clear and accurate summary of the processes we are talking about:

> [E]veryday discrimination [is] powerfully predictive of biological function across a broad range of indicators in multiple countries and it documents that how we relate and treat each other on a day-to-day basis may not just matter for how they make the person feel or their mental health, but it's

---

[3] In his book, *The Pocket Guide to Polyvagal Theory*, Dr. Stephen Porges (whom we quoted earlier) provides an accessible overview of people's physical reactions to stress and how they can endanger people's health.

literally leading to pathogenic processes within the body and people were adapting and were making changes in their life based on the reality that they thought they could be a victim [34].

Very few diseases have a single cause. A person's heredity, gender, age, lifestyle, diet, daily habits, where they live, and the germs and toxins these environments expose them to (see Chapter 3) all affect their health. Nevertheless, despite all the other things that can affect people's health, there is still a reliable and significant link between the experience of racial discrimination and health problems and even death. That is, the "signal" created by racial discrimination can be clearly detected amid the "noise" of all the other things that can affect a person's health.

Racial Discrimination and Specific Diseases: Documenting the Relationship

Coleman A. Young, the first Black mayor of Detroit, Michigan, once observed, "Racism is something like high blood pressure – the person who has it doesn't know he has it until he drops over with a goddamned stroke" [35]. Indeed, racism is like a disease that erodes the health of Black people in a broad range of ways. The list of specific health problems and diseases that are directly associated with experiencing racial discrimination is very long. Table 2.1 presents many, but certainly not all, of these associations. The relationships between directly or indirectly encountering racial discrimination and the incidence of certain diseases and mortality invariably involve three things: chronic stress, elevated levels of stress hormones, and allostatic load.

One of the medical problems that is often associated with racial discrimination is cardiovascular disorders. Cardiovascular disorders (also sometimes called cardiovascular conditions) include a number of specific diseases that all contribute significantly to the higher mortality rates among Black Americans than White Americans. Dr. La Princess Brewer, professor of medicine at the Mayo Clinic, and Dr. Lisa Cooper, professor of medicine at John Hopkins Medical School, are two physicians who are among the leading authorities on the health effects of exposure to racist actions. They conclude, "There is now compelling evidence linking the perception of racism to cardiovascular health" [36, 37].[4]

[4] Dr. Cooper has recently published a book on racism and health, *Why Are Health Disparities Everyone's Problem?*

Table 2.1 *A list of diseases linked to the experience of discrimination through allostatic load*

System/Part	Condition or Disease
Cardiovascular and metabolic systems	Hypertension
	High cholesterol
	Obesity
	Heart disease (e.g., atherosclerosis, coronary artery disease)
	Heart attack
	Cardiac arrest
	Stroke
	Diabetes
Immune system	Immune deficiency
	Autoimmune disease (e.g., lupus, asthma)
	Some cancers (e.g., breast cancer, ovarian cancer)
	Chronic fatigue
Brain	Depression
	Anxiety
	Post-traumatic stress disorder
	Sleep deprivation
	Impaired cognitive functioning

Hypertension

One kind of cardiovascular disorder is hypertension, commonly referred to as high blood pressure. Data from numerous national surveys show that the percentage of Black people diagnosed with this very dangerous disease is about 10 to 15 percent higher than among White people [38]. The American Medical Association uses the term "rampant" to describe the incidence of this health problem among Black Americans [39]. One of the most dangerous aspects of hypertension is that it is a "silent killer." Often there are no symptoms until it is too late, and then the person suffers a stroke or a heart attack.

One study that documented the relationship between experiencing racial discrimination and hypertension was a meta-analysis. As we explained in Chapter 1, meta-analysis is a way of combining a number of different research findings into one overall estimate of how strongly two things are related. This particular meta-analysis combined the results of 44 studies with 32,000 participants and revealed a consistent association between the experience of racial discrimination and hypertension [40]. People who reported medium to high levels of past discrimination were

30 to 50 percent more likely to develop hypertension than those who experienced low levels.

Hypertension is usually considered part of allostatic load. That is, high blood pressure is one of the physiological responses to chronic stress along with other biomarkers of allostatic load, such as chronically high levels of epinephrine and norepinephrine and the buildup of cholesterol and fats in the walls of arteries. These interfere with blood flow and increase a person's blood pressure.

Heart Disease

In the 2018 study of what factors people perceived as affecting their health, which we described earlier, another young Black woman was asked about the causes of her health problem. She responded that "your heart can only function so much, so there's more stress on it. And, uh, when your heart is – when the stress is there, uh, you're just not able to function like you normally would be because of all that stress on your heart" [23].

Racial discrimination plays an important role in the incidence of heart disease among Black Americans. The experience of discrimination is also related to heart disease among members of other groups. For instance, one study asked both Black people and White people about the age at which they believed that they had first been exposed to discrimination and then whether had they experienced any cardiovascular problems. The younger the people were when they were first exposed to discrimination, the greater the likelihood that both Black people and White people would experience cardiovascular problems as an adult [41]. Another meta-analytic study combined the results of 84 different studies conducted over 33 years and found that, irrespective of race, people who had experienced higher levels of past discrimination were more likely to experience angina pain and heart attacks [42].

So, let us be very clear once again: There is nothing unique about Black people that makes them the only ones whose heart health is harmed by chronic stress. Stress is dangerous for everyone. What makes things much more dangerous for Black people is their much greater exposure to the pervasive racial discrimination and experience of the "universal context of racism," which create stress and sets this perilous process into motion. Black Americans are about 25 percent more likely to die from heart disease than White Americans [43].

Once again, the elevated levels of stress hormones, which are part of allostatic load, play an important role in this relationship. Experiencing discrimination, which increases the levels of stress hormones in a person's body, has downstream consequences for heart disease [44]. One of the primary causes of heart disease is unhealthy levels of certain fats in a person's blood, such as cholesterol. Actually, there are good and bad kinds of cholesterol, meaning that one kind reduces the probability of a heart attack and the other increases this probability. We are only going to focus on the bad kind, which is called *low-density lipoprotein* (LDL). Black Americans who report more experiences of anti-Black discrimination have higher LDL levels than do Black Americans who report fewer experiences with discrimination [45]. Thus, it is not surprising that higher levels of past discrimination are also associated with coronary obstructions (blockages due to deposits of cholesterol and other substances) [46].

Diabetes

There are two types of diabetes. Type 1 diabetes involves the absence of the hormone insulin that controls the amount of glucose in the blood. It is primarily a genetic disorder. Type 2 diabetes reflects problems in how the body processes and regulates a person's glucose levels. Although there may also be a genetic predisposition toward developing it, type 2 diabetes is much more affected by a person's life experiences and lifestyle. About 10 percent of all Americans have diabetes, but the percentage is much higher among Black Americans (11.7 percent) and Indigenous Peoples (14.7 percent) than it is among White Americans (7.5 percent). Black people are also up to two and a half times more likely to suffer a limb amputation and over five times more likely to suffer kidney damage from diabetes than are White people [47]. (Part of these particular health disparities is almost surely due to systemic and individual racism in healthcare, which we discuss in Chapters 5 and 6.)

There is strong evidence that the experience of discrimination is associated with increased risk of diabetes, especially type 2 [48]. A longitudinal study tracked the health of 59,000 women over 16 years found that women who reported the highest level of discrimination over their lifetime were 30 percent more likely to develop diabetes than the women who reported the lowest levels. In addition, among people who already have diabetes, the experience of discrimination makes things more difficult. Among women with type 2 diabetes, higher levels of discrimination are associated with greater insulin resistance (i.e., the blood cells do not process the insulin) and higher levels of glucose in their blood.

One Black patient described the role of stress in her diabetes this way: "I think mine was stress induced ... at the time that I found out I had diabetes, my meal everyday was peppermints and Pepsi. And I was working in a daycare and that's all I was able to pop them peppermints in my mouth all day long and drink a Pepsi ... and it was a stressful time in my life. So, it was probably going to catch up with me. ... Then I think stress just pulled that trigger" [49]. The role of stress in diabetes can be directly traced to allostatic load. One way this occurs is that chronically high levels of cortisol impair the ability of insulin to affect the level of glucose in a person's blood, that is, high levels of cortisol produce insulin resistance.

Almost every recommendation for reducing the incidence of type 2 diabetes and/or controlling it involves losing weight because excess weight is a serious risk factor for type 2 diabetes. However, experiencing racism is associated with significant weight *gain*. A recent report from The Samuel DuBois Cook Center on Social Equity at Duke University succinctly summarized the research findings on racial discrimination and weight problems: "Discrimination's adverse effect on maintenance of healthy weight and well-being is virtually as pernicious as its effects on employment and income" [50]. Consistent with this conclusion, a study of over 5,000 Black Americans found that higher levels of everyday discrimination were associated with greater weight.

Once again, the allostatic load associated with stress responses plays a critical role in this process. When the body needs to respond to a threat, cortisol levels rise, and glucose and fats are released into the blood system to give the person energy to respond to the threat. In the case of prolonged stress, this is accompanied by an increased appetite for foods that are high in carbohydrates, fat, and sugar (Big Macs, for example). This is not unique to humans. The preference for foods high in fat and sugar following stress is also found in other animals [51]. This effect of stress significantly increases the chances that a person will gain a significant amount of weight.

Immune Disorders

Science writer Matt Richtel titled his best-selling book about the immune system, *An Elegant Defense* [52].[5] The immune system is indeed that. It

---

[5] The full title of his book is *An Elegant Defense: The Extraordinary New Science of the Immune System: A Tale in Four Lives*. It is an excellent source for lay readers interested in what the immune system is and how it works.

uses some very complex biochemical processes to shield us from a multitude of different viral and bacterial diseases. Of course, heredity and overall health affect how well the immune system works, but prolonged stress by itself significantly alters how immune systems function. It does this in two ways. First, stress causes an immune system to become deficient and unable to provide sufficient protection against some invading pathogen – viruses and/or bacteria that cause disease. Second, it causes the immune system to overreact and essentially attack the person's own body.

One good example of how stress impairs the immune system involves the body's ability to fight off influenza, or the "flu." The flu is not viewed as that much of a danger today, but 100 years ago it killed a third of the world's population (about 50 million people) and in the United States it still kills about 35,000 to 40,000 people per year [53]. When the influenza virus enters the body, the immune system normally detects it as a "foreign invader" and attacks and destroys it with various antibodies. However, research in psychoneuroimmunology has clearly established that prolonged exposure to stress impairs the body's ability to fight off the flu (as well as other kinds of viral infections) [54]. For example, during stressful examination periods, the immune systems of medical students become much less effective. Stress appears to have these effects because of increased levels of the stress hormones that are part of allostatic load. Oversimplified, these hormones suppress the actions of immune cells that would normally respond to the flu. Thus, stress and the resultant weakened immune systems partially explain why Black Americans are more likely to get the flu than White Americans and are about twice as likely to be hospitalized for it [55]. This weakening of the immune system was also a likely cause of the higher rates of COVID-19 infections and deaths among Black Americans than White Americans during at least the first two years of the pandemic [56].

Stress also diminishes the efficacy of vaccines designed to protect people from the flu and several other diseases. The development of vaccines against various kinds of viral infections has been one of the signal achievements of medical science. At the simplest level, vaccines make immune systems more active and create antibodies that help a person fight off infections. However, high levels of stress diminish the impact of many vaccines on the immune system, making them less effective. One specific example of this has been seen in a study that focused on people who provided care for other family members with dementia. The more stressed these caretakers were, the less effective the flu vaccine was for them [57]. It appears that the high levels of cortisol and other stress hormones in the caretakers' systems interfered with the ability of the vaccines to activate the antibodies needed to fight off the flu [58].

The list of vaccines whose effectiveness is diminished by high levels of stress includes vaccinations for hepatitis, herpes, pneumonia, and rubella to mention a few. Dr. Janice Keicolt-Glaser, professor of medicine at Ohio State University, and one of the people who did the seminal work on stress and the effectiveness of vaccines, believed this may apply to COVID-19 vaccinations as well [59]. Thus, when the COVID-19 vaccines first came out, she suggested that people get vaccinated when they are not stressed. But, of course, this may not be possible for people living with the chronic stress induced by racial discrimination.

Autoimmune Disorders

There are also a number of medical problems that occur when the immune system overreacts and identifies certain chemicals that our own body has produced as foreign invaders (i.e., pathogens). Autoimmune disorders are often also called inflammatory disorders because inflammatory responses are normally one way the body fights off many viral and bacterial diseases. (Inflammatory responses are why we feel a fever when we get sick.) Autoimmune diseases involving inflammation include lupus, rheumatoid arthritis, and irritable bowel syndrome.

As is true with immune deficiencies, racial discrimination and stress are involved in inflammatory immune responses. As Dr. April Thames, professor of psychiatry and biobehavioral sciences at University of California, Los Angeles explains, "Stress from racial discrimination alters the innate immunity of a host [and] promote[s] abnormal inflammatory responses" [60]. Stress and the resultant physiological reactions to stress significantly increase the chances that the immune system will overreact and make some serious "mistakes" [61]. One example of this involves interleukin 6, a protein that activates inflammatory responses in the immune system. In the short run, such responses are beneficial, helping the immune system fight off various pathogens. However, if the immune system remains chronically inflamed, a host of autoimmune disorders and other diseases occur. It has been found that, among Black Americans, feelings associated with racial discrimination, such as stress and a sense of isolation, increase the production of interleukin 6 (and other inflammatory proteins). The chronically high levels of inflammation caused by these proteins, in turn, endanger the health of Black Americans [62].

One autoimmune disorder associated with the overproduction of interleukin 6 is lupus. Lupus' symptoms include fatigue, joint pain, facial rashes, skin lesions, and fever. While a relatively rare disease, lupus is at least twice as common among Black Americans as White Americans. Several studies have found that more experiences with anti-Black racism are associated with more serious cases of lupus [63].

Asthma is another example of discrimination contributing to autoimmune disorders. Asthma, a respiratory condition causing difficulty in breathing, is an important aspect of racial health disparities. While it is only somewhat more common among Black Americans than White Americans, it is much more deadly for Black Americans – the mortality rate is more than twice as high among Black Americans than White Americans [64]. As we discuss in Chapter 3, the poor air quality in many of the economically disadvantaged and under-resourced neighborhoods where Black Americans live does increase the incidence and severity of asthma attacks. However, discrimination plays an important role as well. One study, conducted with about 3,500 people of color who ranged in age from 8 to 21, found that those who reported having experienced some discrimination in the past were almost twice as likely to develop and have difficulties with asthma as were people of color who did not report any experiences with discrimination [65].

Mental Health Problems

Racial discrimination is also associated with poorer mental health. A part of the report from *Mental Health America, 2021* summarizes this relationship quite well: "People of color and all those whose lives have been marginalized by those in power experience life differently from those whose lives have not been devalued. They experience overt racism and bigotry far too often, which leads to a mental health burden that is deeper than what others may face" [66].

There are a wide variety of mental health problems that people experience, ranging from those that cause some degree of discomfort and disruptions in a person's daily life to those that require institutionalization. Among the most common mental health problems in the United States are prolonged periods of anxiety and/or depression. People with an anxiety disorder tend to respond to certain situations or people whom they encounter with excessive fear or concerns about their own safety. People with depression feel persistently sad and lose interest in activities. Although Black Americans are not, on average, more likely to report anxiety or depression, they are more likely to be disabled by it. And they are much more likely to report higher levels of personal distress.

Black people do not have to be the direct recipient of racial discrimination for it to affect their mental health. As we noted earlier, Black Americans' mental health is associated with events such as news reports of violence against Black people (e.g., police killings and hate crime murders). One study looked at "poor mental health days" among Black Americans over five years and found that these days were much more likely to occur during weeks when such acts of racial violence received considerable attention in the media. These incidents did not have similar effects on the mental health of White Americans [67]. It is also true that heightened levels of vigilance for acts of racial discrimination are associated with higher levels of depression [68].

Direct experiences with racial discrimination are closely linked to mental health problems. An extensive meta-analysis that combined data from 293 studies conducted over 30 years found a systematic association between experiencing racial discrimination and a decline in a person's mental health. Greater exposure to racial discrimination was associated with greater depression, anxiety, and other kinds of psychological distress [69]. A longitudinal study of over 40,0000 people conducted in the United Kingdom showed how discrimination predicted the mental health of not only individuals who self-identified as Black but also other individuals of color from countries in South Asia (e.g., India, Pakistan) [70]. Across the various groups of people of color (i.e., BIPOC participants) studied, the greater the level of discrimination they experienced at the beginning of the study, the more psychological distress they reported two years later. This effect was not observed among the White participants in this study.

The association between allostatic load and different aspects of mental illness is not quite as clear-cut as it is in the other diseases we have discussed. It may be mitigated by the ways in which a person deals with their stress. For example, when people who are high in neuroticism – the tendency to see the world as threatening and unsafe – experience stress, they show much greater increases in their allostatic load than do people with lower levels of neuroticism [71].

The kind of research that best documents the causal impact of stress and allostatic load on mental health often involves experimental studies on nonhuman animals, so-called animal model studies. Animals are used in these studies, because the experiments can deliberately create enduring and serious disruptions in their lives (e.g., isolating them for long periods of time) and, thus, prolonged and serious stress. It would be highly unethical to do this with human participants. (Of course, some people would also argue that it is just as unethical to do this with other animals.) Researchers then compare a group of highly stressed animals (usually rats or mice) to a group of animals with no exposure to stress. Animals who experience prolonged stress show greater release of catecholamine hormones, which is one indicator of allostatic load. High levels of catecholamine hormones in the brain cause increases in activity in the amygdala and impair activity in the prefrontal cortex (an area of the brain associated with problem-solving). Humans are not the same as laboratory animals, but we share many of the same brain structures and functions with them. Thus, we can extrapolate from the results of these animal studies to humans' physiological reactions to chronic stress. If a person is chronically stressed, the person's amygdala functions are enhanced while their prefrontal cortex functions (i.e., higher-level brain functions) are impaired. Thus, when humans are stressed, they experience quite strong emotions (because of heightened activity in the amygdala), but they are unable to regulate these emotions with higher-order brain functions that would produce more logical thinking (because of impairments in the prefrontal cortex). This makes them more likely to attend negative information, which threatens their mental health.

Studies of naturally occurring adverse events and stress in humans also find that higher levels of stress are associated with less gray matter in the prefrontal cortex. As a result, people may be more likely to pay attention to negative information and possibly experience greater anxiety and be more vulnerable to anxiety and perhaps even depressive disorders [72]. There is also evidence that dysfunction in these areas caused by stress may play a role in post-traumatic stress disorder (PTSD) [73].

The Health Challenges of Black Americans

One cannot overstate the impact of pervasive racial discrimination on the health of Black Americans. This is widely agreed upon by epidemiologists who study racial health disparities. Dr. Michelle Williams, dean of Harvard T.H. Chan School of Public Health, for example, wrote that "in addressing the health outcomes of individuals facing racial and ethnic discrimination, it is important to change the nature of the discussion we are having." She continued, "We are led to believe, on one side, that this is an issue of political correctness, and on the other, that there is only a need to respond to individual instances of micro-aggressions. But the long-term impact of these broad patterns of discrimination on health and economic outcomes must be our shared focus" [74].

Discrimination and Allostatic Load: Racism Gets under the Skin

One way to carry out Dr. Williams' suggestions for research is to take advantage of national databases that tell us about racial differences as a key element of racial disparities in health and allostatic load. This was done by Dr. Arline Geronimus, professor of health behavior and health education at the University of Michigan Medical School. In collaboration with her colleagues, Dr. Geronimus examined data from the National Health and Nutrition Survey to compare the levels of different kinds of biomarkers of allostatic load in Black Americans and White Americans. They found that at every age between 20 and 64, Black Americans' allostatic load was higher than the allostatic load of White Americans [75]. Other studies, each using different measures of perceived discrimination and different kinds of biomarkers for allostatic load, have further documented that more experiences with discrimination are associated with greater allostatic load [66]. For example, one study found that people who reported experiencing high levels of discrimination over the course of 20 years were likely to exhibit what is known as a "blunted" diurnal cortisol profile [76]. In a "blunted" profile, a person's cortisol levels decline more slowly over the course of a day than is normal. It is another widely used and reliable biomarker for allostatic load.

Dr. Geronimus' extensive investigations into the relationships among racial discrimination, allostatic load, and a person's longevity have led her to propose the concept of "weathering." She argues that the continuous higher levels of stress among Black people due to discrimination physically "weathers" them in the same way storms would weather a building. She was not being metaphorical: Dr. Geronimus literally meant that persistent high levels of stress due to challenging social, environmental, and economic conditions cause higher levels of allostatic load that physically wear down Black people and make them more susceptible to certain diseases, age more quickly, and therefore be more likely to die younger than other groups of people.

In a 2017 interview with NPR, Dr. Geronimus described what she meant by the weathering process by recounting another interview she had heard with a woman named Emerald Snipes Garner. Ms. Garner is the daughter of Eric Garner, who was killed in 2014. He died of asphyxiation that resulted from a New York City police officer holding him in a prolonged chokehold. But in this interview, Ms. Garner was not talking about the death of her father. Rather, she spoke of her sister, who died in her mid-20s.

Recalling the interview, Dr. Geronimus shared that Ms. Garner "talked about the stresses that she felt led to [her sister's] death at age twenty-seven as being like if you're playing the game Jenga." (Jenga is a game in which people try to remove blocks from a wooden tower without it collapsing.) "I'm paraphrasing her," Dr. Geronimus continued, "but I thought that the Jenga metaphor was very apt because you start losing pieces of your health and well-being, but you still try to go on as long as you can. Even if you're disabled, even if it's hard, that you have a certain tenacity and hope, and sense of collective responsibility whether that's for your family or community. But there's a point where enough pieces have been pulled out of you, that you can no longer withstand, and you collapse" [77].

Other research supports Dr. Geronimus' ideas about the stress associated with racial discrimination, allostatic load, and mortality. One study examined public health records of a large group of Black Americans and White Americans and found that higher levels of allostatic load largely explained the disparity in mortality between the Black people and White people in the study. This was true even when the researchers controlled for two powerful predictors of people's health – their socioeconomic status and history of health-related behaviors [78].

Epigenetic Effects of Racial Discrimination: Racism Gets Way under the Skin

The health effects of stress go beyond just the physiological changes in people's blood and immune systems. As Dr. Geronimus argued, the conditions associated with experiencing racial discrimination can induce *epigenetic* alterations in a person's genome, which make people more vulnerable to disease and age more rapidly.

Epigenetics is still a relatively new science that focuses on our genome and its effects on people's health. Epigenetics does not primarily concern any physical changes in our genes but rather the impact of a person's life experiences on what their genes do or do not do. The DNA in our genes affects our health through the proteins they tell our cells to produce. But this "gene expression" can be affected by messenger RNA and other processes that can turn certain protein-producing genes on or off. Gene expression can also act as a "volume control," affecting the amount of a protein the genes tell the cells to make. Epigenetic events occur when the social conditions people experience affect their gene expression, and this has serious consequences for the person's health.

When Dr. Geronimus introduced her weathering hypothesis about stress, epigenetic changes, and the longevity of Black people, there were a lot of doubters. They did not believe that a social phenomenon – racial discrimination – could induce the kinds of epigenetic events that would put a Black person's health at risk. There is now compelling evidence, however, that social experiences, such as racial discrimination and stress, in fact, activate epigenetic processes that decrease a person's ability to fight off certain diseases and shorten their lives.

Feeling Lonely: Emotions and Genetic Responses
One clear example of the epigenetic effects of stress is how it can affect a person's ability to fight off certain diseases. This involves an epigenetic response formally known as the "conserved transcriptional response to adversity," which involves a very specific group of genes. These are genes that specifically react to a person's feelings and emotions, especially feelings of loneliness and isolation. When activated, the genes simultaneously increase a person's resistance to bacterial infections and decrease their resistance to viruses [79].

The primary explanation of why this occurs lies in humans' evolutionary history and the kinds of health threats they encountered under different circumstances. The ecosystems in which our ancestors lived were ones in which if they were alone (hunting, for example), they were much more likely to be physically attacked (perhaps by an animal or members of another tribe) than if they were surrounded by other people. Animal bites (or wounds from weapons) usually cause bacterial infections. Being part of a group of other people usually decreases the likelihood of such attacks and, thus, bacterial infections. But the close presence of other people also increases the likeli-hood of a viral infection because viruses are transmitted from one person to another. So, through natural selection humans evolved such that certain different social conditions (i.e., feeling the support of others versus feeling alone) influenced which genes would be expressed (that is, "up-regulated") and which genes would be suppressed (that is, "down-regulated"). Perceived racial discrimination is one of those social circumstances that makes some genes up-regulate and others down-regulate.

Experiencing discrimination or feeling stressed arouses feelings of being alone and isolated. Thus, the genes that would activate anti-bacterial defenses are over-expressed and those that would activate anti-viral defenses are under-expressed [69]. In essence, the signal to certain genes is, "Hey, don't worry about other people infecting you; you are all alone." As a consequence, people who experience more discrimination tend to become more susceptible to viral infections. This epigenetic process provides yet another explanation of why feeling stressed reduces a person's ability to fight off the flu and other viruses. This may be an explanation of why during the COVID-19 pandemic there was a greater number of COVID infections and deaths among Black people living in communities that had higher levels of racial inequalities [80].

Methylation

Another epigenetic phenomenon involves a chemical process known as methylation or methylation patterns, which can control which genes are expressed or suppressed. Methylation is a complex process, in which chemicals called methyls are added to a person's DNA (i.e., their genes). These methyls act like a light switch, turning on or off particular genes. Methylation is a normal part of how genes operate. However, life experiences can disrupt the methylation patterns, causing changes in how genes normally function. Not surprisingly, such disruption of genes by methylation patterns has been linked to a wide range of diseases such as cardiovascular disorders, diabetes, autoimmune diseases, and cancer. Research has shown experiencing discrimination disrupts normal DNA methylation patterns; this, in turn, can cause harmful alterations in the expression of the genes that regulate particular stress reactions [81].

Telomere Length

A third epigenetic phenomenon is telomere length. Telomeres are DNA and protein structures located at the end of chromosomes that essentially protect them. They are kind of like the plastic caps at the end of shoelaces that keep the laces from fraying. Telomere length is an important indicator of biological aging: As we age, our telomeres become shorter. Shorter telomeres are less protective of our DNA and negatively affect the structure and function of vital organs through a degeneration of their tissues. Critically, shorter telomere length is associated with a wide range of aging-related diseases, such as cardiovascular disease, diabetes, dementia, Alzheimer's, arthritis, and even death among people who are considered relatively young chronologically [82].

Change in telomere length is another epigenetic event that is associated with a person's life experiences, including discrimination [83]. For example, Dr. David Chae, professor of public health and tropical medicine at Tulane University, and his colleagues have examined the association between the experience of anti-Black discrimination and telomere length. In several different studies, they and other researchers have shown that higher reported levels of anti-Black discrimination are associated significantly with shorter telomere length [84]. That is, experiences with anti-Black discrimination are accelerating biological aging among Black people; this seems to be especially true for those who experience other kinds of social disadvantages, such as lower levels of education [85].

As we said, epigenetics is a relatively new field of science and much remains to be studied before we will fully know how these processes operate. However, the available evidence rather strongly supports Dr. Geronimus' core thesis about adverse epigenetic effects of chronic exposure to racial discrimination.

There are, however, things in a person's life that can lessen some of the negative epigenetic effects of racial discrimination. Some studies of discrimination and biological aging in Black men find that having a supportive family environment weakens the relationship between discrimination and telomere length. Higher levels of education also appear to have this effect. This highlights a more general and significant fact – having more positive and supportive social and family environments mitigate some of the harmful health effects of racial discrimination.

Racial Discrimination, Stress, and Health Behaviors

As we discussed in Chapter 1, in the late nineteenth century and early twentieth century, government officials and people we would now probably call epidemiologists began to systematically study the health of all Americans. It soon became quite clear that Black Americans were dramatically less healthy than White Americans. This was largely due to the appallingly unhealthy conditions of the neighborhoods where most Black people were forced to live. However, this idea was rejected by many scientists and in the media of the time. Rather, these huge racial health disparities were attributed to either (1) the biological inferiority of Black people or (2) another racist trope – Black Americans were doing things that made them less healthy than White Americans. They do unhealthy things and do not take care of themselves.

Alas, this idea is still alive. In 2020, Ohio State Senator Daniel Huffman offered the following racist explanation for why so many more Black Americans than White Americans were dying from COVID-19: "Could it just be that African-Americans, or the colored population, do not wash their hands as well as other groups or wear a mask or do not socially distance themselves? Could that be the explanation of why the higher incidence?" [86]

We believe there are much more valid and reasonable explanations for racial health disparities than those offered by Senator Huffman. They involve chronic stress due to experiencing racial discrimination. In addition to its physiological effects, racial discrimination can actually cause people to engage in behaviors that induce pleasurable feelings that reduce discrimination-related stress, but these behaviors could put their health at risk. A meta-analysis, which combined the results of studies involving about 15,000 people, found a significant relationship between the biomarkers indicating greater stress-induced allostatic load and more engagement in a variety of unhealthy behaviors, including overeating and substance use, as well as other generally risky behaviors [87]. Moreover, two national longitudinal studies with Black participants showed that greater engagement in unhealthy behaviors (e.g., use of tobacco, alcohol, and consumption of fast food) weakened the association between transitory symptoms of nonspecific distress (such as feeling overwhelmed, upset, and anxious) and serious depression. Black people who experienced higher levels of stress were less likely to develop a depressive disorder apparently because they engaged in stress-coping behaviors that are physically unhealthy in the long run.

It has also been found that, activation of the amygdala and the hormonal activity associated with stress can impair higher-order cognitive functions. This interference with more rational and logical thinking can reduce self-control, making it more likely a person will focus on immediate gratification over the long-term consequences of their actions. It may also reduce their ability to self-regulate their unhealthy behaviors once they have begun [87]. Engaging in actions that produce immediate gratification and having problems in self-regulation lead to higher levels of health compromising behaviors.

In the following section, we discuss specific stress-coping behaviors that may appear maladaptive and could in the long run be quite dangerous to the health of Black people. Talking candidly about these phenomena raises the possibility that we could end up, like Senator Huffman, appearing to blame the victims. So, let us be very clear: The root cause of the problematic health-related behaviors that we review is *anti-Black racism*.

Smoking

One major reason why people smoke is because they are stressed, and smoking temporarily reduces stress [88]. Although Black Americans, on average, experience much more stress than White Americans, the percentage who say they smoke is actually about the same as White Americans (about 15 percent). Yet, it appears that the smoking behaviors of the two groups may differ. Black smokers report greater difficulty in quitting. Historically, one reason for this is that they are much more likely to smoke menthol cigarette brands, which have a much higher nicotine content, and thus are more addictive [89].[6] But there is more to this picture. Another meta-analysis of the results of 27 studies with over 4,000 Black participants found a consistent trend across the studies that Black smokers who report greater experiences of racial discrimination are more likely to smoke [90]. As a result, Black Americans have greater total exposure to the dangerous contents of cigarettes, resulting in greater mortality rates from smoking among Black Americans than White Americans [91].

Black people do not need to be the direct targets of racism for it to affect how much they smoke. This behavior can also be affected by the stress induced by racial discrimination in the neighborhoods where they live. Recall from the Introduction chapter that so-called stop and frisk laws disproportionately target Black people. A group of researchers at Tulane University looked at how the relative incidence of Black people being subjected to these searches in New Orleans, Louisiana affected smoking and some other health-related behaviors of people in predominantly Black neighborhoods. They found, first, that police in New Orleans stopped Black people at three times the rate they stopped White people in stop and frisk incidents. The researchers also found that even after they had statistically equated different neighborhoods for socioeconomic status and other factors that might affect smoking, the greater the number of stop and frisks incidents in a neighborhood, the more the residents smoked (and the less they exercised). Presumably this was because of the stress induced by the systemic racism embedded in the city's stop and frisk operations [92]. Of course, this exacerbates the already higher stress levels that result from living in the high-poverty and under-resourced Black neighborhoods where these searches are most likely to occur.

---

[6] In the past, tobacco companies specifically promoted menthol cigarettes to Black people. This marketing effort is documented in *Pushing Cool: Big Tobacco, Racial Marketing and the Untold Story of the Menthol Cigarette* by Keith Wailoo. In May 2021, the FDA announced it would ban the production and distribution of menthol-flavored cigarettes. This may help reduce future racial disparities in deaths from smoking.

Alcohol Use

Excessive use of alcohol is a serious problem in the United States. According to the CDC, about 25 percent of the people they surveyed reported that there was least one day in the past year when they had four to five drinks, which classifies them as "heavy drinker" [93]. Alcohol use seems to be much more of a problem for White Americans than Black Americans. White Americans are somewhat more likely to be "regular drinkers" (12 drinks in the last year) than are Black Americans and are about twice as likely as Black Americans to report being heavy drinkers [94].

Dr. Jessica Desalu, a clinical psychologist at Howard University, and her colleagues conducted a meta-analysis of the research on racial discrimination and alcohol use among Black Americans, combining data from 27 different studies that together had studied over 26,000 Black people. Greater perceived racial discrimination was positively associated with the amount of alcohol people drank, binge drinking, and drinking that might put the person or others at risk (e.g., a pregnant woman who drinks, driving while intoxicated) [95]. The underlying reasons for these associations are not yet understood, but we know that alcohol provides short-term relief from stress. Thus, it seems likely that one way Black Americans cope with stress from anti-Black racism is by drinking alcohol, which can contribute to many of the health problems that accompany drinking too much alcohol.

Recreational Drug Use

Overall, Black Americans are no more likely to use recreational drugs than White Americans. In fact, cocaine and heroin use is substantially greater among White Americans [96]. Research shows, however, that recreational drug use among Black Americans is positively associated with being the target of racial discrimination. Dr. Rick Gibbons and Dr. Meg Gerrard, professors of psychological sciences at the University of Connecticut, recruited a very large number of Black adults and their children as study participants and collected information from them at several different points in time [97]. At the beginning of their study, they asked the children about perceived racial discrimination and their willingness to engage in the use of substances such as recreational drugs; at the same time, they asked the parents about discrimination and their actual use of these substances. Later on, both parents and children were again asked about using recreational drugs. Dr. Gibbons, Dr. Gerard, and their colleagues found that perceived discrimination measured at the beginning of the study was associated with actual use of these substances among both parents and their children at a later time. Sometimes this relationship was present for as long as five years [97].

The relationship between discrimination and drug use, however, is neither automatic nor unchangeable. In these studies, we again see an example of the mitigating effects of a person's family life. Supportive parenting greatly reduced the associations between discrimination and both children's intentions and their willingness to use drugs [98]. This is important because it reveals yet again that there are things that can mitigate the negative impact of racial discrimination on racial health disparities in America.

Unhealthy Diets

As discussed earlier, unhealthy eating in response to stress is not a phenomenon limited to Black people. Looking for "comfort" foods in times of stress is a widespread phenomenon. You can see examples of this in the memes that appear on social media, such as: "*To relieve stress: Please follow these instructions carefully 1) Eat a handful of your favorite chocolate; 2) Repeat nine more times.*" But unhealthy eating patterns are often more of a problem for Black people and other racial/ethnic minority groups. In large part, this is because they are likely to experience more stress and discrimination in their day-to day lives [99]. Research consistently shows a relationship between experiences of racial discrimination and unhealthy eating. (Also see the discussion in Chapter 3 of food deserts and food swamps in poor, predominantly Black neighborhoods.)

At least a partial explanation of why stress affects what people eat lies in allostatic load, discussed earlier in this chapter. When stressed, the body "thinks" it needs more energy to respond to the stressor. Thus, higher levels of cortisol are secreted, and greater cortisol secretion increases people's appetite for foods that are high in carbohydrates, fat, and sugar. This is at least in part why people turn to foods like pizza, ice cream, and various fast foods when they are stressed out [87].

So, the tendency to eat potentially unhealthy foods, like all reactions to discrimination and stress, is not peculiar to Black people. However, the relationship may pose special risks for Black people. Two researchers at the University of Michigan, Dr. Briana Mezuk, professor of epidemiology, and Dr. James S. Jackson, professor of psychology, have proposed an intriguing theory of how the environment in which one lives may affect what one eats in response to stress, and this may result in yet another racial health disparity. The theory begins with the idea that the range of behaviors people can engage in to cope with stress is largely determined by the availability of resources in their immediate environment. Disparities in resources may result in disparities between how Black people and White people cope with discrimination that could produce differences in their health-related behaviors [100].

This idea was based on some earlier research findings. The first of these was that because of greater exposure to racial discrimination, Black people experienced more day-to-day stress than White people and were more likely to report transitory symptoms of nonspecific distress, such as feeling overwhelmed, upset, and anxious, than were White people. But contrary to what one might expect, these transitory symptoms of nonspecific distress were less likely to develop into major depression and/or anxiety disorders in Black people than in White people. To explain this unanticipated second finding, Dr. Mezuk and Dr. Jackson proposed that it was due to the characteristics of the neighborhoods where Black Americans and White Americans typically live, as well as differences in cultural backgrounds and social norms.

When people search for behaviors to mitigate their stress, their choices are limited by what their environment makes available (i.e., "affords") to them. Because of the racial, social, and economic disparities that exist in the United States, the number of behaviors available to address stress among people, who live in under-resourced neighborhoods may be appreciably less than those available to White people. For example, as we discuss in detail in Chapter 3, under-resourced and segregated Black neighborhoods have lots of stores selling alcohol and tobacco products, as well as many fast-food restaurants. However, grocery stores that sell healthy foods and places that offer recreational opportunities that might enable people to work off their stress are in short supply. Further, social norms and the cultural milieu in some neighborhoods may make some choices to reduce stress more attractive than others. One consequence may be that when Black residents of segregated neighborhoods are looking for ways to reduce their stress, the limited options they have may be less healthy than those available to people who live in wealthier White or integrated neighborhoods. Also, the social norms within a neighborhood will also affect what people are inclined to eat.

However, the less healthy options that are available (e.g., comfort foods, smoking) may actually offer immediate gratification and relief from stress.

In higher socioeconomic status, predominantly White neighborhoods, the alternatives people might choose (e.g., exercise or meditation) would take much longer to have such effects. These unhealthy eating or drinking behaviors that are readily available in some neighborhoods may be much more effective in quickly reducing stress, and thus in also reducing its more serious longer-term psychological consequences.

Dr. Mezuk and Dr. Jackson predicted that when they compared the impact of unhealthy eating choices among Black people and among White people, the choice of the less healthy foods would reduce the strength of the association between stress and serious anxiety or depression among Black people but not White people. Findings from two national longitudinal studies supported their predictions. Among the Black participants in these studies, greater engagement in unhealthy behaviors (e.g., use of tobacco, alcohol, and consumption of fast food) weakened the association between transitory symptoms of nonspecific distress and serious depression. But, by contrast, among White participants, engaging in unhealthy behaviors tended to increase their levels of stress-related depression. Thus, the paradoxical conclusion from this research is that environmental constraints (e.g., the neighborhoods where they live, lower incomes) and social norms may offer Black people fewer ways to reduce their stress. But this may make it easier for them to quickly choose those behaviors that offer fast relief. Still, these same environmental constraints and social norms mean that the choices available to them are more likely to involve unhealthy behaviors, with substantial consequences for their physical health.

Thus far, the studies we have presented show consistent associations between exposure to racial discrimination and unhealthy behaviors. Dr. Laura Smart Richman, professor of population health science at Duke University, and her colleagues conducted an experiment that was intended to determine whether exposure to racial discrimination could *cause* unhealthy behaviors, including food choices. The researchers divided the Black participants in the study into two groups. For one group, they increased the participants' awareness of racial discrimination by asking them to think of and then write about the death of Trayvon Martin. In 2012 Martin, an unarmed Black teenager, was on his way home from a convenience store where he had purchased some candy, when he was confronted by and killed by George Zimmerman, a member of a neighborhood watch, who suspected Martin of committing some unspecified crime. For the other group, the researchers asked Black participants to think and write about something unrelated to discrimination – the weather.

Dr. Richman and her colleagues then presented both groups with a list of health-related behaviors involving food, including things such as eating fried foods or buying fresh produce. Compared to Black participants who just thought about the weather, those who thought of and wrote about the death of Trayvon Martin were more likely to indicate that eating unhealthy foods is something they would do [101]. This experiment therefore provides evidence that when Black Americans attend more to racial discrimination, it causes them to make food choices that are less healthy. Presumably this is because of the stress induced by the impact of racial discrimination on a Black person.

Of course, in the final analysis individuals bear some personal responsibility for their health-related behaviors. However, the root cause of these racial disparities in health-related behaviors is the pervasive anti-Black racism that creates the predominantly Black and under-resourced neighborhoods that are typical of most large American cities. Black people living in these neighborhoods do not eat healthy food because of some self-destructive urge. Rather their food choices reflect the limited options available to them. For many Black Americans, these choices may effectively reduce stress but at the cost of subsequent poorer health.

Health Benefits of a Strong Black Racial Identity

While the previous sections have identified a range of activities and choices that put Black Americans' health at risk, we reemphasize that the problem is not being Black, it is the experience of racial discrimination. However, there are things that can mitigate the health effects of exposure to racial discrimination. One of them is strongly identifying as a Black person and being proud to be a member of this social group. This kind of identification can result in an increased sense of personal strength and resilience when a Black person confronts the challenges of anti-Black racism.

Having a strong sense of racial identity can improve a person's psychological and physical well-being in a number of ways [102]. One reason for this is that a strong racial identity increases a sense of connectedness with others, which buffers the negative impact of discrimination and increases social support when a person is exposed to various difficulties. Another benefit is that a strong identity increases a person's sense of meaning, purpose, and personal worth. While the "universal context of racism" has the potential to lead Black Americans to accept and internalize their negative treatment, a strong racial identity helps Black Americans see the barriers they face as the result of racism directed at Black people as a group, not them as individuals. Thus, a strong racial identity can protect an individual Black person against the negative effects of self-blame and self-doubt. This perhaps explains why, despite their exposure to persistent and pervasive racial discrimination, most Black Americans' self-esteem remains comparable to that of White Americans [103]. Finally, a strong racial identity can increase Black people's sense of control and self-determination [104]. This identification permits them to make choices that ultimately benefit them, their health, and other members of their group.

Turning to specific health benefits, a strong positive racial identity is associated with lower levels of smoking or use of recreational drugs among Black children, better immune responses (i.e., lower levels of cytokines) among Black adolescents, lower likelihood of having hypertension among older Black adults, and better overall general health among Black adults. In sum, a strong racial identity can at least partially protect Black Americans against the corrosive effects of exposure to racial discrimination on their health [105–107].

Putting It All Together

The key to understanding the path from racial discrimination to racial health disparities is to remember that racial discrimination is what Thomas of Aquinas and other philosophers would call the "prime mover." To be sure, stress is part of everyone's daily lives, and Black Americans would still experience some forms of stress even if all anti-Black racism somehow magically disappeared. But it has not disappeared, and it causes a particular form of chronic stress in Black people. This stress begins a dangerous cascade, which can end in death. Thus, pervasive racial discrimination creates some special dangers to the health of Black Americans. These involve both physiological and psychological processes that occur in response to racial discrimination.

Of course, there are things that can disrupt these dangerous paths. They are really not that complicated; they all involve changing some aspects of the social, economic, and psychological race-related conditions that confront many Black Americans in their daily lives. This would serve to reduce the level of chronic stress that many Black Americans experience. But, doing this will require broad and sincere commitments from individual Americans and the government to address these conditions. The reality, however, is that we as a country have been unwilling to make such commitments for over 400 years.

REFERENCES

1. Centers for Disease Control and Prevention. (2021, April 8). *Media statement from CDC Director Rochelle P. Walensky, MD, MPH, on Racism and Health.* www.cdc.gov/media/releases/2021/s0408-racism-health.html

2. Whitaker, B. (2021, April 18). Racism's corrosive impact on the health of Black Americans. *CBS News.* www.cbsnews.com/news/60-minutes-disease-black-americans-covid-19-2021-04-18/

3. Holland, B., Dozier, L., & Holland, E. (1965). *Nowhere to run, nowhere to hide.* Motown.

4. Jones, J. M., Engleman, S., Turner, C. E. Jr., & Campbell, S. (2009). Worlds apart: The universality of racism leads to divergent social realities. In S. Demoulin, J. -P. Leyens, & J. F. Dovidio (Eds.), *Intergroup misunderstandings: Impact of divergent social realities* (pp. 117–133). Psychology Press.

5. Loh, T. H., Coes, C., & Buthe, B. (2020, December 16). Separate and unequal: Persistent residential segregation is sustaining racial and economic injustice in the US. *Brookings.* www.brookings.edu/essay/trend-1-separate-and-unequal-neighborhoods-are-sustaining-racial-and-economic-injustice-in-the-us/

6. Horowitz, J. M., Brown, A., & Cox, K. (2019, April 9). *Race in America 2019.* Pew Research Center. www.pewresearch.org/social-trends/2019/04/09/race-in-america-2019/

7. Asmelash, L. (2020, May 30). Michelle Obama: It's up to everyone to root out racism. *CNN Politics.* www.cnn.com/2020/05/30/politics/michelle-obama-george-floyd-statement-trnd/index.html

8. Wilkerson, I. (2020). *Caste: The origins of our discontents.* Random House. https://books.google.com/books?id=_er2DwAAQBAJ

9. Stone, A., Katersky, A., & Ghebremedhin, S. (2021, January 8). Woman accused of attacking teen in NY hotel arrested after fleeing, boy's family speaks out. *ABC News.* https://abcnews.go.com/US/woman-accused-attacking-teen-ny-hotel-arrested-california/story?id=75124832

10. O'Hare, J. (2017, June 1). LeBron James: 'Racism will always be part of the world'. *Global Citizen.* www.globalcitizen.org/en/content/lebron-james-racism-hate-crime-emmet-till/

11. Harvard T. H. Chan School of Public Health, National Public Radio, Robert Wood Johnson Foundation. (2018, January). *Discrimination in America: Final summary.* https://cdn1.sph.harvard.edu/wp-content/uploads/sites/94/2018/01/NPR-RWJF-HSPH-Discrimination-Final-Summary.pdf

12. Lee, R. T., Perez, A. D., Boykin, C. M., & Mendoza-Denton, R. (2019). On the prevalence of racial discrimination in the United States. *PLoS ONE, 14* (1), e0210698. https://doi.org/10.1371/journal.pone.0210698

13. Abrajano, M., & Alvarez, R. M. (2018). Answering questions about race: How racial and ethnic identities influence survey response. *American Politics Research, 47*(2), 250–274. https://doi.org/10.1177/1532673X18812039

14. U.S. Department of Justice. (2021). *2021 Hate Crime Statistics.* www.justice.gov/hatecrimes/hate-crime-statistics

15. Anti-Defamation League. (2020, November 16). *Alabama only state in U.S. to report zero hate crimes.* https://atlanta.adl.org/news/alabama-only-state-in-u-s-to-report-zero-hate-crimes/?
gclid=CjwKCAjwzruGBhBAEiwAUqMR8NseA2D_xojFGeMS62bE8OH-HCI-gutFNCMGl9ssk3afHJvUl8oz3sxoCfZgQAvD_BwE

16. Statista. (2023). *Rate of fatal police shootings in the United States from 2015 to March 2023, by ethnicity.* www.statista.com/statistics/1123070/police-shootings-rate-ethnicity-us/

17. Pickett, J. T., Graham, A., & Cullen, F. T. (2022). The American racial divide in fear of the police. *Criminology, 60*(2), 291–320. https://onlinelibrary.wiley.com/doi/10.1111/1745-9125.12298

18. Hamel, L. K., A., Kearney, A., Lopes, L., Munana, C., & Brodie, M. (2020, June 26). *KFF health tracking poll – June 2020.* KFF. www.kff.org/racial-equity-and-health-policy/report/kff-health-tracking-poll-june-2020/

19. Perez, A., & Mendoza-Denton, R. (2019). On the prevalence of racial discrimination in the United States. *PLoS One, 14*(1), e0210698. www.ncbi.nlm.nih.gov/pmc/articles/PMC6328188/

20. Young, K. (2020, June 28). A Black mother reflects on giving her 3 sons 'The talk … again and again. National Public Radio. www.npr.org/people/469530441/kenya-young

21. Fowers, A. (2020, June 12). Depression and anxiety spiked among black Americans after George Floyd's death. *The Washington Post.* www.ncbi.nlm.nih.gov/search/research-news/10210/

22. Sellers, R. M. (2020, May 29). Op-Ed: I am so tired. University of Michigan. https://odei.umich.edu/2020/05/29/i-am-so-tired/

23. Der Ananian, C., Winham, D. M., Thompson, S. V., & Tisue, M. E. (2018). Perceptions of heart-healthy behaviors among African American Adults: A mixed methods study. *International Journal of Environmental Research and Public Health, 15*(11), 2433. https://doi.org/10.3390/ijerph15112433 24.

24. American Psychological Association. (2020, October). Stress in America 2020: A mental health crisis. www.apa.org/news/press/releases/stress/2020/sia-mental-health-crisis.pdf

25. Chae, D. H., Yip, T., Martz, C. D., Chung, K., Richeson, J. A., Hajat, A., Curtis, D. S., Rogers, L. O., & LaVeist, T. A. (2021). Vicarious racism and vigilance during the COVID-19 pandemic: Mental health implications among Asian and Black Americans. *Public Health Reports, 136*(4), 508–517. https://doi.org/10.1177/00333549211018675

26. Wells, C. (2018, October 11). *Microaggressions: What they are and why they matter.* Race, Racism, and the Law. https://racism.org/articles/defining-racism/2283-microaggressions-what

27. Sue, D. W., Capodilupo, C. M., Torino, G. C., Bucceri, J. M., Holder, A. M. B., Nadal, K. L., & Esquilin, M. (2007). Racial microaggressions in everyday life: Implications for clinical practice. *American Psychologist, 62*(4), 271–286. https://doi.org/10.1037/0003-066X.62.4.271

28. American Medical Association. (2020, September 9). Aletha Maybank, MD, MPH, explores the context of public health to improve equity. www.ama-assn .org/delivering-care/health-equity/aletha-maybank-md-mph-explores-context-public-health-improve-equity

29. Porges, S. W. (2004). Neuroception: A subconscious system for detecting threats and safety. *Zero to Three, 24*(5), 19–24. https://eric.ed.gov/?id= EJ938225

30. Goleman, D. (1989, August 15). Brain's design emerges as a key to emotions. *New York Times.* www.nytimes.com/1989/08/15/science/brain-s-design-emerges-as-a-key-to-emotions.html?pagewanted=all

31. Godoy, L. D., Rossignoli, M. T., Delfino-Pereira, P., Garcia-Cairasco, N., & de Lima Umeoka, E. H. (2018). A comprehensive overview on stress neurobiology: Basic concepts and clinical implications [Review]. *Frontiers in Behavioral Neuroscience, 12*(127). https://doi.org/10.3389/fnbeh.2018.00127

32. Porges, S. W. (2017). *The pocket guide to the polyvagal theory: The transformative power of feeling safe.* WW Norton & Co.

33. Jones, J. M. (2003). TRIOS: A psychological theory of the African legacy in American culture. *Journal of Social Issues, 59*(1), 217–242. https://doi.org/10 .1111/1540-4560.t01-1-00014

34. McKenna, H. (2019). *Professor David Williams on racism, discrimination and the impact they have on health.* In The King's Fund podcast. https://kingsfund .libsyn.com/professor-david-williams-on-racism-discrimination-and-the-impact-it-has-on-health

35. McGraw, B. (2005). *The quotations of Mayor Coleman A. Young.* Wayne State University Press.

36. Brewer, L. C., & Cooper, L. A. (2014). Race, discrimination, and cardiovascular disease. *Virtual Mentor, 16*(6), 270–274. https://doi.org/10.1001/ virtualmentor.2014.16.06.stas2–1406

37. Cooper, L. (2021). *Why are health disparities everyone's problem?* JHU Press.

38. Hertz, R. P., Unger, A. N., Cornell, J. A., & Saunders, E. (2005). Racial disparities in hypertension prevalence, awareness, and management. *Archives of Internal Medicine, 165*(18), 2098–2104. https://doi.org/10.1001/archinte .165.18.2098

39. Berg, S. (2018, April). *Racial health disparities are rampant in hypertensions.* American Medical Association. www.ama-assn.org/delivering-care/hyperten sion/racial-health-disparities-are-rampant-hypertension

40. Dolezsar, C. M., McGrath, J. J., Herzig, A. J. M., & Miller, S. B. (2014). Perceived racial discrimination and hypertension: A comprehensive systematic review. *Health Psychology, 33*(1), 20–34. https://doi.org/10.1037/ a0033718

41. Cuevas, A. G., Ho, T., Rodgers, J., DeNufrio, D., Alley, L., Allen, J., & Williams, D. R. (2021). Developmental timing of initial racial discrimination exposure is associated with cardiovascular health conditions in adulthood. *Ethnic Health, 26*(7), 949–962. https://doi.org/10.1080/13557858.2019 .1613517

42. Panza, G. A., Puhl, R. M., Taylor, B. A., Zaleski, A. L., Livingston, J., & Pescatello, L. S. (2019). Links between discrimination and cardiovascular health among socially stigmatized groups: A systematic review. *PLoS ONE, 14* (6), e0217623. https://doi.org/10.1371/journal.pone.0217623

43. Centers for Disease Control and Prevention. (2020). *Health, United States. Spotlight: Racial and ethnic disparities in heart disease; 2019.* www.cdc.gov/nchs/hus/spotlight/HeartDiseaseSpotlight_2019_0404.pdf

44. Homandberg, L. K., & Fuller-Rowell, T. E. (2020). Experiences of discrimination and urinary catecholamine concentrations: Longitudinal associations in a college student sample. *Annals of Behavioral Medicine, 54*(11), 843–852. https://doi.org/10.1093/abm/kaaa033

45. Mwendwa, D. T., Sims, R. C., Madhere, S., Thomas, J., Keen, L. D., III, Callender, C. O., & Campbell, A. L., Jr. (2011). The influence of coping with perceived racism and stress on lipid levels in African Americans. *Journal of the National Medical Association, 103*(7), 594–601. https://doi.org/10.1016/s0027–9684(15)30385-0

46. Ayotte, B. J., Hausmann, L. R., Whittle, J., & Kressin, N. R. (2012). The relationship between perceived discrimination and coronary artery obstruction. *American Heart Journal, 163*(4), 677–683. https://doi.org/10.1016/j.ahj.2012.01.006

47. DeNoon, D. J. (2005). *Why 7 deadly diseases strike Blacks most.* WebMD. www.webmd.com/hypertension-high-blood-pressure/features/why-7-deadly-diseases-strike-blacks-most

48. Whitaker, K. M., Everson-Rose, S. A., Pankow, J. S., Rodriguez, C. J., Lewis, T. T., Kershaw, K. N., Diez Roux, A. V., & Lutsey, P. L. (2017). Experiences of discrimination and incident Type 2 Diabetes Mellitus: The multi-ethnic study of atherosclerosis (MESA). *American Journal of Epidemiology, 186*(4), 445–455. https://doi.org/10.1093/aje/kwx047

49. Shiyanbola, O. O., Ward, E. C., & Brown, C. M. (2018). Utilizing the common sense model to explore African Americans' perception of type 2 diabetes: A qualitative study. *PLoS One, 13*(11), e0207692. https://doi.org/10.1371/journal.pone.0207692

50. Duke Today. (2019, July 22). *How segregation and discrimination racialized the obesity epidemic.* https://today.duke.edu/2019/07/how-segregation-and-discrimination-racialized-obesity-epidemic2051

51. Koob, G. F., & Volkow, N. D. (2016). Neurobiology of addiction: A neurocircuitry analysis. *The Lancet Psychiatry, 3*(8), 760–773. https://doi.org/10.1016/S2215–0366(16)00104-8

52. Richtel, M. (2019). *An elegant defense: The extraordinary new science of the immune system: A tale in four lives.* William Morrow

53. Centers for Disease Control and Prevention. (2020). *Past season's estimated influenza disease burden.* www.cdc.gov/flu/about/burden/past-seasons.html?web=1&wdLOR=cA3736C8C-D6E7-D148-93B8-6D7C016E23E1

54. Glaser, R., & Kiecolt-Glaser, J. K. (2005). Stress-induced immune dysfunction: Implications for health. *Nature Reviews Immunology, 5*(3), 243–251. https://doi.org/10.1038/nri1571

55. Centers for Disease Control and Prevention. (2021). Flu disparities among racial and ethnic minority groups. www.cdc.gov/flu/highrisk/disparities-racial-ethnic-minority-groups.html?web=1&wdLOR=c77CED519-F457-3F44-A425-B4073317D23F

56. Centers for Disease Control and Prevention. (2022, November, 22). *People with certain medical conditions.* www.cdc.gov/coronavirus/2019-ncov/need-extra-precautions/people-with-medical-conditions.html#immunocompromised

57. Glaser, R., & Kiecolt-Glaser, J. (2009). Stress damages immune system and health. *Discovery Medicine, 5*(26), 165–169. www.discoverymedicine.com/Ronald-Glaser/2009/07/18/stress-damages-immune-system-and-health/

58. Madison, A. A., Shrout, M. R., Renna, M. E., & Kiecolt-Glaser, J. K. (2021). Psychological and behavioral predictors of vaccine efficacy: Considerations for COVID-19. *Perspectives in Psychological Science, 16*(2), 191–203. https://doi.org/10.1177/1745691621989243

59. Kiecolt-Glaser, J. K. (2021, January 15). *How can stress affect COVID-19 vaccine immune response?* The Ohio State University. https://wexnermedical.osu.edu/blog/how-can-stress-affect-covid19-immune-response

60. Thames, A. (2020, June 10). *Question: How does racism affect the immune system?* The National Interest. https://nationalinterest.org/blog/reboot/question-how-does-racism-affect-immune-system-161921

61. Liu, Y. Z., Wang, Y. X., & Jiang, C. L. (2017). Inflammation: The common pathway of stress-related diseases. *Frontiers of Human Neuroscience, 11*(6), 316. https://doi.org/10.3389/fnhum.2017.00316

62. Cunningham, T. J., Seeman, T. E., Kawachi, I., Gortmaker, S. L., Jacobs, D. R., Kiefe, C. I., & Berkman, L. F. (2012). Racial/ethnic and gender differences in the association between self-reported experiences of racial/ethnic discrimination and inflammation in the CARDIA cohort of 4 US communities. *Social Science and Medicine, 75*(5), 922–931. https://doi.org/10.1016/j.socscimed.2012.04.027

63. Chae, D. H., Drenkard, C. M., Lewis, T. T., & Lim, S. S. (2015). Discrimination and cumulative disease damage among African American women with Systemic Lupus Erythematosus. *American Journal of Public Health, 105*(10), 2099–2107. https://doi.org/10.2105/ajph.2015.302727

64. Centers for Disease Control and Prevention. (2021). *Most recent national asthma data.* www.cdc.gov/asthma/most_recent_national_asthma_data.htm

65. Thakur, N., Barcelo, N. E., Borrell, L. N., Singh, S., Eng, C., Davis, A., Meade, K., LeNoir, M. A., Avila, P. C., Farber, H. J., Serebrisky, D., Brigino-Buenaventura, E., Rodriguez-Cintron, W., Thyne, S., Rodriguez-Santana, J. R., Sen, S., Bibbins-Domingo, K., & Burchard, E. G. (2017). Perceived discrimination associated with asthma and related outcomes in minority youth: The GALA II and SAGE II Studies. *Chest, 151*(4), 804–812. https://doi.org/10.1016/j.chest.2016.11.027

66. Mental Health America. (n. d.). *Racism and mental health.* https://mhanational.org/racism-and-mental-health

67. Curtis, D. S., Washburn, T., Lee, H., Smith, K. R., Kim, J., Martz, C. D., Kramer, M. R., & Chae, D. H. (2021). Highly public anti-Black violence is

associated with poor mental health days for Black Americans. *Proceedings of the National Academy of Sciences, 118*(17). www.pnas.org/content/pnas/118/17/e2019624118.full.pdf

68. Himmelstein, M., Young, D., Sanchez, D., & Jackson, J. (2014). Vigilance in the discrimination stress model for Black Americans. *Psychology & Health, 30*(3), 252–267. https://doi.org/10.1080/08870446.2014.966104

69. Yoon, E., Coburn, C., & Spence, S. A. (2019). Perceived discrimination and mental health among older African Americans: The role of psychological well-being. *Aging and Mental Health, 23*(4), 461–469. https://doi.org/10.1080/13607863.2017.1423034

70. Wallace, S., Nazroo, J., & Bécares, L. (2016). Cumulative effect of racial discrimination on the mental health of ethnic minorities in the United Kingdom. *American Journal of Public Health, 106*(7), 1294–1300. https://doi.org/10.2105/ajph.2016.303121

71. Barlow, D. H., Ellard, K. K., Sauer-Zavala, S., Bullis, J. R., & Carl, J. R. (2014). The origins of neuroticism. *Perspectives on Psychological Science, 9*(5), 481–496. https://doi.org/10.1177/1745691614544528

72. Ansell, E. B., Rando, K., Tuit, K., Guarnaccia, J., & Sinha, R. (2012). Cumulative adversity and smaller gray matter volume in medial prefrontal, anterior cingulate, and insula regions. *Biological Psychiatry, 72*(1), 57–64. https://doi.org/10.1016/j.biopsych.2011.11.022

73. Arnsten, A. F., Raskind, M. A., Taylor, F. B., & Connor, D. F. (2015). The effects of stress exposure on prefrontal cortex: Translating basic research into successful treatments for Post-Traumatic Stress Disorder. *Neurobiology of Stress, 1*(1), 89–99. https://doi.org/10.1016/j.ynstr.2014.10.002

74. Harvard T. H. Chan School of Public Health. (2018). *Discrimination in America*. Harvard Public Health: Magazine of the Harvard T.H. Chan School of Public Health. www.hsph.harvard.edu/magazine/magazine_article/discrimination-in-america/

75. Geronimus, A. T., Hicken, M., Keene, D., & Bound, J. (2006). "Weathering" and age patterns of allostatic load scores among blacks and whites in the United States. *American Journal of Public Health, 96*(5), 826–833. https://doi.org/10.2105/ajph.2004.060749

76. Van Dyke, M. E., Baumhofer, N. K., Slopen, N., Mujahid, M. S., Clark, C. R., Williams, D. R., & Lewis, T. T. (2020). Pervasive discrimination and allostatic load in African American and White adults. *Psychosomatic Medicine, 82*(3), 316–323. https://doi.org/10.1097/psy.0000000000000788

77. Demby, G. (2018, January 14). *Making the case that discrimination is bad for your health*. NPR. www.npr.org/sections/codeswitch/2018/01/14/577664626/making-the-case-that-discrimination-is-bad-for-your-health

78. Duru, O. K., Harawa, N. T., Kermah, D., & Norris, K. C. (2012). Allostatic load burden and racial disparities in mortality. *Journal of the National Medical Association, 104*(1–2), 89–95. https://doi.org/10.1016/s0027-9684(15)30120-6

79. Brown, K. M., Diez-Roux, A. V., Smith, J. A., Needham, B. L., Mukherjee, B., Ware, E. B., Liu, Y., Cole, S. W., Seeman, T. E., & Kardia, S. L. R. (2019).

Expression of socially sensitive genes: The multi-ethnic study of atherosclerosis. *PLoS One, 14*(4), e0214061. https://doi.org/10.1371/journal.pone.0214061

80. Tan, S. B., deSouza, P., & Raifman, M. (2022). Structural racism and COVID-19 in the USA: A county-level empirical analysis. *Journal of Racial and Ethnic Health Disparities, 9*, 1–11. https://doi.org/10.1007/s40615–020-00948-8

81. Crusto, C. A., Sun, Y. V., & Taylor, J. Y. (2018). Perceived racial discrimination and DNA Methylation among African American women in the InterGEN Study. *Biological Research for Nursing, 20*(2), 145–152. https://journals.sagepub.com/doi/10.1177/1099800417748759

82. Adwan-Shekhidem, H., & Atzmon, G. (2018). The epigenetic regulation of telomere maintenance in aging. In A. Moskalev & A. M. Vaiserman (Eds.), *Epigenetics of aging and longevity* (Vol. 4, pp. 119–136). Academic Press. https://doi.org/https://doi.org/10.1016/B978–0-12-811060-7.00005-X

83. Chae, D. H., Wang, Y., Martz, C. D., Slopen, N., Yip, T., Adler, N. E., Fuller-Rowell, T. E., Lin, J., Matthews, K. A., Brody, G. H., Spears, E. C., Puterman, E., & Epel, E. S. (2020). Racial discrimination and telomere shortening among African Americans: The Coronary Artery Risk Development in Young Adults (CARDIA) Study. *Health Psychology, 39*(3), 209–219. https://doi.org/10.1037/hea0000832 https://doi.org/https://doi.org/10.1016/j.psyneuen.2020.104766

84. Thomas, M. D., Sohail, S., Mendez, R. M., Márquez-Magaña, L., & Allen, A. M. (2020). Racial discrimination and telomere length in midlife African American women: Interactions of educational attainment and employment status. *Annals of Behavioral Medicine, 55*(7), 601–611. https://doi.org/10.1093/abm/kaaa104

85. Calado, R. T., & Young, N. S. (2009). Telomere diseases. *The New England Journal of Medicine, 361*(24), 2353–2365. https://doi.org/10.1056/NEJMra0903373

86. Chiu, A. (2020, June 11). Ohio GOP lawmaker fired from ER job over remarks about 'colored population' and covid-19. *The Washington Post.* www.washingtonpost.com/nation/2020/06/11/black-coronavirus-ohio-gop/

87. Suvarna, B., Suvarna, A., Phillips, R., Juster, R.-P., McDermott, B., & Sarnyai, Z. (2020). Health risk behaviours and allostatic load: A systematic review. *Neuroscience & Biobehavioral Reviews, 108*(1), 694–711. https://doi.org/https://doi.org/10.1016/j.neubiorev.2019.12.020

88. Stubbs, B., Veronese, N., Vancampfort, D., Prina, A. M., Lin, P. Y., Tseng, P. T., Evangelou, E., Solmi, M., Kohler, C., Carvalho, A. F., & Koyanagi, A. (2017). Perceived stress and smoking across 41 countries: A global perspective across Europe, Africa, Asia and the Americas. *Scientific Reports, 7*(1), 7597. https://doi.org/10.1038/s41598–017-07579-w

89. University of North Carolina Gillings School of Public Health. (2018, August 31). *Study finds menthol cigarette marketing targets African-Americans.* https://sph.unc.edu/sph-news/study-finds-menthol-cigarette-marketing-targets-african-americans/

90. Sartor, C. E., Woerner, J., & Haeny, A. M. (2021). The contributions of everyday and major experiences of racial discrimination to current alcohol use and regular smoking in Black adults: Considering variation by demographic characteristics and family history. *Addictive Behaviors, 114*(3), 106711. https://doi.org/10.1016/j.addbeh.2020.106711

91. Center for Disease Control and Prevention. (2010, November). *Racial disparities in smoking-attributable mortality and years of potential life lost: Missouri, 2003–2007.* www.cdc.gov/mmwr/preview/mmwrhtml/mm5946a4.htm

92. Theall, K. P., Francois, S., Bell, C. N., Anderson, A., Chae, D., & LaVeist, T. A. (2022). Neighborhood police encounters, health, and violence in a southern city. *Health Affairs, 41*(2), 228–236. https://doi.org/10.1377/hlthaff.2021.01428

93. Centers for Disease Control and Prevention. (2018, March 16). *QuickStats: Age-adjusted percentages of adults aged ≥18 years who are current regular drinkers of alcohol, by sex, race, and Hispanic origin – National Health Interview Survey, 2016.* www.cdc.gov/mmwr/volumes/67/wr/mm6710a8.htm

94. Partnership to End Addiction. (2012, October). *African-American youth see higher levels of alcohol advertising, study finds.* https://drugfree.org/drug-and-alcohol-news/african-american-youth-see-higher-levels-of-alcohol-advertising-study-finds/

95. Desalu, J. M., Goodhines, P. A., & Park, A. (2019). Racial discrimination and alcohol use and negative drinking consequences among Black Americans: A meta-analytical review. *Addiction, 114*(6), 957–967. https://doi.org/10.1111/add.14578

96. Schuler, M. S., Schell, T. L., & Wong, E. C. (2021). Racial/ethnic differences in prescription opioid misuse and heroin use among a national sample, 1999–2018. *Drug and Alcohol Dependence, 221*(4), 108588. https://doi.org/10.1016/j.drugalcdep.2021.108588

97 Gibbons, F. X., Gerrard, M., Cleveland, M. J., Wills, T. A., & Brody, G. (2004). Perceived discrimination and substance use in African American parents and their children: A panel study. *Journal of Personality and Social Psychology, 86*(4), 517–529. https://doi.org/10.1037/0022-3514.86.4.517

98. Gibbons, F. X., Etcheverry, P. E., Stock, M. L., Gerrard, M., Weng, C. Y., Kiviniemi, M., & O'Hara, R. E. (2010). Exploring the link between racial discrimination and substance use: What mediates? What buffers? *Journal of Personality and Social Psychology, 99*(5), 785–801. https://doi.org/10.1037/a0019880

99. Cheng, H.-L. (2014). Disordered eating among Asian/Asian American women: Racial and cultural factors as correlates. *The Counseling Psychologist, 42*(6), 821–851. https://doi.org/10.1177/0011000014535472

100. Mezuk, B., Abdou, C. M., Hudson, D., Kershaw, K. N., Rafferty, J. A., Lee, H., & Jackson, J. S. (2013). "White Box" epidemiology and the social neuroscience of health behaviors: The environmental affordances model.

Society and Mental Health, *3*(2), 79–95. https://doi.org/10.1177/2156869313480892

101. Smart Richman, L., Blodorn, A., & Major, B. (2016). An identity-based motivational model of the effects of perceived discrimination on health-related behaviors. *Group Processes & Intergroup Relations*, *19*(4), 415–425. https://doi.org/10.1177/1368430216634192

102. Jetten, J., Haslam, S. A., Cruwys, T., & Branscombe, N. R. (2018). Social identity, stigma, and health. In B. Major, J. F. Dovidio, & B. G. Link (Eds.), *The Oxford handbook of stigma, discrimination, and health* (pp. 301–316). Oxford University Press. https://psycnet.apa.org/record/2017-57025-016

103. Crocker, J., & Major, B. (1989). Social stigma and self-esteem: The self-protective properties of stigma. *Psychological Review*, *96*(4), 608–630. https://doi.org/10.1037/0033-295X.96.4.608

104. Zapolski, T. C. B., Beutlich, M. R., Fisher, S., & Barnes-Najor, J. (2019). Collective ethnic-racial identity and health outcomes among African American youth: Examination of promotive and protective effects. *Cultural Diversity and Ethnic Minority Psychology*, *25*(3), 388–396. www.ncbi.nlm.nih.gov/pmc/articles/PMC6579722/

105. Thomas Tobin, C. S., Gutierrrez, A., Norris, K. C., & Thorpe, R. J., Jr. (2022). Discrimination, racial identity, and hypertension among Black Americans across young, middle, and older adulthood. *Journals of Gerontology, Series B*, *77*(11), 1990–2005. https://doi.org/10.1093/geronb/gbac068

106. Lewis, F., Boutrin, M-C., Dalrymple, L., & McNeil, L. H. (2018). The influence of Black identity on wellbeing and health behaviors. *Journal of Racial and Ethnic Health Disparities*, *5*, 671–681. https://link.springer.com/article/10.1007/s40615-017-0412-7

107. Greenaway, K. H., Haslam, S. A., Cruwys, T., Branscombe, N. R., Ysseldyk, R., & Heldreth, C. (2015). From "we" to "me": Group identification enhances perceived personal control with consequences for health and well-being. *Journal of Personality and Social Psychology*, *109*(1), 53–74. https://doi.org/10.1037/pspi0000019

CHAPTER 3

"Two Americas"
The Effects of Racial Residential Segregation on the Health of Black Americans

> There are two Americas. Every city in our country has this kind of dualism ... split at so many parts, and so every city ends up being two cities rather one. .... [And in one part] millions of people are forced to live in distressing housing conditions.
> —Dr. Martin Luther King Jr., March 14, 1968 [1]

Dr. King was assassinated shortly after he gave the speech quoted above, in which he characterized the United States as a divided nation wherein millions of Black Americans suffer from poor housing conditions. One consequence of his tragic death, however, was a swell of support for the passage of the Fair Housing Act of 1968. The Act, which Congress passed about a month after Dr. King's death, was a follow-up to the Civil Rights Act of 1964. It specifically prohibited discrimination concerning the sale, rental, and financing of housing based on race, religion, national origin, or sex. Although the 14th Amendment, passed in 1868, gave all citizens "equal protection under the laws," the Fair Housing Act was needed because racial segregation in housing had always been part of federal, state, and local governments' policies. Moreover, as recently as 2020, opposition to the Act's basic principles was still being voiced by some prominent political figures.

During his 2020 presidential campaign, former president Donald Trump tweeted, "I am happy to inform all of the people living their Suburban Lifestyle Dream that you will no longer be bothered or financially hurt by having low income housing built in your neighborhood... Your housing prices will go up based on the market, and crime will go down. I have rescinded the Obama-Biden AFFH Rule. Enjoy!" [2]. The Affirmatively Furthering Fair Housing (AFFH) Rule was a federal housing regulation designed to eliminate racial disparities in housing in the suburbs. Political experts described this tweet as an effort to win over suburbanites, particularly White women, by promising them protection from the supposed crime, racial unrest, and financial loss that would result from

124

this rule. It does not take great insight to see how the phrase "low-income housing" was a not-so-subtle code for housing in which Black people (and other BIPOC people) would live. As he often did, Trump was appealing to the worst of White people's attitudes. In this case, it was a very old and widely held sentiment among White Americans that they do not want to live in close proximity to Black Americans [3]. Indeed, over 50 years after Dr. King's speech and the passage of the Fair Housing Act, de facto residential segregation is still a fact of life in almost all American cities.

Racially Segregated Neighborhoods: Divided We Live

We use the term "racially segregated neighborhoods" to describe neighborhoods whose residents are predominantly economically disadvantaged Black people. The neighborhoods are also typically under-resourced in terms of housing, economic opportunities, and the quality of life available to the residents. There are multiple dangers to the residents' health in these neighborhoods, including substantial difficulties in the access to sometimes even basic healthcare. Clearly, not all majority-Black neighborhoods have predominantly poor residents or are under-resourced. There are many predominantly Black neighborhoods where the residents are wealthy, and the neighborhoods are well-resourced. Nevertheless, on average, the residents of most predominantly Black neighborhoods are much more likely to be poor than are residents of predominantly White neighborhoods. Poor Black Americans are three times more likely than poor White Americans to live in neighborhoods where the poverty rate is 40 percent or more. As the US Partnership on Mobility from Poverty puts it, racial segregation in housing has forced a "racialized concentration of poverty" [4].

Segregation and Poverty: Exceptions to the Rule

We note that it is not only poor Black people who live in these racially segregated, under-resourced, and generally unhealthy neighborhoods. A large percentage of middle- and upper-income Black Americans also live in low-income racially segregated neighborhoods. In fact, middle-class Black families are much more likely to live in high poverty areas than are low-income White families [4]. One study found that relatively affluent Black families (income more than $75,000) were over twice as likely as relatively affluent White families to live in high poverty neighborhoods [5]. For example, in Detroit and Cleveland, over 25 percent of affluent Black families live in high poverty, predominantly Black neighborhoods. Some of these higher-income Black families may have chosen to live in neighborhoods with people who are racially similar to them. However, because of the realities of pervasive racism and the de facto housing segregation that still exist in the United States, it is likely that many Black families' choices of where they might live and be accepted by their neighbors are much more limited than the choices of White families with comparable incomes. In the United States, race and racism still matter a lot in determining where a person lives.[1]

Racially segregated neighborhoods are not only the *result* of racism; they are also a major cause of racial inequities in all facets of their residents' lives, including their health and healthcare. The city of Baltimore, Maryland, provides a case study of racial segregation of neighborhoods and its consequences for the people who live in them.

Baltimore: A Portrait of Racial Residential Segregation

Baltimore, Maryland, is a city of nearly 600,000 residents that hugs the Chesapeake Bay at a picturesque harbor, with deep channels that sweep gracefully from the shoreline to the bay. This harbor defines the city's culture and economy. For well over 300 years, Baltimore has been home to generations of people attracted by the abundance of the bay. The region's first inhabitants were the Indigenous Lumbee people, who prospered before being colonized by Europeans in the early seventeenth century. Baltimore's natural harbor later attracted Scottish settlers and, after that, immigrants from Italy, Ireland, and other European countries [6].

The tobacco industry in Maryland led to the importation of large numbers of enslaved Black people. Black people, both enslaved and free, have always been a prominent demographic group since Baltimore's formal founding as a city in 1729. Today, 63 percent of Baltimore residents are people who self-identify as Black or African American [7]. While Black people and White people may share this city, they live in two very different kinds of neighborhoods.

Residential Segregation in Baltimore
The racial segregation of Baltimore neighborhoods can, in part, be traced back to 1911, when the City Council was the first in the country to pass a

[1] A book by Dr. Matthew Desmond, professor of sociology at Princeton University, titled *Eviction: Poverty and Profit in the American City* provides a very informative firsthand account of the unique life challenges faced by poor Black Americans living in a highly segregated American city.

segregation ordinance dictating where Black people could live. When the Supreme Court struck down a similar ordinance in Kentucky, the Baltimore mayor ordered city housing inspectors to issue a housing code violation to any person who sold or rented property in a predominantly White area to a Black person. The customs and traditions of racial housing segregation continue to today. As it was in the past, Baltimore is currently among the most racially segregated large cities in the United States.

Most Black residents are concentrated in older neighborhoods circling the city center, whereas White residents live in wealthier neighborhoods such as those with luxury condominiums circling the harbor, as well as leafy, tree-lined neighborhoods at the city's northern and western edges. The predominantly White neighborhoods are characterized by higher quality housing with a variety of high-end grocery stores nearby. There are also substantial healthcare facilities and many other amenities available to the residents. By contrast, the Black segregated neighborhoods are characterized by overcrowded housing, an absence of supermarkets and a glut of fast-food restaurants, high rates of poverty, relatively few healthcare facilities, and few, if any, of the amenities that would make the residents' lives easier.

Health in Black and White
In Baltimore, as in almost every major US city, place, race, and socioeconomic status (SES) matter in important ways for health. The people who live in the predominantly Black and under-resourced Baltimore neighborhoods have an average life expectancy that is 30 years less than it is in the predominantly White and wealthy neighborhoods – 60 years versus 90 years. Additionally, the premature death rate (e.g., dying before age 75) in these predominantly Black neighborhoods is 1.8 times higher than in the predominantly White neighborhoods [8]. However, it is important to understand that it is the nature of the neighborhoods and the health risks they contain, not their residents' race, that are primarily driving these health problems. White people in Baltimore who live under similar conditions as Black people suffer the same kinds of health problems [9].

These health differences between predominantly White and predominantly Black geographic areas within major cities are not unique to Baltimore. Figure 3.1 shows a map of the Chicago elevated transit system and the locations of some of its stations [10]. It also shows people's life expectancies in the neighborhoods surrounding these stations. The distance from the predominantly White neighborhood near the "Loop" station (the area around downtown Chicago is called the "Loop") to the predominantly

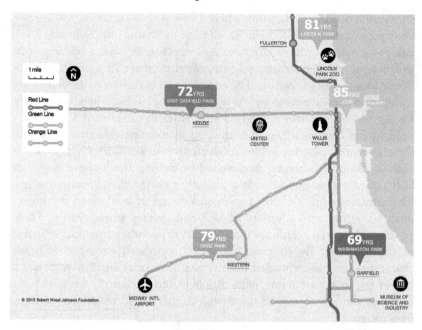

Figure 3.1 Neighborhoods' location and life expectancy: This is a map of stations in the Chicago subway and rail system. The distance from the "Loop Station" to the "Washington Park Station" is only about four miles. The life expectancy at birth of people living in the predominantly Black and poor neighborhood surrounding the Washington Park Station is, on average, 18 years less than the life expectancy of people living in the predominantly White and wealthy neighborhood surrounding the Loop Station.
Source: VCU Center on Society and Health. societyhealth@vcu.edu

Black neighborhood near the Washington Park station is only about four miles. The difference in life expectancy at birth is 16 years. The same kind of pattern exists in New York City and in most other major American cities [11]. Relative to other Americans, Black people who live in poor and under-resourced racially segregated neighborhoods, on average, have much poorer health. National data also show that the higher the percentage of Black residents in a neighborhood, the shorter is their life expectancy.[2]

[2] This may partly be due to the higher homicide rates among Black Americans. However, overall, homicides account for only 2 percent of all the deaths of Black Americans, which are far less than the deaths due to a host of different diseases. Moreover, the higher homicide rates are yet another indicator of the effects of systemic racism in the forms of forced racial segregation and the social inequities that exist in segregated and under-resourced neighborhoods. Violent crime rates are substantially greater in the most under-resourced and segregated neighborhoods. https://equitablegrowth.org/new-research-documents-the-high-cost-of-residential-racial-segregation-in-northern-cities-of-the-united-states/

A Nation Divided: How We Got Here

There are several ways to quantify how segregated American cities really are. One common measure of residential segregation by race in a city or metropolitan area is called the "dissimilarity index." It is the percentage of people in each of two racially or ethnically different groups who would need to move to achieve complete integration in a defined geographic area. For example, a dissimilarity index of 80 means that 80 percent of Black residents and White residents of a city would need to move to different neighborhoods to achieve full racial integration – an index of zero. The higher the dissimilarity index, the greater the racial segregation in housing.

The most recent US Census data available at the time of our writing this book puts the national Black–White dissimilarity index at about 70. This is down considerably from the index of 93 in 1970; so, the United States has made progress in integrating some neighborhoods and communities since the passage of the 1964 Civil Rights Act and the 1968 Fair Housing Act. However, the United States is still a very racially segregated country. This is especially true in large cities. In 2021, the Roots of Structural Racism Project at the University of California, Berkeley, reported that the most segregated large cities in the United States were Milwaukee, Wisconsin; Philadelphia, Pennsylvania; Chicago, Illinois; Detroit, Michigan; and Cleveland, Ohio. All of these cities had dissimilarity indices of 74 or more [12]. In sum, most Americans still live in neighborhoods where the majority of their neighbors are of the same race or ethnicity as them.

The story of how America became so racially divided in housing largely begins in the 1920s. Of course, racial residential segregation was already an integral part of the Jim Crow race laws that were in force in the southern United States. But, concerns about where Black people lived was not a major issue in most northern, more industrialized cities simply because before the 1930s there were so few Black people living in them. Ninety percent of all Black Americans lived in the rural South [13].

This all changed with the "Great Migration," during which approximately six million Black people moved from the South to cities in the Midwest and other northern urban centers over the course of about 50 years (the Great Migration is also discussed in Chapter 1). As a result, cities such as Detroit and Chicago, which had been almost all-White at the beginning of the twentieth century, saw incredible increases in the number of Black residents. In Detroit, the increase was over 500 percent, and Chicago experienced about a 150 percent increase. In Baltimore, the proportion of population that identified as Black tripled.

However, as we said in Chapter 1, these new Black residents were not welcomed with open arms. Rather, there was widespread resistance to their arrival in most northern cities and even more opposition to any racial integration in housing. This opposition took many forms, which created the legacy of the pervasive racial residential segregation that is part of America today.

Sundown Towns

There is a town in Illinois named "Anna" that Dr. James Loewen, professor of sociology and history at the University of Vermont, visited in 2001. "Is it true," Loewen asked a clerk in a store, "that Anna stands for 'Ain't No Niggers Allowed'?" "Yes," she answered with some embarrassment. Anna was (and Loewen suggests still may be) a "Sundown Town" [14]. These were places where Black people could visit during the day, but they were not allowed to live there: They had to leave before sundown. If a Black person somehow remained after dark, they faced at least arrest and often much worse consequences at the hands of the town's residents [15].

Sundown towns and regions were once a fact of American life: Between the 1890s and the 1960s, there were over 10,000 of them spread all over America. There was at least one Sundown state, Oregon, that legally excluded all Black people until 1926 [16]. Federal and state laws now prohibit towns and states from excluding people because of their race, but the laws in these places affected subsequent housing patterns and created areas where few Black people live today. For example, in Oregon, the percentage of residents who identify as Black is just over 2 percent. The comparable percentage in neighboring California is six times as great.

Restrictive Zoning and Covenants

Most large cities and suburbs were not formal Sundown towns, but systemic racism in the form of local housing laws and ordinances were often just as effective in creating large-scale racial residential segregation. Racial zoning ordinances were one such mechanism of exclusion. They prohibited Black people from living in certain parts of the city and prevented White owners from selling homes to them. In the 1920s, for example, city officials divided most of Atlanta, Georgia, which had a fairly large Black population, into "R-1 White Districts" and "R-2 Black Districts" [17]. When legal challenges made cities change such racial zoning ordinances, Atlanta and many other cities created other barriers to integrated housing. One way in which cities did this was to restrict population density in some neighborhoods so that only single-family detached homes could be built in them. This policy effectively excluded most Black residents because they could not afford such homes.

Another way of achieving the same exclusionary goal was by enacting "restrictive covenants." These were statements in real estate deeds that legally bound a buyer not to later sell a property to a Black person or members of other certain racial or ethnic minority groups. For example, a restrictive covenant written sometime before 1950 for Edina, a suburb of Minneapolis, Minnesota, stated that "no lot shall ever be sold, conveyed, leased, or rented to any person other than one of the white or Caucasian race, nor shall any lot ever be occupied or used for any person other than one of White or Caucasian race, except such as may be serving as domestics for the owner or tenant" [18].[3] While ordinances and covenants like this are no longer allowed, they established the templates for the residential segregation that we continue to see in cities and suburbs today.

The Federal Government's Role in Racial Residential Segregation: Color-Coded Public Housing

There is no doubt that individual acts of housing discrimination have contributed significantly to racial residential segregation today. But, the policies and practices of the federal and local governments played a much larger role in creating segregated housing and, thus, the contemporary health problems it has produced. In his comprehensive book on racial residential segregation in America, *The Color of Law: A Forgotten History of How Our Government Segregated America*, Richard Rothstein, senior fellow at the Haas Institute, University of California Berkeley, writes that racial residential segregation was "not merely a project of southerners in the former slaveholding Confederacy." He argued that, "[It was] a nation-wide project of the federal government in the 20th century" [18].

---

[3] These exclusionary covenants did not only apply to Black people. Many also applied to religious and ethnic minorities, including those whose ancestors were Jewish, Irish, or Italian. However, probably because these groups were identified as White people, residential restrictions fell much more rapidly for those ethnic groups than those for Black people.

Later in his book, Rothstein notes that the federal government's segrega-
tionist policies were accompanied by similar housing policies of state and
local governments "to create segregation in ways that still survive."

The systematic attempts by the federal government to separate where
Black Americans and White Americans live began in the 1930s, when
there was a serious housing shortage. As part of the "New Deal," the
government began to build public housing – large apartment complexes
that offered more affordable housing for both Black Americans and White
Americans because the government subsidized the rents. But, the pervasiveness of anti-Black racism in most large American cities caused the
federal government to construct separate housing for Black Americans
and White Americans. The federal agency responsible for this housing,
the Public Works Program, established a rule that the race of the residents
who would live in a new housing project must reflect the racial composition of the neighborhood in which it was built. That is, there should be
Black residents in the public housing in Black neighborhoods and White
residents in White neighborhoods [18]. Not only did the federal government, thus, actively promote racial segregation in housing, it compounded
the problem by frequently placing the public housing for Black people in
neighborhoods that were already poor and disadvantaged.

The government policies that created large-scale public housing for
Black Americans produced crowded high-rise buildings mostly occupied
by poor families. For example, the Henry Horner project in Chicago, built
in an under-resourced, predominantly Black neighborhood in 1957, contained more than 19 high-rise apartment buildings, with over 2,300
individual units. The buildings often did not have on-site managers
responsible for their care and were frequently poorly maintained [19]. In
most buildings there was little in the way of security. Law enforcement
agencies typically avoided them, and the complexes often became breeding
grounds for gangs. The apartments were infested with rats and other
vermin. They were often poorly ventilated – too hot in the summer and
too cold in the winter, and the plumbing frequently did not work.

In 1992, author Alex Kotlowitz chronicled the life of a Black family
living in the Henry Horner housing project on the west side of Chicago
over the course of several years [20].[4] Many years later, he described how

---

[4] Kotlowitz's book, *There Are No Children Here: The Story of Two Boys growing Up in the Other
America*, is a compelling account of the tragic lives of two children living in a large urban housing
project. The life circumstances for families like the one he wrote about have not changed much in
the 30 years since the book's publication.

he felt the first time he set foot in the housing project: "I trembled – not out of fear, but out of shame. How could it be possible that people in the world's richest nation lived in such intolerable conditions?" [21]. The Henry Horner project was typical of the housing projects in Chicago and other large cities. They were generally constructed within already predominantly Black and poor neighborhoods. Rather than providing residents with relief from their past housing problems, they became anchors for existing disadvantaged and under-resourced neighborhoods. This kind of public housing "became a bulwark of urban segregation" [22].

In the end, many city governments finally acknowledged the failure of these "projects" and literally blew some of them up. In many instances, they were replaced by row houses and "mixed income" housing, which usually could accommodate only a fraction of the original residents of the projects. In Chicago, many of the former residents of Henry Horner and other large public housing projects had to move to other under-resourced segregated neighborhoods in the south and west sides of the city.

The Interstate Highway System and Racial Residential Segregation

Public housing was not the only way in which the federal government facilitated racial residential segregation. The separation of Black neighborhoods and White neighborhoods was often intentionally facilitated by where major highways in a city were located. When the federal government began to build the interstate highway system in the 1950s, many of the new highways were specifically built in locations that created physical barriers between Black neighborhoods and White neighborhoods. For example, when an interstate highway was built through Atlanta, Georgia in the 1950s, the city's mayor explicitly said that the purpose of its winding route through the city was to create the "boundary between the white and negro communities" [22]. Similar kinds of physical barriers to racial integration were built in cities such as Chicago, Milwaukee, Pittsburgh, and St. Louis. It is more than a coincidence that these highways were placed where they were at a time when successful legal challenges to racial discrimination in housing were increasing. Because of the passage of the Fair Housing Act of 1968 and court rulings that followed, these structural barriers are more permeable today, yet they still serve their original purpose. One of these places is Minneapolis, Minnesota where an interstate highway separates the predominantly Black neighborhood where George Floyd lived from the predominantly White suburbs [23]. Similar highways that furthered racial segregation in housing can be found in Detroit, Cincinnati, and other major American cities [24].

It is also true that, over the years, the construction of new highways was used as a means to remove Black families from areas where they were not wanted. Homes were seized, usually by the state or local government, often over the protests of the owners, and then destroyed. As the result of coordinated efforts between local and federal agencies, thriving Black neighborhoods were replaced with multi-lane highways, and Black residents were forced to find other places to live in rigidly segregated cities.

Some cities have finally acknowledged what they did. Rochester, New York, has already destroyed one such highway and replaced it with locations where people can build homes. Detroit, Michigan, is planning to do the same thing by demolishing an interstate highway and making the area available for the kinds of Black-owned residences and businesses that existed before the highway destroyed them [25]. There are still, however, very many places in US cities where the thriving Black neighborhoods that once existed are gone forever. One of these is the neighborhood once called "Black Wall Street" in Tulsa, Oklahoma. The Black residents of the area destroyed in the infamous riot of 1921 rebuilt much of the neighborhood. In the 1950s and 1960s, however, it was destroyed once again by the construction of interstate highways where the revitalized neighborhood once stood [26].[5]

Black Americans and Home Ownership: A Long Story of Exclusion

The home ownership rate among Black Americans is about 30 percent lower than that of White Americans, and the gap has actually grown in recent years [27]. An immediate and too simplistic explanation of this huge disparity would be the much lower average income and total wealth among Black Americans than White Americans. This is part of the reason, but this disparity has a much longer and more malevolent history.

In the aftermath of the communist takeover of the Russian government early in the twentieth century, there was a widespread "red scare" (i.e., fear of communism) in the United States. Government leaders believed that one major way to fight communism was to make most Americans better

---

[5] Another way in which Black neighborhoods are displaced is through gentrification – real estate developers purchase property in poor neighborhoods with desirable locations and create housing that the neighborhood residents cannot afford. Black people are forced to leave and the neighborhood is gentrified, as in wealthy White "gentry." One book on this is *Capitol City: Gentrification and the Real Estate State* by Samuel Stein.

capitalists by helping them acquire their own home. The federal government was able to get lenders to reduce down payments on mortgages from a prohibitive 50 percent to much lower percentages and extend the length of time to repay mortgages, making monthly mortgage payments much lower. As a result, many more Americans could afford to buy homes.

To further facilitate private home ownership, the US government also established the Federal Housing Authority (FHA) in 1934. One of the FHA's major functions was to underwrite or guarantee private bank loans to potential homeowners. This dramatically increased the number of home loans banks made available to prospective homeowners – but mostly for White people. The FHA told banks that in order to obtain this guarantee, they should avoid loans that promoted "inharmonious racial or nationality groups" and only give loans in areas where there were natural or man-made barriers to preserve racial segregation in neighborhoods. That barrier might be a river or a bridge, or a large thoroughfare or highway. In one instance, the FHA would not underwrite a development unless the developer built a six-foot high wall between the planned all-White neighborhood and a nearby Black neighborhood [28].

After World War II ended, the US government attempted to actively help the massive number of returning veterans get their own piece of the American dream by underwriting their mortgage applications. The government essentially eliminated a bank's financial risk in giving a veteran a mortgage by underwriting the loan. This policy helped a substantial portion of White Americans to achieve their dream of owning their own home, but Black Americans were largely excluded from getting these guaranteed loans and, thus, home ownership.

For example, the FHA actively and directly supported the development of entire communities of new single-family homes in areas that explicitly excluded Black residents. Perhaps the most infamous instance of this was the creation of several small cities across the United States, all called "Levittown". The government largely funded the creation of these cities and carefully monitored every aspect of their development, including who was (or was not) able to buy homes in them. As Richard Rothstein explains, "The FHA financed Levittown on the condition that ... it be all White, with no foreseeable change in its racial composition." (p. 71). Six years after the Levitt family broke ground on their first development, there were 70,000 people living in this new community – and not one of them was Black [29]. The significant long-term financial impact of these kinds of policies on home ownership among Black Americans is discussed in detail later in this chapter. Other kinds of government policies further contributed to racial disparities in the kinds of housing available to Black Americans and White Americans.

Redlining: The Color of Neighborhood Decline

The government also limited the ability of Black people (including veterans) to buy their own homes through its approach to "risk assessment" in mortgage lending. In the 1930s and 1940s, the federal housing agencies, which underwrote most home loans, set rules for the acceptable level of risk a bank should take when issuing a home mortgage loan. If a loan exceeded this level, they would probably not underwrite it. Risk, though, was not primarily based on individual loan-seekers' credit rating; rather, it was determined by government guidelines concerning how likely it was that people living in different neighborhoods would default on their loans. To help the banks, neighborhoods were color-coded. Those neighborhoods whose residents were predominantly Black people (or other racial/ ethnic minorities, such as Asian or Latinx) were almost always considered to have the highest level of financial risk and were therefore colored red on government-issued maps. Those neighborhoods deemed to have lower risk – those whose residents were overwhelmingly White – were colored green (safest investments) or blue (safer investments). This practice thus earned the name "Redlining."

Although decisions to redline neighborhoods were made some time ago, their consequences are still felt. Nearly three-fourths of the neighborhoods that were redlined in the 1930s and 1940s are now classified as low-to-moderate income areas, and the residents are predominantly Black. By contrast, 91 percent of the original "green" neighborhoods are now classified as upper-income areas; not surprisingly, in almost all of these areas, the residents are predominantly White. Figure 3.2 shows a redlining map for Baltimore, Maryland created in 1937. There is almost a perfect geographical overlap between the redlined districts in 1937 and the predominantly Black and under-resourced neighborhoods in Baltimore in 2022 that we described earlier in this chapter [30].

Redlining not only served to discourage individual home ownership in predominantly Black neighborhoods, it also reduced the ability of private sector investors to acquire loans to do business in these areas. As Torey Edmonds, a Black resident of a redlined area in Richmond, Virginia, puts it, "If the bank's not lending, then things deteriorate" [31]. So, another major consequence of redlining was that neither existing businesses nor new businesses that wanted to open in these neighborhoods could get

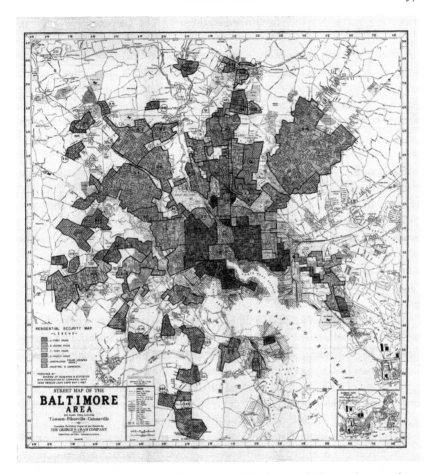

Figure 3.2   A 1937 "Residential Security Map," indicating the least and most safe Baltimore neighborhoods. Such maps were given to banks to assess their risk in making private and commercial loans. The supposedly least safe neighborhoods were colored red or "Redlined." These are the darkest regions on the map. Neighborhoods "Redlined" then are still economically disadvantaged and under-resourced over 80 years later.
Source: Digital Scholarship Lab. https://s3.amazonaws.com/holc/tiles/MD/Baltimore/1937/holc-scan.jpg

loans. Jobs disappeared from these neighborhoods, unemployment increased, residences fell into disrepair, and the overall quality of life declined. Some scholars, such as Dr. William Julius Wilson, professor of sociology at Harvard University, have argued that these kinds of neighborhood characteristics are responsible for a broad swath of social problems, many of which are linked to the health of the people who live in these areas [32].[6]

One important long-term consequence of government policies that reduced home ownership among Black Americans is that they created enormous racial disparities in the wealth of Black Americans and White Americans today. For most Americans, the way in which they accumulate wealth is through inheritance from their parents. This typically occurs by either inheriting their family's home or receiving the proceeds of the sale of the home. The government mortgage subsidies for White people (but not Black people) who wanted to buy a home in the 1940s and 1950s meant that many of the White people who bought homes at the time did not need to put much money into down payments. And, in many instances, the value of their homes increased by as much as 100-fold over the next 50 or 60 years. This created inter-generational wealth that could be passed on to the next generation of a family through inheritance. Further, even non-subsidized homes in so-called low-risk areas appreciated in value much more than did those undervalued homes in redlined areas, resulting in less wealth for Black people to inherit. A contemporary consequence of these earlier federal housing policies and practices is the current large disparity in the wealth of Black families and White families in the United States. A survey by Federal Reserve System showed that the median wealth of a White American family is about $170,000, whereas the median wealth of a Black family is about $17,000, or about 10 percent of that of White families [33]. This is one of the major reasons why home ownership among Black Americans is 30 percent less than among White Americans [34].

The US government's housing policies over the course of many years are an exemplar of systemic racism in practice. Systemic racism can sometimes occur in the absence of individuals consciously intending to harm Black people. In most instances, however, government housing policies were specifically crafted to separate the neighborhoods where White people lived from those where Black people lived. Across many administrations, the US government was thus a critical force in creating and then sustaining segregated housing and racial separation in American cities. It is a major reason for the racial residential segregation that we see today.

Systemic racism can also operate in less direct ways to restrict where Black Americans can live. One way it does this is through its impact on Black Americans' ability to get a home loan. When deciding whether to

---

[6] His book is titled *When Work Disappears: The World of the New Urban Poor.*

give an applicant a loan for a mortgage or home improvements, financial institutions give considerable weight to the applicant's annual income and wealth (which includes, for example, savings, investments, the value of any property the person owns). As discussed in the Introduction chapter, because of systemic racism, there are large disparities in the annual incomes of Black Americans and White Americans and, as we just discussed, the systematic exclusion of Black families from federal home loan programs produced even greater disparities between Black families' and White families' inherited wealth. In addition, if the home a Black family already owns is in a neighborhood that has an "undesirable" zip code, it will be assigned a lower value than the same house in a "better" neighborhood. As a result of these things, Black applicants for home loans often have lower credit ratings, and their loans are judged to be riskier (i.e., greater probability of default) than White applicants. Thus, in 2020, lenders were 80 percent more likely to deny a mortgage to Black applicants than to White applicants [35]. The Fair Housing Act of 1968 prohibited many explicit kinds of racial discrimination in determining who could qualify for a loan. However, because of the financial disparities we have discussed, which have their origins in systemic racism, today racial disparities in obtaining loans can happen even without a lender knowing the applicant's race.

Individual-Level Racial Biases and Racial Residential Segregation

It is also true that, independent of these "objective" financial factors, individual-level racial biases do contribute to racial residential segregation. In 2018, the Center for Investigative Reporting found that even when applicants for a loan have similar credit and financial backgrounds, lenders turn down Black applicants for home mortgages much more often than they turn down White applicants [36].

In 2022, the *New York Times* reported on this phenomenon by way of a troubling story about a Black couple who wanted to refinance their home. The couple had substantial equity in the home and an excellent credit rating. They applied for a loan to refinance their home, which required a new appraisal of their home. They had originally paid $450,000 for the home five years earlier and made substantial improvements. Further, home values in the area where they lived had risen by 42 percent. Nevertheless, the appraiser valued the home at only $472,000, and they were rejected for the loan. Then, the couple removed all the family photos from their home and asked a White friend to pretend to be the home owner. The new appraiser valued the house at $750,000! [37]. The family is currently suing the initial appraiser and the mortgage company.

There are many other documented instances in which professionals hired to assess the value of homes have appraised these homes as worth less when the owners were believed to be Black people than when the owners were believed to be White people. Because of such stories, real estate websites, such as Zillow, have been developed to allow people to search for places to live without using a real estate agent who would know their race. Yet, as late as 2019, some Zillow home sale listings still contained phrases like "no Blacks near me" [38].

Violent Resistance to Integration
Individual and collective acts of violence have also helped keep many neighborhoods all-White. When he was 10 years old, one of the co-authors (LAP) was a passenger in a car that was driving on a street that ran through the center of a working-class neighborhood on the far south side of Chicago, Illinois. A Black man was driving the car directly in front of the car the co-author was in. A mob blocked his path, smashed all the car's windows, pulled him onto the street, and, as Chicago Police officers idly watched, severely beat him with fists and a baseball bat. As the man lay bleeding on the ground, the terrified 10-year-old and his companions were allowed to pass unharmed because someone had looked into the car and yelled, "They're OK. They're White."

This horrific scene was part of the 1953 Trumbull Park Race Riot. The riot, which was one of many "race riots" in the 1950s, began when a single Black family was allowed to move into one of the 460 apartments in the Trumbull Park public housing development [39]. The violence continued for many months, and it was not until 10 years later that Black people felt safe walking in the Trumbull Park area [40]. Thirteen years after the Trumbull Park riots, but before the Fair Housing Act had been passed, Dr. Martin Luther King Jr. led a demonstration against de facto segregation in housing in the southwest part of Chicago. After being confronted by an angry mob, Dr. King said, "I have never seen, even in Mississippi and Alabama, mobs as hateful as I've seen here in Chicago" [41].

Violence as a tool against racial integration was a frequent occurrence up until the last part of twentieth century. Black people living in formerly all-White neighborhoods were frequently the victims of vandalism, arson, and even physical beatings. Moreover, government agencies across the country sometimes tacitly and sometimes not-so-tacitly approved this kind of violent resistance to residential integration.

Block Busting and White Flight

In the 1950s and 1960s, the economic status of many Black Americans began to improve, and more egalitarian laws and housing ordinances were passed. Black people began moving into neighborhoods where they had previously been excluded. During this period, however, many real estate agents unethically exploited Black people's desire to live in better neighborhoods and many White people's fear of or dislike for Black people. Their practices maintained or even increased racial segregation in housing in American cities.

Realtors frequently engaged in a practice called "block busting," in which a real estate agent would find homes for sale in an all-White neighborhood, purchase a few houses, and then sell some of them to Black families – often at a substantially lower price than the agent paid for them. The agent would be willing to absorb this initial loss because they knew that White families, fearing that more Black families would move into their neighborhood, would begin to panic and offer to sell their homes at a much lower price than they were worth. The agent would then find more Black families looking for a better neighborhood and sell the houses at highly inflated prices. After an initial trickle of new Black families, even more White residents would be likely to place their homes for sale, which, in turn, allowed more Black families to purchase homes in previously all-White neighborhoods [42]. This pattern caused many neighborhoods to change from being all-White to all-Black in a matter of months. Two of the co-authors saw these kinds of dramatic transitions first hand in the neighborhoods where they grew up.

One common result of block busting was a substantial decline in property values. In many cases, this decline reduced local tax bases, which then led to a decline in municipal services and resources for things like public schools and streetlights. Block busting was therefore a reinforcing cycle of residential segregation produced by capitalizing on individual racism. While block busting was formally outlawed in 1968, its legacy – like many of the practices discussed here – lives on in the racially segregated neighborhoods that it created.

Indeed, as new federal and state laws allowed more Black people to find places to live in many American cities, many White people began to flee in what is known as "White flight." They left large metropolitan areas in numbers that far exceeded the number of Black families who moved into these areas. For example, in 1950, 85 percent of the residents of people Chicago, Illinois were White people; today White people comprise less than 50 percent of the city's population [43]. About 55 percent of the residents of major American cities currently identify as White, a significant decline from past years, but the percentage of White people who live in predominantly White neighborhoods within these cities has not declined over time – it approaches 80 percent [44].

One of this book's authors (BDS) vividly recalls the impact of White flight from his Detroit neighborhood in the 1960s. At that time, it was an integrated neighborhood with the kinds of duplexes and single-family homes that had attracted blue-collar families after World War II. However, as Black families began to move into this neighborhood in the mid-1960s, White families began to quickly flee the neighborhood, with nearly two to three "For Sale" signs popping up per block each month. Housing prices plummeted, which made homes more available and afford-able for Black families. But, a rapid change in the racial composition of the neighborhood (there were now only Black families) meant that homes became less valuable, and the property tax base for the neighborhood declined. The majority of new Black residents of this neighborhood maintained neat properties and lawns, often leading to informal competi-tion among neighbors to claim the title of "greenest grass" and "most immaculate" property. But, the high mortality among Detroit's Black residents (described in the Introduction chapter) and the lack of commer-cial investment in the neighborhood resulted in the abandonment of some properties and a large number of vacant lots. Today, in this neighborhood, it is not uncommon to find neatly maintained homes that are right next to dilapidated, abandoned properties. This further undercuts the efforts of the remaining residents to preserve the value of homes and the quality of life in the neighborhood.

The Health Effects of Racial Residential Segregation

Dr. Douglas Massey, professor of sociology at Princeton University, and his colleagues have conducted extensive studies of the health consequences of poverty and racial residential segregation. In 2018, his research team concluded that "the combination of high poverty and high residential segregation uniquely exposes African Americans to spatially concentrated disadvantage, yielding a prolonged exposure to stress, with potential adverse health consequences later in life" [45]. Indeed, an overwhelming amount of research evidence shows that living in poor, segregated, and under-resourced or disadvantaged neighborhoods is strongly associated with poorer health and greater mortality among Black Americans [46]. The specific kinds of health problems include, but are not limited to, more preterm and low-weight births, higher incidences of infectious diseases (such as tuberculosis), heart and cardiovascular disease, several kinds of cancer, and diminished cognitive functioning [47–50]. Living in a segregated and under-resourced neighborhood is also associated with a weakened immune system and even with how people's genes are expressed [51, 52]. This involves some of the epigenetic processes discussed in Chapter 2.

Income and Health

As discussed in the Introduction chapter, the association between people's SES, especially their income, and their health is very strong. Indeed, other than congenital or inherited diseases, a person's income is probably the best single correlate of the individual's health. As we have already discussed, one clear distinction between predominantly Black, under-resourced neighborhoods and predominantly White, well-resourced neighborhoods is that, on average, Black people who live in these neighborhoods are substantially poorer than White people or Black people who live in integrated, well-resourced neighborhoods.

It has also been suggested that living in a segregated and under-resourced neighborhood may be a cause of poverty. For example, Dr. David Williams, professor of public health at Harvard University, and Dr. Chiquita Collins, professor of sociology at the University of Texas, have argued that "segregation is a primary cause of racial differences in socioeconomic status (SES)" because it determines a person's access to education and employment opportunities [53]. Their argument is that people living in racially segregated neighborhoods experience a vicious circle of poverty in which they start out poor, and being poor makes their continued poverty more likely. But, whether poverty causes Black Americans to live in segregated neighborhoods or is the result of living in these neighborhoods, poverty among Black Americans is largely concentrated in segregated and under-resourced neighborhoods. Being poor often means working in more physically demanding and dangerous jobs (e.g., having to work outside the home in close contact with other people during the COVID-19 pandemic), having less access to healthy food, facing more difficulty obtaining needed medicines and medical care, and other things that directly threaten a person's health.

But, what would happen if poor Black people were able to leave these segregated and under-resourced neighborhoods? In 1994, the US Department of Housing and Urban Development funded the "Moving to Opportunity" experiment, which partially addresses this question [54].

Researchers randomly selected low-income families living in public housing in some of the country's most disadvantaged neighborhoods and gave them rent vouchers that enabled them to move into private housing in less distressed, lower poverty rate neighborhoods. Ten to 15 years later, they were compared to families who were given rent vouchers for public housing in the same neighborhoods where they currently lived or no vouchers at all. The adults in the families who were able to move showed improvements in their health, such as lower diabetes rates and improved mental health. Their female children showed improvement in their mental health. Also, if the children were relatively young when their family moved from the poorer neighborhoods, there were economic and educational benefits for them as adults. Their incomes as adults were 31 percent higher than children in the other groups, and they were also more likely to attend college. But this was not true for the adults or children who were older when they moved. Overall, this study suggested that the longer a person lives in a disadvantaged neighborhood, the harder it is to reverse its impact on their lives [55]. This is because the poverty in many segregated Black neighborhoods combines with other aspects of these neighborhoods to create enduring threats to their residents' health.

Environmental Toxins and Health

One health-related characteristic common to many predominantly Black, segregated, and under-resourced neighborhoods is that the quality of the water residents drink and the air that they breathe are of poorer quality than in wealthier, predominantly White, and well-resourced neighborhoods. There are many reasons for this, but certainly the most parsimonious and direct explanation of these conditions is long-standing government, state, and local policies regarding where Black Americans were allowed (or required) to live and the limited protections from various environmental poisons in these areas. For a very long time, governmental protections from environmental toxins were typically not enforced in predominantly Black, segregated neighborhoods. In many instances, governmental regulatory decisions about where industries could be located failed to take into consideration their environmental impact on the poor and politically weak Black communities that were near them [56].[7]

---

[7] An excellent overview of the effects of environmental toxins on residents of poor and Black neighborhoods can be found in Harriett Washington's book, *A Terrible Thing to Waste: Environmental Racism and Its Assault on the American Mind*.

Water Quality: The Case of Flint, Michigan

A familiar, tragic story of environment toxicity comes from Flint, Michigan. Flint is a city with a predominantly Black population. It was once a thriving industrial center, but after General Motors and other companies left in the 1980s, it became, according to one newspaper, "one of the poorest and most dangerous cities in the United States" [57]. It was in the top 10 percent nationally in both poverty and crime rates. Flint's current notoriety, however, comes not from these grim statistics, but from the results of a cost-cutting measure initiated by the governor of Michigan. In 2011, Flint was in financial free fall when the then governor of Michigan, "Rick" Snyder, appointed an emergency manager to take control of the city. In 2014, this emergency manager decided that one way to save money was by switching Flint's water supply from the one provided by the city of Detroit to one that came from the Flint River. This was done pretty much without any analysis of the quality of the water in the river, not much publicity, and little, if any, consultation with the people who lived in Flint.

The switch to water from the Flint River quickly caused both the city's and individual homeowners' lead water pipes to corrode. The result was a dramatic increase in the levels of lead in the water people drank. For a large proportion of Flint's population, the lead level in their water far exceeded the amount that would normally lead a government to take some sort of remedial action. Of course, lead contamination was not the only problem. The Flint River had long ago become polluted with industrial waste and sewage. The city failed to provide adequate chlorine in the water supply after the switch was made, resulting in the third largest outbreak of Legionnaires' Disease in American history.

Over the course of 18 months, about 9,000 children in Flint drank lead-contaminated water [58]. As Dr. Mona Hanna-Attisha, the Flint pediatrician who eventually exposed this scandal, said, "Lead is one of the most damning things you can do to a child in their entire life-course trajectory" [59]. Flint, however, is but one example of the problem of lead poisoning among Black children. From before birth and long after, Black children in poor, segregated neighborhoods are exposed to higher levels of lead than are White children [60]. Nationally, Black children are 1.6 times more likely to test positive for lead in their blood than are White children [61]. In Flint, the source was primarily the water, but the main source of lead poisoning nationally is the lead paint that is quite common in homes in poor and segregated Black neighborhoods. The paint chips to give off lead-laden dust, and these particles find their way into the children's bodies. High levels of lead can result in lower IQ and attention deficit disorders, resulting in poor performance in school [62, 63].

While the dust particles from lead paint can be difficult to see, the effects of the pipe corrosion in Flint were not. The water coming out of people's faucets was badly discolored and had a foul smell. There were numerous individual complaints and organized and spontaneous protests, but for 18 months the state government did nothing; the predominantly Black and poor protestors were dismissed as people with a political agenda. We can see this in an email from one of the people on the governor's staff, "In a Nutshell: Agitators [are] claiming 'environmental racism' and comparing Flint water to the gas chambers at concentration camps. But Flint water [is] still determined to be safe" [64].

Dr. Hannah-Attisha reports that when she tried to present her findings about the effects of the contaminated water on her patients to the state government, the state officials said that "I was an unfortunate researcher, that I was causing near-hysteria, that I was splicing and dicing numbers. ... It's very difficult when you are presenting science and facts and numbers to have the state say that you are wrong" [59].[8] And, when a mother from Flint complained to a state nurse about the impact of the lead poisoning on her child's IQ, the nurse replied, "It's just a few IQ points ... it's not the end of the world" [64]. In fact, a difference of five IQ points is not trivial. In her book on the effects of environmental toxins, Harriet Washington explains that if nationally every child's IQ became five points lower, there would be a 57 percent increase in the number of children labeled as "intellectually impaired," and the number of children being classified as "gifted" would decline by about a third [56].

Several former Michigan state officials, including former governor Rick Snyder, faced civil and criminal charges for their callous indifference to the complaints of the largely poor and Black residents of Flint. However, in 2022, all charges against them were dismissed or reduced to minor offenses. The State of Michigan did agree to a final settlement amounting to $626 million dollars as compensation for the damage it had caused to the citizens of Flint [65]. A large portion of the pipes have been repaired. Nevertheless, among Flint's residents, the fear of the water they drink persists, as does the permanent damage the lead laden water has done to the people who live there.

---

[8] Dr. Hanna-Atisha has written a book about her experiences in Flint, titled *What the Eye's Don't See: A Story of Crises, Resistance and Hope*.

Air Quality

Black Americans are also exposed to significantly higher levels of air pollution than are White Americans [66]. For example, a 2007 study conducted for the United Church of Christ Justice and Witness Ministries found that the percentage of racial and ethnic minority group members living near incinerators was much higher than the national median. Twenty percent of Black Americans in this study were likely to live less than two miles from one of the nation's commercial hazardous waste facilities. If we include Latinx (Hispanic) Americans as well, the percentage of members of these minority groups who live in such highly polluted regions was 89 percent higher than the national average. There is no evidence that these percentages have changed appreciably since this study was completed [67]. As the climate activist Abhijit Naskar mused, "Roses are red, violets are blue, bad hair days are okay, but bad air days will screw you" [68]. Importantly, part of this problem is another legacy of government housing policies enacted long ago. Neighborhoods that were redlined (i.e., were rated as risky investments) 70 to 80 years ago have poorer air quality today than neighborhoods that were not redlined [69].

One kind of air pollution is fine particulate matter (known as $PM_{2.5}$). It is a grave danger to people's health and is responsible for 63 percent of all deaths from environmental causes and 3 percent of deaths from any causes. The location of companies that produce this pollutant in America is yet another example of a racial injustice. Companies producing the pollutant are more likely to be in close proximity to under-resourced, predominantly Black neighborhoods than well-resourced, predominantly White neighborhoods. Nationally, Black Americans are 1.5 times more likely to live in areas with high levels of this form of air pollution [70].

Another element of this racial disparity involves who produces $PM_{2.5}$. It is not only produced by industrial emissions from factories, it is also generated by individuals' overall consumption of goods and services (e.g., residential and business construction, production of appliances, vehicle usage and traffic, food consumption, electrical usage). Because of the disparate income levels of Black Americans and White Americans, many more of these goods and services are consumed by White Americans. Thus, much more $PM_{2.5}$ is produced per capita by wealthy White Americans than by poor Black Americans. But, there is a large inequity in who is eventually *exposed* to this kind of air pollution. Black Americans are exposed to 21 percent more $PM_{2.5}$ than the national average. Put simply, on average, Black Americans create less air pollution than do White Americans but are exposed to higher levels of it. Researchers who study this phenomenon call this difference "pollution inequity," and it is greatest in cities with the highest levels of racial segregation in housing [71].

High levels of fine particulate matter have a multitude of negative effects on people's health. The most obvious of these is the effect on respiratory diseases. The asthma rates for Black Americans are double the rates for White Americans. This is not, however, the only health consequence of this kind of air pollution. It is also associated with cardiovascular diseases, reproductive and neurological problems, and cancer [72–74]. And, a 2021 study linked higher concentrations of $PM_{2.5}$ to a higher incidence of Alzheimer's disease among Black women [75].

Other Environmental Toxins
Ozone levels are also much higher in Black neighborhoods than White neighborhoods. Ozone has health consequences similar to those of fine particulate matter [76]. Additionally, people living in racially segregated neighborhoods are more likely to be exposed to pollutants that cause cancer. There is a strong and consistent positive association between living in segregated Black neighborhoods and a higher incidence of cancer [77].

Racially Segregated Neighborhood Characteristics and Health

Where people live significantly shapes their access to essential resources and exposure to physical environments that can jeopardize health. Many of these are not immediately apparent as threats to people's health. But, their effects are cumulative and ultimately harmful.

Restricted Food Choices: Too Little or Too Much
A significant difference between most poor, segregated, and under-resourced neighborhoods and wealthy, well-resourced neighborhoods is the kinds of food available to the residents. In poor, segregated, and under-resourced Black neighborhoods, there is usually not enough healthy food and too much unhealthy food.

With regard to the first problem, one characteristic of many of these neighborhoods is that they are "food deserts." The US Department of Agriculture defines a food desert as "a low-income census tract where a substantial number or share of residents [have] low access to a supermarket or large grocery store" [78]. Geographically, an area is identified as a food desert if the distance to the nearest supermarket is one mile or more. In the United States, over 23 million people live more than one mile from any supermarket. Nationally, Black Americans are twice as likely as White

Americans to live in food deserts [79]. One mile is a significant distance for people who have limited or no access to public or private transportation, which is often the case in poor, predominantly Black neighborhoods. Thus, it will be very difficult for these members of the community to purchase affordable healthy foods, including things such as fresh fruits and vegetables from stores beyond this distance.

A study conducted in Washington, DC found that there was one supermarket for every 70,000 people in the poorest Black neighborhoods, compared to one for every 12,000 people in the wealthiest White neighborhoods. Indeed, in some large predominantly Black cities, such as Detroit, it has only been in the last 8 to 10 years that there have been *any* large supermarkets [80]. This situation has improved somewhat in several American cities in the last 10 or so years, largely because of state and federal programs, such as the Federal Food Financing Initiative, which provides resources to stores that sell healthy foods in under-resourced segregated neighborhoods [81]. There is now actually a Whole Foods store in central Detroit and a few more large chain stores in other neighborhoods. But, food deserts are still a fact of life for most Black Americans living in racially segregated, and particularly poor, neighborhoods. Food activist Karen Washington, who advocates for more food choices in poor, segregated neighborhoods, compares this situation to the system of racial separation that existed in South Africa for many years: "What I would rather say instead of 'food desert' is 'food apartheid,' because 'food apartheid' looks at the whole food system, along with race, geography, faith, and economics. [When] you say 'food apartheid'... you get to the root cause of some of the problems around the food system" [82].

Large grocery chains have long been reluctant to place their stores in low-income, predominantly Black neighborhoods because their executives believe these stores will not produce a profit [83]. They assume that because of the high level of poverty among the people in these neighborhoods, the prices in the stores will be too high for them. Actual crime levels or, perhaps more importantly, perceptions about crime levels in these neighborhoods, may also lead executives to expect large-scale pilferage of the stores' products. Profit margins on sales in retail groceries are very small (usually about 2 percent), and the executives thus conclude – often in the absence of any actual data – that a supermarket in a high poverty Black neighborhood will not make any money. As another food activist has put it, these grocery chains have redlined food availability in poor Black neighborhoods in the same way that the government redlined housing availability in the 1930s [84].

But, the people in food deserts still need to eat. So, the large supermarkets are often replaced by small convenience stores. Small convenience stores are about 10 times more likely to be in these neighborhoods than are supermarkets. Moreover, the poorer a Black neighborhood is, the larger this ratio becomes. These small convenience stores primarily offer canned goods because of the greater difficulties and higher costs involved in keeping perishable items fresh. As a result, the products sold in these stores are likely to be low in nutritional value and high in fat, sodium, and sugar. The owners of these stores are obviously not trying to make their customers less healthy, but this is a clear consequence of what they are able to offer to them and still stay in business. This increases the health risks for Black residents of highly segregated neighborhoods, particularly when these are also low-income areas [85].

One of these risks concerns people's weight. Being substantially above the average weight for one's height often represents an increased risk to a person's health. According to the National Institute of Health, it is associated with a wide range of chronic diseases, which include type 2 diabetes, high blood pressure, heart disease, stroke, various gastrointestinal diseases, higher cholesterol levels, diseases of the kidney, and certain cancers [86]. A national study that examined the long-term effects of living in a segregated neighborhood on female residents' weight found that the longer women lived in these neighborhoods, the more weight they gained [87]. Another national study looked at the relationship between living in a food desert and having above-average weight. The greater the difficulty of getting food from grocery stores in the neighborhood, the greater the risk of having above-average weight. This association was the strongest for residents of food deserts who are female and Black [88].[9]

Another food problem for many poor, predominantly Black, and under-resourced neighborhoods is that they may also be "food swamps." A food swamp is an area where, in addition to there being a relative dearth of healthy food, there is an overabundance of unhealthy foods. These neighborhoods are much more likely to be food swamps than are wealthier, predominantly White, and well-resourced neighborhoods [89]. This relationship holds even when a study controls for population density and income levels within these neighborhoods [90]. Food swamps are easily identifiable because of the very high concentrations of fast-food restaurants

---

[9] No one is exactly sure why these relationships are stronger for Black women than Black men. Some authors suggest that women may be more likely to sacrifice their own diets for their children. Perhaps because they are on limited budgets, they save the healthier and more expensive food for their children.

like McDonald's, Taco Bell, Popeyes, and similar businesses. Consider the experience of Anthony, a teenager who lives in a poor and predominantly Black neighborhood in Washington, DC. Anthony lives in a food swamp. When asked why he eats at McDonald's more than any other restaurant, Anthony explained that "it is cheap and there is one every three blocks." There is also, he noted, a Subway and a Pizza Hut nearby. Anthony neither likes nor dislikes his food options because, as he puts it, "I'm used to it, it's all I know" [91].

Large restaurant chains place easily accessible fast-food restaurants that offer cheap meals in poor and under-resourced neighborhoods because of the absence of supermarkets, people's limited financial resources, and many residents' frequent inability to go elsewhere for food because of the lack of public and private transportation. Such characteristics create a ready market for these restaurants and substantial profits for their owners. Indeed, this is why these corporations spend so much money on advertising that specifically targets people living in such neighborhoods.

A neighborhood being a food swamp is actually an even stronger predictor of health problems among its residents than it being a food desert. This is because the kinds of food available in fast-food restaurants (and small convenience stores) in under-resourced neighborhoods are usually quite flavorful – fried foods probably taste better than fresh vegetables – but they are, as we already noted, also quite unhealthy. Thus, fast-food restaurants play a direct role in weight gain among residents of these poor and under-resourced neighborhoods. Nationally, the number of fast-food restaurants in a geographic area is related to higher average weights among the residents of that area [92]. This relationship cannot be explained by the number of supermarkets, average income, or the availability of recreational facilities in an area.

Further, the poor nutrition created by food deserts and food swamps can cause a host of other health problems that extend beyond substantial weight gain. For example, high levels of trans fats and saturated fats in fried foods and snack foods, like chips and donuts, can cause chronic inflammation. They also increase bad cholesterol in the blood and, thus, increase the chances of heart disease [93].

The kinds of food that are either not available or too easily available in poor, segregated, and under-resourced neighborhoods are the product of another aspect of systemic racism. The companies making decisions about where to place their stores and restuarants did not create racial segregation in housing, and it seems very unlikely that there has been a conscious intention to put the health of the people who live in these neighborhoods at risk. However, it also seems that there has been an almost total lack of concern for the health of the people who eat the food they provide. Thus, their institutional practices have done great harm to the Black Americans who live in poor and under-resourced neighborhoods. Some of these companies have begun to realize this harm and are now creating healthier menus, but it has been a very slow process. Food swamps are still part of most poor Black neighborhoods.

The Built Environment

In 2008, Dr. Nancy Krieger, professor of social epidemiology at Harvard University, observed that "we literally embody, biologically, the societal and ecological conditions in which we grow up, develop and live" [94]. One key element of our living conditions is the "built environment." A built environment consists of the physically constructed features of a neighborhood in which people live and work. It includes the quality of housing and the amount of green space (parks and recreational facilities) in the area. These and many other different but related features make up a neighborhood's built environment.

It is overwhelmingly the case that the built environments in predominantly Black, under-resourced neighborhoods in the United States are lower in quality than in neighborhoods that are well-resourced. Such environmental disparities can be directly linked to systemic and individual racism in housing. Historically, Black people have been forced to live in under-resourced and disadvantaged neighborhoods, and the problem has been exacerbated by the absence of investment in these neighborhoods by both private and public institutions.

Part of the quality of a neighborhood's built environment is the extent to which there is physical decay – buildings in substantial disrepair (e.g., broken windows and doors), vacant or abandoned buildings, broken streetlights, and other damaged public structures. Research shows that the worse the physical decay of a built environment is, the poorer is the health of the people who live in these environments [95]. Physical decay in a geographic region is associated with the incidence of health problems, such as cardiovascular disease, diabetes, asthma, and depression. It is also true that the poorer the quality of the built environment in a neighborhood, the higher the level of interpersonal violence [96]. High levels of violence in a neighborhood is a chronic stressor for its residents. And, as we discussed in Chapter 2, high levels of chronic stressors are associated with a multitude of different diseases.

The quality of housing in which Black Americans and White Americans live represents one more racial disparity in the built environments. Black

Americans are significantly more likely than White Americans to live in substandard housing [97]. Substandard housing can contribute to poor health in a number of ways, including the health hazards we have discussed, such as exposure to the lead present in many of these homes. But, there is more. Substandard apartments or houses are typically poorly ventilated and often fairly noisy because of high density and poor construction. They are also more likely to contain pests, allergens, and mold, and have higher levels of radon, which is associated with pancreatic cancer among Black Americans [98]. Substandard homes usually have poor toilet and hygiene facilities, and they are often located in poorly maintained buildings containing structures and equipment that are likely to cause accidents and injuries. Each of these characteristics has been linked to poorer health and/or greater mortality [99].

Population Density
High population density in a neighborhood and large numbers of people living in the same dwellings in that neighborhood also contribute to the higher incidence of infectious diseases. In the United States, Black people are much more likely to live in a high-density neighborhood and have more people living under the same roof than are White Americans. This may be, at least in part, responsible for the higher rates of COVID-19 transmission that occurred in Black, segregated neighborhoods [100].

Open Green Space
Another thing that differentiates poor, under-resourced neighborhoods from wealthy, well-resourced neighborhoods is access to parks and other green spaces. The amount of green space in Black neighborhoods is usually much less than in White neighborhoods – and the more segregated a city is, the greater the disparity. In general, neighborhoods in which residents have lower income and less education tend to have less green space [97]. However, it is hard to see how these attributes of a neighborhood's residents could *cause* it to have fewer public parks [101]. There are more plausible explanations. Perhaps the most plausible of these is that lower income levels, less education, and fewer green spaces are all the *results* of the systemic racism that created racially segregated neighborhoods. Historically, city governments were reluctant to spend money on almost anything in poor and predominantly Black neighborhoods. Additionally, largely because of redlining, private investments that would produce new business opportunities, improve schools, or create new parks and green

space have, at least up until recently, been in very short supply in poor, segregated Black neighborhoods.

The amount of green space in a neighborhood has implications for people's health because green spaces provide opportunities for physical activity and a better quality of life. A national study found that adolescents who had inadequate access to green spaces in their neighborhood were less likely than adolescents who had adequate access to engage in physical activity and had higher levels of above-average weight. More green space in a neighborhood is also associated with less air pollution and better mental health and lower stress levels [102].

Access to Healthcare: Less Is Less
The amount of access to healthcare that a neighborhood's residents have is also quite relevant to their health. People living in zip codes with predominantly Black populations are substantially less likely than people living in zip codes with predominantly White populations to have had an office visit with a physician, nurse, or any other kind of healthcare professional during the past year. This is true even after statistically controlling for other aspects of a neighborhood that might affect the likelihood of visiting a healthcare professional, such as the number of people who have health insurance, the percentage living in poverty, and the average level of educational attainment. Notably, such disparities in access on a regular basis to healthcare providers are also true for people living in zip codes with predominantly Latinx populations [103].

Researchers believe that the lower use of healthcare in these neighborhoods may, in part, be due to some residents' attitudes toward healthcare. For very good reasons, which we discuss in detail in Chapter 6, the level of medical mistrust among Black people is much higher than among White people. So, in part, there may be a greater reluctance among residents of poor, Black neighborhoods to seek medical care in poor, Black neighborhoods.

However, a neighborhood's location also plays a very important role in people being simply able to find healthcare. Many poor, predominantly Black neighborhoods are "medical deserts," where there is very limited availability of healthcare [104]. A ratio of greater than 3,500 people to one primary care provider is the usual definition of a shortage of physicians in a geographic region. Black Americans are much more likely than White Americans to live in a neighborhood with such a shortage of physicians. The greater the level of racial segregation in an area, the greater the shortage of primary care providers in the that location [105].

There are also fewer hospitals in highly segregated areas. An example of one possible consequence of there being fewer hospitals in neighborhoods where most of the residents are poor and Black can be found in the COVID-19 pandemic. An article published in 2021 in the *Journal of the American Medical Association Network* concluded that a major reason for the higher overall COVID-related mortality rates among Black Americans was that Black Americans with COVID-19 were much less likely than White Americans to go to a hospital for their medical problems [106]. One likely reason for this is that there are simply fewer hospitals in the neighborhoods where they live. We discuss other problems for hospitals and other medical facilities located in poor, segregated neighborhoods in Chapter 5.

All of this begs the question of why there are such large racial disparities in the availability of healthcare in racially segregated Black neighborhoods. In an article in the *New England Journal of Medicine*, three public health researchers offered an answer. They argued that the historical lack of public and private investments in segregated Black neighborhoods has resulted in under-resourced health facilities with fewer clinicians, "which makes it more difficult to recruit experienced and well-credentialed primary care providers and specialists." This reduces people's access to and utilization of healthcare. They further argued that "Black communities became medical training grounds and a source of profit, reinforcing the American medical caste system that we have today. Regardless of intent, actions by parties ranging from medical schools to providers, insurers, health systems, legislators, and employers have ensured that racially segregated Black communities have limited and substandard care" [107].

Community-Level Racial Bias and the Health of Its Black Residents

In addition to the physical environment, the social environment in which one lives is also systematically related to health. While systemic racism's impact on where Black people live is certainly a major contributor to the health challenges they face, individual racism in an area appears to also play a role. Dr. David Chae, professor of public health and tropical medicine at Tulane University, and his colleagues conducted an innovative study of how individual racism in geographic regions across the country might be related to the health of the Black people who live in those regions.[10] They did this by counting the number of Google searches in 196 different

---

[10] Dr. Chae's work on the epigenetic effects of racial discrimination is discussed in Chapter 2.

"markets" (that is, geographic areas) that used the "n-word," and then they examined the relationship between this number and data from the CDC on mortality rates over five years for Black people and for White people living in each market. The researchers found that the higher the number of searches for the "n-word" in an area, the higher the number of deaths among Black people, but not White people in that area. The primary causes of Black people's deaths were diseases such as heart ailments, cancer, and strokes. Chae and his colleagues estimated that, nationwide, 30,000 more Black people died each year in the high n-word search regions than in regions where such searches were less frequent [108].

Other researchers have looked at different indicators of community-level racial bias and their association with the health of Black people. For example, one group used CDC mortality data and the results of an annual national survey of American racial attitudes (the *General Social Survey*). These researchers broke down data from each source by geographic region. They found that the higher the community levels of racial prejudice (as measured by the survey questions), the higher the mortality rates for both Black residents and White residents in that community [109].

Still other researchers have used a unique database called "Project Implicit" to gain information on racial attitudes in a given community. Through Harvard University, Project Implicit maintains a website where a person can anonymously take tests that measure their attitudes toward Black people and toward White people. Project Implicit not only collects self-reported racial attitudes (i.e., explicit attitudes) but also assesses people's automatic, nonconscious attitudes (i.e., implicit attitudes) toward Black people and toward White people (explicit and implicit racial attitudes are also discussed at length in Chapters 1 and 6). This data source provides researchers with information on average levels of explicit and implicit bias for a geographic region, such as a zip code, census tract, or county.

The general finding from studies that use data from Project Implicit is that there is a significant relationship between both kinds of racial bias (i.e., explicit and implicit) and people's health. For example, one study found that the level of racial bias in a county is associated with the number of preterm births and deaths from circulatory diseases among the Black – but not the White – people who live there [110]. In 2022, a group of public health researchers did a comprehensive review of all the published studies on the association between area-level racial prejudice and health. These studies found that a higher level of prejudice in an area was associated with more negative health outcomes for members of racial and ethnic minority groups in that area. In a few studies, racial prejudice was also associated with negative health outcomes for White residents in a given geographic area [111].

It is a bit difficult to interpret the results of these community-level studies because they do not tell us *why* the level of racial bias in a community is related to the health of people in that community. One possibility is that the healthcare system in the more racist areas is of poorer quality and less available to all people who live there. But, this would not explain those instances for which the relationship between community-level racial bias and health is only present among Black residents. It seems quite possible, however, that a higher level of racial bias in a region results in higher levels of both social and structural racial inequities that in some way exact a physiological and psychological toll on the Black residents of these communities. This is certainly a reasonable explanation, but it needs to be tested.

Putting It All Together

Most Americans live in racially segregated neighborhoods. In part, this reflects the impact of race relations in the United States on individuals' preferences about the kind of people they do or do not want to have as neighbors. But, a major reason why housing in America is usually racially segregated and why Black people are much more likely to live in poor and disadvantaged neighborhoods is systemic racism. For over 100 years after the abolition of slavery, federal, state, and local governments enacted laws and engaged in practices that created segregated neighborhoods and then vigorously maintained racial residential segregation in America. Neighborhoods where Black people were allowed to live were usually undesirable places with few resources, isolated from the surrounding communities, and deprived of the kinds of public and private investments often made in predominantly White neighborhoods.

The living conditions in many poor, under-resourced, predominantly Black neighborhoods create serious and direct threats to the health of their residents. They perpetuate poverty, which directly and indirectly harms people's health. These neighborhoods also contain health hazards that range from the poor quality of the water people drink and the air they breathe in to the dearth of healthy foods and an excess of unhealthy foods. They also create difficulties for community residents to access medical care when they become sick.

Racial residential segregation is a social injustice with significant implications for the health of all Americans, but especially for the residents of poor Black neighborhoods. Effectively addressing this pervasive systemic racism will require large-scale programs designed to significantly change where and/or how many Americans live.

REFERENCES

1. King, M. L., Jr. (1968, March 14). The Other America. https://the-other-america.com/speech

2. Trump tweets about "suburban lifestyle dream" after revoking Obama-era rule to diversify suburbs. (2020, July 29). ABC 7 Chicago https://abc7chicago.com/trump-tweet-suburban-lifestyle-dream-suburb/6340805/

3. Krysan, M. et al. (2009). Does race matter in neighborhood preferences? Results from a video experiment. *American Journal of Sociology, 115,* 527–559. https://www.ncbi.nlm.nih.gov/pmc/articles/PMC3704191/

4 Greene, S. T., Austin, M., & Gourevitch, R. (2017, August 29). Racial residential segregation and neighborhood disparities. U.S. Partnership on mobility from poverty. www.mobilitypartnership.org/publications/racial-resi dential-segregation-and-neighborhood-disparities

5 Logan, R. (2011, July). Separate and unequal: The neighborhood gap for Blacks, Hispanics, and Asians in Metropolitan America. US 2010. www .russellsage.org/sites/all/files/US2010/US2010_Logan_20110727.pdf

6. Spiegel, I. (2020, October 5). A Native American community in Baltimore reclaims its history. *Smithsonian Magazine.* www.smithsonianmag.com/smith sonian-institution/native-american-community-baltimore-reclaims-its-his tory-180975948/

7. United States Census Bureau. (2019, July 1). QuickFacts: Baltimore City, Maryland; United States. www.census.gov/quickfacts/fact/table/baltimoreci tymaryland,US/PST045219

8. Joint Center for Political and Economic Studies. (2012, November). Place Matters for Health in Baltimore: Ensuring Opportunities for Good Health for All. www.nationalcollaborative.org/wp-content/uploads/2016/02/ PLACE-MATTERS-for-Health-in-Baltimore.pdf

9. LaVeist, T., Pollack, K., Thorpe, R. Jr., Feshazion, R., & Gaskin, D. (2011). Place not race: Disparities dissipate in southwest Baltimore when black and whites live under similar conditions. *Health Affairs,* October *30*(10), 18890–1887. https://doi.org/10.1377/hlthaff.2011.0640

10. Mapping Life Expectancy. Virginia Commonwealth University Center on Society and Health. 16 Years in Chicago, Illinois. https://societyhealth.vcu .edu/work/the-projects/mapschicago.html

11. Mapping Life Expectancy. Virginia Commonwealth University Center on Society and Health. https://societyhealth.vcu.edu/work/the-projects/map ping-life-expectancy.html

12. The Roots of Structural Racism Project. (2021). belonging.berkeley.edu/roots-structural-racism

13. Wilkerson, I. (2016, September). The long-lasting legacy of the great migration. *Smithsonian Magazine.* www.smithsonianmag.com/history/long-lasting-legacy-great-migration-180960118/

14. Loewen, J. (2005). *Sundown towns: A hidden dimension of American racism.* The New Press.

15. Sullivan, T. N., & Nasir, N. (2020, October 14). AP road trip: Racial tensions in America's "Sundown Towns." https://apnews.com/article/virus-outbreak-race-and-ethnicity-violence-db28a9aaa3b800d91b65dc11a6b12c4c

16. The Oregon Social Justice Documentation Project. The Oregon black laws. https://blogs.oregonstate.edu/oregonsocialjustice/oregon-black-laws/

17. Taylor, K. (2021, January 6). Exclusionary policies of the past and present: How single-family zoning structures inequality. Atlanta Department of City Planning. www.atlcitydesign.com/blog/2021/1/5/exclusionary-policies-of-the-past-and-present-how-single-family-zoning-structures-inequality

18. Rothstein, R. (2017). *The color of law: A forgotten history of how our government segregated America.* Liveright Publishing.

19. HealthyPeople.gov. (2020). Quality of Housing. www.healthypeople.gov/2020/topics-objectives/topic/social-determinants-health/interventions-resources/quality-of-housing

20. Kotlowitz, A. (1992). *There are no children here: The story of two boys growing up in the other America.* Anchor.

21. Petty, A. (2013). *High rise stories: Voices from Chicago public housing.* McSweeney's.

22. Kruse, K. M. (2019, August 14). How segregation caused your traffic jam. *New York Times.* www.nytimes.com/interactive/2019/08/14/magazine/traffic-atlanta-segregation.html?mtrref=undefined&gwh=D39823A1609E24C83C5D78EC89A5DFD2&gwt=pay&assetType=PAYWALL

23. Poon, L. (2020, June 3). The racial injustice of American highways. Bloomberg CityLab. www.bloomberg.com/news/articles/2020-06-03/what-highways-mean-to-the-george-floyd-protesters

24. DiMento, J. F., & Ellis, C. (2012). *Changing lanes: Visions and histories of urban freeways.* MIT Press.

25. Spruill, L. (2021, June 15). The future of the I-375 boulevard project and the history behind it. Click On Detroit. www.clickondetroit.com/news/local/2021/06/15/the-future-of-the-i-375-boulevard-project-and-the-history-behind-it/

26. Moreno, C. (2021, June 2). Decades after the Tulsa race massacre, Urban "Renewal" sparked Black Wall Street's second destruction. *Smithsonian Magazine.* www.smithsonianmag.com/history/black-wall-streets-second-destruction-180977871/

27. Cozzi, L. (2023, March 2). More Americans own their homes, but Black-White homeownership rate gap is biggest in a decade, NAR Report Finds. *National Association of Realtors.* www.nar.realtor/newsroom/more-americans-own-their-homes-but-black-white-homeownership-rate-gap-is-biggest-in-a-decade-nar

28. Gross, T. (2017, May 3). A "forgotten history" of how the U.S. government segregated America. *National Public Radio*. www.npr.org/2017/05/03/526655831/a-forgotten-history-of-how-the-u-s-government-segregated-america

29. Galyean, C. Levittown: The imperfect rise of the American suburbs. *U.S. History Scene*. https://ushistoryscene.com/article/levittown/

30. George F. Cramer Company. Street map of Baltimore Area, 1937. https://s3.amazonaws.com/holc/tiles/MD/Baltimore/1937/holc-scan.jpg

31. Godoy, M. (2020, November 19). In U.S. cities, the health effects of past housing discrimination are plain to see. *National Public Radio*. www.npr.org/sections/health-shots/2020/11/19/911909187/in-u-s-cities-the-health-effects-of-past-housing-discrimination-are-plain-to-see

32. Wilson, W. J. (2011). *When work disappears: The world of the new urban poor*. Vintage.

33. Shiro, A. G., Pulliam, C., Sabelhus, J. S., & Smith, E. (2022, June 29). Stuck on the Ladder: Intragenerational wealth mobility in the United States. Brookings. www.brookings.edu/research/stuck-on-the-ladder-intragenerational-wealth-mobility-in-the-united-states/

34. Cozzi, L. (2023, March 2). More Americans own their homes, but Black-White homeownership rate gap is biggest in a decade, NAR Report Finds. *National Association of Realtors*. www.nar.realtor/newsroom/more-americans-own-their-homes-but-black-white-homeownership-rate-gap-is-biggest-in-a-decade-nar

35. Brancaccio, D. C., & Conlon, R. (2021, August, 25). How mortgage algorithms perpetuate racial disparity in home lending. *Marketplace*. www.marketplace.org/2021/08/25/housing-mortgage-algorithms-racial-disparities-bias-home-lending/

36. Glantz, A. M., & Martinez, E. (2018, February 15). For people of color, banks are shutting the door to homeownership. *Reveal News*. https://revealnews.org/article/for-people-of-color-banks-are-shutting-the-door-to-homeownership/

37. Kamin, D. (2022, August 25). Home Appraised with a Black Owner: $472,000. With a White Owner: $750,000. *New York Times*. www.nytimes.com/2022/08/18/realestate/housing-discrimination-maryland.html

38. Kearns, P. (2019, April 1). Zillow accused of allowing housing discrimination in listings. *Inman*. www.inman.com/2019/04/01/zillow-accused-of-allowing-housing-discrimination-in-listings/

39. North American Newspaper Alliance. (1957, February 24). Site of race riots in 1953 now calm; Conflict set off by negroes moving into Chicago area seems to be over at last. *New York Times*. www.nytimes.com/1957/02/24/archives/site-of-race-riots-in-1953-now-calm-conflict-set-off-by-negroes.html

40. Taylor, P. Trumbull Park Homes Race Riots, 1953–54. A case study of racial issues in Chicago, Illinois. https://raceinchicago.weebly.com/trumbull-park-homes-race-riots.html

41. Pearce, M. (2016, January 18). When Martin Luther King Jr. took his fight into the North, and saw a new level of hatred. *Los Angeles Times*. www.latimes.com/nation/la-na-mlk-chicago-20160118-story.html

42. Zacks, S. (2020, August 13). How blockbusting and real estate profiteers cash in on racial tension. *Dwell.* www.dwell.com/article/blockbusting-housing-segregation-real-estate-8e76fd46

43. Gorey, J. (2020, August 15). How "white flight" segregated American cities and suburbs. *Apartment Therapy.* www.apartmenttherapy.com/white-flight-2-36805862

44. Frey, W. H. (2020, March 23). Even as metropolitan areas diversify, white Americans still live in mostly white neighborhoods. *Brookings.* www .brookings.edu/research/even-as-metropolitan-areas-diversify-white-ameri cans-still-live-in-mostly-white-neighborhoods/

45. Massey, D. S., Wagner, B., Donnelly, L., McLanahan, S., Brooks-Gunn, J., Garfinkel, I., Mitchell, C., & Notterman, D. A. (2018). Neighborhood disadvantage and telomere length: Results from the fragile families study. *The Russell Sage Foundation Journal of the Social Sciences: RSF, 4*(4), 28–42. https://doi.org/10.7758/RSF.2018.4.4.02

46. White, K., & Borrell, L. N. (2011). Racial/ethnic residential segregation: Framing the context of health risk and health disparities. *Health & Place, 17* (2), 438–448. https://doi.org/10.1016/j.healthplace.2010.12.002

47. Jang, J. B., Hicken, M. T., Mullins, M., Esposito, M., Sol, K., Manly, J. J., Judd, S., Wadley, V., & Clarke, P. J. (2021). Racial segregation and cognitive function among older adults in the United States: Findings from the reasons for geographic and racial differences in stroke study. *The Journals of Gerontology: Series B, 77*(6), 1131–1143 https://doi.org/10.1093/geronb/gbab107

48. Landrine, H., Corral, I., Lee, J. G. L., Efird, J. T., Hall, M. B., & Bess, J. J. (2017). Residential segregation and racial cancer disparities: A systematic review. *Journal of Racial and Ethnic Health Disparities, 4*(6), 1195–1205. https://link.springer.com/article/10.1007/s40615-016-0326-9

49. Acevedo-Garcia, D. (2000). Residential segregation and the epidemiology of infectious diseases. *Social Science & Medicine, 51*(8), 1143–1161. https://doi .org/10.1016/S0277-9536(00)00016-2

50. Kershaw, K. N., & Albrecht, S. S. (2015). Racial/ethnic residential segrega-tion and cardiovascular disease risk. *Current Cardiovascular Risk Reports, 9*(3), 10. https://pubmed.ncbi.nlm.nih.gov/25893031/

51. Martin, C. L., Ward-Caviness, C. K., Dhingra, R., Zikry, T. M., Galea, S., Wildman, D. E., Koenen, K. C., Uddin, M., & Aiello, A. E. (2021). Neighborhood environment, social cohesion, and epigenetic aging. *Aging, 13*(6), 7883–7899. https://doi.org/10.18632/aging.202814

52. Baumer, Y., Farmer, N., Premeaux, T. A., Wallen, G. R., & Powell-Wiley, T. M. (2020). Health Disparities in COVID-19: Addressing the role of social determi-nants of health in immune system dysfunction to turn the tide [Perspective]. *Frontiers in Public Health, 8*(589). https://doi.org/10.3389/fpubh.2020.559312

53. Williams, D. R., & Collins, C. (2001). Racial residential segregation: A fundamental cause of racial disparities in health. *Public Health Reports, 116* (5), 404–416. https://www.ncbi.nlm.nih.gov/pmc/articles/PMC1497358/

54. National Bureau of Economic Research. Moving to Opportunity (MTO) for Fair Housing Demonstration Program. www2.nber.org/mtopublic/

55. Rothwell, J. (2015, May 6). Sociology's revenge: Moving to Opportunity (MTO) revisited. *Brookings.* www.brookings.edu/blog/social-mobility-memos/2015/05/06/sociologys-revenge-moving-to-opportunity-mto-revisited/

56. Washington, H. A. (2019). *A terrible thing to waste: Environmental racism and its assault on the American mind.* Hachette UK.

57. Wildt, T. (2019, February 7). 6 Michigan cities make list of worst places to live in America. *Detroit Free Press.* www.freep.com/story/news/local/michigan/2019/02/07/worst-cities-united-states-michigan/2804613002/

58. Denchak, M. (2018, November 8). Flint water crisis: Everything you need to know. *NRDC.* www.nrdc.org/stories/flint-water-crisis-everything-you-need-know

59. Hanna-Attisha, M. (2019). *What the eyes don't see: A story of crisis, resistance, and hope in an American city.* One World.

60. Cassidy-Bushrow, A. E., Sitarik, A. R., Havstad, S., Park, S. K., Bielak, L. F., Austin, C., Johnson, C. C., & Arora, M. (2017). Burden of higher lead exposure in African-Americans starts in utero and persists into childhood. *Environment International, 108,* 221–227. https://doi.org/10.1016/j.envint.2017.08.021

61. Dissell, R., & Zeitner, B. (2015, October 22). Race, racism and lead poisoning: Toxic neglect. *Cleveland Plain Dealer.* www.cleveland.com/healthfit/2015/10/race_racism_and_lead_poisoning.html

62. Bellinger, D. C. (2017). Childhood lead exposure and adult outcomes. *JAMA, 317*(12), 1219–1220. https://doi.org/10.1001/jama.2017.1560

63. Center for Disease Control and Prevention. Prevent children's exposure to lead. www.cdc.gov/nceh/features/leadpoisoning/

64. Detroit Free Press Staff. (2016, February 29). The 9 most troubling quotes from Gov. Rick Snyder's office e-mail dump. *Detroit Free Press.* www.freep.com/story/news/local/michigan/flint-water-crisis/2016/02/29/10-most-troubling-quotes-snyder/81109548/

65. Egan, P. (2021, November 10). Federal judge gives final approval to $626.25M settlement in Flint water crisis. *Detroit Free Press.* www.freep.com/story/news/local/michigan/flint-water-crisis/2021/11/10/federal-judge-approves-settlement-flint-lead-poisoning-case/5556131001/

66. Morello-Frosch, R. (2004). Separate but unequal? Residential segregation and air quality in U.S. metropolitan areas. *Epidemiology, 15*(4), S134. https://journals.lww.com/epidem/Fulltext/2004/07000/SEPARATE_BUT_UNEQUAL__RESIDENTIAL_SEGREGATION_AND.347.aspx

67. Bullard, R., Mohai, P. Saha, R., & Wright, B. (2007, March). Toxic wastes and race at twenty 1987–2007. www.nrdc.org/sites/default/files/toxic-wastes-and-race-at-twenty-1987-2007.pdf

68. Goodreads. Air Pollution Quotes. www.goodreads.com/quotes/tag/air-pollution

69. Wamsley, L. (2002, March 10). Even many decades later, redlined areas see higher levels of air pollution. *NPR.* www.npr.org/2022/03/10/1085882933/redlining-pollution-racism

70. Mikati, I., Benson, A. F., Luben, T. J., Sacks, J. D., & Richmond-Bryant, J. (2018). Disparities in distribution of particulate matter emission sources by race and poverty status. *American Journal of Public Health, 108*(4), 480–485. https://doi.org/10.2105/AJPH.2017.304297

71. Woo, B., Kravitz-Wirtz, N., Sass, V., Crowder, K., Teixeira, S., & Takeuchi, D. T. (2019). Residential segregation and racial/ethnic disparities in ambient air pollution. *Race and Social Problems, 11*(1), 60–67. https://pubmed.ncbi.nlm.nih.gov/31440306/

72. Genc, S., Zadeoglulari, Z., Fuss, S. H., & Genc, K. (2012). The adverse effects of air pollution on the nervous system. *Journal of Toxicology*, 2012, Article ID 782462. https://doi.org/10.1155/2012/782462

73. Brook, R. D., Franklin, B., Cascio, W., Hong, Y., Howard, G., Lipsett, M., Luepker, R., Mittleman, M., Samet, J., Smith, S. C., Tager, I., Expert Panel on, P., & Prevention Science of the American Heart, A. (2004). Air pollution and cardiovascular disease: A statement for healthcare professionals from the Expert Panel on Population and Prevention Science of the American Heart Association. *Circulation, 109*(21), 2655–2671. https://doi.org/10.1161/01.cir.0000128587.30041.c8

74. Turner, M. C., Andersen, Z. J., Baccarelli, A., Diver, W. R., Gapstur, S. M., Pope, C. A., 3rd, Prada, D., Samet, J., Thurston, G., & Cohen, A. (2020). Outdoor air pollution and cancer: An overview of the current evidence and public health recommendations. *CA Cancer: A Journal for Clinicians*, (70), 460–479. https://doi.org/10.3322/caac.21632

75. Younan, D., Wang, X., Gruenewald, T., Gatz, M., Serre, M. L., Vizuete, W., Braskie, M. N., Woods, N. F., Kahe, K., Garcia, L., Lurmann, F., Manson, J. E., Chui, H. C., Wallace, R. B., Espeland, M. A., & Chen, J.-C. (2021). Racial/Ethnic disparities in Alzheimer's Disease Risk: Role of exposure to ambient fine particles. *The Journals of Gerontology: Series A, 77*(5), 977–985. https://doi.org/10.1093/gerona/glab231

76. Jones, M. R., Diez-Roux, A. V., Hajat, A., Kershaw, K. N., O'Neill, M. S., Guallar, E., Post, W. S., Kaufman, J. D., & Navas-Acien, A. (2014). Race/ethnicity, residential segregation, and exposure to ambient air pollution: The Multi-Ethnic Study of Atherosclerosis (MESA). *American Journal of Public Health, 104*(11), 2130–2137. https://doi.org/10.2105/AJPH.2014.302135

77. Landrine, H., Corral, I., Lee, J. G. L., Efird, J. T., Hall, M. B., & Bess, J. J. (2017). Residential segregation and racial cancer disparities: A systematic review. *Journal of Racial and Ethnic Health Disparities, 4*(6), 1195–1205. https://pubmed.ncbi.nlm.nih.gov/28039602/

78. U.S. Department of Agriculture. (October 2022). Food Access Research Atlas. www.ers.usda.gov/data-products/food-access-research-atlas/documentation/

79. Sevilla, N. (2021, April 2). Food Apartheid: Racialized access to healthy affordable food. *NRDC*. www.nrdc.org/experts/nina-sevilla/food-apartheid-racialized-access-healthy-affordable-food

80. New York Law School Racial Justice Project. (2012, June). Unshared bounty: How structural racism contributes to the creation and persistence of food

deserts. (with American Civil Liberties Union). https://digitalcommons.nyls.edu/cgi/viewcontent.cgi?article=1002&context=racial_justice_project

81. America's Healthy Food Financing Initiative Reinvestment Fund. www.investinginfood.com/

82. Brones, A. (2018, May 7). Karen Washington: It's not a food desert, it's food apartheid. *Guernica*. www.guernicamag.com/karen-washington-its-not-a-food-desert-its-food-apartheid/

83. Bower, K. M., Thorpe, R. J., Jr., Rohde, C., & Gaskin, D. J. (2014). The intersection of neighborhood racial segregation, poverty, and urbanicity and its impact on food store availability in the United States. *Preventive Medicine, 58*, 33–39. https://doi.org/10.1016/j.ypmed.2013.10.010

84. Agyeman, J. (2021, March 9). How urban planning and housing policy helped create "food apartheid" in US cities. *The Conversation*. https://theconversation.com/how-urban-planning-and-housing-policy-helped-create-food-apartheid-in-us-cities-154433

85. Holzer, H., Schanzenbach, D. W., Duncan, G. J., & Ludwig, J. (2007). *The economic costs of poverty in the United States: Subsequent effects of children growing up poor*. Center for American Progress.

86. National Institute of Diabetes and Digestive and Kidney Diseases. Health risks of overweight & obesity. www.niddk.nih.gov/health-information/weight-management/adult-overweight-obesity/health-risks

87. Pool, L. R., Carnethon, M. R., Goff, D. C., Jr., Gordon-Larsen, P., Robinson, W. R., & Kershaw, K. N. (2018). Longitudinal associations of neighborhood-level racial residential segregation with obesity among Blacks. *Epidemiology, 29* (2), 207–214. https://doi.org/10.1097/ede.0000000000000792

88. ScienceDaily. (2019, January 23). Those with inadequate access to food likely to suffer from obesity. www.sciencedaily.com/releases/2019/01/190123144522.htm

89. Hilmers, A., Hilmers, D. C., & Dave, J. (2012). Neighborhood disparities in access to healthy foods and their effects on environmental justice. *American Journal of Public Health, 102*(9), 1644–1654. https://doi.org/10.2105/AJPH.2012.300865

90. James, P., Arcaya, M. C., Parker, D. M., Tucker-Seeley, R. D., & Subramanian, S. V. (2014). Do minority and poor neighborhoods have higher access to fast-food restaurants in the United States? *Health & Place, 29*, 10–17. https://doi.org/10.1016/j.healthplace.2014.04.011

91. New York Law School Racial Justice Project. (2012, June). Unshared bounty: How structural racism contributes to the creation and persistence of food deserts. (with American Civil Liberties Union). https://digitalcommons.nyls.edu/cgi/viewcontent.cgi?article=1002&context=racial_justice_project

92. Cooksey-Stowers, K., Schwartz, M. B., & Brownell, K. D. (2017). Food swamps predict obesity rates better than food deserts in the United States. *International Journal of Environmental Research and Public Health, 14*(11), 1366. https://doi.org/10.3390/ijerph14111366

93. Mayo Clinic Staff. (2020, February 13). Trans fat is double trouble for your heart health. *Mayo Clinic*. www.mayoclinic.org/diseases-conditions/high-blood-cholesterol/in-depth/trans-fat/art-20046114

94. Frederick, R. (2018, May 10). The environment that racism built. Centre for American Progress. https://americanprogress.org/article/environment-racism-built/

95. Aboelata, M. J., Mikkelsenm, L., Cohen, L., Fernandes, F., Silver, M., Parks, L. F., & DuLong, J. (2004, July). The built environment and health: 11 Profiles of neighborhood transformation. www.preventioninstitute.org/sites/default/files/publications/ENV_BEP_Wray%20CO_web_040511.pdf

96. Gracia, E., López-Quílez, A., Marco, M., Lladosa, S., & Lila, M. (2015). The spatial epidemiology of intimate partner violence: Do neighborhoods matter? *American Journal of Epidemiology, 182*(1), 58–66. https://doi.org/10.1093/aje/kwv016

97. Yang, Y., Cho, A., Ngyuyen, Q., & Nsoesie, E. (2023). Association of neighborhood racial and ethnic composition and historical redlining with built environment indicators derived from street view images in the US. JAMA Open Network. https://jamanetwork.com/journals/jamanetworkopen/article-abstract/2800557

98. Reddy, N. K., & Bhutani, M. S. (2009). Racial disparities in pancreatic cancer and radon exposure: A correlation study. *Pancreas, 38*(4), 391–395. https://journals.lww.com/pancreasjournal/Fulltext/2009/05000/Racial_Disparities_in_Pancreatic_Cancer_and_Radon.6.aspx

99. Gordon-Larsen, P., Nelson, M. C., Page, P., & Popkin, B. M. (2006). Inequality in the built environment underlies key health disparities in physical activity and obesity. *Pediatrics, 117*(2), 417–424. https://doi.org/10.1542/peds.2005-0058

100. Anderson, K., Lopez, A., & Simburger, D. (2021). Racial/Ethnic Residential Segregation and the First Wave of SARS-CoV-2 Infection Rates: A Spatial Analysis of Four U.S. Cities. *Sociological Perspectives, 64* (5), 804–830. www.ncbi.nlm.nih.gov/pmc/articles/PMC8404417/

101. Saporito, S., & Casey, D. (2015). Are there relationships among racial segregation, economic isolation, and proximity to green space? *Human Ecology Review, 21*(2), 113–132. www.jstor.org/stable/24875135

102. Wolf, K. L. (2017, April 3). The health benefits of small parks and green spaces. *Parks & Recreation Magazine.* www.nrpa.org/parks-recreation-magazine/2017/april/the-health-benefits-of-small-parks-and-green-spaces/

103. Gaskin, D. J., Dinwiddie, G. Y., Chan, K. S., & McCleary, R. (2012). Residential segregation and disparities in health care services utilization. *Medical Care Research and Review, 69*(2), 158–175. https://doi.org/10.1177/1077558711420263

104. Best medical degrees. Medical Deserts. www.bestmedicaldegrees.com/medical-deserts/

105. Gaskin, D. J., Dinwiddie, G. Y., Chan, K. S., & McCleary, R. R. (2012). Residential segregation and the availability of primary care physicians. *Health Services Research, 47*(6), 2353–2376. https://doi.org/10.1111/j.1475-6773.2012.01417.x

106. Lopez, L., III, Hart, L. H., III, & Katz, M. H. (2021). Racial and ethnic health disparities related to COVID-19. *JAMA, 325*(8), 719–720. https://doi.org/10.1001/jama.2020.26443

107. Bailey, Z. D., Feldman, J. M., & Bassett, M. T. (2021). How structural racism works – racist policies as a root cause of U.S. racial health inequities. *New England Journal of Medicine, 384*(8), 768–773. https://doi.org/10.1056/NEJMms2025396

108. Chae, D. H., Clouston, S., Hatzenbuehler, M. L., Kramer, M. R., Cooper, H. L. F., Wilson, S. M., Stephens-Davidowitz, S. I., Gold, R. S., & Link, B. G. (2015). Association between an internet-based measure of area racism and black mortality. *PLoS ONE, 10*(4), e0122963. https://doi.org/10.1371/journal.pone.0122963

109. Lee, Y., Muennig, P., Kawachi, I., & Hatzenbuehler, M. L. (2015). Effects of racial prejudice on the health of communities: A multilevel survival analysis. *American Journal of Public Health, 105*(11), 2349–2355. https://doi.org/10.2105/AJPH.2015.302776

110. Orchard, J., & Price, J. (2017). County-level racial prejudice and the black-white gap in infant health outcomes. *Social Science & Medicine, 181*, 191–198. https://doi.org/10.1016/j.socscimed.2017.03.036

111. Michaels, E. Board, C., & Allen, A, (2022). Area-level prejudice and health: A systematic review. *Health Psychology, 41*(3), 211–224. www.ncbi.nlm.nih.gov/pmc/articles/PMC8930473/

CHAPTER 4

Racism in American Medicine
Do No Harm to Some; Do Great Harm to Others

The practice of the negro doctor [should be] limited to his own race. [1]
Abraham Flexner, 1910

In the two chapters that follow this one, we describe how systemic racism and individual racism create substantial disparities in the quality of the health*care* Black patients and White patients receive today. These present-day disparities must, however, be placed in a historical context. Anti-Black racism has plagued American medicine for several centuries. This shameful history has created a legacy for many of the contemporary racial disparities in healthcare. For example, the legal racial segregation of medical facilities that existed over several centuries plays a major role in the continued de facto segregation of medical care in the United States. Also, the blatant anti-Black racism exhibited by White physicians until well into the twentieth century contributes to the current higher levels of mistrust of physicians among Black patients than White patients [2]. As Dorothy Roberts, professor of law and sociology at the University of Pennsylvania, explained, "It's not that Black people have an irrational fear of [individual physicians], it's that they have an awareness of a long history of being disrespected, mistreated, and violated by the government and by healthcare professionals" [3].

We begin with a discussion of anti-Black racism in the public and private entities that controlled the practice of medicine and medical education in the United States in the early twentieth century. The signal event that shaped modern American medicine occurred in 1910. Concerned about the state of medical education, the American Medical Association (AMA) contracted with the Carnegie Foundation for the Advancement of Teaching to produce a report on the current status of physicians' training. The Foundation engaged a noted educator, Abraham Flexner, to examine current practices and issue a report with recommendations for changes that needed to be made in how physicians were educated. Flexner documented the abysmal quality of most medical schools and recommended that many of them be closed and the remaining schools be graded according to the quality of their training. He argued for a standard curriculum across medical schools, which would include science education, experience with dissections, and seeing patients. This resulted in a significant change in medical education in the United States. Specifically, the worst private medical schools, which were mostly "diploma mills," were closed and a large portion of medical training was moved to medical schools that were part of research universities. The result was a substantially higher quality of medical training and the integration of medical practice with medical science, which eventually resulted in a significant improvement in medical care.[1]

But there was an ugly, racist side to Flexner's report. In it, he addressed the training of Black physicians and their roles in medical care, recommending that medical schools continue to be segregated and that Black students be trained differently from White students. He proposed that Black students be trained in "hygiene rather than surgery," and that they should primarily work as "sanitarians" – health workers whose main responsibility was "protecting Whites" from diseases common in Black communities [4]. And finally, as quoted at the beginning of this chapter, Flexner advocated for the continued segregation of medical care, with Black physicians only treating Black patients.

Flexner's racism was not unusual among prominent people in the medical community at that time. It reflected the anti-Black racism that was already deeply entrenched in American medicine. This involved systemic racism by federal, state, and local governments, as well as professional medical organizations. This systemic racism was typically accompanied by substantial individual racism among White physicians. The first and most pervasive kind of systemic racism was the denial of medical care to most Black people, combined with a dramatically lower quality of the limited medical care that was available to them.

Racial Exclusion in Medical Care before 1964: Quite Separate and Very Unequal

At the time of the Civil War, almost 90 percent of all Black people in the United States were enslaved and held captive by slaveholders. Although

[1] In his book, *The Great Influenza: The Story of the Deadliest Pandemic in History*, Dr. John Barry, professor of public health and tropical medicine at Tulane University, provides an insightful history of the state of American medicine at the turn of the twentieth century. This is a prelude to his discussion of the flu pandemic of 1918, which killed as many as 100 million people. Many of his descriptions of how America responded to that flu pandemic are disturbingly close to the responses to the COVID-19 pandemic 100 years later.

free Black people at that time faced many serious health challenges, including their ability to obtain decent medical care, the situation for most enslaved people was especially dire. The decisions made about medical care for Black people who were enslaved were largely in the hands of the people who owned them. Because slaveholders considered their slaves to be an investment in a piece of property, decisions about their medical care (or lack thereof) were almost exclusively based on whether they were able to perform some kind of work on a plantation.[2]

When enslaved Black people were finally set free, many of them were released without any money or other personal resources and had to fend for themselves without jobs or places to live. Few had access to even the minimal medical care they had received on the plantations. As a consequence, Black Americans in the South started to die in alarming numbers. This massive public health problem led to the establishment of medical facilities known as "Freedmen Hospitals." These facilities were intended to only serve Black patients. Although some of the Freedmen Hospitals did significantly reduce mortality rates, most were dependent on local and state governments, which provided sparse funding, and the conditions in the hospitals reflected the widespread mistreatment of Black people at the time. The hospitals were grossly understaffed and in very short supply. For example, in 1865, there were about 80 physicians and a dozen hospitals available to treat four million formerly enslaved Black people [5].[3]

The Jim Crow race laws that were enacted across the South in the 1870s and largely remained in force until the mid-twentieth century severely limited Black people's rights. (These race laws were more fully discussed in the Introduction chapter.) This included their right to access to the same kinds of medical care that were available to White people. White physicians were either prohibited from treating Black patients entirely or were only allowed to treat them after they had treated all their White patients. In many states, Black people were denied admission to most public and private medical facilities [6]. The limited number of hospitals that did serve Black patients and White patients were required to have separate

---

[2] However, as Sharla Fett discusses in her book, *Working Cures: Healing, Health and Power on Southern Plantations*, there were various forms of healthcare provided by enslaved people themselves, some of which reflected the healing traditions they brought with them from Africa. Black women on the plantations also served as midwives for both other Black women and sometimes for the White plantation owners.

[3] A good historical account of the very serious post-Civil War health problems among formerly enslaved Black people and of the establishment of "Freedmen Hospitals" can be found in *Sick from Freedom: African American Illness and Suffering During the Civil War and Reconstruction* by Dr. Jim Downs, professor of civil war era studies and history at Gettysburg College.

wards for Black patients and White patients, and medical treatments for Black patients and White patients were usually performed in separate areas of a hospital. For example, in 1935, a Georgia law stated, "The Board of Control shall see that proper and distinct apartments are arranged for said patients, so that in no case shall Negroes and White persons be together" [7].

Even in the hospitals that admitted Black patients, the wards that housed them were under-resourced and understaffed, in large part (as we discuss later in this chapter) because of the barriers to the professional education of Black people. These wards were also located in the least desirable parts of the hospital (usually the basements). Many years after legal segregation ended, Mabel Williams, a Black nurse who had worked at one of these hospitals, described what it was like for their Black patients: "Black people were in the basement, admitted to the basement of the hospital. And the White people were on the upper level. . . . the plumbing that took care of the hospital was placed in the [Black] patients' rooms. . . . Babies . . . were taken into the utility room, where we had to empty and wash out bed pans [8]." Even the equipment and instruments hospital staff used were labeled "white" or "colored." Some White nurses and physicians were willing to work in Black wards, but this was very rare. As late as 1956, only 6 percent of the hospitals in the South offered fully integrated services [9]. Thirty-one percent still refused to admit Black patients under any conditions.

When millions of Black people began to move from the southern to the northern parts of the United States during the Great Migration of the early twentieth century, the medical care they received in northern hospitals was dramatically inferior to that received by White patients. There was typically de facto segregation. In Chicago, Illinois, for example, the only hospitals that would accept Black patients were in the predominantly Black neighborhoods and, as in the South, were understaffed and under-resourced [10]. The hospitals that eventually did accept Black patients were built in such a way that Black patients were on different floors or in different wings from White patients.

The major consequence of all of these laws and policies was that many Black Americans who had migrated to northern cities were unable to obtain adequate medical care. There were some Black physicians and nurses in northern urban centers, but their number was very small relative to the need for their services. Black people who were ill were often treated by other family members or in many cases by Black midwives, who expanded their activities from assisting in the deliveries of babies to the treatment of many different kinds of medical problems. But the AMA actively tried to prohibit midwives from providing these types of services because, the organization claimed, their practices did not meet the standards that the medical profession had established [11]. This opposition grew as more male physicians began practicing obstetrics, suggesting that the AMA may have been trying to stifle competition [12].

One consequence of the lack of an adequate amount of formal medical care was a significant number of deaths that could have been prevented if Black people had more access to hospitals and medical facilities. The infant son of Dr. W. E. B. Du Bois, the eminent sociologist whom we have already mentioned as one of the pioneers in identifying the true causes of racial health disparities, died from diphtheria because the medical treatments that could have saved the boy were not available to Black people like the Du Bois family. In his book, *Souls of Black Folk*, Du Bois mournfully described his son's passing: "He died at eventide, when the sun lay like a brooding sorrow above the western hills, veiling its face; when the winds spoke not, and the trees, the great green trees he loved, stood motionless. I saw his breath beat quicker and quicker, pause, and then his little soul leapt like a star that travels in the night and left a world of darkness in its train" [13].

Small Steps Forward

The enactment of the Social Security Act in 1935, as well as the establishment of various health programs under President Franklin Roosevelt's "New Deal," did much to improve the health of Black Americans, especially those living in the South. Programs of the Public Health Service improved sanitation in areas where Black Americans lived, provided healthcare to both Black Americans and White Americans who were unemployed, and later funded large-scale public health programs for maternal and infant care that dramatically reduced the infant and maternal mortality rates of Black women living in southern states.

Furthermore, legal challenges to racial segregation in medical care and other services began to emerge in the 1930s. State governments in the South did not end segregated medical care in response to these challenges. Rather, several of them responded by creating supposedly "separate but equal" medical institutions and care. In other words, in an effort to maintain segregation, they sought to improve the institutions that only served Black people. A leading Black newspaper of the time called these actions "Deluxe Jim Crow Laws" [14]. Although these changes constituted an insidious new strategy to maintain the racist foundation of Jim Crow laws, they did, in conjunction with the Public Health Service (PHS) and pressure from various advocacy groups, improve the healthcare available to Black Americans and thus their health. But both healthcare for and the health of Black Americans still remained quite poor and lagged far behind that of White people.

During World War II, the expansion of the military draft brought national attention to the poor health of many White Americans and the much poorer health of most Black Americans. A significant number of all draftees were rejected for service because of their poor health, but the percentage of Black Americans who were rejected was astoundingly high. In North Carolina, for example, 71 percent of the Black draftees were rejected primarily because of their poor mental or physical health [14].

In response, the federal government initiated a few programs intended to improve the overall health of all Americans. Some of these involved greatly expanding the Public Health Service, which gave special attention to the quality of medical care for Black Americans living in the South. Some federal programs also successfully reduced public health problems such as the levels of sexually transmitted diseases and maternal mortality, which were both higher among Black Americans – again especially those living in the South [14]. However, because of the race-based laws and racist sentiments, large numbers of these programs failed, and none significantly reduced the level of legal segregation in medical care in the United States even after World War II. For example, the Veterans Administration hospitals, which were supposed to serve all military vet-erans, were not fully integrated until 1953 [15].

True integration of medical care and facilities would have reduced many of the racial disparities in twentieth-century health and mortality, but powerful forces opposed it. The AMA was one of them. For example, in 1946, the US Congress passed the Hill–Burton Act, which provided federal funding for hospital construction. With the AMA's support, however, the Act permitted these hospitals to be segregated. The AMA endorsed the idea that under the patently false principle that "separate but equal" medical facilities provided equal medical care. In the 1960s, the National Medical Association, which represented Black physicians, appealed to the AMA to support an amendment to the Hill–Burton Act that would have prohibited federal support for segregated hospitals, but the AMA refused to do so. It claimed that giving the federal government such control over hospitals' admission policies would lead to "socialized medicine" [16].

More generally, the AMA vigorously opposed any sort of nationalized healthcare or health insurance programs. Such programs would have almost certainly improved access to healthcare among both poor Black Americans and White Americans. As programs like Medicare and Medicaid eventually did, they also would have greatly reduced segregation in medical care. But from the 1930s through at least the 1970s, the AMA quite actively and successfully prevented federal programs that would have reduced the enormous racial disparities in access to medical care. In 1956, the AMA made a statement to Congress about broadening the healthcare services offered under the Social Security. The statement proclaimed, "The American Medical Association is vigorously opposed to the proposed changes. ... We are opposed to those changes because they are needless, wasteful, dangerous, and contrary to the established policy of gradual Federal withdrawal from local public assistance programs" [16].[4]

Even in the 1960s, when the national zeitgeist began to move in favor of more civil rights for Black Americans, the AMA resisted government initiatives that would have increased racial equity in general, and specifically in healthcare. For example, the AMA did not support the 1964 Civil Rights Act, even though it contained a provision that prohibited racially segregated hospitals [16]. (There were still many such hospitals in 1964, primarily in the South.) The AMA also opposed the establishment of the Medicare and Medicaid programs that were eventually enacted in 1965, both of which included a requirement that participating physicians sign a statement that they would not racially discriminate in their practice. Indeed, the AMA later successfully fought to get that provision eliminated from the programs [17, 18].

Eventually, the enactment of Medicare and Medicaid made racial segregation in healthcare the exception rather than the rule in the United States. For example, in the four months after the passage of Medicare, about 1,000 previously segregated hospitals became integrated. The major reason for this was that the federal agency administering Medicare would not provide funding to a hospital unless the hospital certified that it was no longer segregated [19]. More recently, racial disparities in access to healthcare were further reduced by the Affordable Care Act (ACA), which went into full force in 2014 and substantially increased the number of Black Americans with health insurance. Black Americans are still less likely to have health insurance than White

---

[4] Material on the history of the AMA and racism in medicine can be found in studies the AMA commissioned and have recently been published. Part of this history is in appendices to the public document, "Organizational Strategic Plan to Embed Racial Justice and Advance Health Equity 2021–2023" www.ama-assn.org/about/leadership/ama-s-strategic-plan-embed-racial-justice-and-advance-health-equity?

Americans, but the racial gap in insurance coverage has since been cut in half [20].

Importantly, the political stance of the AMA has changed dramatically in the 50 years since the passage of Medicare. In 2008, the AMA formally apologized for a century of "past wrongs" [17]. And more recently, the AMA publicly supported the passage of the ACA. Nevertheless, while segregation and the legalized denial of medical care to Black Americans is a thing of the past, the legacy of almost 100 years of racial segregation and exclusion in medical care still plays a significant role in contemporary racial disparities in healthcare access, utilization, and outcomes.

Segregated Medical Education and Practice

The problem of inadequate healthcare for Black Americans before and long after the Civil War was compounded by the dearth of Black physicians. The main reason for this was simply that Black people were excluded in one way or another from medical schools and opportunities to practice medicine.

Exclusion of Black Physicians

In their chronicling of Historically Black Colleges and Universities (HBCUs), the US Department of Education and the Office of Civil Rights note that before the Civil War there was no structured higher education specifically for Black students, and the few institutions that called themselves "universities" very likely only provided primary and secondary education [21]. Thus, there were no Black medical schools and only a very small number of Black Americans who received medical education. This situation improved somewhat after the end of the Civil War due to the major health crisis among former slaves, discussed earlier. The Freedmen Hospital in Washington, DC, for example, led to the establishment of a medical school for Black students at Howard University in 1868, and Meharry Medical College in Tennessee was established in 1876 with the support of the Methodist Episcopal Church and private donors. Nine other medical schools for Black students were established in the following years.

Some of the medical schools associated with White universities also started to admit Black students. Among them was the University of Pennsylvania Medical School, but it was not a welcoming environment. Dr. Nathan Francis Mossell, the first Black student who enrolled there encountered enormous racist hostility and numerous threats to his safety, which forced him to carry a gun for protection. For a time, the medical school required him to sit behind a screen that hid his face during medical lectures [22]. Despite these obstacles, he graduated in 1882. Systematic exclusion of Black students from predominantly White medical schools continued in some form until it became illegal in 1964.

Graduation from medical school did not mean the end of challenges for Black physicians. White physicians refused to collaborate with them, and most hospitals refused to grant them admitting and treatment privileges. The primary rationale given for these exclusory practices was that Black physicians had not been accepted into local medical societies, which was a requirement for granting hospital privileges. In most instances, though, Black physicians had been refused membership in these societies solely because of their race. Black physicians were therefore often unable to earn a living practicing medicine full-time. They took other jobs and practiced part time, often as "sundown doctors," who saw patients in the hours after White physicians had stopped treating patients [6].

The AMA did little, if anything, to challenge the local medical societies' policies of racial exclusion in medical practice and, in fact, tacitly supported them. In 1870, three Black physicians applied for AMA membership. The men had been trained in traditional medicine, were experienced, and licensed to practice in Washington, DC. They belonged to a small, integrated local medical society. However, they had been denied membership to the much larger all-White Medical Society of Washington, DC, because of their race. And, because the AMA had a policy of not admitting physicians to membership if they were not members of their local medical society, it ultimately refused membership to these Black physicians. There was substantial debate among AMA members over the issue, and the organization acknowledged that the Black physicians were excluded from the Medical Society of Washington, DC only because they were Black. But it was concluded that the decision did "not come into conflict with any part of the AMA's code of ethics" [18].

Black medical schools and individual Black physicians in practice have long been the targets of systemic racist practices by powerful medical associations. When the grading system proposed by the Flexner Report of 1910 led to a dramatic reduction in the number of medical colleges across the United States, it disproportionality targeted Black medical schools. The report directly resulted in the closure of five Black medical schools and the demotion of two other Black medical schools, Howard and Meharry, to a "Class B" status, thus classifying them as inferior to most

White medical colleges [1, 23]. By 1923 Howard and Meharry were the only two Black medical schools that remained open. As discussed earlier, the AMA's policy of requiring membership in local medical societies before they would admit a physician as an AMA member – and their refusal to challenge those societies that excluded Black physicians solely because of their race – continued for almost 100 more years. Finally, if a Black physician *was* granted membership in the AMA, the physician was listed as "colored" in the organization's directory, a practice that often made it harder for Black physicians to obtain liability insurance [18].

In response to their exclusion from the AMA, Black physicians formed the National Medical Association (NMA) in 1895. Since then, the NMA has been a strong, effective voice for racial equality in the training of physicians and the provision of comparable medical treatment to Black patients and White patients. The NMA's activities somewhat reduced the effects of the de facto and de jure segregation on the practice of medicine by Black physicians and thus did much to make healthcare more available to Black patients.

Many of the AMA's discriminatory practices remained in place until they were rendered moot by the 1964 Civil Rights Act. At that point, all Black physicians with the proper credentials could join the AMA. While the AMA's formal positions have become much more progressive on issues related to reducing healthcare disparities over the past 30 years or so, the AMA did not formally apologize for its past history of effectively barring Black members until 2008 [17]. Fortunately, there has since been a rapprochement between the AMA and the NMA, and they now collaborate on a number of issues related to equitable healthcare.

Exclusion of Black Nurses

There have been Black nurses for a very long time, but this was an informal role, often assumed by enslaved women who had no formal training. These women were critical to the survival of the other enslaved people living with them on plantations. During the Civil War Black women also served as nurses for the Union Army, but almost always only for Black soldiers. Among women who did this were Harriet Tubman and Sojourner Truth, better known for their courageous exploits freeing enslaved people in the underground railroad [24]. However, even long after nursing became an established medical profession, Black women (at least until the later part of the twentieth century, almost all nurses were women) were still discouraged from pursuing a career in nursing because the women who became nurses were supposed to embody the notions of "dignity, purity, morality, and virtue." The prevalent racist stereotype at that time was that Black women could not have possessed these characteristics.

Established nursing schools in the South refused to admit Black students, and there were rigid racial quotas at northern schools [25]. For example, the nursing school at the New England Hospital for Women and Children stated in its charter that the hospital would admit "one Negro and one Jew" to each year's class [25]. The only nursing schools in the South that did admit Black students were quite small, segregated facilities that served very few patients. It was not until 1881 that the first formally recognized nursing school for Black women in the South was established at Spelman College in Atlanta, Georgia [26].

Black women who graduated with nursing degrees were subjected to the same kinds of racism and exclusion as were Black physicians [27]. They were excluded from most local nursing societies, almost always because of their race. This, in turn, prevented them from joining the American Nursing Association, which like the AMA required membership in the local professional organization. Because of this, they were often refused employment at local hospitals. Those hospitals that did hire Black nurses typically restricted their activities to the wards for Black patients, where the conditions were significantly worse than in the wards for White patients [28]. This practice continued in many states until it became illegal in 1964.

One of the main employment opportunities for all nurses has been serving in the military, but this opportunity was severely limited for Black nurses during the first half of the twentieth century. During World War I, the Army Nursing Corps and the American Red Cross, which procured nurses for the Army, opposed allowing Black nurses into the military. In what would have almost certainly been a maddening "Catch-22" situation for Black nurses, this was because membership to the American Nursing Association was required for joining the Red Cross. However, as we have mentioned earlier, the American Nursing Association denied Black nurses membership because of the racist admission policies of the local nursing societies. It was not until 1918 that Black nurses could enlist in the Army. Their numbers were, however, extremely small [28]. Their inability to join the Red Cross also denied them the opportunity to serve as public health nurses during the 1918 "Spanish Flu" pandemic. This was despite the fact that nurses were desperately needed to treat American soldiers and civilian victims of this pandemic.

There was another severe shortage of nurses during World War II. In fact, it was so serious that at one time the US government was considering drafting American women. Despite this, the Army rejected the applications of about 9,000 Black nurses. After they submitted their applications, many of them received a letter that said, "Your application to the Army Nurses Corps cannot be given favorable consideration as there are no provisions in Army regulations for the appointment of colored nurses in the Corps" [29, 30]. Congressman Adam Clayton Powell, who actively lobbied against this exclusory policy, issued the following statement: "It is ... unbelievable that these leaders have become so blindly and unreasonably un-American that they have forced our wounded men to face the tragedy of death rather than allow trained nurses to aid[them] because these nurses' skins happen to be of a different color" [31, 32]. When a small number of Black nurses were finally admitted into the Nursing Corps, initially, they were not allowed to treat White American soldiers. Rather, they were almost all assigned to camps that held German prisoners and later to military hospitals or wards that only served Black soldiers. They were also segregated from White military nurses, a practice that continued until 1948, when President Harry S. Truman ordered the military to treat all personnel equally and end segregation [33].

The professional exclusion of Black nurses in the early twentieth century led to the creation of the National Association of Colored Graduate Nurses (NACGN), which advocated for the rights of Black nurses. Partially as a result of their advocacy, at least one national nursing association no longer barred Black nurses from membership, and by 1948, only the District of Columbia and nine states barred Black nurses from their state organizations [33]. In 1951, the NACGN merged with the American Nursing Association. However, as was the case with Black physicians, formal exclusion and segregation in the education and employment of Black nurses did not really end until 1964, when such discrimination became prohibited under the Civil Rights Act.

Medical Training and Research: The Abuse of Black People's Bodies

The systemic anti-Black racism that was endemic in American medicine from at least the eighteenth century until the mid-twentieth century also led to widespread abuse of Black patients and laypeople by both medical institutions and individual physicians. While Black physicians and nurses were being systematically excluded from professional schools and professional practice, Black laypeople were playing an essential role in medical training in the United States. However, almost always this was as victims of anti-Black racism. That is, this medical abuse of Black people was always in some way predicated on the idea that they were inferior to and biologically different from White people, and thus White people had the right to exert power over them.

Medical schools of the nineteenth century were only profitable if they could enroll enough tuition-paying students, as tuition was their only income source. Consequently, there was often fairly fierce competition for new students. In this context, one major inducement medical schools could offer was that there would be plenty of patients for students to study – and plenty of cadavers to dissect. However, at this time, relatively few White people actually sought medical care and even fewer went to hospitals, because hospitals were often accurately considered more dangerous to people's health than staying at home. So, medical schools had to look elsewhere for patients and cadavers. They turned to Black communities. In both the northern and southern United States, a very large percentage of the live patients and the cadavers that medical schools provided to their students were Black people. White medical students learned how to treat patients by practicing on Black people, and they learned the secrets of human anatomy by studying them. As one medical school advertised, "The number of negroes in our factories will furnish support of an extensive hospital and afford the student the great desideratum – clinical instruction" [34].

In many instances, medical schools used local hospitals to obtain large numbers of Black patients for White students to study. Prior to the Civil War, these Black patients were often sick enslaved people who were treated at local hospitals because their owners were encouraged to send them. Later, destitute free Black people would often go to hospitals that offered to treat them for free. These hospitals were associated with medical training, and these Black patients would be used to "promote the interest of medical education within their native state and city" [35]. Accordingly, the Black people in these hospitals were not so much patients as they were what we might today call "teaching tools." Black patients in the hospitals were probably not deliberately mistreated, but the primary reason they were admitted was not to treat them but to use them to teach White medical students.

The medical exploitation of Black people continued even after they were dead. Medical schools promised their students that they would be taught about human anatomy, and at the time the dissection of human cadavers was the only way to do so. Harriett Martineau, a Black woman living in Baltimore in 1838, recounted that "the bodies of colored people exclusively are taken for dissection because the whites do not like it, and the colored people cannot resist" [34]. Even in death, enslaved Black people were powerless and exploited. After they died, their bodies were often either sold or given to medical schools as a donation to the public good and the advancement of medical education.

Grave Robbing

Before the Civil War, the use of Black corpses in medical schools was a widespread phenomenon. In 1833, the Kentucky legislature narrowly defeated a law that would have allowed judges to distribute the bodies of dead Black people to chartered colleges "for dissection and experiment" [35]. After the Civil War, it was not quite as easy for medical schools to simply claim the body of a Black person after they died. Their families had rights, although still limited, to deceased relatives' bodies. This new situation created somewhat of a shortage of cadavers. In response, the medical community in southern states both openly and – more often – covertly turned to grave robbing. People were hired to enter cemeteries containing dead Black people and steal their corpses. Journalist Antero Pietila, the author of *The Ghosts of Johns Hopkins*, graphically described the process: "The plunderers began by shoveling at the head of a freshly buried coffin, breaking the lid, placing a hook around the deceased's neck or armpit and, with the help of a rope, easing the body out of the grave. For shipment elsewhere, the corpses were folded into barrels filled with whiskey – to mask the odor. At the destination, a medical school took the remains for dissection" [36].

According to Harriett Washington's book, *Medical Apartheid: The Dark History of Medical Experimentation on Black Americans from Colonial Times to the Present*, and other histories of racism in medicine, grave robbing in Black cemeteries was not restricted to the southern US. In fact, archaeological excavations provide evidence of grave robbing that benefited private medical schools at Harvard, Columbia University, New York University, and state universities in Maryland, Michigan, and Pennsylvania [37, 38].

Grave robbing was not a short-lived phenomenon. For example, sometime in the 1850s the Medical College of Georgia began using an enslaved man named Grandison Harrison to surreptitiously steal bodies from a Black cemetery. He was freed after the Civil War, but his work continued for another 50 years [36]. Even today, long after the passage of many laws protecting the legal rights of Black families, there are still instances of exploitation of dead Black people's bodies. In April 2021, various media outlets reported on one such instance. It involved the bones of a Black girl in her early teens who had been killed about 35 years earlier when the Philadelphia police had bombed a house that belonged to a Black resistance movement called "Move." She was one of the 11 people who died in the fire that followed the bombing. Their bones were initially given to Dr. Allen Mann, professor of anthropology at the University of Pennsylvania, in the hope that some of the deceased people could be identified. Sometime later, he gave two bones from the young Black teenager to a visiting professor at Princeton University, Dr. Janet Monge.

Neither Monge nor Mann ever obtained permission from any living relative to show the bones publicly. However, Monge displayed them in her online forensic anthropology classes, which included a lecture about the police raid. She described the girl's remains to her class in this way: "The bones are juicy, by which I mean you can tell they are the bones of a recently deceased individual. If you smell it, it doesn't actually smell bad – it smells kind of greasy, like an older-style grease" [39].

The history of grave robbing to provide medical schools with Black cadavers is well-known in many Black communities and has become part of certain folk legends. To this day, a disproportionate number of Black people are used as cadavers in medical training. This is largely because of the social, political, and economic forces that make it much more likely that the body of a Black person will be unclaimed or unknown than the body of a White person. As a result, Black people are more likely than White people to be used as cadavers in some medical schools. Thus, both historical and contemporary practices regarding the bodies of dead Black people provide substantial reasons for Black Americans' widespread mistrust of the medical community. As noted by Dr. Shawn Utsey, professor of psychology at Virginia Commonwealth University, "Black folks knew they were more vulnerable to grave robbing. I think the tension is still there" [40].

Medical Experimentation on Black Americans: The Banality of Evil

The end of World War II in 1945 led to the liberation of prisoners in concentration camps where the German government had imprisoned and executed large numbers of Jews, Roma, and other groups deemed undesirable by Germany's Nazi leadership. When the concentration camps that held these people were finally liberated, the former prisoners and the soldiers who freed the prisoners let the world know about the unethical and horrendous medical experiments that German physicians carried out on those imprisoned in the camps. A substantial number of these physicians were subsequently tried and convicted for war crimes.

This awful part of the Nazi legacy led to the creation of the Nuremburg Code in 1947. It was a statement of principles intended to prevent any more of this kind of experimentation on human beings. The Nuremburg Code included the following principles: subjects in medical (and other) experiments have to be told that their participation is voluntary, they have the right to end their participation in the study, and researchers have to ensure that their experiments will not do physical or mental harm to the subjects [41]. The Nuremburg Code became the informal standard for medical experimentation in the United States. And at the time, many Americans felt quite proud that American physicians had never done or would do anything as awful as had the German physicians.

In fact, starting perhaps as early as the eighteenth century and continuing at least to the 1990s, there were medical studies conducted on Black people that grossly violated any code of human decency. According to Harriett Washington, despite claims to the contrary, these studies were not the work of some isolated "mad" scientists who fit the Dr. Frankenstein stereotype. She writes that, in fact, "researchers who exploit [ed and horribly abused] African Americans were the norm for much of our nation's history, when Black [people] were commonly regarded as fit subjects for nonconsensual, nontherapeutic research" [37]. That is, the Black subjects were the victims of both systemic and individual anti-Black racism.

The Horrific Gynecological Experiments of Dr. James Marion Sims
The history of medical abuses of Black people is greatly intertwined with the abuses of slavery. From almost the beginning of the importation of Black Africans, physicians were enlisted to determine the worth of enslaved Black people for sale in the slave markets [42]. It was also quite common for physicians to use enslaved individuals as unwilling subjects in medical experiments. One of the most famous (or infamous) instances of this were the gynecological experiments performed by Dr. James Marion Sims in the 1840s. All of his initial subjects were enslaved Black women. Some were lent to Sims by the women's enslavers, but many more were enslaved women purchased by Sims for the sole purpose of conducting his research on them. The women could not refuse to be subjects in his research and likely faced substantial risk if they even complained. He performed

painful, invasive, and dangerous surgical procedures on these enslaved women without any apparent regard for their welfare.

Although other physicians in the South had discovered in 1839 that ether could be used during surgeries (notably, by experimenting on a Black child they had seized from the streets), Sims chose not to use it with the Black women who were the victims of his surgeries. Generally, ether was reserved for White surgical patients [43]. Sims believed in the racist trope that Black people experience much less pain than White people. However, the excruciating pain of the women who were his subjects must have been obvious to him, as they screamed out while he performed his surgeries. It seems likely that he simply did not care.

He operated on one enslaved woman, whose name was Anarcha, at least 30 times without giving her any ether. Instead, he had his assistants and/or colleagues hold her down as he made the incisions. It was reported that Sims once said that he considered the Black women upon whom he performed his experimental surgeries as sacrifices on the "altar of science" [44].

Dr. Sims' abuse of enslaved Black women extended beyond the surgeries. He frequently had them undress and kneel in a position that exposed their vagina as he and other physicians took turns examining the women with his speculum. On some occasions, these humiliating examinations were opened to the public and, according to Sims, the voyeurs "saw everything as no man had seen before" [37]. Sims also experimented on enslaved Black children, conducting operations in which he used a shoemaker's tool to pry their bones apart and loosen their skulls. He believed that Black people were less intelligent than White people because their skulls grew too quickly [44].

Although he conducted his gynecological studies over 180 years ago, Dr. Sims created instruments and procedures that are still used in gynecology. For example, he developed the vaginal speculum, a device used to examine a woman's vagina. He also developed many currently used surgical procedures for gynecological disorders [45]. Sims went on to become one of the leading physicians of the nineteenth century and even served as president of the AMA in 1876. Overlooking and even tacitly condoning the brutality and horror of Sims' experiments, for a long time the medical establishment continued to honor Sims as the "father of gynecology." There is even a hospital named after Sims, and the South Carolina Medical Association still has an annual award in his name [46]. Until 2018, there was a statue in honor of him in New York City. It is only relatively recently that the horrors of his treatments of enslaved women have been publicly acknowledged and some of these tributes have been withdrawn.[5]

The exploitation of Black people in the name of medical advancement was by no means restricted to Dr. Sims' medical research. In the nineteenth century, Black people were also disproportionality used as "guinea pigs" in new eye surgeries, experimental cesarean deliveries, and treatments for asthma and malaria. In one infamous example of this kind of experimentation, a physician and slave owner named Thomas Hamilton wanted to discover the best way to treat heat stroke. He borrowed an enslaved man named "Fed" and placed him in a large hole in the ground, which he heated to a very high temperature. Hamilton forced Fed to sit naked on a stool in the pit, with wet blankets placed over the opening to retain the heat. The experiment continued for two or three weeks, with Hamilton forcing Fed to take medicines Hamilton believed might cure heat stroke. Remarkably, Fed survived the experiment, escaped slavery, and lived to talk about the abuse [37].

Tuskegee and Other Atrocities
Unethical and harmful medical studies that used Black people as subjects did not end with the abolishment of slavery; they continued in abundance throughout the twentieth century. The most well-known of these is the "Tuskegee Study of Syphilis in Untreated Black Males" [47]. This study did great harm to many Black people's lives over a long period of time.

The rationale for the Tuskegee study was polygenism, a theory that was a part of scientific racism. It proposed that Black people and White people are genetically distinct species (see Chapter 1). Thus, many physicians at the time believed that whereas syphilis attacked the nervous system and brain of White people, the disease attacked the cardiovascular system of Black people. This idea never really had any scientific basis and has long since been discarded.

Ironically, the events that eventually led to this notorious study actually began with an attempt to address pervasive treatment inequities in Alabama in the 1930s. Syphilis among Black men had approached a

---

[5] In 2021 The American College of Obstetricians and Gynecologists, representing a broad coalition of medical societies involved in women's productive health, issued a statement acknowledging the enslaved women who were unwilling subjects in Sims' experiments and the past racist injustices committed by him and many other physicians of the nineteenth and twentieth centuries. The statement contains a commitment to end the systemic and individual racism that is pervasive in US healthcare. It can be found at www.acog.org/news/news-articles/2021/02/collective-action-addressing-racism-acknowledging-betsey-lucy-and-anarcha

pandemic level in Macon County, and the state of Alabama was doing little, if anything, to address it. The state did not offer even the most basic kinds of public health services to any of the Black people living in the region. In response, a large private foundation called the Rosenwald Fund partnered with the Public Health System (PHS) to provide some basic healthcare to Black residents. However, these efforts to treat and control syphilis in this community were soon abandoned – in part because of cost, but primarily because the government officials came to believe that the Black men could not learn ways to control the disease or practice better health habits in general. More ominously, some White people in the region even believed that, left untreated, syphilis might provide an end to the "negro problem" in Macon County [48].

But the PHS researchers saw the substantial numbers of Black men who had syphilis and who supposedly had not received any treatment as providing a research opportunity that seemed too good to pass up. There had been a recent study on the disease's long-term effects on Norwegian men, but reflecting their polygenetic beliefs, the American researchers decided to study the course of the disease in untreated Black men by comparing various aspects of the long-term health of the Black men who did have syphilis with those men who did not have syphilis. The study was, however, fatally flawed. To begin, although the treatments for syphilis at that time were only marginally effective, they were better than no treatments. And some of the men in the syphilis group had actually received minimal treatments before the beginning of the study. This was not, however, systematically recorded. So, while these men were all described as "untreated," treatment actually varied from person to person, pretty much invalidating the study from the start. Furthermore, when any of the initially uninfected men *became* infected, they were simply moved to the infected group – which is not a correct procedure in any comparative study of this kind. This is because these newly infected individuals were quite different in a multitude of ways from those originally identified as infected. Thus, any valid scientific comparison between the men in the two groups became impossible. The study, which was originally supposed to last for 6 months, actually continued for about 40 years. Premised on a myth from scientific racism and poorly designed, the Tuskegee syphilis study was, in fact, incapable of making any contribution to a medical understanding of the course of syphilitic infections in Black people or anyone else.

But the real tragedy of this study was not the poor science but rather what it did to the men who were subjects and their families. To induce men to participate in this study, the PHS officials offered them free medical examinations, certain limited kinds of medical care, and financial incentives. The biggest incentive offered, however, was the promise that the men would be treated for their "bad blood," meaning syphilis. In fact, no treatments were ever actually provided. Rather, the men were deliberately given ineffective sham treatments while being subjected to painful and invasive diagnostic procedures like spinal taps. Further, about 10 years after the study began, penicillin became widely available for the treatment of syphilis. It was not, however, offered to any of the men. In fact, the PHS officials actually intervened with the local draft board to prevent men in the study from being drafted during World War II because the military physicians would have detected the men's syphilis infections and treated them with penicillin [47].[6]

Because the men were left untreated over the course of so many years, the disease was spread to their sexual partners and from them to their children. It is estimated that the study may have eventually affected the lives of 9,000 Black people scattered around the United States. The PHS continued to study the Tuskegee survivors until the early 1970s, but kept the study hidden from the public. However, in 1972, a physician who worked for PHS grew frustrated with their lack of candor and told a reporter for the Associated Press about the study and PHS' refusal to make it public. The study was finally exposed in the *Washington Star* on July 25, 1972. About eight months later the study was terminated [48]. Shortly after that, the US Senate opened a public hearing on the Tuskegee experiment, and the American public became aware of what had been done to the men in the study and their families. In 1974, the surviving men and their families eventually filed a class action suit and received a $10 million out-of-court settlement [47]. It took 15 more years before President Clinton finally issued a formal apology to the Black residents of Macon County, Alabama for what the US government had subjected them to for over 40 years.

This was, however, far from the end of the medical abuse of Black people. In the 1950s and 1960s, government agencies, such as the CIA and the Department of Defense, joined with chemical companies to fund other studies that grossly mistreated their Black subjects. One of these involved Dr. Harry Bailey, an acclaimed Australian brain researcher, who came to Tulane University to begin a series of experiments with Dr. Robert Heath.

[6] A complete description of the Tuskegee experiment and its aftermath can be found in *Bad Blood: The Tuskegee Syphilis Experiment* by Dr. James H. Jones, professor of history at the University of Arkansas.

Their goal was to learn more about the nature of human emotions. Their series of experiments involved implanting electrodes into a subject's brain, which activated their limbic system at random times, in order to see what emotions the subjects experienced. Today, experimental surgical procedures, including implanting electrodes in the brain, are only done on humans after extensive testing of their safety with animals. But Dr. Bailey, Dr. Heath, and their colleagues did not bother with any animal studies before implementing this new, untested, and potentially dangerous surgical procedure. They went straight to human subjects, all of whom were Black. As far as we know, these subjects were never informed of the purpose of these studies, and they never gave written consent to be in them. In some instances, the implants remained in place for as long as three years.

About 25 years later, Bailey was asked why they did not use animals in these experiments. His reply is an exemplar of virulent anti-Black racism: "So, in New Orleans, it was . . . cheaper to use [N-word]s than cats because they were everywhere and cheap experimental animals" [49]. According to Bailey, the Black victims of his experimentation were "basically worthless," and "shooting them" was really the only alternative he saw to using them as test subjects.

At about the same time as Bailey and Heath were conducting their studies, Dr. Albert Kligman was conducting research on prisoners in Philadelphia, most of whom were Black men. Kligman was a dermatologist at the University of Pennsylvania, and his work was supported by the Dow Chemical Company. As part of his research, some of the prisoners were intentionally exposed to pathogens that caused skin infections such as the herpes virus. Other prisoners were given a known carcinogen, dioxin. Dow Chemical later supplied dioxin to the US military in the form of "Agent Orange," the infamous airborne chemical that killed an untold number of Vietnamese people and American soldiers. The prisoners were paid for their participation in Kligman's study, but they never gave any written consent for their participation. To Dr. Kligman, they were not even human beings. Rather, in an interview with the *Philadelphia Bulletin* in 1966, he referred to them as "acres of skin" [50, 51].

Black Participants in Radiation Studies
Yet another significant episode in the medical abuse of Black Americans were the radiation studies that began at the turn of the twentieth century and continued in various forms through the 1970s. Almost as soon as physicists began to write about their discoveries with radiation and its

effects on humans, medical researchers began to perform experiments on Black people. In the early 1900s, for example, Black subjects were exposed to high levels of radiation in an attempt to turn their skin color white. In the words of one 1905 New York newspaper article, the purpose of such studies was to make "all coons to look white." The newspaper, perhaps like the researchers themselves, believed this would solve the race problem in the United States [37].

One of the subjects in early radiation experiments was a five-year-old Black child named Vertus Hardiman, living in Lyles Station, Indiana, in 1928. He was taken, along with several other Black children, to a local county hospital. Their parents were told that their children were going to be part of a study on how to cure ringworm. However, they were really subjects in a study on the effects of radiation on people's bodies and minds. The experiment left Vertus Hardiman horribly scarred with open head wounds for the rest of his life [52]. For 80 years, he never told anyone what had been done to him and wore wigs or hats to hide the massive disfiguration of his scalp and the hole in his head.

Seventy years after Mr. Hardiman's ordeal began, there were still radiation experiments being conducted primarily on Black people and funded by government agencies such as the Department of Defense and the Department of Energy. One of these was a large research program on the effects of exposure to radioactive materials led by Dr. Eugene L. Saenger at the University of Cincinnati from 1960 to 1972. In these studies, almost 100 cancer patients, the majority of whom were Black, were exposed to either total (TBI) or partial (PBI) body irradiation [53]. Today, TBI is sometimes used as a cancer treatment, but the primary purpose of this study was to inform the military about what to expect if soldiers were exposed to an atomic bomb. The amount of radiation the TBI patients received was equivalent to about 60 X-rays. The results were lethal. Over a quarter of these patients died within a few weeks of the treatment, and more than 75 percent died within 1 year; this mortality rate was much greater than for the patients who received PBI [54].

Dr. Saenger later insisted the patients had given written informed consent, but a descendant of one of the Black women in the study reported her surprise when she was shown her grandmother's "signed" informed consent – her grandmother could neither read nor write. Indeed, families of the people in these experiments sued the University of Cincinnati and eventually received over $4 million in compensation. As Gwendon Plair, the daughter of one victim of the experiments, wrote, "It's a great tragedy to lose a loved one. That tragedy is made all the worse when that loved one is taken purposely by one's own government" [55].

Around the same time as Saenger's radiation studies, similar studies were being conducted at the Medical College of Virginia with the goal of seeing whether Black people could tolerate more radiation than White people. This hypothesis was largely based on the old racist myth that Black people could tolerate more pain than White people. In this instance, researchers believed that Black people's skin was thicker and that their bones were harder and denser [37].[7]

The studies we have presented are only a portion of the many dangerous and unethical medical studies carried out on countless Black people. Whether enslaved or free, they were usually unable to refuse to participate or were simply never told they were in an experiment. As far as we know, these kinds of blatantly dangerous and unethical studies are no longer being conducted, but they leave a stained legacy of anti-Black racism in American medicine and almost certainly contribute to the higher level of medical mistrust among Black Americans than White Americans. Further, the story of the victimization of Black people in the name of science does not end with these medical studies.

Henrietta Lacks: Her Unacknowledged Contribution to Medical Science
Henrietta Lacks was a Black woman being treated for cervical cancer at Johns Hopkins Hospital in the early 1950s. At the time, this hospital was the only medical facility in the Baltimore area that would treat Black patients. There is no clear evidence that Ms. Lacks received inferior treatment because of her race but, while she was a patient, cells were taken from a biopsy of her tumor and cultured so they could be used as a "cell line" or "culture" for further medical research. Cell lines grown outside the human body enable researchers to observe the effects of certain medications on human cells in a controlled laboratory setting. It was very difficult to grow such cell lines in the early 1950s, but Ms. Lacks' cells were, for unknown reasons, very resilient. They became so widely used for research that they were given their own name: "HeLa (**He**nrietta **La**cks) cells." HeLa cell lines were used in medical experiments for many decades after Ms. Lacks' death in 1951 [56].

Pharmaceutical companies developed many drugs using HeLa cells, including the first polio vaccines. Yet, while they earned hundreds of

---

[7] In his book, *Contested Medicine: Cancer Research and the Military*, Gerald Kutcher describes these experiments and other instances of questionable research done for the US military.

millions of dollars from these drugs, Ms. Lacks was never even told that her cells had been harvested. Indeed, she never formally consented to the use of her cells for any purpose, nor was anyone in her family initially aware of what had happened to her cells. Many years later, when the truth came out, the family asked for compensation. But they were refused. "I always thought it was strange," Ms. Lacks' daughter stated, "If our mother's cells done so much for medicine, how come her family can't afford to see no doctors? People got rich off my mother without us even knowing about them takin' her cells, now we don't get a dime" [56].

The public became aware of this episode in medical science in 2010 with the publication of *The Immortal Life of Henrietta Lacks* by Deborah Skloot. As a result, the Johns Hopkins Hospital faced intense criticism for their role in the exploitation of Ms. Lacks. While they have formally honored Ms. Lacks, they still claim that they never financially benefited from the HeLa cells and, thus, have never apologized to her family or offered them any financial compensation. The pharmaceutical companies also refused to compensate her family. However, in the summer of 2020, a major bio-medical research organization did finally give the surviving members of the Lacks family a large donation to partially compensate for the fact that the cells had been taken from Ms. Lacks without consent [57]. In 2021, Ms. Lacks' family initiated a suit against the pharmaceutical companies that had profited from her cells. As of 2023, the suit is still in litigation [58].

Unethical Research despite Government Regulations
Disclosures about the Tuskegee study and several of the other studies discussed here led the federal government to issue the Belmont Report. Published in 1978, the report contained three principles that researchers were supposed to follow when their subjects were human beings: obtaining informed consent, minimizing any risk to the subjects, and treating all research subjects fairly and equally. Subsequently, in 1981, these principles became part of a federal regulation for human experimentation. The regulation required that all institutions receiving any kind of federal funding must establish an Institutional Review Board to review and certify the ethics of all research with human subjects. The government also established much stricter guidelines for research with prisoners who, because of their confinement, were deemed much more likely to be coerced into being research subjects. This regulation greatly reduced the likelihood that Black participants in medical experiments would be abused in the way that they had been for over 200 years, but, tragically, such abuses did not end altogether.

In the early 1990s, the Kennedy Krieger Institute and Johns Hopkins University jointly embarked on a study intended to find ways to lower the level of poisoning from lean-laden paint in low-income housing in Baltimore, Maryland. At the time of the study, about 95 percent of the housing in Baltimore occupied by Black residents was contaminated with lead-infused paint. As we discussed in Chapter 3, lead poisoning is an extremely pernicious threat to the normal intellectual development of children. The specific purpose of this study was to develop the most cost-effective strategy for lead abatement in contaminated homes – an admirable objective. The researchers could have conducted a controlled laboratory experiment, in which they would simply systematically manipulate levels of lead in a closed environment and determine their effects on laboratory animals. Instead, the researchers conducted a field experiment and measured its success by assessing levels of lead poisoning in Black children.

The researchers selected 108 buildings in Baltimore, all of which housed Black residents. They then randomly divided the dwellings into three groups. The first group received minimal repairs and maintenance to remove the lead paint, and the other two groups each received progressively more extensive repairs and maintenance. To ensure they had enough children in the study, the researchers gave the owners of the homes financial incentives specifically to rent to families with young children. They also gave the parents a small financial incentive to be in the study and to allow the researchers to draw blood samples from their children. The effectiveness of the three levels of lead abatement was assessed by "measuring the extent to which the ... healthy children's blood became contaminated with lead and comparing that contamination with levels of lead dust in the houses over the same periods of time" [59].

Over the course of the study, the researchers periodically drew blood samples, and they measured and compared the levels of lead in the blood of the children living in three groups of homes. Importantly, the parents were never informed of the dangers of the lead poisoning to which their children were being exposed. In fact, the parents were told that the study would help protect their children from lead-infused paint. This was at best a half-truth. To be sure, eventually the lead levels in some of the children started to go down because of the improvements, but the children were never really "protected," and the reduction in lead levels occurred only after prolonged and very dangerous exposure to lead-infused paint. Compounding this endangerment, the parents were never told what the actual levels of lead in their children's blood were, even as the lead levels tripled in some children. If the parents had known, they very likely would have sought medical care for their children. The researchers, of course, were well aware of these dangerous increases in lead poisoning and the damage it could do to the children, but no treatment was ever offered for its effects even after the study was over. The parents were, in essence, asked to put their children in harm's way without any potential benefits for the children and no awareness of the dangers.

This study was a clear violation of federal guidelines regarding how children should be treated in research. While it does not appear that the researchers intended to harm the children involved, their unwillingness to inform parents about the lead levels or provide necessary treatment had consequences that seem indistinguishable from a desire to actually do such harm. In almost every respect, the children were treated as if they were laboratory animals in an experiment rather than human beings. When some of the parents later sued the Kennedy Krieger Institute and Johns Hopkins University, the university's defense was basically that the study was really a private contract between themselves and the parents rather than research. Thus, the university argued, the laws regarding the ethical treatment of human subjects did not apply. However, the judge who heard the case disagreed and ruled in the parents' favor. In his decision, he said that the children were like the "canaries in mines" – sacrificed in order to warn others of dangerous conditions [59].

The Eugenics Movement: A Social Movement That Became a Racist Tool

The final way in which Black people have suffered medical abuses because of systemic and individual anti-Black racism has a more circuitous path than the ones we have discussed so far. It begins with a flawed theory proposed by a prominent English intellectual, Sir Francis Galton, a leading British statistician and polymath (and cousin of Charles Darwin). In the late nineteenth century, Galton began to study English families from different social classes. He quickly saw that wealthy and powerful parents usually had wealthy and powerful children, and poor and powerless families usually had poor and powerless children. Rather than attributing these differences to the rigid social class system that existed in England at the time, Galton turned to the genetic theories that were then popular among members of the British intellectual community – specifically, theories about the transmission of inherited characteristics. His interpretation of the differences he observed was that privileged children inherited their superior characteristics from their superior parents, and underprivi-leged children inherited their inferior characteristics from their inferior parents [60]. Galton coined a term for his theory: eugenics. Eugenics means "well-born." Based on his theory, Galton believed the British government should limit reproduction among the lowest social classes in their country.

Today, we know that the transmission of certain traits from parents to their children is infinitely more complex than the early eugenicists thought. To be sure, there are similarities between parents and their children, but a child's intellect or other complex characteristics are deter-mined by a host of complex genetic and environmental factors. Thus, attempting to "breed" humans in the manner that hunting dogs are bred is not only immoral but also it is impossible to do. Galton's gross misun-derstanding of how heredity actually works and his failure to acknowledge that political, social, and economic factors were the root causes of the class differences he observed led to much more than just another theory of the origins of differences among people. He strongly advocated that govern-ments should encourage reproduction among the "best" of their citizens and discourage it among the "worst," and Galton actively promoted his ideas among the powerful political and social circles of the time [61].

When eugenics was first introduced in the United States, it was strongly supported by Alexander Graham Bell, Clarence Darrow, Helen Keller, Margaret Sanger (founder of Planned Parenthood), Theodore Roosevelt, and many other prominent people of the early twentieth century [62]. Originally, the eugenics movement in the United States was "passive." It advocated achieving its goals by isolating different racial and ethnic groups, so they could not "intermingle," discouraging reproduction among certain socially and economically disadvantaged groups, and restricting the immi-gration of specific groups of people (e.g., Chinese, Italians, and Jews) who differed in some way from the majority White northern European popu-lation.[8] These efforts were often successful. For example, beginning in the 1920s they led to severe limitations on who could immigrate to the United States. However, passive genetics soon evolved into "active" eugenics, which became more dominant in the United States. Active eugenics soon

---

[8] For more information on the eugenics movement in the United States, see Daniel Okrent's book, *The Guarded Gate: Bigotry, Eugenics and the Law That Kept Two Generations of Jews, Italians and Other European Immigrants Out of America*. Okrent shows how many of the ideas of American eugenics influenced Adolph Hitler and provided the rationale for the Holocaust against Jews and other racial/ethnic minorities. Also see Adam Cohen's book, *Im-be-ciles: The Supreme Court, American Eugenics and the Sterilization of Carrie Buck*.

became intermingled with anti-Black racism, with disastrous consequences for Black Americans, especially Black women.

Active Eugenics and Racist Public Policies

Active eugenic policies go far beyond simply isolating social groups from one another; they are intended to proactively limit the level of procreation among members of certain disadvantaged groups. Sometimes this limitation was achieved through birth control, but very often it was accomplished through government-enforced sterilizations of Black people and other groups designated as "undesirable." Surprisingly, when sterilization and other types of birth control for Black people were first proposed in the 1920s, this idea was initially supported by some Black leaders, including W. E. B. Du Bois, as a means of reducing crowding and improving the living conditions in segregated Black neighborhoods [62]. But it quickly became clear that sterilization was being used as a means to carry out racist policies and diminish the power of Black Americans, and this support vanished.

As part of the active eugenics movement in the twentieth century, it is estimated that well over 60,000 American citizens were forcibly sterilized [63]. Black women were not the only targets of government-sponsored sterilization programs, but they (and other minority women) were substantially more likely to be involuntarily sterilized than were White women. These sterilizations were either enforced by laws or, in many cases, simply done extralegally without a woman's knowledge. One notorious example of the latter involves Fannie Lou Hammer, a Black woman living in Mississippi. Ms. Hammer was a courageous and eloquent civil rights advocate who led the effort to integrate the Democratic party in Mississippi in 1964. But a few years earlier, at the age of 34, she had gone to a hospital to have a benign fibroid tumor removed. Her physicians did more than remove the tumor, however. They also removed her uterus, rendering her unable to ever have children. Ms. Hammer's experience was not an isolated instance. Indeed, the involuntary sterilization of Black women in Mississippi was so common it came to be called the "Mississippi Appendectomy" [64].[9]

The horror and the long-term trauma of these operations were recently captured in a 2022, *New York Times* interview. The reporter spoke with two Black women (sisters) from Alabama, both of whom had undergone

---

[9] A good biography of Ms. Hammer's life and important accomplishments is *Walk With Me: A Biography of Fanny Lou Hammer* by Kate Clifford.

legally authorized involuntary surgical sterilizations 50 years earlier. One of the women told the reporter, "I can show you what they did to me." She then lifted up her T-shirt and revealed a jagged horizontal scar that extended across her entire abdomen. "That's where they cut me. It might have happened a long time ago, but it still brings back memories. We're still thinking about it" [65].

In North Carolina, the Eugenics Control Board sterilized about 7,600 people between 1929 and 1973. Black women represented a much larger percentage of the sterilizations than their percentage of the state's population [66]. Researchers who have examined the historical trends of sterilizations in North Carolina have noted that this racial disparity increased in the 1960s when the state had to integrate its schools and Black people were gaining more political power in the state [67]. These researchers suggest that the increased sterilizations of Black women may have been intended to limit the political influence of Black North Carolina residents.

Nationally, most sterilizations occurred when pregnant Black women were told they would lose public assistance for their babies and families if they were not sterilized after their babies were born. To justify this policy, the state agencies that provided welfare benefits argued that these women would not take care of their children, would endanger their lives, and would create too big a burden on the welfare system. This echoes yet another racist myth that dates back to at least the time of slavery – that Black women are bad or even abusive mothers. For example, in the 1850 census, suffocation was very frequently listed as the cause of death among the children of enslaved Black women. At that time, it was widely believed that Black women either failed to properly care for their children or often killed them by rolling over on their infants when they were sleeping.[10] The twentieth-century involuntary sterilization policies were, at least in part, due to this long-held racist stereotype about Black women [67].

The involuntary sterilization of Black women (and women who were Indigenous Peoples or Latina) was not just a problem in the South. It existed throughout the United States. In 1973, a lawsuit was filed to end federally funded sterilizations. Although Black Americans comprised less than 15 percent of the total population in the United States, over 50 percent of the women who were sterilized were Black. In many instances,

---

[10] In *Medical Apartheid*, Harriett Washington points out that the census takers of the time had no formal training in the identification of diseases; there were no guidelines for recording the causes of mortalities; and there was political pressure to justify slavery. The findings about the health of enslaved Black people from census of the time are, thus, highly suspect.

these sterilizations were not, strictly speaking, involuntary. Rather, as in North Carolina, they involved poor women being offered a terrible choice – be sterilized or lose the benefits they were receiving to support their families. Indeed, in the 1973 lawsuit, a court ruled that such policies were "arbitrary and unreasonable," and the court prohibited the further use of federal funds for involuntary sterilization and the practice of coercing women who were on welfare [68]. In response, the US Department of Health Education and Welfare stopped providing funds for these kinds of sterilizations. The two Black sisters, whose ordeals we presented earlier, were the plaintiffs in this lawsuit.

Some states, however, continued to fund forced sterilizations. A total of 1,400 female prisoners in California, most of whom were Black or Latina, underwent involuntary sterilizations between 1997 and 2003. There were likely many more, as the practice continued until 2014 when California's governor banned this practice [69]. One of the Black women involuntarily sterilized was 24 years old when she underwent this procedure. Speaking about these sterilization programs many years later, she said that this "is one of the things that has happened to the African American Black woman: We're seen as welfare recipients. And we're seen as burdens on the system" [69].

More recently, the targets of forced sterilization have been Latina immigrants. In 2018, these were instances of involuntary sterilization of Latina prisoners in Georgia, and in 2020 there were accusations that women of color (primarily Latina) who were being held at the US Immigration and Customs Detention Center in Irwin County, Texas, were receiving hysterectomies at a "seemingly high rate" [70].

Birth Control: A Hidden Path to Racial Eugenics

Even as involuntary sterilizations became less common, other ways of limiting Black women's reproductive rights became more common [71]. These primarily involved birth control programs by state and local governments that largely targeted poor and Black women and promoted the increased use of oral and other types of contraceptives. One such widely used contraceptive was Norplant. Norplant was an inexpensive form of birth control in which small rods were implanted in a woman's arms in a minor surgical procedure. The rods contained hormones that prevented a woman from becoming pregnant. While no longer used, it was considered safe and effective at the time it was introduced [72].

Norplant was the drug of choice in an especially egregious instance of White city officials trying to reduce pregnancy rates among Black women. In Baltimore, Maryland in the 1990s, city officials decided to implant the Norplant rods in the arms of a very large number of Black girls between the ages of 13 and 19. Norplant had never been tested on teenagers, and it was placed in the Black girls' arms without their parents' knowledge or consent. The rationale for the program was that it would stem the allegedly increasing tide of pregnancies among Black girls. According to a spokesperson for the school district, officials were seeing a high pregnancy rate and were "looking for any innovative, sound, medically proven ways to deal with this complex issue." Or as the superintendent of schools for the Baltimore Archdiocese put it in support of the program, young people "can't say no" [73].

But these ideas about high pregnancy rates among teenage Black girls were largely another kind of racist myth. The pregnancy rate among White teenagers was actually higher than among Black teenagers. Further, nationally, the steepest decline in teenage pregnancies was among Black girls [37]. Yet not only was Norplant regularly implanted in Black teenagers, but it (and various oral contraceptives) was also widely advocated for use with poor Black women. The justification, yet again, was that doing so would protect the welfare of Black women's children and/or prevent Black women from abusing the welfare programs that provided them public assistance.

Some people believe, however, that there was a different reason for administering contraceptives to Black women. For example, a Black minister from Baltimore, Reverend Melvin Tuggle, decried such practices as genocide: "One third of us are in jail and another third is killing us, . . . and now they're taking away the babies" [74]. There is good reason to think Reverend Tuggle was correct about the intent of these birth control programs. At the peak of forced sterilizations and the widespread use of Norplant among Black girls and women, Frederick Osborn, one of the founders of a prominent pro-eugenics organization, wrote that "birth control and abortions are turning out to be one of the great eugenic advances of our time" [75].

While Osborn believed that the eugenics purpose would best be served by not acknowledging it publicly, not all proponents felt the same need to hide their intentions. The desire to limit reproduction among poor and Black women was, for example, quite publicly expressed in an infamous 1990 editorial in the *Philadelphia Inquirer* titled, "Poverty and Norplant: Can Contraception Reduce the Underclass?" The editorial writers decried the supposedly increasing number of children being born into poor Black families and proposed a solution: "It's very difficult to undo the damage of being born into a dysfunctional family. So why not make a major effort to reduce the number of children of any race?" [76] Such publicly expressed views may explain why surveys today find that Black Americans are more likely than White Americans to believe that the government encourages contraceptive use to limit minority populations [77].

Putting It All Together

American medicine has a long and shameful history of anti-Black racism. The blatant racism in the healthcare of the past is largely gone, but it continues to influence contemporary racial disparities in healthcare. The medical abuse of Black Americans has taken many different forms over the past several centuries, but they all did untold harm to Black people and their families. For almost 100 years after the end of slavery, Black people were largely unable to obtain adequate healthcare. Systemic and individual racism excluded Black people from most of the medical care that was available to White people. The problem was seriously compounded by the severe shortage of Black physicians and nurses who would have been willing to treat Black patients. Indeed, for a long time Black Americans were largely excluded from professional medical training and, if they were able to become physicians or nurses, they faced innumerable barriers in offering their services to anyone. The result of these circumstances is that a large number of Black people died because they could not find someone to provide medical treatment for them.

In addition, horrific medical experiments were conducted on Black people over the course of at least 200 years. This kind of cruel exploitation created a legacy of justifiable medical mistrust among Black Americans that continues to this day. Further eroding Black Americans' trust in the medical establishment is the willing role played by medical professionals in eugenics-inspired practices intended to limit the reproductive rights of Black women. (This mistrust and its role in healthcare disparities are discussed in Chapter 6.)

To be sure, governmental actions and social changes have greatly improved the quality of the healthcare available to Black Americans today and made it more accessible to them. Most of the laws and customs that did so much medical harm to Black people are part of a shameful past. Moreover, almost all professional medical organizations have acknowledged and apologized for the past brutality and injustices of racist medical practices within their specialties. These organizations now clearly denounce racism in American healthcare. Yet the impact of the long history of racism in American medicine remains and has formed an enduring legacy that still influences racial disparities in healthcare.

REFERENCES

1. Savitt, T. (2006). Abraham Flexner and the black medical schools. 1992. *Journal of the National Medical Association, 98*(9), 1415–1424. https://pubmed.ncbi.nlm.nih.gov/17019906/

2. Dovidio, J. F., Penner, L. A., Albrecht, T. L., Norton, W. E., Gaertner, S. L., & Shelton, J. N. (2008). Disparities and distrust: The implications of psychological processes for understanding racial disparities in health and health care. *Social Science and Medicine, 6*(3), 478–486. https://doi.org/10.1016/j.socscimed.2008.03.019

3. Young, S. (2021). *Black vaccine hesitancy rooted in mistrust, doubts.* WebMD. www.webmd.com/vaccines/covid-19-vaccine/news/20210202/black-vaccine-hesitancy-rooted-in-mistrust-doubts

4. Laws, T. (2021). How should we respond to racist legacies in health professions education originating in the Flexner Report? *AMA Journal of Ethics, 23*(3), 271–275. https://journalofethics.ama-assn.org/article/how-should-we-respond-racist-legacies-health-professions-education-originating-flexner-report/2021-03

5. Downs, J. (2012). *Sick from freedom: African-American illness and suffering during the Civil War and Reconstruction.* Oxford University Press.

6. Byrd, W. M., & Clayton, L. A. (2000). *An American health dilemma: A medical history of African Americans and the problem of race: Beginnings to 1900.* Routledge.

7. Hunkele, K. L. (2014). *Segregation in United States healthcare: From reconstruction to deluxe Jim Crow.* (Unpublished Honors Thesis). University of New Hampshire. https://scholars.unh.edu/cgi/viewcontent.cgi?article=1189&context=honors

8. Williams, M. (1999, August 20). Unhealthy conditions in black area of a segregated hospital [Interview]. Documenting the American South. https://docsouth.unc.edu/sohp/K-0266/excerpts/excerpt_8777.html

9. Cornely, P. B. (1957). Trend in racial integration in hospitals in the United States. *Journal of the National Medical Association, 49*(1), 8–10. https://pubmed.ncbi.nlm.nih.gov/13385679

10. Dorsey, K. (2000, April 12). Exhibit explores city's history of segregation. *The Daily Northwestern.* https://dailynorthwestern.com/2000/04/13/archive-manual/exhibit-explores-citys-history-of-segregation/

11. Reynolds, P. P. (2004). Professional and hospital discrimination and the US Court of Appeals Fourth Circuit 1956–1967. *American Journal of Public Health, 94*(5), 710–720. https://doi.org/10.2105/ajph.94.5.710

12. Radosh, P. F. (1986). Midwives in the United States: Past and present. *Population Research and Policy Review, 5*(2), 129–146. https://doi.org/10.1007/BF00137177

13. Du Bois, W. E. B. (1903). *The souls of Black folk.* A. C. McClurg & Co.

14. Thomas, K. K. (2011). *Deluxe Jim Crow: Civil rights and American health policy, 1935–1954.* University of Georgia Press.

15. Museum of the American Military Family. (2016, August 1). *End of racial segregation in VA Hospitals.* We served too. https://weservedtoo.wordpress.com/2016/08/01/end-of-racial-segregation-in-va-hospitals/

16. U.S. Congress. House Committee on Ways and Means. (1956). Public Assistance Titles of the Social Security Act, Hearings on H.R. 9120. 84th Congress, Second Session. www.ssa.gov/policy/docs/ssb/v19n9/v19n9p3.pdf

17. Washington, H. A. (2008, July 29). Apology shines light on racial schism in medicine. *New York Times.* www.nytimes.com/2008/07/29/health/views/29essa.html

18. Baker, R. B. (2014). The American Medical Association and race. *AMA Journal of Ethics, 16*(6), 479–488. https://journalofethics.ama-assn.org/article/american-medical-association-and-race/2014-06

19. Sternberg, S. (2015, July 29). Desegregation: The hidden legacy of Medicare. *US News & World Report.* www.usnews.com/news/articles/2015/07/30/desegregation-the-hidden-legacy-of-medicare

20. Chaudry, A., Jackson, A., & Glied, S. A. (2019, August 21). *Did the Affordable Care Act reduce racial and ethnic disparities in health insurance coverage?* The Commonwealth Fund. www.commonwealthfund.org/publications/issue-briefs/2019/aug/did-ACA-reduce-racial-ethnic-disparities-coverage

21. U.S. Department of Education. (1991, March). Office for Civil Rights. Historically black colleges and universities and higher education desegregation. https://files.eric.ed.gov/fulltext/ED330264.pdf

22. Press, R. (2017, February 6). In his own words: Nathan Francis Mossell, Penn Medicine's first Black graduate. *Penn Medicine News.* www.pennmedicine.org/news/news-blog/2017/february/in-his-own-words-nathan-francis-mossell

23. Wright-Mendoza, J. (2019, May 3). The 1910 report that disadvantaged minority doctors. *JSTOR Daily.* https://daily.jstor.org/the-1910-report-that-unintentionally-disadvantaged-minority-doctors/

24. Jefferies, K. (2020, May 11). Recognizing history of Black nurses a first step to addressing racism and discrimination in nursing. *The Conversation.* https://theconversation.com/recognizing-history-of-black-nurses-a-first-step-to-addressing-racism-and-discrimination-in-nursing-125538

25. Bennett, C., Hamilton, E. K., & Rochani, H. (2019). Exploring race in nursing: Teaching nursing students about racial inequality using the historical lens. *OJIN: The Online Journal of Issues in Nursing, 24*(2). https://ojin.nursingworld.org/MainMenuCategories/ANAMarketplace/ANAPeriodicals/OJIN/TableofContents/Vol-24-2019/No2-May-2019/Articles-Previous-Topics/Exploring-Race-in-Nursing.html

26. Carnegie, M. E. (1999). *The path we tread: Blacks in nursing worldwide, 1854–1994* (3rd ed.). Jones & Bartlett.

27. Farrow, S. (2021, August 13). This day in history, August 13th. *The Hub news.* https://thehub.news/this-day-in-history-august-13th/

28. Bellafaire, J. The Army nurse corps in World War II. AMEDD Center of History & Heritage. https://achh.army.mil/history/ancwwiibook-introduction

29. Clark, A. (2018, May 15). The army's first Black nurses were relegated to caring for Nazi prisoners of war. *Smithsonian Magazine.* www.smithsonianmag.com/history/armys-first-black-nurses-had-tend-to-german-prisoners-war-180969069/

30. National Women's History Museum. (2019, July 8). *African American nurses in World War II.* https://www.womenshistory.org/articles/african-american-nurses-world-war-ii

31. Tomblin, B. (1996). *GI Nightingales: The army nurse corps in World War II.* University Press of Kentucky.

32. The New York Public Library Archives & Manuscripts. National Association of Colored Graduate Nurses records 1908–1958. https://archives.nypl.org/scm/20744

33. Scrubs Editor. (2016, February 25). Historical moments for African American nurses. *Scrubs Magazine.* https://scrubsmag.com/historical-moments-for-african-american-nurses/

34. Savitt, T. L. (1982). The use of Blacks for medical experimentation and demonstration in the Old South. *The Journal of Southern History, 48*(3), 331–348. https://doi.org/10.2307/2207450

35. Kentucky General Assembly. House of Representatives. (1833). Journal of the House of Representatives of the Commonwealth of Kentucky, December 1, 1833 - February 24, 1834. Journals of the General Assembly of the Commonwealth of Kentucky. https://uknowledge.uky.edu/ky_state_journals/16/

36. Pietila, A. (2018, October 25). In need of cadavers, 19th-century medical students raided Baltimore's graves. *Smithsonian Magazine.* www.smithsonianmag.com/history/in-need-cadavers-19th-century-medical-students-raided-baltimores-graves-180970629/

37. Washington, H. (2006). *Medical apartheid: The dark history of medical experimentation on black Americans from colonial times to the present.* Anchor Books

38. Berry, D. R. (2018, February 3). Beyond the slave trade, the cadaver trade. *New York Times.* www.nytimes.com/2018/02/03/opinion/sunday/cadavers-slavery-medical-schools.html

39. Pilkington, E. (2021, April 23). Bones of Black children killed in police bombing used in Ivy League anthropology course. *The Guardian.* www.theguardian.com/us-news/2021/apr/22/move-bombing-black-children-bones-philadelphia-princeton-pennsylvania

40. Griset, R. (2011, November 15). Transmission of the body snatchers. *Style Weekly.* www.styleweekly.com/richmond/transmission-of-the-body-snatchers/Content?oid=1633570

41. Shuster, E. (1997). Fifty years later: The significance of the Nuremberg Code. *New England Journal of Medicine, 337*(20), 1436–1440. https://doi.org/10.1056/nejm199711133372006

42. Levin, M. (2020). "Putrid disorders and dangerous diseases": Slave ship surgeons' journals and medicine on the middle passage. *Yale Historical Review.* www.yalehistoricalreview.org/putrid-disorders-and-dangerous-dis eases-slave-ship-surgeons-journals-and-medicine-on-the-middle-passage/

43. McGregor, D. K. (1990). *Sexual surgery and the origins of gynecology: J. Marion Sims, his hospital, and his patients.* Taylor & Francis.

44. Holland, B. (2018, December 4). *The 'Father of Modern Gynecology' performed shocking experiments on enslaved women.* History.com. www.history.com/news/the-father-of-modern-gynecology-performed-shocking-experiments-on-slaves

45. Stamatakos, M., Sargedi, C., Stasinou, T., & Kontzoglou, K. (2014). Vesicovaginal fistula: Diagnosis and management. *Indian Journal of Surgery, 76*(2), 131–136. https://www.ncbi.nlm.nih.gov/pmc/articles/PMC4039689/

46. South Carolina Public Health Association. (2018). Award Eligibility 2018. www.scpha.com/resources/Documents/2020%20Awards%20Eligibility.pdf

47. Jones, J. H. (1981). *Bad blood: The Tuskegee syphilis experiment.* Simon and Schuster.

48. US Centers for Disease Control and Prevention. (n. d.). The Tuskegee timeline. https://www.cdc.gov/tuskegee/timeline.htm

49. TulaneLink.com. (2004, June). Changing people's minds, Tulane style. www.tulanelink.com/tulanelink/twoviews_04a.htm

50. Adamson, A., & Lipoff, J. (2021, January 4). Penn must cut ties with Dr. Albert Kligman, who conducted unethical human research on Black men. *The Philadelphia Inquirer.* www.inquirer.com/opinion/commentary/albert-kligman-holmesburg-prison-black-men-retina-a-medical-experiments-20210104.html

51. Hornblum, A. M. (1998). *Acres of skin: Human experiments at Holmesburg prison.* Routledge.

52. Black Youth Project. (2011, April 8). *A hole in my head: A life revealed – the story of Vertus Hardiman.* http://blackyouthproject.com/a-hole-in-my-head-a-life-revealed-the-story-of-vertus-hardiman/

53. Wolfe, A. J. (2010). A shameful system of research. *Nature Medicine, 16*(6), 633. https://www.nature.com/articles/nm0610-633

54. Stephens, M. (2002). *The treatment: The story of those who died in the Cincinnati radiation test.* Duke University Press.

55. Grim, R. (2002). American Mengele: Human radiation experiments. *The Brooklyn Rail.* https://brooklynrail.org/2002/10/express/american-mengele-human-radiation-experim

56. Skloot, R. (2010). *The immortal life of Henrietta Lacks.* Broadway Paperbacks.

57. Witze, A. (2020). Wealthy funder pays reparations for use of stolen cells. *Nature, 587*(7832), 20–21. https://pubmed.ncbi.nlm.nih.gov/33122840/

58. Gaskill, H. (2022, May 17). Judge weighing motion to dismiss Henrietta Lacks' family lawsuit against biotech firm. *Maryland Matters.* www

.marylandmatters.org/2022/05/17/judge-weighing-motion-to-dismiss-hen rietta-lacks-family-lawsuit-against-biotech-firm/

59. Buchanan, D. R., & Miller, F. G. (2006). Justice and fairness in the Kennedy Krieger Institute lead paint study: The ethics of public health research on less expensive, less effective interventions. *American Journal of Public Health, 96* (5), 781–787. https://doi.org/10.2105/AJPH.2005.063719

60. Facing History & Ourselves. (2015). The Origins of eugenics. www .facinghistory.org/resource-library/origins-eugenics

61. Gillham, N. W. (2001). Sir Francis Galton and the birth of eugenics. *Annual Review of Genetics, 35,* 83–101. https://doi.org/10.1146/annurev.genet.35 .102401.090055

62. Bouche, T., & Rivard, L. (2014, September 18). America's hidden history: The Eugenics Movement. *Scitable by Nature Education.* www.nature.com/ scitable/forums/genetics-generation/america-s-hidden-history-the-eugenics-movement-123919444/

63. Singleton, M. M. (2014). The 'science' of eugenics: America's moral detour. *Journal of American Physicians and Surgeons, 19*(4), 122–126. www.jpands .org/vol19no4/singleton.pdf

64. Pearce, J. (2020, October 28). Mississippi appendectomies: Reliving our pro-eugenics past. *Ms Magazine.* https://msmagazine.com/2020/10/28/ice-immigra tion-mississippi-appendectomies-usa-eugenics-forced-coerced-sterilization/

65. Villarosa, L. (2022). The long shadow of eugenics in America. *New York Times.* https://www.nytimes.com/2022/06/08/magazine/eugenics-movement-america.html

66. Rose, J. (2011, December 28). A brutal chapter in North Carolina's eugenics past. *National Public Radio.* www.npr.org/2011/12/28/144375339/a-brutal-chapter-in-north-carolinas-eugenics-past

67. Stern, A. M. (2020, August 26). Forced sterilization policies in the US targeted minorities and those with disabilities – and lasted into the 21st century. *The Conversation.* https://theconversation.com/forced-sterilization-policies-in-the-us-targeted-minorities-and-those-with-disabilities-and-lasted-into-the-21st-century-143144

68. Southern Poverty Law Center. (1973). Relf v. Weinberger. www.splcenter .org/seeking-justice/case-docket/relf-v-weinberger

69. Naftulin, J. (2020, November 24). Inside the hidden campaign to forcibly sterilize thousands of inmates in California women's prisons. *Insider.* www .insider.com/inside-forced-sterilizations-california-womens-prisons-documen tary-2020-11

70. Campoamor, D. (2020, September 16). Mass hysterectomies' at ICE happened on Trump's watch. But they're America's problem. *NBC News.* www.nbcnews.com/think/opinion/mass-hysterectomies-ice-happened-trump-s-watch-they-re-america-ncna1240238

71. Lennard, N. (2020, September 17). The long, disgraceful history of American attacks on Brown and Black women's reproductive systems. *The Intercept.* https://theintercept.com/2020/09/17/forced-sterilization-ice-us-history/

72. Burrell, D. E. (1994). The Norplant solution: Norplant and the control of African-American motherhood. *UCLA Women's Law Journal,* 5(2), 401–402 https://escholarship.org/content/qt9861n279/qt9861n279.pdf

73. Portner, J. (1992, December 16). Baltimore plan to offer Norplant raises ethical, medical, legal questions. *Education Week.* www.edweek.org/education/baltimore-plan-to-offer-norplant-raises-ethical-medical-legal-questions/1992/12

74. Wingert, P. (1993, February 14). The Norplant debate. *Newsweek.* www.newsweek.com/norplant-debate-195258

75. Horvath, A. (n. d.). Frederick Osborn: "Birth control and abortion are turning out to be great eugenic advances." Eugenics.US. https://www.azquotes.com/quote/1068479

76. Poverty and Norplant. (1990, December 12). The Philadelphia Inquirer. www.newspapers.com/clip/24246037/the-philadelphia-inquirer/

77. Payne, C., & Fanarjian, N. (2014). Seeking causes for race-related disparities in contraceptive use. *AMA Journal of Ethics, 16*(10), 805–809. https://journalofethics.ama-assn.org/article/seeking-causes-race-related-disparities-contraceptive-use/2014-10

CHAPTER 5

Not Part of the Solution
Systemic Racism in Contemporary Healthcare

> There has never been any period in American history where the
> health of blacks was equal to that of whites. Disparity is built into
> the system. [1]
>> Dr. Evelynn Maxine Hammonds, Barbara Guttman Rosenkrantz
>> Professor of History of Science, Harvard University

In 1985, the US Department of Health and Human Services (DHHS)
issued *The Report of the Secretary's Panel on Black and Minority Health,* an
eight-volume document also known as the Heckler Report [2]. For the first
time, a US government agency formally acknowledged the existence of
enormous disparities between the health of White Americans and the health
of members of racial and ethnic minority groups in the United States.

The report contained several useful and constructive recommendations.
For example, it proposed increasing Black Americans' (and members of
other racial/ethnic minority groups') access to healthcare services, improving the quality of healthcare services they receive, and collecting and
coordinating the data gathered about existing significant health disparities.
The remaining recommendations concerned various ways to increase
health-related knowledge in Black communities, with a special emphasis
on helping members of these communities become aware of the causes of
certain diseases and how to prevent them.

Overall, the Heckler Report resulted in the implemention of some badly
needed changes in federal government policies. It led to the establishment of
federal offices devoted to minority health and health equity in many key
government agencies such as the Centers for Disease Control and
Prevention (through its Office of Minority Health and Health Equity)
and the National Institutes of Health (through its Office of Minority
Programs). It also contributed significantly to a growing recognition of racial
health disparities among healthcare professionals and the general public.

In retrospect, however, there are several problems with the report. First,
although the recommendations to educate Black people on disease

prevention and control are well-intentioned, they imply that a large part of the problem resides with the members of these communities – that these community members lack the knowledge that would make them healthier. This seems to be a newer version of earlier explanations of why Black people are less healthy than White people – *they* are doing something wrong. Therefore, to reduce health disparities, they are the ones who need to change.

Moreover, the report omitted discussion of any important underlying causes of racial health disparities. For example, the report does discuss the relative dearth of medical professionals in predominantly minority neighborhoods, but never addresses the underlying reasons for this. That is, the report did not substantively address whether the healthcare system itself was failing to provide comparable care to minority Black Americans and majority White Americans. More broadly, the report failed to address the critical role of individual and systemic racism in the health problems of Black Americans.

About 15 years later, the US Congress requested the Institute of Medicine (IOM) of the National Academies (now called the National Academy of Medicine) to conduct another study that was similarly concerned with racial health disparities. The IOM study, however, addressed a different question about racial health disparities than did the Heckler Report. Although the IOM Committee that conducted the study was interested in disparities such as access to and utilization of healthcare, its primary interest was in disparities in the quality of the healthcare provided to patients from racial and ethnic minority groups. A key question the Committee asked was, "Did some groups of patients receive poorer care than others?" And if there were such disparities, what were the reasons for them? Although the charge to the Committee did not include identifying structural reasons for healthcare disparities, the report also included these (e.g., lack of healthcare facilities in certain neighborhoods). The work of the IOM Committee resulted in the publication of a seminal work on racial and ethnic healthcare disparities, *Unequal Treatment: Confronting Racial and Ethnic Disparities in Healthcare* in 2003. Dr. Brian Smedley, who was the director of the IOM study and the lead editor of the volume that resulted from the Committee's work, is one of the co-authors of this book. Another co-author of this book, Dr. John Dovidio, was a member of the Committee.

The major new conclusion of the IOM report, which surprised and challenged many people in healthcare professions, was that patients who were members of racial and ethnic minority groups consistently "receive a

lower quality and intensity of healthcare and diagnostic services across a
wide range of procedures and disease areas [and] these disparities in care
have been linked to poorer clinical outcomes and higher mortality among
minorities" [3].

The publication of *Unequal Treatment* eventually led to widespread
recognition by both lay people and medical professionals that racial
disparities in healthcare are indeed a major public health problem. The
IOM report also stimulated an explosion of research on these healthcare
disparities and the reasons behind them. We present some of that research
in this and the next chapter. The division of material in the two chapters
basically follows the way in which the IOM panel divided the primary
causes of large and persistent racial healthcare disparities. In this chapter,
we examine the structural-level causes of contemporary healthcare disparities. Specifically, we discuss how the general socioeconomic disparities
between Black Americans and White Americans – disparities created by
systemic racism in society – and certain kinds of systemic racism within
the American healthcare system produce significant racial disparities in the
quality of healthcare Black patients and White patients receive.[1] In the
next chapter, we focus on individual-level causes and discuss how
the thoughts and actions of people giving or receiving care can affect the
quality of the healthcare that Black patients receive.

"It's the Same Old Song" [4]: How America's Healthcare System Disadvantages Black Americans

Healthcare disparities between White Americans and Black Americans
(and other racial or ethnic minority groups) are a piece of the larger mosaic
of racial disparities in the health of Black Americans and White Americans.
Disparities in *health*, as we have already discussed, are the product of past
and present systemic and individual racism. For example, the health of
many Black Americans suffers because of persistent exposure to racial
discrimination (see Chapter 2), as well as the unhealthy environments that
commonly exist in predominantly Black and under-resourced neighborhoods. As explained in Chapter 3, these segregated neighborhoods are
primarily the result of racist private and public housing policies. Thus,
even if there were no racial disparities in the American healthcare system,
Black Americans would, on average, still have poorer health than White

[1] An excellent book on racial disparities in healthcare from a lawyer's perspective is *Just Medicine: A Cure for Racial Inequality in American Health Care* by Dayna Bowen Matthew, JD.

Americans. However, large and egregious racial disparities in the healthcare that Black Americans and White Americans receive greatly exacerbate the health disparities between Black Americans and White Americans.

One Significant Challenge: Unequal Access to Healthcare

One of the major reasons why Black Americans receive poorer healthcare than White Americans is that in the United States most people are responsible for the cost of their healthcare. A family's income plays a critical role in whether they will get adequate healthcare. Serious medical problems create a much greater burden on people with limited financial resources, and Black Americans, on average, have more limited financial resources than do White Americans. Thus, it is not surprising that a national survey conducted by the Pew Research Center in 2020 found that nearly three-quarters of the Black respondents said they did not have the funds needed to cover a long-term medical problem in their family [5]. This was true for less than 50 percent of White respondents.

The Affordable Care Act (ACA, often referred to as Obamacare), which was passed in 2010 and came into full force in 2014, was intended to reduce the financial burden of serious diseases on lower-income American families by making healthcare services much more affordable and accessible. These objectives were primarily accomplished by reducing the cost of individual health insurance for many people, requiring that insurance companies provide coverage for new patients who had preexisting health conditions, and expanding access to publicly supported insurance for low-income Americans (i.e., Medicaid). In general, these goals were achieved; in this respect, the ACA was a dramatic success. It significantly increased the number of people in America who had public or private health insurance. This resulted in greater racial and economic equity with regard to health insurance coverage, which was a very important achievement. However, a key question is whether the ACA actually decreased racial disparities in healthcare and health in the United States. The answer is, not nearly as much as was hoped.

A study published in 2021 in the *Journal of the American Medical Association* (JAMA) supports this conclusion. Shiwani Mahajan, a hospital resident at Yale University, and her colleagues analyzed the responses of about 600,000 Americans who were interviewed for the National Health Interview Survey between 1999 and 2018 [6]. Although White Americans were still more likely to have health insurance (and especially private health insurance) than Black Americans, the researchers found a significant decline over this time period in the percentage of Black Americans who were uninsured. This largely occurred after the ACA took effect. However, the trends in measures of healthcare *access* (e.g., having a usual source of care, talking to a medical professional in the last year, and delaying medical care due to cost) were less encouraging. For example, the percentage of Black respondents who reported talking to a healthcare professional in the past year increased only among middle- and high-income Black people. There was no improvement overall in Black respondents' reports of having a consistent source of medical care. This was true even among wealthier Black respondents. More troubling was the finding that over the period of time examined in this study, there was actually an increase in the likelihood of Black respondents having to delay medical care because of its cost. Finally, and most importantly, the percentage of Black respondents who reported that their health was only "fair" or "poor" did not improve significantly over the 20-year period, and that percentage was still substantially higher than the comparable percentage for White respondents.

Thus, while the ACA achieved a number of its objectives, it still failed to address the long-standing reality that Black Americans are less able to access healthcare services than White Americans and are, on average, substantially less healthy. A major reason for this is that the ACA alone could not really remediate the long history and present reality of systemic and individual racism in the United States. That is, it could not change the pervasive disparities in the economic, social, and political status of Black Americans and White Americans, which, in turn, results in racial disparities in the quality of healthcare people receive.

A Glaring Disparity: Patient Race and Healthcare Quality

Beyond the differences between Black Americans and White Americans in getting access to healthcare, there are also racial disparities in the quality of care they actually receive. The Agency for Healthcare Research and Quality (AHRQ) of the DHHS issues regular reports on "quality of care" in the United States [7]. The 2021 report included the results of all the studies published between 2017 and 2019 that examined Black–White disparities in the overall quality of care [8]. These studies used observations of actual medical interactions, data from medical records, and patient self-reports. In 42 percent of these studies, Black patients received a lower quality of care than did White patients. In contrast, White patients received a poorer quality of care than Black patients in about 11 percent of the studies. Some examples of the lower-quality care provided to Black patients include a greater number of deaths following bypass surgery, less provision of post-surgery radiation treatments for women with breast cancer, and fewer tests for viral load among patients with HIV. The level of disparities in the quality of care was virtually unchanged from previous reports by the AHRQ. Thus, even after the ACA came into force and Medicaid was expanded, Black patients continued to experience poorer quality healthcare than do White patients.

Another major aspect of the quality of care that patients receive is continuity among the medical personnel who treat them. Continuity of care requires a coordinated plan for treating a patient. This requires effective communication among members of a patient's care team, comparable treatments across healthcare providers, and good coordination when a patient moves from one clinic setting to another. In general, patients tend to receive better medical care when there is continuity of care among the different healthcare providers they see.

In 67 percent of the studies reported by AHRQ, Black patients had poorer continuity of care than did White patients; only one study found they had better continuity of care. One major cause of less continuity of care and a number of other disparities in quality of care is that Black patients and White patients are likely to see healthcare providers in different kinds of healthcare facilities.

American Healthcare: Still Separate and Unequal

It has been about 60 years since segregated healthcare facilities and the refusal to treat a person because of their race were ruled unconstitutional or prohibited by laws passed at both federal and state levels. The reality, however, is there is still a substantial amount of de facto discrimination in the medical care that Black Americans and White Americans receive. One imortant aspect of this is that the social disadvantages and economic inequities that are consequences of systemic racism still significantly influence where Black people seek medical care.

The Choice of Healthcare Facilities: What Is Available and Affordable

Social and economic factors are major reasons why Black patients, especially those who are poor, are disproportionately more likely than White patients to be seen in community health centers and/or hospital emergency departments [9]. To be clear, because White people are a numerical majority in the United States, the absolute number of White patients who are seen at community health centers and emergency departments is much greater than the number of Black patients. However, in terms of proportions within each group, Black patients are dramatically overrepresented at these kinds of facilities.

Walk Right In: Community Health Centers and Emergency Departments
Community health centers are nonprofit clinics that primarily serve uninsured or publicly insured patients. They are supported in part by a government program separate from Medicaid [10]. These facilities are typically located in neighborhoods where it has been determined there is the greatest need for more medical care. The rationale for where these centers are usually located makes sense. For example, the Philadelphia neighborhoods chosen to house community health centers were determined by the percentage of residents who had no health insurance or who had public health insurance [11]. Although there is no evidence that locations for community health centers are determined by the racial composition of a neighborhood, the reality is that community health centers in urban areas are predominately located in neighborhoods with fewer resources and greater poverty, and these are very often neighborhoods in which most of the residents are Black. In contrast, most well-resourced private medical centers are located in relatively affluent and predominantly White areas.

Black people are also about 1.5 times more likely to use emergency departments at hospitals for their medical care than are members of any other racial or ethnic group [12]. The ACA reduced the usage of emergency departments for many groups of Americans, but it did not affect the percentage of Black patients who use emergency departments for their medical care. Emergency departments are open 24 hours a day and required to treat any patient who requests care whether or not they have insurance.[2]

There are a number of possible reasons why Black patients are disproportionally more likely to be seen at community health centers or emergency departments. Lower direct costs of receiving medical care almost certainly play a role. Community health centers often have sliding fee schedules based on a patient's ability to pay and, as we said, emergency departments are at least theoretically supposed to treat anyone who comes

---

[2] However, some private hospitals do engage in inappropriate "dumping." This is a practice in which they tell indigent patients they must go to public hospitals.

to them even if the patient is not able to pay for the treatment. In short, the out-of-pocket costs of medical care may be less at these facilities than at private for-fee medical practices or at for-profit urgent care centers run by these practices.

It is also likely true that for many Black Americans community health centers and emergency departments may provide more accessible and convenient healthcare than do private medical practices. With regard to accessibility, most private medical practices require an appointment with a specific healthcare provider. Making such an appointment is relatively simple for individuals who have an ongoing relationship with their health-care providers. However, as already noted, Black Americans are much less likely to have such relationships than are White Americans. Community health centers and emergency departments do not require appointments; usually, patients can simply walk in.

In addition, most private medical practices have "regular" business hours. That is, they may only be open from 8:00 a.m. to 5:00 or 6:00 p. m., with only limited appointments in the evening or on weekends. Community health centers are often open outside this limited time corri-dor (e.g., during weekend hours). Emergency departments, of course, are open 24 hours a day, seven days a week. Thus, these kinds of healthcare facilities may be a more convenient place to receive medical care for people whose work schedules might prevent them from getting care at private medical practices. Seeing a physician during normal working hours is not a problem for people who can take time off work without any loss of salary, but for people who have an hourly job without such benefits, the loss of salary produces an additional nonmedical cost beyond what a physician may charge. In the United States, there are very many people who will lose pay if they have to see a physician, which forces some hard choices. There are endless iterations of how this can affect patient care.

For example, as part of a research project, one of the co-authors (LAP) shadowed a pediatric oncologist as he spoke to an adult accompanying a young cancer patient. The adult was unable to answer almost any of the physician's questions about the child's health status. After the adult and child left the room, the co-author expressed surprise at how little the person he assumed to be the parent seemed to know about their critically ill child's health status. The physician turned and, with some irritation at the insensitivity of this comment, explained that the adult was not the child's parent. He was the child's uncle; he had been recruited to take the child to the needed appointment because the child's mother could not get time off from work. Actually, this was a common kind of problem for many of the low-income families seen at this clinic. In interviews about the challenges they faced, parents at this cancer clinic quite frequently talked about the serious problem of finding child care for the patient's siblings. Sometimes they even had to reschedule appointments for the child with cancer because there was no one to take care of their other children.

There are no precise statistics that we are aware of that document how many Black Americans are employed in hourly as opposed to salaried jobs, but Black workers are almost twice as likely to be in hourly minimum-wage jobs as are White workers. Also, across all jobs, Black workers' salaries are about 70 percent lower than those of White workers [13, 14]. Thus, it seems reasonable to speculate that because of the hours they are open, community health centers and emergency departments may provide a way for many Black Americans to obtain medical care without incurring these additional nonmedical costs of lost wages. There are, however, drawbacks to receiving healthcare at these kinds of facilities.

Walk-in Care and Healthcare Disparities
Because patients are frequently "walk-ins," it is unlikely that they will see the same healthcare professional from one visit to the next. As we noted earlier, when there is better continuity of care (e.g., regularly seeing the same physician), the quality of care received is generally higher. One reason for the lack of continuity is that there are often no medical records readily available for walk-ins. As a result, the healthcare professionals who serve these patients may only have patients' self-reports of what medications they are using and what past medical problems they may have had. It is very difficult for patients to provide accurate information about the medications they are taking and to accurately recall medical problems that occurred more than a few months earlier. Usually, only about 50 percent of this kind of information is accurate, and the percentage is worse for patients who did not complete high school [15]. Thus, important information needed for accurate diagnoses and treatments may be missing or even wrong. Moreover, although the ACA and other government programs did much to improve the quality of care provided at community health centers, these centers are still likely to provide much poorer continuity of care for patients than would be the case for patients who have a regular medical provider [16].

There are also racial disparities in the quality of care that Black patients and White patients receive in emergency departments. A study of about one million patients admitted to emergency departments over 12 years found that Black patients were less likely than White patients to be classified as needing immediate or urgent care [17]. They were also less likely to receive blood tests, any sort of imaging, or treatment procedures that would address the problem that brought them to the hospital. Additionally, fewer Black patients than White patients were subsequently admitted as patients by the hospitals associated with emergency departments [18]. Of course, it is possible that these kinds of disparities may be due in part to Black patients being more likely to use emergency departments for routine medical care. Thus, they may be less likely to be admitted to the hospital after emergency department visits than White patients because, on average, their medical needs were not as serious.

However, there are other racial disparities in treatment at emergency departments that seem to be determined more by a patient's race than by the patient's medical conditions. Differences in medical needs are only a part of the story. One of the more dramatic examples of racial inequities in emergency departments is the use of physical restraints. One study showed that, even after statistically controlling for things such as history of violence, homelessness, and medical diagnosis, Black patients were significantly more likely to be put in restraints when they visited an emergency department [19]. Further, as we discuss in Chapter 6, there are widespread disparities in the treatments that hospitalized Black patients and White patients receive for the same medical problems.

There is also considerable evidence that when Black patients come to emergency departments, they experience longer wait times than do White patients. This is true even when Black patients and White patients have equally serious medical problems when they arrive [17]. Longer wait times lead to patients being more likely to leave without being seen, and Black patients and low-income, poorly insured patients are more likely than other patients to leave an emergency department without having been seen by a healthcare provider [20, 21]. This, in turn, may be due to something that we discussed Chapter 3: There are fewer hospitals and other kinds of healthcare facilities available for the residents of predominantly Black neighborhoods, so their emergency departments may be more crowded with longer wait times.

Hospital Inequality: Another Healthcare Disparity

Black (and Latinx) patients are disproportionately more likely than White patients to be treated at so-called safety-net hospitals. These are hospitals that have high numbers of Medicaid and uninsured patients. Reflecting the very well-documented racial and economic disparities in health, which we discussed in the Introduction chapter, so-called safety-net hospitals are also likely to treat sicker patients [22–24]. The ACA and the expansion of Medicaid were expected to eliminate racial imbalances in the kind of hospitals where Black patients and White patients are treated, but overall, they have not [25]. As a group, the hospitals where Black patients are more likely to be treated are of lower quality than those where White patients are more likely to be treated. For example, a study that collected data from 26 states found that indicators of poor surgical practices (e.g., number of respiratory failures, infections, and/or blood clots after surgeries) were substantially higher in the hospitals where Black patients were overrepresented than in those where White patients were overrepresented [26]. Another study showed that as the percentage of Black patients in a hospital increased, so did the incidence of problems with patient safety. The patients in these hospitals were more at risk for developing bedsores, having adverse reactions to some drug given to them, and contracting new infections while they were patients at these hospitals [27].

Of course, ratings of hospitals' quality of care and safety record sometimes reflect factors beyond the control of hospital administrators and staff. Such ratings are often based on how many patients are readmitted shortly after they are discharged. This outcome is, however, often determined as much by the characteristics of patients when they enter a hospital as the hospital's practices. Not only are the patients treated at safety-net hospitals likely to be sicker than those treated at better-resourced hospitals, but also they are more likely to be poor, unemployed, without health insurance, and have limited education (i.e., they are at greater social risk) [28]. These factors may create post-discharge health problems for the patients discharged from safety-net hospitals and it is more likely they will need to return to the hospital for further care.

Being judged as a lower-quality hospital may, in turn, create a vicious circle. As an incentive to improve hospital quality, government healthcare programs base a certain portion of their reimbursements on specific performance measures [29, 30]. Such penalties can cost a hospital in excess of $200,000 per year. Thus, a program reasonably intended to reduce government healthcare expenditures may further lower the quality of the care poor and/or Black patients receive at these hospitals.

Another factor that may affect the quality of safety-net hospitals is the kind of insurance that their patients have. Medicaid reimbursements for hospital care are substantially lower than those from either private insurance or Medicare [31]. As a consequence, hospitals that treat high percentages of Medicaid patients often have fewer and lower-quality resources to treat patients. The physicians at these hospitals who treat Medicaid patients also receive lower payments than they would receive from private insurance or even Medicare patients [32]. The level of payment a physician receives for their services is a strong predictor of what type of patients the physician will choose to see. For example, a study of physicians in general practice found they would accept 90 percent of new patients who have private insurance but less than 70 percent of new patients covered by Medicaid [33]. A consequence of this discrepancy is that there are fewer physicians willing to work at these safety-net hospitals.

The persistence of these kinds of healthcare disparities does not mean that Medicaid has failed in its mission to broaden healthcare for people who are economically disadvantaged. Medicaid patients still have better healthcare access than those without any insurance [34]. Rather, our point is that the economics of healthcare in the United States play a critical role in the racial disparities that exist within US healthcare systems.

"Steering" and Healthcare: Patient, "Go Where I Send Thee"

When there is a medical emergency, hospitals of higher and lower quality should be equally available to patients. However, Black patients are more likely than White patients to be taken to a lower-quality hospital. This kind of "steering" was once a common practice in real estate. It involved real estate agents only showing their clients homes or apartments in neighborhoods where the race of the majority of residents matched that of the clients. White people were only taken to predominantly White neighborhoods, and Black people were only taken to Black neighborhoods. Steering in real estate is now illegal, and the increasing use of online real estate listings probably has made it much less common than it once was. It turns out, however, that race-based steering in the choice of hospitals where patients are taken is still alive and fairly active.

This can be clearly seen in where emergency medical services (EMS) take patients with a medical emergency. One might assume that in a medical emergency the race or ethnicity of a patient should not make any difference in terms of which hospital an EMS crew chooses for them. However, a nationwide study of where EMS crews take patients found that among Black patients and White patients living in the same zip code and with similar healthcare coverage (i.e., Medicare patients), White patients were more likely to be taken to the closest hospital than were Black patients. Black patients were significantly more likely than White patients to be taken to a safety-net hospital, even though another hospital might have been much closer [35].

New York City provides a case study of these kinds of disparities. The majority of White New Yorkers are treated at hospitals that belong to large healthcare systems with substantial resources. In contrast, the majority of Black New Yorkers needing hospitalization are treated at public hospitals (or small independent ones) with fewer resources. These hospitals are located in low-income neighborhoods and have high numbers of uninsured or Medicaid patients. This disparity cannot be explained by whether or not a patient had health insurance or the geographic location of a hospital. For example, the New York University Langone Medical Center, one of the premier hospitals in the United States in terms of care and research, is located literally next door to the publicly funded Bellevue Hospital. In 2020, 9 percent of the patients at Langone were Black compared to 26 percent at Bellevue [36].

There is some reason to believe that these patterns concerning where Black patients and White patients will be taken for treatment may primarily reflect the past history of de jure or de facto racial segregation in the hospitals where Black patients and White patients were usually treated. Healthcare providers (and perhaps even patients) may continue these racial patterns without any conscious intent to provide Black people with poorer care [37]. Nonetheless, a patient's race should not influence where they are taken for medical care. Because resources vary between hospitals, this likely has the effect of increasing racial disparities in the quality of care that Black patients and White patients receive.

The kind of hospitals where Black patients are likely to be taken to receive medical care can have serious medical consequences for them. As we discussed in the Introduction chapter, the COVID-19-related mortality rates for Black people have been substantially higher than those for White people, and Black patients and White patients with COVID-19 were frequently treated at different hospitals. A 2021 article reported on the JAMA Network looked at the impact of hospital characteristics on racial disparities in mortality rates among patients with COVID-19. The authors of this study gathered data on patient characteristics (e.g., age, comorbidities, and income) and hospital characteristics (e.g., rural or urban, large or small, profit or nonprofit) from 1,200 hospitals. The researchers found that, in the hospitals they studied, the mortality rates for Black patients were much higher than for White patients. Significantly, the researchers also showed that the characteristics of the hospitals where patients were treated predicted patient mortality much better than did patients' personal characteristics. In essence, the kind of hospital where a patient with COVID-19 was treated was at least as important a predictor of patient mortality as their race or medical condition when they entered the hospital.

The researchers then conducted a computer-generated simulation in which they examined what the disparity in mortality rates would have been if Black patients had been treated at hospitals with the same characteristics as those that had treated White patients. The simulation showed that if the hospitals that had disproportionately treated Black patients had the same characteristics as the hospitals that had disproportionately treated the White patients, the mortality rate for Black patients with COVID-19 would have been significantly reduced. Indeed, it would have been almost exactly the same as it had been for White patients [38].

"Out of Pocket": Income and Disparities in Healthcare

All of these findings lead to the clear conclusion that Black Americans are significantly disadvantaged relative to White Americans when it comes to the quality of the healthcare they receive. These disparities cut across specific diseases and geographic regions. While many of these disparities have been reduced in recent years, they stubbornly persist. They reflect the impact of the large-scale historical, social, economic, and political inequalities that exist in America. That is, the one common factor underlying all of the healthcare inequities we have discussed thus far is the large disparity in income and wealth between Black Americans and White Americans.

One major reason for this is that America does not have a single-payer system for supporting all of the costs of all Americans' healthcare. A single-payer system is one in which a single government agency would pay for all or a substantial portion of all Americans' medical care. Medicare is an example of a single-payer system for Americans over 65. Medicare, however, only covers 80 percent of patients' often substantial medical fees and, for most Americans, the system in place is a patchwork of private and public insurance plans that often only partially pay for their healthcare. These plans frequently result in there being large unpaid balances for healthcare that are the responsibility of an individual patient and/or their family. The United States is fairly unique in this respect. Healthcare systems that provide comprehensive or "universal" payments for all or most of their citizens' healthcare costs are the norm in Europe (e.g., the United Kingdom and Germany), Asia (e.g., Japan and Pakistan), Australia, South America (e.g., Chile and Peru), and other countries in North

America (Canada, Mexico) [39]. The United States is the only industrialized country in the world without a government-sponsored single-payer system for all of its citizens [40].

This does not mean that some sort of single-payer system would eliminate all racial and ethnic disparities in healthcare in the United States. These kinds of healthcare disparities still exist within countries that have single-payer systems. However, the way in which healthcare is financed in the United States means that a primary determinant of the quality of the healthcare people receive is, as we noted earlier, their economic status. This is reflected in the fact that the best single predictor of an American's health is their socioeconomic status – the higher their socioeconomic status, the healthier they are.

Although there may be some specific instances in which explicit and virulent individual racism results in a Black person being deprived of healthcare, that is really not the problem we are addressing here. The kinds of widespread and formal racial animus that existed in the US medical system until the mid-twentieth century are not the major reasons for the kinds of healthcare disparities that exist today. However, the systemic racism that exists in the United States is. And, as we have suggested elsewhere, in many ways this is a much more insidious and difficult problem to solve because contemporary systemic racism operates in a more subtle and less blatant manner than the overt racism of the past. Thus, the effects of systemic disparities are far less likely to be viewed as a *racial* injustice that needs to be addressed.

"Physician, Heal Thyself": Systemic Racism within American Medicine [41]

In February 2021, JAMA presented a podcast of a conversation between two of their editors, Edward Livingstone, MD, and Mitchell Katz, MD, both of whom had substantial reputations in the medical community. The podcast featured their views on whether racism was a major problem in the practice of medicine. They did not think it was. Here are two quotes from the podcast that caught many people's attention: "No physician is a racist, so how can there be structural [i.e., systemic] racism in health care?" And, "What you are talking about isn't so much racism . . . it isn't their [i.e., the patients'] race, it isn't their color, it's their socioeconomic status."

A few days after this podcast first appeared, it was withdrawn. It was a major embarrassment for JAMA and the journal's sponsor, the AMA. After taking the podcast off the air, the editor-in-chief of JAMA publicly denounced the comments made in it as "inaccurate, hurtful, and inconsistent with the standards of JAMA" [42].[3] The opinions expressed in the podcast were certainly unique in their insensitivity to the problem of racism in America, in general, and in healthcare, in particular. The participants in the podcast demonstrated a remarkable lack of understanding of what racism is, how it affects the medical profession, and the ways it influences the lives of Black Americans (as well as other racial and ethnic minorities) who need medical care. They seemed oblivious to the ways in which systemic (and individual) racism directly affects how healthcare is provided in the United States. In the following pages, we provide further evidence concerning how systemic racism in American medicine produces significant racial disparities in healthcare. This evidence directly refutes the positions of the two physicians. We begin with the dearth of Black physicians.

The Very Narrow and Leaky Pipeline: The Dearth of Black Healthcare Professionals

Black people are seriously underrepresented in the healthcare professions. Black Americans comprise about 15 percent of the US population. However, less than 10 percent of registered nurses in the United States self-identify as Black. Black people represent less than 4 percent of the rapidly expanding profession of physicians' assistants [43]. But, the racial disparity with the greatest impact on healthcare in the United States is the dearth of Black physicians. In 2019, about 5 percent of all active physicians self-identified as Black or African American. Over the last 80 years, the percentage of Black male physicians has increased by .01 percent, and the percentage of Black female physicians has grown only by 2.7 percent [44]. There is little evidence that this pattern will change in the future. This is in contrast to the awarding of advanced degrees in other disciplines. While there is still substantial underrepresentation of Black people in graduate schools, there has been a very steady increase in the number of Black students earning doctorates in nonmedical disciplines in the past 20 years [45].

In specialty areas of medicine, such as cancer, the underrepresentation of Black physicians is much greater [46]. In 2019, for example, about

---

[3] Although the podcast no longer exists on the JAMA website, Dr. Clarence Gravlee, professor of anthropology at the University of Florida, was able to post a transcript of it. Interested readers may be able to find it at https://static1.squarespace.com/static/5d7d985bfc6bb40f1dfae872/t/6061d1425689961a044a3ac0/1617023298545/Transcript+-+Structural+Racism+for+Doctors.pdf.

2 percent of all the medical oncologists were Black. This means that out of the almost 13,000 medical oncologists in the United States, just 430 identify as Black. Yet, the most recent estimate available is that about 2,000,000 Black people have been diagnosed with cancer in the past ten years [47]. Thus, the ratio of Black patients to Black oncologists is about 4650-to-1. The ratio of White patients to White oncologists is about 1440-to-1.

The dearth of Black physicians rather obviously reflects the very limited population of Black medical students. Black students comprise less than 3 percent of the current enrollment at medical schools and about 6 percent of their graduates [48, 49]. The reasons why relatively few Black people are currently pursuing medical degrees begin long before a student applies to medical school. There are huge racial disparities in the quality of K–12 education for Black children and White children, who even today largely attend de facto segregated schools [50]. It is beyond the scope of this book to discuss all these educational disparities in the detail they deserve. Many of them, however, involve the absence of math and science classes and programs specifically designed to prepare students for college science curricula. These educational disparities reduce the chances that a Black college student will successfully complete a major in premedical studies (i.e., a premed major).

There are also serious financial roadblocks in the path of Black undergraduate college students, who might be interested in a postgraduate career in medicine. They are much less likely than White students to be supported by their families and must therefore finance their education on their own, usually by holding part- or full-time jobs [51, 52]. Only 29 percent of Black college students report feeling financially secure while in college. This usually means that it is harder for them to graduate college in four years and makes it more likely that they will accumulate substantial debt. Black students are five times more likely to default on their student loans than White students [53].

Furthermore, the costs of getting a medical degree are extremely high. In 2022, the average per year cost for a student at a US medical school was over $57,000, and the total cost of medical training was just over $230,000 [54]. There are some scholarships, but most medical students have to borrow money to attend medical school and graduate with enormous debt. These financial factors alone would deter many Black students from considering medical school, especially those students already saddled with substantial debt from their undergraduate education.

Academic practices at many universities also may make it less likely that a Black student can go on to medical school. There is a very low completion rate among Black undergraduate students who enroll in pre-med studies at most predominantly White colleges and universities; this is especially true if the Black student is also poor [55]. This is not simply because Black students are less successful in these majors; rather, it involves something often called a "leaky pipeline." This term refers to the fact that Black students leave these majors and transfer to another major at higher rates than do White students. Some observers might interpret this difference as due to low levels of interest and motivation among Black premed majors, but there is one very significant fact that contradicts this explanation: This pattern of Black students prematurely leaving premed majors is much less common at most historically Black colleges and universities (HBCUs).

Although they represent only 3 percent of all degree-granting institutions, HBCU graduates make up 17 percent of all the Black applicants to medical schools [56]. Further, many of these Black students are accepted to medical schools and go on to become physicians. Overall, 50 percent of all Black physicians in the United States obtained their undergraduate degrees at a HBCU. Just one historically Black university, Xavier University in New Orleans, has consistently graduated many more successful medical school applicants and graduates than have much larger public universities, as well as private universities with a strong focus on medicine. This includes universities such as Harvard and Johns Hopkins [57]. There is no single explanation for this striking disparity, but a major factor appears to be the way that Xavier (along with many other HBCUs) approaches the education of premed students. It stands in stark contrast to most large, predominantly White institutions.

At many universities with small enrollments of minority students, a major part of a premed curriculum includes culling out the supposedly "weaker" students. This is a process that is sometimes called "creaming" because these schools only want to graduate the "cream of the crop." Premedical curricula at these schools often include courses that are specifically designed to weed out supposedly weaker students [58]. Although many universities are now trying to find ways to address racial and ethnic disparities in how well students are prepared for premed and similar majors, such programs are not yet very effective in achieving these goals. Thus, selective policies of this sort are likely to have a disproportionately negative impact on Black students and members of other socioeconomically disadvantaged racial and ethnic minorities.

At many HBCUs, however, there are often much more extensive and focused attempts to address these possible problems and to provide support for students who want to pursue a career in medicine.[4] These institutions offer different kinds of help and resources to students encountering difficulties in their premed major in order to maximize rather than minimize the number of students who successfully complete a premed curriculum. The result is that although the HBCUs typically have substantially fewer resources than many other colleges and universities in the United States, they do a much better job of graduating Black students who go on to medical school. Nonetheless, the challenges facing those Black students who enter predominantly White medical schools are significant.

Medical Schools: White on White

Black people are dramatically underrepresented in the faculties of medical schools. In 2020, about 63 percent of the faculty self-identified as White. Black men comprised 2.8 percent of all medical school faculty, and Black women represented 5.1 percent. Eighty-two percent of the department chairs and 90 percent of the deans at medical schools were also White [59, 60]. Independent of any explicit or implicit racism among the White faculty or students, this very limited representation of Black faculty members in medical schools hardly makes it a welcoming environment for Black students.

Racial Bias in Medical School Curricula
Compounding the problems facing Black medical students is how topics related to race are often taught in medical schools. In 2021, 11 physicians reported on a project in which they systematically analyzed the content of a large number of lectures given in the preclinical (or basic) curriculum at a number of different medical schools [61]. The authors began by noting that although race is a socially constructed category "that reflects the impact of unequal social experiences on health, ... medical education and practice have not evolved to reflect ... the relationships among race, racism, and health." The evidence the authors presented in support of this claim showed that the misuse of the term "race" and racial stereotyping was quite common in medical school lectures and curricula.

---

[4] The author, Malcolm Gladwell, has a podcast called "The Dillard Project" as part of his "Revisionist History" series. It discusses some of the differences between how premed majors are treated at HBCUs and predominantly White universities that have small numbers of Black students. Its insights into the racial disparities in higher education extend far beyond just the preparation of physicians.

Instructors often use outdated terms for different racial groups, which implicitly (or maybe explicitly) suggests there are biological differences among these groups. To wit, it is relatively common for faculty to use the term "Caucasian" to describe White people. This term has its origins in the scientific racism of the eighteenth century and was used by the German philosopher Cristoph Meiners to describe a skull found in the Caucasus region of Russia. Meiners believed that people from this region were the Whitest people in the world, and that people from outside this region were "inferior" and "animal-like" [62]. The term "Caucasian" has long been abandoned by geneticists and other scientists who study differences in human populations. However, it seems to be alive and well in the lectures given in medical schools.

Another related practice is calling all Black patients "African Americans." In one case, for example, an instructor described a patient born and raised in Nigeria as "African American." Such an approach ignores the enormous diversity among Black people who live in the United States. Today, Black people in America come from a variety of different places around the world, and many would not identify their heritage as American. Using the term "African American" to describe this very diverse group of people suggests that "one size would fit them all" when it comes to their medical care.

The authors also found that it was common for instructors to fail to explain why certain diseases, such as sickle cell diseases are much more prevalent in Black Americans than White Americans. As we discussed in the Introduction chapter, sickle cell disease is common among any group of people whose origins are in areas where populations are at risk for malaria. (The sickle cell anomaly provides some protection against malaria.) Yet, this explanation why sickle cell disease patients in the United States are much more likely to be Black people is generally omitted, which could lead to the conclusion that only Black people develop sickle cell disease. This kind of conclusion is not only wrong, it also has significant potential ramifications in the treatment of Black patients. Compounding this type of problem, when instructors talked about differences between Black Americans and White Americans in the incidence of certain diseases, they rarely included any discussion of possible social determinants of such differences. For example, the higher rates of asthma among Black Americans are discussed without mentioning the presence of environmental hazards and low air quality in many under-resourced, predominantly Black neighborhoods (see Chapter 3).

Moreover, while there are now some very serious questions about how a patient's race is used in medical diagnoses and treatments (discussed later in this chapter), this topic was not presented in the medical school lectures that the researchers surveyed. Other studies conducted in clinical settings find that when supervising physicians say that Black patients and White patients should receive different drugs for the same disease, they typically fail to explain why or provide the scientific basis for this distinction. In one instance, when a Black medical student asked the supervising physician *why* they should administer different blood pressure drugs to Black patients and White patients, the physician did not give a reason. The physician simply replied that it was "the standard of care" [63]. This was a description of what is done, not an explanation of why.

Returning to the analyses of medical school lectures in the article, the authors reported there was also a tendency to pathologize Black patients. That is, there was a consistent message in the lectures that there is something about Black people that puts them at much greater risk for poor health. According to the authors of this study, "The cumulative effect of overrepresenting minorities as high-risk is the creation of an implicit link between race and predisposition to disease, which reinforces the view that race/ethnicity disparities in health stem from innate racial differences." The faculty members basically ignored the impact of systemic and individual racism on Black people's health despite the voluminous amount of research that demonstrates this causal relationship.

Further, racial stereotypes were often part of how Black patients were presented to medical students. In a separate report on the shortcomings in how medical schools address race-related issues, Naomi Nkinsi, a fourth-year medical student at the University of Washington, recounted that when her professors presented students with pictures of Black patients and White patients, the White patients were much more likely to seem happy and well-to-do. She continued, "We [i.e., Black people] were only ever depicted when they are talking about STIs [sexually transmitted infections], diabetes, or dying during childbirth. It's almost as though we don't exist in medicine outside of this context." She concluded by saying, "It's not hard to imagine why people go out and practice medicine with so much bias. That's how we are being taught to practice it. The fact that professors and administrators don't see these issues until it's pointed out to them shows they were taught with the same bias" [64].

Racial Bias in Medical Training and Beyond
Compounding the troubling racial biases that percolate throughout medical curricula is the fact that medical schools are not immune from the kinds of individual racism that exist within society at large. Dr. Damon

Tweedy, the author of *Black Man in a White Coat*, recounts a painful experience from his own time in medical school. He had just entered a lecture hall when the instructor in his class approached him and asked, "Are you here to fix the lights?" When Dr. Tweedy responded "no," the instructor frowned and said, "Then what are you doing here?" Dr. Tweedy's experiences are similar to those reported by many other Black medical students. They report feeling socially isolated, have a lower sense of belonging, and that they are often the targets of racial stereotyping and overt discrimination [65, 66]. A survey of graduates of all the accredited medical schools in the United States disclosed that about 20 percent of the graduates who were members of a racial or ethnic minority reported that they had experienced discrimination based on their race or ethnicity [67]. Discrimination came from both other students and faculty members, and was often manifested in faculty members' letters of recommendation for residencies. Black students were much less likely than White students to be described with words such as "exceptional," "best," or "bright," but there did not appear to be any objective difference in the two groups of students' academic records that would account for the differences in the words selected [68].

The contents of such letters of recommendation can have significant career consequences for Black medical students. Being accepted for training in medical specialties, for example, usually requires strong recommendations from the physicians who practice these specialties. And, race sometimes plays a bigger role in these recommendations than actual qualifications. For example, one Black physician recalls what happened when he asked the chair of neurosurgery at the medical school he was attending for advice on how to become a neurosurgeon. The physician, who knew nothing about him other than he was Black said, "Why are you asking this? You have to be smart to be a neurosurgeon." It is worth noting, however, that the Black physician persevered and is now chair of neurosurgery at a large medical school [69].

Practicing Black physicians are also often the recipients of racist words and deeds from both colleagues and patients. Dr. Milton Little, one of the very few Black orthopedic trauma surgeons in the United States, described some of his own experiences, "I can't count how many times I walked into a patient's room and they asked if I was the person who would be transporting them. I've had patients refuse my care because I was black" [70]. Other Black physicians, especially women, report that patients mistaking them for janitors or food service workers is a fairly common experience [69].

We were unable to find comprehensive data on attrition and graduation rates for Black medical students and White medical students nationally, but a survey of the top 14 medical schools in the United States reported in the *Journal of Blacks in Higher Education* indicated that graduation rates for Black medical students were generally equal to that of White students [71]. However, the cost of medical school and awareness of the racial climate at many medical schools may still have a "chilling effect" on Black students considering a medical career. That is, many talented and qualified Black undergraduates may simply decide not to apply to medical school because of what they know about the serious financial and interpersonal challenges they would likely face.

We do not want to suggest that medical schools are totally insensitive to the challenges faced by Black students or the problems in the content of some medical curricula. In recent years, there has been a dramatic increase in the number of programs designed to address this aspect of systemic racism in medical education. It is an effort strongly endorsed by organizations like the American Association of Medical Colleges and the American Medical Association. It is too soon, however, to determine whether such efforts will increase the number of Black students who attend and graduate from medical schools or change the way race and racial health disparities are taught in medical schools. But such changes are critical to the reduction of racial health disparities in the United States.

It Pays to Be a Physician, But Not as Much If You Are a Black Physician
Currently in the United States, there are large racial disparities in the average incomes of Black physicians and White physicians. When compared to White male physicians, Black male physicians earn about $65,000 less a year; a Black female physician earns about $85,000 less. This disparity is smaller when Black female physicians are compared to White female physicians; however, this primarily reflects the fact that, overall, women in medicine generally make much less than men [72]. Thus, there is less room for a racial salary gap.

Although our primary emphasis in this chapter has been on Black physicians, many of the same barriers that exist for them also exist for Black nurses. For example, Black nurses' hourly wage is 97 percent of that of White nurses [73]. When multiplied by 40 hours and 52 weeks, this becomes a substantial racial disparity in the annual salaries of Black nurses and White nurses.

There is no simple explanation as to why Black healthcare professionals earn so much less than White healthcare professionals. Racial discrimination that occurred earlier in their careers may play an important role. For example, a key factor in an early career physician being accepted for a residency in the most competitive (and highest paying) medical specialties (e.g., plastic surgery, radiation oncology) is whether they had been chosen for the medical honor society, Alpha Omega Alpha, when they were in medical school. White medical students are six times more likely to be inducted into this honor society than are Black medical students, even when the two groups have comparable scores on medical licensing examinations and a similar number of scientific publications [74].

There may also be reasons for the racial disparity in incomes other than discrimination. One of these may be what kind of medical career Black physicians and White physicians want to pursue. A 2019 survey conducted by the American Association of Medical Colleges found that whereas 60 percent of Black medical students say they plan to practice in a medically underserved area, only about 34 percent of White medical students express the same kind of interest. As already discussed, physician salaries are lower in most medical facilities located in these medically underserved areas.

Some Black physicians claim that all these factors combine to cause more Black physicians than White physicians to leave the field [75]. We could not locate data that support this statement. Still, it is hard to imagine that the kinds of experiences we have presented do not affect Black physicians' decisions about continuing in this profession. The formal and informal barriers to Black people becoming physicians and other kinds of healthcare providers are, in and of themselves a social injustice. However, they also has important implications for racial disparities in health and healthcare.

The Impact of Racial Concordance between Patients and Physicians on Medical Outcomes

Does a Black patient seeing a physician of the same race make a difference in medical outcomes? The view of the Association of American Medical Colleges is that similarities between patients and their physicians, including being of the same race (i.e., race concordance), are quite important. The Association concludes that having these similarities is particularly valuable for patients from underserved groups: "When health care providers have life experiences that more closely match the experiences of their patients, patients tend to be more satisfied with their care and to adhere to medical advice. This effect has been seen in studies addressing racial, ethnic, and sexual minority communities when the demographics of health care providers reflect those of underserved populations" [76]. Research shows that there is, in fact, a substantial benefit to Black patients from seeing Black physicians rather than White physicians [77].

For example, Black patients feel they are more involved in their medical visits when their physician is also Black [78]. Adherence to medication routines is also greater among Black patients who see Black physicians than among Black patients who see White physicians [79]. One study found Black patients with a coronary problem were more likely to consider having a coronary bypass procedure when they saw a Black physician than when they saw a White physician [80].

The Benefits of Racial Concordance: Experimental Evidence

A very innovative experiment conducted in Oakland, California, by Dr. Marcella Alsan, professor of public policy and health at Harvard University, and her colleagues demonstrated other benefits of racial concordance for Black patients [81]. The researchers recruited 1,300 Black men from the Oakland community for their study and essentially created their own health clinic by enlisting the assistance of eight Black physicians and six non-Black physicians. Neither the physicians nor their patients were aware of the study's purpose. When the patients arrived at the clinic, they were given a list of preventive health services they could receive for free. These services included assessments of their weight and blood pressure and more invasive procedures that required a blood draw, such as testing for diabetes and cholesterol levels. Patients were asked to indicate which of these preventive services they were willing to have done. Not surprisingly, patients were generally more reluctant to receive the more invasive tests. The study participants were then randomly assigned to meet with one of the Black physicians or one of the non-Black physicians. All of the physicians were instructed to try to get the patients to receive the more invasive – but potentially more medically beneficial – tests. The results show the strong effects of the physicians' race on Black patients' decisions.

The Black participants who met with a Black physician were significantly more willing to receive the invasive tests than they had been prior to seeing a physician. In contrast, there was no increase in willingness to receive the invasive tests among the Black patients who saw a non-Black physician. Figure 5.1 shows the differences in the percentage of Black male patients who were willing to have one particular invasive test – a blood draw to measure their cholesterol – after seeing a Black physician versus those who saw a non-Black physician. Seeing a Black physician made the Black patients in the study more willing to have their blood drawn. And, this kind of difference was not limited to blood draws: Black patients who saw Black physicians were also more willing to receive flu vaccinations.

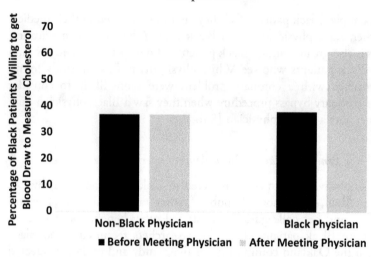

Figure 5.1   The benefits of racial concordance for Black patients. The percentage of Black patients who agreed to an invasive medical test before and after they were asked to take it by a non-Black physician or a Black physician.

Source: Alsan, M., Garrick, O., & Graziani, G. (2019). Does diversity matter for health? Experimental evidence from Oakland. *American Economic Review*, *109* (12), 4071–4111. Reproduced with permission of the American Economic Review. https://www.nber.org/system/files/working_papers/w24787/w24787.pdf

Racial Concordance and Patient Mortality

There is also evidence to suggest that race concordance between physicians and patients can reduce mortality rates for Black patients. Dr. Brian Greenwood, professor of information systems and operations at George Mason University, and his colleagues examined data for 1.8 million live births in the United States over a 23-year period [82]. The researchers compared infant mortality rates during their first year among Black newborns treated by Black physicians to mortality rates among Black newborns treated by White physicians. As discussed in the Introduction chapter, the mortality rate for Black babies is substantially higher than the mortality rate for White babies. The question in this study was whether being treated by a Black physician would reduce this racial disparity. The answer was "yes." The mortality rate among Black newborns treated by a White physician was 430 per 100,000 more than White newborns. However, the mortality rate among Black newborns treated by a Black physician was 173 per 100,000 more than White newborns. This was a 58 percent reduction in the racial mortality disparity. Notably, the race of a physician had no impact on mortality among White newborns. (Physician race also did not affect racial disparities in maternal mortality.)

This strong positive impact of physician–patient race concordance for the health of Black people was further demonstrated in a large study conducted in Florida. This research revealed that Black hospital patients who were assigned to Black physicians when they were admitted had significantly lower mortality rates than Black patients assigned to White physicians. Importantly, this was not because of higher mortality rates among the Black patients with White physicians; that is, having a White physician did not make it more likely that a Black patient would die. Rather, there was a decline in mortality among the Black patients with Black physicians relative to *all* patients in the hospital. In some as yet unspecified way, having a Black physician made it less likely that Black patients would die while they were in the hospital [83].

These kinds of data send a strong message about some of the actual medical consequences stemming from the dearth of Black physicians. However, the data do *not* indicate that having a White physician jeopardizes the health of Black patients or that Black patients should only see Black physicians. In fact, suggesting that racial concordance between physicians and their patients is the only factor that determines medical outcomes would essentially echo the arguments made in the early twentieth century by people like Abraham Flexner. When Flexner issued his report on the quality of medical education in the United States (see Chapter 4), he proposed that only Black physicians should treat Black patients. Such positions led to the continuation of the rigidly segregated practice of medicine that existed in America until about 60 years ago. Rather, the point here is that there are some potential advantages for Black patients being treated by Black physicians, but it is difficult for them to actually find the relatively few Black physicians.

Beyond the argument that Black patients might have better medical outcomes if there were more Black physicians, there is the matter of allowing Black patients (and other minority patients) to have the same range of options when they choose a physician as do White patients. Right now, the limited availability of Black physicians generally precludes this freedom of choice. Moreover, as long as the racial ratios in medical training and practice continue to not reflect the diversity of the US population, the voices and opinions of Black and other minority-group physicians may not be part of the development of professional and governmental health-related policies that affect all Americans.

The Use of Patient Race in Healthcare Decisions: A Lesson in Getting Things Wrong

Contemporary medicine continues to struggle with the best ways to consider the impact of a patient's assigned race on medical decisions. Although it is unlikely that any physician, if asked directly, would say that race is a biological fact rather than a social construct, race continues to be used in that way in many diagnoses. In addition, when resources are limited and decisions have to be made about how to allocate costly medical care, there may be a failure to adequately consider the impact of racial healthcare disparities on Black patients' need for such care.

Diagnostic Algorithms: An Incorrect Correction

A common part of contemporary medical care is to conduct a large number of standardized diagnostic tests, usually before a patient meets with their physician. The tests gather what are called biomarkers. Biomarkers are measurable substances in a person's body, such as the chemicals in a person's blood or urine. They provide information on the presence of certain diseases, infections, and other kinds of medical problems. Typically, biomarkers are entered into an algorithm. This is a mathematical equation that gives each of the biomarker measures and other patient attributes (e.g., age, weight, and very often their race) a numerical value, which reflects the importance it has been assigned, and then uses these values to compute a score. This score is supposed to be a precise estimate of how well specific bodily functions are working (e.g., how well a person's liver or kidney is functioning). The validity of such algorithms is rarely challenged by patients or their physicians because it is assumed they are based solely on objective medical science. The reality is quite different. Including patient race in the equations is often based on earlier racist theories of biological differences between Black people and White people. Moreover, many physicians may be unaware of how patient race originally became part of these algorithms and how race is actually being used in them.

Racist Myths and Estimates of People's Health
One example is that the lung capacity of patients identified as Black is assumed to be inherently less than those identified as White. In *Breathing Race into the Machine: The Surprising Career of the Spirometer from Planation to Genetics*, Dr. Lundy Braun, professor of pathology and

laboratory medicine at Brown University, traces this assumption back to racist medical theories in the nineteenth century. In particular, Dr. Brown disclosed the role of a southern physician, Dr. Samuel Cartwright, who was quite well known for his beliefs about the innate inferiority of Black people and his passionate support of slavery [84]. Cartwright used a device called the spirometer to measure the lung capacity of enslaved Black people and found that their lung capacity was less than that of White people.[5] Cartwright did not attribute this difference to the brutal conditions of slavery; rather, in keeping with his racist views, Cartwright claimed it was due to an innate difference between Black people and White people – a "deficiency in the negro" [85].

Although other studies conducted around the same time with free Black people did not show this difference, Cartwright's view prevailed and still shapes medical practice today. Currently, when the results of a spirometer test are entered into the algorithm used to compute what is "normal" lung capacity, race is also included. As a consequence of including race in the diagnostic equation, a lung capacity that would be considered abnormally low for a White person is often considered normal for a Black person. This could result in lung disease being underdiagnosed and thus undertreated in Black patients. This racial difference in diagnoses because of the fallacious "race correction" may have especially serious consequences for the many Black Americans who live in neighborhoods with toxic environments that can cause significant respiratory problems (see Chapter 3).

Another powerful example of the misuse of race in medical diagnoses has been estimates of kidney functions [86]. When a person receives a test for their kidney function, the estimate of how well their kidney is functioning is the Estimated Globular Filtration Rate (eGFR). The estimate is primarily, but not completely, based on how much creatinine a person has in their kidney. The more creatinine they have, the poorer is their kidney function, which is reflected in a lower eGFR value. Until 2022, the algorithm used to compute a patient's eGFR always included a patient's race. This inclusion almost always resulted in a patient identified as Black receiving a substantially higher eGFR score than a comparable patient identified as White. That is, because of the race correction, a Black person with exactly the same creatinine level as a White person would be diagnosed as having a healthier kidney function. The origins of this race correction appear to be the belief that Black people naturally release more

---

[5] The spirometer test involves a patient blowing as hard as they can into a device that assesses how easily and quickly a person can expel air from their lungs. It is still used to estimate lung capacity.

creatinine into their blood because they are more muscular than White people. This belief is rooted in very old racist stereotyping and myths about the strength of enslaved Black people – there is no scientific evidence that being Black is associated with naturally higher creatinine levels [86].

Another algorithm used to assess kidney problems also uses patients' assigned race. The STONE algorithm for identifying the presence of a kidney stone assumes that flank pain (pain in the lower back) is a much better indicator of kidney disease for non-Black patients than it is for Black patients [87]. Flank pain is therefore not given the same diagnostic value for Black patients as it is for White patients. The people who developed this scale do not provide any rationale for this race correction. However, as noted in several places in this book, underestimating the pain of Black people is embedded in the long history of slavery and racism in the United States. Its legacy in contemporary medicine has profound and pervasive effects on patient care and outcomes. As is the case in the race-corrected estimates of lung capacity, Black people with kidney disease have been underdiagnosed and under-treated. This became especially important in cases of serious kidney disease where the patient may actually need a kidney transplant. Because there are so few kidneys available for transplantation, estimates of kidney function are a major factor in deciding who gets a transplant. Thus, Black patients have been less likely than White patients to get needed kidney transplants due to incorrect race corrections included in diagnoses of this disease.[6]

Today, most professional organizations have issued recommendations that race no longer be included in estimates of kidney function [88]. This change occurred at a large number of medical facilities. Once the recommendation is fully accepted, this particular kind of systemic racism in medical diagnoses may become a thing of the past.[7] However, the fact remains that right now race corrections are still part of many algorithms used in diagnosis and risk assessment for medical procedures throughout the United States despite the absence of empirical data to support this practice (see Table 5.1). As Dr. Andrea Reid, dean at Harvard Medical School, said, "These are not remote historical issues around race-based

---

[6] Similar questionable race corrections exist in predictions of heart failure, transplant failures, hip fractures, developing certain cancers, and the risks of vaginal births.

[7] In 2022 the Board of Directors of the Organ Procurement and Transplantation Network passed a proposal, effective January, 2023, that would eliminate the inclusion of race in the tests used to decide if a patient is eligible for transplantation. https://optn.transplant.hrsa.gov/patients/by-organ/kidney/understanding-the-proposal-to-require-race-neutral-egfr-calculations/) It is too soon to know if the elimination of race in these tests has reduced the racial disparity in kidney transplants discussed earlier.

Table 5.1 *Medical algorithms that include race corrections*

Cardiology:
Heart Failure: Black patients are assumed to be at lower risk. Black patients may be less
  likely to be treated
Cardiac Surgery: Black patients are assumed to be at greater risk. Black patients may be less
  likely to receive surgery

Endocrinology:
Osteoporosis: Black women are assumed to be at less risk. Black women may be less likely
  to receive further evaluations
Bone fracture risk: Black women are assumed to be at lower risk. Black women may be less
  likely to receive therapies to prevent future fractures

Obstetrics:
Risk of vaginal birth after a prior Cesarian delivery: Black women are assumed to be at
  greater risk. Black women may be more likely to have Cesarian delivery, which involves
  more risks and greater costs

Oncology:
Breast Cancer Risk; Black women are assumed to be at lower risk. Black women may be
  discouraged from regular screening for cancer
Rectal Cancer Survival: Black patients are assumed to die sooner. Black patients may be less
  likely to receive additional, aggressive treatments

Urology:
Probability of urinary tract infection in young children; Black children are assumed to be at
  lower risk. Black children may not receive further evaluations

Source: D. Vyas, et al. (2020). Hidden in Plain Sight – Reconsidering the Use of Race
Correction in Clinical Algorithms. *New England Journal of Medicine*, *383*(3), 874–882.

recommendations. These are contemporary issues with disturbing [impli-
cations]" [63]. A clear example of this occurred in 2022. During the
COVID-19 pandemic many prisons released prisoners because they were
at special risk for COVID-19 infections. About 20,00 federal prisoners
have asked for early release because they have medical conditions that
would make them more susceptible to the effects of the COVID-19 virus.
One of these conditions is chronic kidney disease (CKD). Maurice
McPhatter is a Black prisoner who has one kidney and low kidney
function. If the new guidelines eliminating the race correction had been
applied for Mr. McPhatter, he almost certainly would have been released.
But the estimates for kidney function used in the federal prison system still
contain this correction. Thus, Mr. McPhatter was judged not to have a
medical problem that would put him at greater risk from COVID-19, and
he remains in prison [89]. There is currently a lawsuit intended to get the
federal prison system to drop this race correction in the algorithm for how
the kidney functions of Black prisoners are estimated.

Racial Bias and Pulse Oximetry: Ignoring the Obvious

There is another kind of diagnostic error that affects Black patients. It does not seem to be the product of racist myths but rather a systemic lack of concern about possible inaccuracies in estimating the amount of oxygen in a Black person's blood. A patient's blood oxygen level is an important vital sign that is measured in almost every single medical visit. Low blood oxygen levels can result in serious organ (e.g., kidney, liver) failures because they are deprived of critically needed oxygen. The most common way to measure blood oxygen levels is to use a pulse oximeter. This is a device that is simply placed on a person's finger and quickly produces estimates of blood oxygen levels.

In 2022, a group of physicians used data from a large group of patients with COVID-19 to compare how estimates of their blood oxgen levels obtained with a pulse oximeter compared with estimates of their blood oxygen levels obtained by drawing blood from the patients' arms (a more intrusive but more accurate measure) [90]. They expected there would be differences between the two estimates, but their question was whether the differences would be greater for patients in certain racial or ethnic groups. The estimates from the pulse oximeter device yielded substantially less accurate estimates of the oxygen levels for the Black (and Latinx) patients' blood than for the White patients. Importantly, among the Black and Latinx patients the pulse oximeter consistently yielded higher blood oxygen levels than what was actually the case. These inaccurate higher estimates indicated that these patients were in less medical distress, and thus these inaccurate estimates led to delayed treatment for the Black (and Latinx) patients. This kind of delay could have quite serious and dangerous consequences for patients infected with COVID-19.

Other studies disclosed the reason for this diagnostic error. The pulse oximeter works by shining two different lights through a patients' finger and bases the estimate of blood oxygen levels on the difference in how much light is absorbed – essentially how red is the blood. If a patient has darker color skin (as would be the case for many Black and Latinx patients), this distorts the measurement and yields inaccurate estimates, most commonly in the direction of overestimating blood oxygen levels [91].

Remarkably, these inaccuracies in estimating blood oxygen levels had actually been known for about 30 years, but there was no organized effort in the medical community to address this diagnostic error, which could deprive Black (and Latinx) patients of needed care. It is only now because of the spate of publications about this error and its adverse impact on Black and Latinx patients that physicians are calling for much-needed corrections in how the blood oxygen levels of people of color are estimated.

Patient Race and Medical Diagnoses: Another Perspective
Before we leave the topic of race corrections in diagnoses, it is important to note that there is not a consensus among physicians on how to use a patient's race in medical diagnosis and treatment. Some physicians argue that if they totally ignore a patient's race when making their diagnoses, they may miss an important predictor of certain diseases. Or, as Dr. Sally Satel argued in the *New York Times* op-ed, "When it comes to practicing medicine, stereotyping often works" [92]. There are certain diseases that differ in frequency across racial and ethnic groups, so we agree that there may be some instances where awareness of a patient's assigned race might be useful for medical diagnoses. Knowing patients' racial identification may also help physicians better understand Black patients' social background and the race-based challenges they may face in their lives, which can be useful in diagnoses and developing treatment plans.

Still, the fact remains that a physician's judgment of a patient's race is often based solely on the patient's physical appearance. Perceived race represents a highly problematic surrogate for the nature of a patient's genome. Assuming that a patient's race should, per se, always be part of diagnostic formulae or an individual physician's diagnostic judgments without having a clear and accurate scientific rationale for it is just one more way that racism can seriously disadvantage Black Americans. As Dr. Isaac Kahane, professor of biomedical informatics at Harvard Medical School, suggested, "When we use race in medicine and medical education, there ought to be a reason and we need to say what that reason is" [63].

Race and Predicting Need for Care: When Assigned Race Might Matter

Healthcare in America is incredibly expensive. Estimates of annual national health expenditures *before* the COVID-19 pandemic were almost $3.8 trillion dollars [93]. The largest portion of that massive amount of money is spent on hospital care. Thus, it is not surprising that hospital systems are always looking for ways to reduce their costs by conserving available resources. One aspect of this is trying to determine which of their patients need extensive (and expensive) medical care and which do not. In many hospitals, this decision is often determined not by a physician's diagnosis but rather by an algorithm that is computed for every patient. In most algorithms of this type, the greatest importance is assigned to the amount of money that has already been spent on a patient's medical care. This kind of information is very easy to access, and, in principle, it seems logical to use. After all, it is reasonable to assume that sicker people would spend more on their medical care. Hospital algorithms thus often equate greater past spending with greater medical need when they are used to estimate which patients are most in need of extensive medical care. Such estimates of health risk are applied to about 200 million patients each year.

Patient Race and Predictions of Health Risk

Dr. Ziad Obermeyer, professor of public health at the University of California, Berkeley, and his colleagues looked at the impact that this kind of algorithm had on estimates of the health risk for almost 50,000 Black patients and White patients at a large academic hospital over the course of 2 years [94]. These researchers wanted to know whether estimating a patient's medical needs for medical treatment this way might produce racial disparities. To answer this question, the researchers compared the risk level produced by this algorithm to the actual number of chronic diseases among Black patients and White patients. The researchers found that Black patients needed to have many more medical problems than did White patients to be put into the high-risk group – 26.3 percent more to be precise [95]. If they had the same number of medical problems as White patients, Black patients typically fell well below a cut-off score for risk that would result in more intensive medical care. As a result, many Black patients with the same or greater medical problems as White patients were not getting the same quality of care [96].

How can an apparently race-neutral algorithm produce this substantial racial disparity? The answer lies, at least in part, in racial disparities in overall spending for medical care and the kinds of medical care that Black patients and White patients pay for. The cost of care provided to Black patients is, on average, $1,800 less than the cost of care provided to White patients despite the fact that, overall, the health of Black Americans is substantially poorer than White Americans [97]. In addition, Black families consistently spend less out-of-pocket money, in absolute terms, on their medical care than do White families [93].

One of the main reasons for this is simply an economic one discussed earlier: Most health insurance does not cover all of a person's medical expenses, and Black families, on average, have less money to spend on their medical care. Moreover, Black patients (or their insurance companies) are much more likely than White patients to spend money on medical emergencies, such as complications from chronic diseases, rather than spending on regular care. And finally, Black patients tend to spend less money on their medical care when their physician is non-Black than when their physician is also Black.[8] And, as also previously discussed, Black patients are much more likely to be seen by a non-Black physician than a Black one. In short, the amount of money spent on Black patients' overall medical care is typically less than what is spent on White patients' medical care, which directly impacts the results of a hospital's algorithm estimating the need for medical care. As a consequence, the algorithm may result in a racial disparity in which patients get the most intensive medical care that disadvantages Black patients.

Patient Race and Allocation of Hospital Resources
The assessment of the need for medical care is not the only potentially problematic medical algorithm used by hospital administrators. In situations like the COVID-19 pandemic, hospitals may find that their resources are very limited (e.g., very few intensive care unit [ICU] beds or ventilators). Under such circumstances, hospitals will sometimes use other supposedly race-neutral algorithms to decide which patients should *not* receive extensive and expensive medical care. They often use something called a "SOFA" score, which stands for "*s*equential *o*rgan *f*ailure *a*ssessment," to help them make such decisions. The SOFA score involves estimates of factors such as the level of patients' respiratory health, liver and kidney functioning, and their platelet count. Basically, it provides an estimate of how likely it is that a patient's organs will fail and, as a consequence, that they will die. The higher the SOFA score, the worse the expected medical outcomes [98]. If hospital resources are very limited, it is more likely that a patient with a high SOFA score will not get the most aggressive care, with the rationale that the hospital's limited resources would be better allocated to patients more likely to benefit from them.

It turns out, however, that using SOFA scores to make these kinds of decisions disadvantages Black patients. Researchers from Yale University conducted a study of about 2,500 patients with COVID-19 who were admitted to hospitals and found that Black patients had significantly higher SOFA scores than did White patients [99]. The researchers then asked how well these scores actually predicted the Black patients' medical outcomes. The answer was, not very well. Black patients with higher

---

[8] We discuss some of the possible reasons for this in Chapter 6, when we discuss medical mistrust among Black patients.

SOFA scores did not actually have higher rates of mortality while in the hospital, nor were they more likely than White patients to become so sick that they required treatment in an ICU. These researchers therefore concluded that the algorithm commonly used to ration limited resources by giving patients with a high SOFA score a lower priority for receiving these resources might result in "disproportionately denying care to Black patients." The researchers argued that this particular criterion should not have been the only one used to determine which patients with COVID-19 should have access to intensive care.

While the kinds of algorithms discussed here were not created with an intent to deprive very sick Black people of needed medical care, they can clearly have this effect. Understanding the way race is often misused in these algorithms thus provides yet another clear and actionable way that systemic racism in medical care continues to disadvantage Black patients relative to White patients – even in the absence of racist intentions among the individual physicians and hospitals using these widely accepted predictive equations.

Putting It All Together

Since at least 2003, there has been widespread recognition of pervasive racial disparities in the quality of care provided by the American healthcare system. Certainly, initiatives like the enactment of the ACA and the expansion of Medicaid have reduced some health and healthcare disparities, but substantially eliminating them has proven to be much more difficult than many people might have expected it to be in the early part of the twenty-first century. The cost of healthcare in the United States even after the ACA came into force continues to play a critical role in the quality of healthcare received by patients of different assigned races. Black Americans are usually less able to afford healthcare than are White Americans. There also is de facto segregation in the facilities where healthcare is provided and, on average, medical facilities that serve a disproportionate number of Black patients provide a lower quality of care than medical facilities that predominantly serve White patients. Many of such disparities, endemic in healthcare, reflect the general impact of systemic racism in the United States.

There is also systemic racism within medicine that serves to seriously disadvantage Black patients. Its effects include the dearth of Black physicians in medical practice and the inappropriate use of a patient's assigned race in diagnoses and treatment recommendations. The latter is seen in the widespread use of diagnostic equations that implicitly treat race as if it were a biological reality rather than a social construct. The use of problematic formulae for the allocation of medical care can, in fact, incorrectly deny care to seriously ill Black patients.

The systemic racism that exists in society, generally, and in healthcare, specifically, does not, however, provide a complete explanation of why there are large racial disparities in the quality of healthcare patients receive. The race-related thoughts and feelings of individual physicians and patients are a critically important source of racial healthcare disparities in the United States. We turn to this issue in the next chapter.

REFERENCES

1. Frakt, A. (2020, January 13). Bad medicine: The harm that comes from racism. *New York Times.* https://www.nytimes.com/2020/01/13/upshot/bad-medicine-the-harm-that-comes-from-racism.html
2. Centers for Disease Control and Prevention. (1986). Report of the Secretary's Task Force on Black and Minority Health. National Library of Medicine. https://collections.nlm.nih.gov/catalog/nlm:nlmuid-8602912-mvset
3. Smedley, B. D., Stith, A. Y., & Nelson, A. R. (Eds.) (2003). *Unequal treatment: Confronting racial and ethnic disparities in health care.* National Academies Press (US) National Academy of Sciences. https://doi.org/10.17226/12875
4. Holland, B., Dozier, L., & Holland, E. (1965). It's the Same Old Song, (song recorded by The For Tops). *The Four Tops Second Album Motown Records.*
5. Lopez, M., & Budiman, A. (2020, May 5). *Financial and health impacts of COVID-19 vary widely by race and ethnicity.* Pew Research Center. www.pewresearch.org/fact-tank/2020/05/05/financial-and-health-impacts-of-covid-19-vary-widely-by-race-and-ethnicity/
6. Mahajan, S., Caraballo, C., Lu, Y., Valero-Elizondo, J., Massey, D., Annapureddy, A. R., Roy, B., Riley, C., Murugiah, K., Onuma, O., Nunez-Smith, M., Forman, H. P., Nasir, K., Herrin, J., & Krumholz, H. M. (2021). Trends in differences in health status and health care access and affordability by race and ethnicity in the United States, 1999–2018. *Journal of the American Medical Association (JAMA), 326*(7), 637–648. https://doi.org/10.1001/jama.2021.9907
7. Agency for Healthcare Research and Quality. (2021). *National healthcare quality and disparities report.* https://www.ahrq.gov/research/findings/nhqrdr/nhqdr21/index.html
8. Agency for Healthcare Research and Quality. (2021). *Healthcare quality and disparities report.* www.ahrq.gov/sites/default/files/wysiwyg/research/findings/nhqrdr/2021qdr-core-measures-disparities.pdf

9. Shin, P., Alvarez, C., Sharac, J., Rosenbaum, S. J., Vleet, A. V., Paradise, J., & Garfield, R. (2013). *A profile of community health center patients: Implications for policy.* Health Sciences Research Commons. https://hsrc .himmelfarb.gwu.edu/sphhs_policy_ggrchn/43/

10. National Association of Community Health Centers. (2020). *The facts about Medicaid's FQHC prospective payment system (PPS).* www.nachc.org/focus-areas/policy-matters/pps-one-pager-noask-final/

11. Seymour, J. W., Polsky, D. E., Brown, E. J., Barbu, C. M., & Grande, D. (2017). The role of community health centers in reducing racial disparities in spatial access to primary care. *Journal of Primary Care & Community Health, 8* (3), 147–152. https://doi.org/10.1177/2150131917699029

12. Chen, J., Vargas-Bustamante, A., Mortensen, K., & Ortega, A. N. (2016). Racial and ethnic disparities in health care access and utilization under the Affordable Care Act. *Medical Care, 54*(2), 140–146. https://pubmed.ncbi .nlm.nih.gov/26595227/

13. Wursten, J., & Reich, M. (2021). *Racial inequality and minimum wages in frictional labor markets.* Institute for Research on Labor and Employment. https://irle.berkeley.edu/files/2021/02/Racial-Inequality-and-Minimum-Wages.pdf

14. News Release Bureau of Labor Statistics. (2022, October 18). *Usual weekly earnings of wage and salary workers third quarter 2022.* www.bls.gov/news .release/pdf/wkyeng.pdf

15. Laws, M. B., Lee, Y., Taubin, T., Rogers, W. H., & Wilson, I. B. (2018). Factors associated with patient recall of key information in ambulatory specialty care visits: Results of an innovative methodology. *PLoS ONE, 13* (2), e0191940. https://doi.org/10.1371/journal.pone.0191940

16. Lewis, C. G., Getachew, Y., Abrams, M. K., & Doty, M. M. (2019, August 20). *Changes at community health centers, and how patients are benefiting.* The Commonwealth Fund. www.commonwealthfund.org/publications/issue-briefs/2019/aug/changes-at-community-health-centers-how-patients-are-benefiting

17. Schrader, C. D., & Lewis, L. M. (2013). Racial disparity in emergency department triage. *Journal of Emergency Medicine, 44*(2), 511–518. https:// doi.org/10.1016/j.jemermed.2012.05.010

18. Zhang, X., Carabello, M., Hill, T., Bell, S. A., Stephenson, R., & Mahajan, P. (2020). Trends of racial/ethnic differences in emergency department care outcomes among adults in the United States from 2005 to 2016 [Original Research]. *Frontiers in Medicine, 7*(300). https://doi.org/10.3389/fmed.2020.00300

19. Schnitzer, K., Merideth, F., Macias-Konstantopoulos, W., Hayden, D., Shtasel, D., & Bird, S. (2020). Disparities in care: The role of race on the utilization of physical restraints in the emergency setting. *Academic Emergency Medicine, 27*(10), 943–950. https://doi.org/10.1111/acem.14092

20. Hsia, R. Y., Asch, S. M., Weiss, R. E., Zingmond, D., Liang, L. J., Han, W., McCreath, H., & Sun, B. C. (2011). Hospital determinants of emergency department left without being seen rates. *Annals of Emergency Medicine, 58* (1), 24–32.e23. https://doi.org/10.1016/j.annemergmed.2011.01.009

21. Lucas, J., Batt, R. J., & Soremekun, O. A. (2014). Setting wait times to achieve targeted left-without-being-seen rates. *The American Journal of Emergency Medicine*, *32*(4), 342–345. https://pubmed.ncbi.nlm.nih.gov/33128667/

22. Dhuyvetter, A., Cejtin, H. E., Adam, M., & Patel, A. (2021). Coronavirus Disease 2019 in pregnancy: The experience at an urban safety net hospital. *Journal of Community Health*, *46*(2), 267–269. doi.org/10.1007/s10900–020-00940-7

23. Komaromy, M., Harris, M., Koenig, R. M., Tomanovich, M., Ruiz-Mercado, G., & Barocas, J. A. (2021). Caring for COVID's most vulnerable victims: A safety-net hospital responds. *Journal of General Internal Medicine*, *36*(4), 1006–1010. https://www.springermedizin.de/caring-for-covid-s-most-vulnerable-victims-a-safety-net-hospital/18779866

24. Hsu, H. E., Ashe, E. M., Silverstein, M., Hofman, M., Lange, S. J., Razzaghi, H., Mishuris, R. G., Davidoff, R., Parker, E. M., Penman-Aguilar, A., Clarke, K. E. N., Goldman, A., James, T. L., Jacobson, K., Lasser, K. E., Xuan, Z., Peacock, G., Dowling, N. F., & Goodman, A. B. (2020). Race/ethnicity, underlying medical conditions, homelessness, and hospitalization status of adult patients with COVID-19 at an urban safety-net medical center – Boston, Massachusetts, 2020. *Morbidity and Mortality Weekly Report*, *69*(27), 864–869. https://doi.org/10.15585/mmwr.mm6927a3

25. Lasser, K. E., Liu, Z., Lin, M.-Y., Paasche-Orlow, M. K., & Hanchate, A. (2021). Changes in hospitalizations at US safety-net hospitals following Medicaid expansion. *JAMA Network Open*, *4*(6), e2114343–e2114343. https://doi.org/10.1001/jamanetworkopen.2021.14343

26. Gangopadhyaya, A. (2021). *Black patients are more likely than white patients to be in hospitals with worse patient safety conditions*. Urban Institute. www.urban.org/sites/default/files/publication/103925/black-patients-are-more-likely-than-white-patients-to-be-in-hospitals-with-worse-patient-safety-conditions_0.pdf

27. Metersky, M. L., Hunt, D. R., Kliman, R., Wang, Y., Curry, M., Verzier, N., Lyder C. H., & Moy, E. (2011). Racial disparities in the frequency of patient safety events: Results from the National Medicare Patient Safety Monitoring System. *Medical Care*, *49*(5), 504–510. www.jstor.org/stable/23053809

28. Advisory Board. (2021, May 20). 'The gap is not sustainable': Why safety-net hospitals especially struggled amid Covid-19. www.advisory.com/en/daily-briefing/2021/05/20/safety-net-hospitals

29. Center for Medicare & Medicaid Services. (n. d.). Hospital-Acquired Condition Reduction Program. www.cms.gov/Medicare/Medicare-Fee-for-Service-Payment/AcuteInpatientPPS/HAC-Reduction-Program

30. Rau, J. (2021, October 28). Medicare punishes 2,499 hospitals for high readmissions. *Kaiser Health News*. https://khn.org/news/article/hospital-readmission-rates-medicare-penalties/

31. Cunningham, P., Rudowitz, R., Young, K., Garfield, R., & Foutz, J. (2016, June 9). Understanding Medicaid hospital payments and the impact of recent policy changes. Kaiser Family Foundation. www.kff.org/report-section/understanding-medicaid-hospital-payments-and-the-impact-of-recent-policy-changes-issue-brief/

32. Westphal, Z. (n. d.). Physician fee schedules: How do they compare and what's next? *Axene Health Partners.* https://axenehp.com/physician-fee-schedules-compare-whats-next/

33. Holgash, K., & Heberlein, M. (2019, April 10). Physician acceptance of new Medicaid patients: What matters and what doesn't. *Health Affairs Blog.* www.healthaffairs.org/do/10.1377/forefront.20190401.678690/full/

34. Medicaid and CHIP Payment and Access Commission. (n. d.). Key findings on access to care. www.macpac.gov/subtopic/measuring-and-monitoring-access/

35. Hanchate, A. D., Paasche-Orlow, M. K., Baker, W. E., Lin, M.-Y., Banerjee, S., & Feldman, J. (2019, September 6). Association of race/ethnicity with emergency department destination of emergency medical services transport. *JAMA Network Open, 2*(9). https://doi.org/10.1001/jamanetworkopen.2019.10816

36. Caress, B. (2020, September 16). *Hospital care in black and white: How systemic racism persists.* Center for New York City Affairs. www.centernyc.org/urban-matters-2/2020/9/15/hospital-care-in-black-and-white-how-systemic-racism-persists-saved

37. Dimick, J., Ruhter, J., Sarrazin, M. V., & Birkmeyer, J. D. (2013). Black patients more likely than whites to undergo surgery at low-quality hospitals in segregated regions. *Health Affairs, 32*(6), 1046–1053. https://doi.org/10.1377/hlthaff.2011.1365

38. Asch, D. A., Islam, M. N., Sheils, N. E., Chen, Y., Doshi, J. A., Buresh, J., & Werner, R. M. (2021). Patient and hospital factors associated with differences in mortality rates among Black and White US Medicare beneficiaries hospitalized with COVID-19 Infection. *JAMA Network Open, 4*(6), e2112842–e2112842. https://doi.org/10.1001/jamanetworkopen.2021.12842

39. World Population Review. (n. d.). Countries with universal healthcare 2021. https://worldpopulationreview.com/country-rankings/countries-with-universal-healthcare

40. Slaybaugh, C. (n. d.). International healthcare systems: The US versus the world. *Axene Health Partners.* https://axenehp.com/international-healthcare-systems-us-versus-world/

41. Luke 4:23. *The Bible: St. James Version.*

42. Bauchner, H. (2021). Structural racism for doctors – What is it? A response from Howard Bauchner, MD. *JAMA Clinical Reviews.* https://jamanetwork.com/journals/jama/pages/audio-18587774

43. National Commission on Certification of Physician Assistants. (2020). 2019 statistical profile of certified physician assistants. https://prodcmsstoragesa.blob.core.windows.net/uploads/files/2019StatisticalProfileofCertifiedPhysicianAssistants.pdf

44. Ly, D. P. (2021). Historical trends in the representativeness and incomes of Black physicians, 1900–2018. *Journal of General Internal Medicine, 37,* 1310–1312. https://doi.org/10.1007/s11606-021-06745-1

45. National Science Foundation. (2015). Who earns a U.S. doctorate? www.nsf.gov/statistics/2017/nsf17306/report/who-earns-a-us-doctorate/race-and-ethnicity.cfm

46. Hamel, L. M., Chapman, R., Malloy, M., Eggly, S., Penner, L. A., Shields, A. F., Simon, M. S., Klamerus, J. F., Schiffer, C., & Albrecht, T. L. (2015). Critical shortage of African American medical oncologists in the United States. *Journal of Clinical Oncology: Official Journal of the American Society of Clinical Oncology*, *33*(32), 3697–3700. https://doi.org/10.1200/JCO.2014.59.2493

47. American Cancer Society. (2019). Cancer Facts & Figures for African Americans 2019–2021. www.cancer.org/content/dam/cancer-org/research/cancer-facts-and-statistics/cancer-facts-and-figures-for-african-americans/cancer-facts-and-figures-for-african-americans-2019-2021.pdf

48. McFarling, U. L. (2021, April 28). After 40 years, medical schools are admitting fewer Black male or Native American students. *Stat News*. www.statnews.com/2021/04/28/medical-schools-admitting-fewer-black-male-or-native-american-students/

49. Association of American Medical Colleges. (2019). *Diversity in medicine: Facts and Figures 2019*. Figure 13. Percentage of U.S. medical school graduates by race/ethnicity (alone), academic year 2018–2019. www.aamc.org/data-reports/workforce/interactive-data/figure-13-percentage-us-medical-school-graduates-race/ethnicity-alone-academic-year-2018-2019

50. Rothstein, R. (2015). The racial achievement gap, segregated schools, and segregated neighborhoods: A Constitutional insult. *Race and Social Problems*, *7*(1), 21–30. https://link.springer.com/article/10.1007/s12552-014-9134-1

51. Bridges, B. (2018, November 29). *African Americans and college education by the numbers*. United Negro College Fund. https://uncf.org/the-latest/african-americans-and-college-education-by-the-numbers

52. The Postsecondary National Policy Institute. (2021, February 1). *Factsheets: First-generation students*. https://pnpi.org/first-generation-students/

53. Nichols, A. H., & Anthony, M. Jr. (2020, March 5). Graduation rates don't tell the full story: Racial gaps in college success are larger than we think. The Education Trust. https://edtrust.org/resource/graduation-rates-dont-tell-the-full-story-racial-gaps-in-college-success-are-larger-than-we-think/

54. Hanson, M. (2022, December, 2). *Average cost of medical school*. Education Data Initiative. https://educationdata.org/average-cost-of-medical-school

55. Chen, X. (2013). STEM attrition: College students' paths into and out of STEM fields. Statistical Analysis Report. NCES 2014-001. National Center for Education Statistics. https://nces.ed.gov/pubs2014/2014001rev.pdf

56. Gasman, M., Smith, T., Ye, C., & Nguyen, T.-H. (2017). HBCUs and the production of doctors. *AIMS Public Health*, *4*(6), 579–589. https://doi.org/10.3934/publichealth.2017.6.579

57. HBCU College Fair. Did You Know? www.youtube.com/watch?v=zLdYhpKgYDg

58. Tavernier, F. (2018, March 1). *Representation is crucial. So retention of pre-med students of color is imperative*. University of Michigan Health Lab. https://

labblog.uofmhealth.org/med-u/representation-crucial-so-retention-of-pre-med-students-of-color-imperative

59. Association of American Medical Colleges. (2020). U.S. Medical School faculty trends: Percentages. www.aamc.org/data-reports/faculty-institutions/interactive-data/us-medical-school-faculty-trends-percentages

60. Association of American Medical Colleges. (2021). U.S. medical school deans by dean type and race/ethnicity (URiM vs. non-URiM). www.aamc.org/data-reports/faculty-institutions/interactive-data/us-medical-school-deans-dean-type-and-race-ethnicity

61. Amutah, C., Greenidge, K., Mante, A., Munyikwa, M., Surya, S. L., Higginbotham, E., Jones, D. S., Lavizzo-Mourey, R., Roberts, D., Tsai, J., & Aysola, J. (2021). Misrepresenting race: The role of medical schools in propagating physician bias. *New England Journal of Medicine, 384*(9), 872–878. https://doi.org/10.1056/NEJMms2025768

62. Perry, T. (2016, May 3). The racist origins of the word 'Caucasian'. GOOD. www.good.is/articles/the-last-country-to-still-use-the-term-caucasian

63. Dutchen, S. (2021). Field correction. Harvard Medicine. https://hms.harvard.edu/magazine/racism-medicine/field-correction

64. Souter, E. (2021, July 28). How medical schools are fighting racial disparities in health care. WebMD. www.webmd.com/a-to-z-guides/features/med-schools-fight-racism

65. Perry, S. P., Wages III, J. E., Skinner-Dorkenoo, A. L., Burke, S. E., Hardeman, R. R., & Phelan, S. M. (2021). Testing a self-affirmation intervention for improving the psychosocial health of Black and White medical students in the United States. *Journal of Social Issues, 77*(3), 769–800. https://pubmed.ncbi.nlm.nih.gov/34924602/

66. Diaz, T., Navarro, J. R., & Chen, E. H. (2020). An institutional approach to fostering inclusion and addressing racial bias: Implications for diversity in academic medicine. *Teaching and Learning in Medicine, 32*(1), 110–116. https://doi.org/10.1080/10401334.2019.1670665

67. Hill, K. A., Samuels, E. A., Gross, C. P., Desai, M. M., Sitkin Zelin, N., Latimore, D., Huot, S. J., Cramer, L. D., Wong, A. H., & Boatright, D. (2020). Assessment of the prevalence of medical student mistreatment by sex, race/ethnicity, and sexual orientation. *JAMA Internal Medicine, 180*(5), 653–665. https://doi.org/10.1001/jamainternmed.2020.0030

68. Ross, D. A., Boatright, D., Nunez-Smith, M., Jordan, A., Chekroud, A., & Moore, E. Z. (2017). Differences in words used to describe racial and gender groups in Medical Student Performance Evaluations. *PLoS ONE, 12*(8), e0181659. https://doi.org/10.1371/journal.pone.0181659

69. Rosenblum, K. (2020, February 7). *My experience as a Black doctor in 2020.* Cedars Sinai. www.cedars-sinai.org/blog/my-experience-as-a-black-doctor-in-2020.html

70. Goldberg, E. (2020, August 11). For doctors of color, microaggressions are all too familiar. *New York Times.* www.nytimes.com/2020/08/11/health/microaggression-medicine-doctors.html

71. Sullivan, L. W. (2005). A JBHE check-Up on Blacks in US medical schools. *Journal of Blacks in Higher Education, 47,* 76–81. https://www.jbhe.com/features/47_medicalschools.html

72. Ly, D. P., Seabury, S. A., & Jena, A. B. (2016). Differences in incomes of physicians in the United States by race and sex: Observational study. *BMJ, 353,* i2923–i2923. https://doi.org/10.1136/bmj.i2923

73. Moore, J., & Continelli, T. (2016). Racial/ethnic pay disparities among registered nurses in U.S. hospitals: An econometric regression decomposition. *Health Services Research, 51*(2), 511–529. https://doi.org/10.1111/1475-6773 .12337

74. Boatright, D., Ross, D., O'Connor, P., Moore, E., & Nunez-Smith, M. (2017). Racial disparities in medical student membership in the Alpha Omega Alpha Honor Society. *JAMA Internal Medicine, 177*(5), 659–665. https://doi.org/10.1001/jamainternmed.2016.9623

75. Blackstock, U. (2020, January 16). Why Black doctors like me are leaving faculty positions in academic medical centers. *Stat News.* www.statnews.com/2020/01/16/black-doctors-leaving-faculty-positions-academic-medical-centers/

76. Meeks, L., & Jain, N. (2019). *Accessibility, inclusion, and action in medical education: Lived experiences of learners and physicians with disabilities.* Association of American Medical Colleges.

77. Snyder J. E., Upton, R. D., Hassett, T. C., Lee, H., Nouri, Z., & Dill, M. (2023). Black representation in the primary care physician workforce and its association with population life expectancy and mortality rates in the US. *JAMA Network Open.* https://jamanetwork.com/journals/jamanetworkopen/fullarticle/2803898

78. Cooper-Patrick, L., Gallo, J. J., Gonzales, J. J., Vu, H. T., Powe, N. R., Nelson, C., & Ford, D. E. (1999). Race, gender, and partnership in the patient-physician relationship. *Journal of the American Medical Association (JAMA), 282*(6), 583–589. https://doi.org/10.1001/jama.282.6.583

79. Traylor, A. H., Schmittdiel, J. A., Uratsu, C. S., Mangione, C. M., & Subramanian, U. (2010). Adherence to cardiovascular disease medications: Does patient-provider race/ethnicity and language concordance matter? *Journal of General Internal Medicine, 25*(11), 1172–1177. https://pubmed.ncbi.nlm.nih.gov/20571929/

80. Saha, S., & Beach, M. C. (2020). Impact of physician race on patient decision-making and ratings of physicians: A randomized experiment using video vignettes. *Journal of General Internal Medicine, 35*(4), 1084–1091. https://pubmed.ncbi.nlm.nih.gov/31965527/

81. Alsan, M., Garrick, O., & Graziani, G. (2019). Does diversity matter for health? Experimental evidence from Oakland. *American Economic Review, 109*(12), 4071–4111. https://www.aeaweb.org/articles?id=10.1257/aer.20181446

82. Greenwood, B. N., Hardeman, R. R., Huang, L., & Sojourner, A. (2020). Physician-patient racial concordance and disparities in birthing mortality for

newborns. *Proceedings of the National Academy of Sciences, 117*(35), 21194–21200. https://doi.org/10.1073/pnas.1913405117

83. Hill, A., Jones, D., & Woodworth, L. (2020, June 26). Physician-patient race-match reduces patient mortality. *SSRN*. https://dx.doi.org/10.2139/ssrn .3211276

84. James Denny, G. (1968). The pro-slavery arguments of Dr. Samuel A. Cartwright. *Louisiana History: The Journal of the Louisiana Historical Association, 9*(3), 209–227. www.jstor.org/stable/4231017

85. Cartwright, S. (1860). Slavery in the light of ethnology. Cotton is king and pro-slavery arguments. Digital History: ID 275. www.digitalhistory.uh.edu/ disp_textbook.cfm?smtID=3&psid=275

86. Vyas, D. A., Eisenstein, L. G., & Jones, D. S. (2020). Hidden in plain sight: Reconsidering the use of race correction in clinical algorithms. *New England Journal of Medicine, 383*(9), 874–882. https://doi.org/10.1056/NEJMms2004740

87. Chertow, G. M., Hsu, C. Y., & Johansen, K. L. (2006). The enlarging body of evidence: Obesity and chronic kidney disease. *Journal of the American Society of Nephrology, 17*(6), 1501–1502. https://doi.org/10.1681/asn.2006040327

88. Uppal, P., Golden, B., Panicker, A., Kahn, O., & Burday, M. (2022). The case against race-based GFR. *Delaware Journal of Public Health, 8*(3), 86–89. https://www.ncbi.nlm.nih.gov/pmc/articles/PMC9495470/

89. Goldstein, J. (2022, April 25). How a race-based medical formula is keeping some Black men in prison. *New York Times*. www.nytimes.com/2022/04/22/ nyregion/prison-kidney-federal-courts-race.html

90. Fawzy, A., Tianishi, D., Wang, K., Robinson, M., Farha, J., Bradke, A., Golden, S., Yanzun, X., & Garibaldi, B. (2022). Racial and ethnic discrepancy in pulse oximetry and delayed identification of treatment eligibility among patients with COVID-19. *JAMA Internal Medicine, 182*(7), 730–738. https://jamanetwork.com/journals/jamainternalmedicine/fullarti cle/2792653

91. Tobin, M., & Jubran, A. (2022). Pulse oximetry, racial bias, and statistical bias. *Annals of Intensive Care, 22*(19). https://www.ncbi.nlm.nih.gov/pmc/ articles/PMC8723900/

92. Satel, S. (2002, May 5). I am a racially profiling doctor. *New York Times*. www .nytimes.com/2002/05/05/magazine/i-am-a-racially-profiling-doctor.html

93. American Medical Association. (n. d.). Trends in health care spending. www .ama-assn.org/about/research/trends-health-care-spending

94. Obermeyer, Z., Powers, B., Vogeli, C., & Mullainathan, S. (2019). Dissecting racial bias in an algorithm used to manage the health of populations. *Science, 366*(6464), 447–453. doi: 10.1126/science.aax2342

95. Mullainathan, S., & Obermeyer, Z. (2021). On the inequity of predicting A while hoping for B. *AEA Papers and Proceedings, 111*, 37–42. http://ziadobermeyer.com/ wp-content/uploads/2021/08/Predicting-A-While-Hoping-for-B.pdf

96. Ledford, H. (2019). Millions of black people affected by racial bias in health-care algorithms. *Nature, 574*(7780), 608–609. https://pubmed.ncbi.nlm.nih .gov/31664201/

97. Charron-Chénier, R., & Mueller, C. W. (2018). Racial disparities in medical spending: Healthcare expenditures for Black and White households (2013–2015). *Race and Social Problems, 10*(2). https://link.springer.com/arti cle/10.1007/s12552-018-9226-4

98. Roy, S., Showstark, M., Tolchin, B., Kashyap, N., Bonito, J., Salazar, M. C., Herbst, J. L., Nash, K. A., Nguemeni Tiako, M. J., Jubanyik, K., Kim, N., Galusha, D., Wang, K. H., & Oladele, C. (2021). The potential impact of triage protocols on racial disparities in clinical outcomes among COVID-positive patients in a large academic healthcare system. *PLoS ONE, 16*(9), e0256763. https://doi.org/10.1371/journal.pone.0256763

99. Tolchin, B., Oladele, C., Galusha, D., Kashyap, N., Showstark, M., Bonito, J., Salazar, M. C., Herbst, J. L., Martino, S., & Kim, N. (2021). Racial disparities in the SOFA score among patients hospitalized with COVID-19. *PLoS ONE, 16*(9), e0257608. www.ncbi.nlm.nih.gov/pmc/articles/PMC8448580/

CHAPTER 6

A Dangerous Foot in the Door
The Impact of Race-Related Thoughts and Feelings on Healthcare Disparities

Of all the forms of inequality, injustice in healthcare is the most shocking and inhumane because it results in physical death.
Dr. Martin Luther King Jr. (1966 – Press Conference Preceding National Convention of Medical Committee for Human Rights) [1]

On December 20, 2020, Dr. Susan Moore died from COVID-19-related complications. She was a graduate of one of the leading medical schools in the country and a successful practicing family physician. As an experienced physician, Dr. Moore understood the nature of her medical problems and what diagnostic procedures and clinical interventions she needed. However, as a Black patient in a hospital in Indianapolis, Indiana, she was not listened to.

Two weeks before Dr. Moore died, she posted a video about her medical care on her Facebook page; it went viral [2]. In the video Dr. Moore can be seen in her hospital bed with an oxygen tube in her nose. At times, she was in such discomfort that she needed to stop talking. When she was admitted to the hospital, she was in great pain due to swollen lymph nodes in her neck and had great difficulty breathing because of inflammation in her lungs. In the days preceding the video recording, she had asked the attending physician for medication for her pain and remdesivir (an antiviral medication) to treat her worsening viral infection. She was denied the antiviral medication. The physician told her he was not comfortable giving her more pain medication. Dr. Moore described her reaction to this quite clearly, "He made me feel like I was a drug addict." The physician also informed her that, despite her worsening symptoms, they would be sending her home late that coming Saturday night (where she would be alone). She was only provided additional medications after a CAT scan (which she requested) showed the inflammation of her neck and lungs. But it was too late. As Dr. Moore declared in one of her last statements in the video, "I put forth and I maintain, if I was White, I wouldn't have to go through [this]."

The problem confronting Dr. Moore was not the kind of health insurance she had or the quality of the hospital where she was being treated. (It was part of a large, university-based healthcare system.) The problem was the kind of treatment she received from the medical professionals who were in charge of her care. We cannot unambiguously conclude that her race was the primary reason for the abysmal way she was treated, but the fact remains that her story is strikingly similar to other stories of how Black patients in extreme pain and/or with other medical problems have been treated: Their requests and complaints are often ignored.

In the preceding chapter, we addressed how systemic racism in society and within the healthcare system creates racial disparities between the quality of healthcare that Black people and White people receive. In this chapter, we move from a system-level analysis to an individual-level analysis – an examination of how race relations in the United States and individuals' race-related attitudes, beliefs, and behaviors can produce unjustified and harmful racial disparities in the quality of the healthcare Black patients receive. We first present examples of disparities in the treatments received by Black patients and White patients with the same medical problems. This is followed by a discussion of the quality of communication between Black patients and physicians who do not identify as Black.[1] Finally, we present an in-depth analysis of how the race-related feelings and thoughts of both non-Black physicians and their Black patients can jointly contribute to healthcare disparities.

Racial Disparities in the Quality of Medical Treatments: A Disturbing Reality

Racial disparities in healthcare treatment are pervasive. On average, Black patients receive less aggressive and appropriate treatments than White patients across a host of different illnesses and diseases.

The Alleviation of Pain

The first kind of racial treatment disparities that we consider are those for the alleviation of pain. Contrary to the racial stereotypes that were held by

---

[1] We will use the term "non-Black" rather than "White" in order to accurately describe the physicians in the studies we present. Although a clear majority of the physicians were White, a minority of them were either Latinx, Asian (especially South Asia), or from the Middle East. In most studies the number of physicians from these ethnic minorities was too small to determine whether there were any differences between them and White physicians in how they treated their patients or patients reacted to them. However, future research needs to examine if there are such differences.

most physicians in the nineteenth century and that continue to be held by a significant minority of medical professionals today (see Introduction chapter), Black people are no less sensitive to pain than are White people [3]. In fact, because of disparities in access to healthcare and to pharmacies that sell medications to relieve pain, Black Americans, on average, experience more chronic daily pain than do White Americans [4]. Racial disparities in the provision of pain medication include everything from treatments for general chronic pain to specific kinds of pain, ranging from a toothache to chest pain to kidney stones to metastatic gynecologic cancer [5–9]. Black patients experiencing pain are less likely than White patients with comparable levels of pain to receive adequate medications to relieve their distress.

Moreover, even when Black patients and White patients both receive pain medications, there may be disparities in the type of pain medications they are prescribed. For example, Dr. Salimah Meghani, professor of nursing at the University of Pennsylvania, and her colleagues investigated how physicians in a large healthcare system prescribed pain medications to Black patients and White patients with kidney cancer. The researchers found that the physicians in their study were more likely to prescribe morphine than oxycodone to the Black patients, but they were more likely to prescribe oxycodone than morphine to White patients. These medications are both opioids, but morphine has many more adverse side effects for patients with kidney cancer than does oxycodone [10]. In fact, the kind of pain medication given was partially responsible for the Black patients later having more medical complications associated with their cancer than the White patients.

Dr. Meghani and her colleagues could not identify any medical reason for this disparity in the kinds of medications used. They proposed that it was due, at least in part, to physicians' erroneous beliefs that their Black patients were more likely than their White patients to become addicted to oxycodone. This racial stereotype about Black patients having a greater likelihood of becoming addicted to oxycodone or other opioids is simply not true. In fact, a study of over one million patients found that non-Hispanic White patients were substantially more likely than Black (or Latinx) patients to abuse opioids [11]. Nonetheless, these kinds of stereotypes about Black people and drug addiction seem to be an underlying reason for many of the racial disparities in the provision of pain medication. They directly lead to Black patients receiving less effective treatments for their pain than White patients with the same level of discomfort.

Treatment Disparities for the Most Deadly Diseases

Diseases of the heart and various types of cancers are the two leading causes of death in the United States. Disparities in treatments for these diseases are one of the primary reasons for higher mortality rates among Black Americans than White Americans.

Heart Disease

Heart disease is the leading cause of disease-related mortality in the United States. Black patients, on average, receive less aggressive treatments than White patients. This disparity often begins with initial diagnoses and procedures when patients arrive at hospitals with symptoms of a myocardial infarction (i.e., heart attack). There is a consistent pattern of undertreatment of Black patients as compared to White patients with the same symptoms [12, 13]. Black patients are less likely than White patients to receive standard diagnostic procedures, such as electrocardiograms, heart X-rays (angiography), cardiac monitors, or pulse oximeters to check blood oxygen levels. Black patients with heart disease are also less likely than White heart disease patients to receive coronary bypass surgery or other kinds of surgeries for structural defects in their hearts (such as valve replacements). This disparity in surgical treatments also holds true for Latinx patients relative to White patients [14].

Cancer

With regard to cancer, if Black patients and White patients receive comparable treatments, there is virtually no disparity in their mortality rates [15]. But racial disparities in the treatment of cancer are quite common. One of the most striking of these was reported by Dr. Jennifer Griggs, professor of internal medicine, hematology, and oncology at the University of Michigan Medical School, and her colleagues [16]. The context for their research involves the standard treatments for women with breast cancer. When women undergo surgery to remove a malignant tumor, there can often be "malignant recurrence." This is a return of the cancer after surgery despite tests showing that the cancerous tumor is totally gone. This problem is the second leading cause of women's cancer-related deaths in the world [17]. Thus, even after they have had apparently successful surgeries, women very often receive chemotherapy for some period of time. This is called "adjuvant chemotherapy." There is substantial evidence that adjuvant chemotherapy prolongs the lives of the women who receive it [18]. However, a critical determinant of chemotherapy's effectiveness is whether a woman receives the appropriate amount or dosages of the drug. There are well-established, data-based guidelines for the appropriate dosage based on factors such as a patient's height and weight (this is known as the "standard of care"). If the dosages a woman receives are substantially below the recommended level, the odds of a malignant recurrence increase dramatically.

Dr. Griggs and her colleagues examined the adjuvant chemotherapy dosages given to Black women and White women at 10 different cancer clinics. The question they asked was whether a woman's race made any difference in whether they received the recommended dosages. The researchers statistically controlled for any other factors that might affect chemotherapy dosages, such as comorbidities or how long the patient had cancer, in order to be sure that it was only a woman's race that determined the dosage she received. Even after statistically controlling for such factors, the researchers found that Black women were still significantly more likely than White women (39 percent versus 28 percent) to receive first doses of chemotherapy that were well below the standard of care for adjuvant chemotherapy. Black women were also more likely than White women to receive fewer doses of chemotherapy over the course of their treatment. In sum, the Black women were significantly less likely than the White women to get the levels of chemotherapy that would be most effective at preventing a reoccurrence of their cancer [16].[2]

Similar kinds of racial treatment disparities exist for prostate cancer, the most common kind of cancer among men, especially Black men [20, 21]. Overall, Black patients with prostate cancer typically receive less aggressive treatments than do White patients with similar diagnoses. And the more aggressive the prostate cancer is, the greater the racial disparity in treatment [22]. These kinds of disparities may be one of the major reasons why the prostate cancer mortality rate is much greater for Black patients than White patients [23]. Black patients are also less likely to undergo surgery to treat gastrointestinal and pancreatic cancers than are White patients [24, 25].

Treatment Disparities among the Very Old and the Very Young

Racial treatment disparities occur at both ends of people's life cycles. Among the very old these often involve giving Black patients unneeded

---

[2] Chemotherapy is not the only kind of adjuvant therapy. Sometimes adjuvant therapy for breast cancer involves radiation. The findings on racial disparities in radiation-based treatments are mixed, but recent studies suggest there also is racial gap, but it may be closing [19].

treatments; among the very young these often involve not giving Black pediatric patients the treatments they need.

End-of-Life Care: Too Much, Too Late
There is a disturbing exception to the general pattern of Black patients receiving less aggressive treatments, and it highlights yet another way that Black patients may be disadvantaged by decision-making about the medical treatments they receive. We again discuss the treatment of cancer, but from a different perspective. When a patient's cancer has progressed so far that the likelihood the person will survive is exceedingly low, the patient, their family, and the physician face a difficult choice. The patient can either receive further treatment for the cancer such as more chemotherapy, other increasingly invasive treatments, or palliative care. Palliative care focuses not on extending life but rather on reducing the patient's pain and discomfort while optimizing the quality of life for the remaining time patients have [26].

Most oncologists and medical ethicists agree that in the final stages of cancer, palliative care, which is focused mainly on providing relief from symptoms and improving quality of life, is far more preferable than continuing treatment [27]. Active treatment of cancers that have progressed this far is rarely – if ever – successful. It also imposes an additional, serious physical burden on the patient, as well as further financial and psychological burdens on patients and their families [28]. Palliative care, by contrast, may permit patients to spend their final days at home with their families rather than remaining in a hospital bed, where they will likely be receiving medications through needles or tubes inserted into their veins, be fed through feeding tubes, experience the side effects of further chemotherapy, and endure other quite intrusive medical procedures.[3]

It is in these end-of-life situations that Black patients are much more likely than White patients to continue to receive aggressive forms of treatment for their cancer rather than palliative care [29, 30]. To put this differently, Black patients with terminal cancers may often receive more aggressive care than White patients when it does them the least good – and, indeed, when it may cause some substantial harm.

Some people who study healthcare disparities suggest that this particular one may in part reflect Black people's beliefs about their medical care. Black patients may want to continue care because they are more likely to

---

[3] Dr. Siddhartha Mukherjee describes the difficulties of such end-of-life decisions in his brilliant book, *The Emperor of All Maladies: A Biography of Cancer.*

believe that there are cures they have not yet been given. One minister of a predominantly Black church speculated that Black people may "say 'give me everything'. . . . all the treatment there is . . . because we typically don't get the treatment we need" [31]. The available evidence, however, suggests that the disparity is much more likely due to poor communication between non-Black physicians and Black patients and their families [32]. Black patients are, for example, less likely than White patients to be informed about the existence of living wills, which let a patient state their treatment preferences in case they are later unable to do so. They also generally receive less information about what their treatment would actually involve.

Disparities in Pediatric Care: Under-Diagnosed and Under-Treated
Racial treatment disparities are not restricted to the provision of medical care to adults. They can also be found in the treatment of children. Black children admitted to emergency rooms with an appendicitis, for example, receive less pain medication than do White children suffering from the same condition [33].

Another analysis of over one million pediatric visits by over two million Black or White parents and their children highlighted just how pervasive racial treatment disparities are [34]. The researchers looked at cases in which parents brought their children to their pediatrician because they suspected that their child had an acute respiratory infection (e.g., the children were wheezing or coughing). The Black children and the White children were seen by the same pediatricians, which eliminates the possibility that any racial disparities in treatments would be due to the children being seen by different physicians.

The pediatricians in this study were less likely to conclude that a Black child had an infection than a White child had an infection. Moreover, there was a significant racial disparity in whether the physicians followed the established "standard of care" for treatment of the children whom they had diagnosed as having a respiratory infection. The physicians were significantly more likely to prescribe the standard regimen of antibiotics to the White children than to the Black children. This disparity persisted even after the researchers controlled for differences in a child's age, gender, the presence of other health problems, whether their families had insurance, and other similar factors that might explain the difference. In sum, a child's race, by itself, was a significant predictor of this treatment disparity.

Similar disparities exist in the treatment of juvenile diabetes and pediatric cancer. Black children with diabetes are less likely than White children to receive insulin pumps and glucose monitors [35]. Black children with solid tumors and sarcomas (cancers that begin in bones or muscles) are significantly less likely than White children to receive radiation treatments [36, 37]. In addition, Black children with comparable levels of developmental delays or attention deficit disorders as White children are less likely to be diagnosed with and to receive treatment for their condition [38, 39].

Other Treatment Disparities: The List Gets Longer

This list of treatment disparities is far from exhaustive. Other examples of diseases for which Black patients receive less appropriate treatments than do White patients include AIDS, cardiovascular diseases, osteoporosis, Parkinson's disease, mood disorders, as well as life-threatening viral infections [40–45]. In addition, the CDC reported that Black patients hospitalized with the COVID-19 virus were substantially less likely than White patients to receive monoclonal antibody treatments, one of the few effective treatments for this disease. (A similar disparity was found for Latinx patients.) [46].

This discussion of pervasive racial disparities in individual treatments for comparable diseases quite obviously begs the question of the reasons for them. Some people have suggested that they may reflect the de facto segregation of medical facilities discussed in Chapter 5. That is, Black patients may receive poorer medical care because the facilities where they are often treated are simply not as good as the facilities where White patients are treated. However, there are treatment disparities even within the same healthcare systems. For example, within the same hospitals, Black patients experience more adverse safety events (i.e., accidental injuries due to medical errors) than do White patients [47].

More evidence of within-facility racial disparities comes from Dr. Somnath Saha, professor of medicine at Johns Hopkins University, and his colleagues. They conducted an extensive examination of the research literature on racial treatment disparities within the Veterans Administration (VA) medical system, which provides treatments for all military veterans who qualify for treatment in one of the many VA hospitals throughout the country. These researchers concluded that "racial [treatment] disparities exist across a wide range of [VA] clinical areas and service types." Among these were treatments for strokes, heart disease, and management of hypertension [48]. More recent studies have found similar kinds of racial treatment disparities in the VA system. For example, Black patients were less likely than White patients to receive antiviral treatments

for their viral infections and blood thinners to prevent strokes [49, 50].
Thus, it seems that disparities in the quality of medical facilities where
Black patients and White patients are relatively more likely to be treated
are important factors, but they cannot fully explain the kinds of treatment
disparities we have presented. We must consider other reasons for them.

As we discussed in Chapter 5, socioeconomic factors almost certainly
play a role in treatment disparities. Not only do they affect simple access to
healthcare, but they influence the quality of healthcare as well. Consider
again racial disparities in the treatment of cancer. Because cancer is such a
pervasive and deadly disease, enormous amounts of money are invested in
developing new and better ways to treat it. Dr. Parisa Tehranifar, professor
of epidemiology at Columbia University, and her colleagues have argued
that advances in cancer treatments are not, however, shared equally among
all patients. They proposed the reality is that "individuals with greater access
to important social and economic resources (e.g., knowledge, income, and
beneficial social relations)" are more able to "delay and avoid death from
cancer" [51]. In support of this argument, the researchers showed that those
cancers for which the greatest treatment advances have been made are also
the types of cancer that display the largest disparities in survival rates for
Black patients and White patients: The survival rates are much lower for
Black patients than for White patients. On average, White people, compared to Black people, are disproportionately more likely to possess the
resources needed to access these latest and most effective treatments.

We are not proposing that every single instance in which Black patients
and White patients receive different treatments can be attributed to some
aspect of anti-Black racism. As Chapter 5 shows, systemic inequities lead
to many kinds of treatment disparities, and the reality is that we do not
know the percentage of instances in which Black patients and White
patients receive different treatments because of some aspect of anti-Black
racism. But the evidence contained in the seminal Institute of Medicine
(IOM) report on racial and ethnic healthcare disparities (see Chapter 5)
and the large body of research that followed it rather strongly suggest that
factors related to the ways in which Black Americans and White Americans
interact with one another and racial bias both play important roles.

Physician–Patient Interactions and Healthcare Disparities: The "Art" of Medicine

A person's race, which plays such an important role in social interactions,
also has an important role in medical interactions and the interpersonal

dynamics between physicians and patients that can influence treatment decisions. The medical profession now clearly recognizes how important the dynamics of physician–patient interactions can be in the medical outcomes for the patients. Thus, students who graduate from medical schools are now often asked to swear to a part of the modern Hippocratic Oath that states, "I will remember that there is art to medicine as well as science, and that warmth, sympathy, and understanding may outweigh the surgeon's knife or the chemist's drug."[4] This powerful statement emphasizes a major change in how the medical establishment views the most critical aspects of treating a patient. Historically, physicians were taught that their job was to cure diseases (e.g., diabetes, cancer, organ failure). In essence, the patient was merely a "vessel" that contained a medical problem. Today physicians realize that they are treating more than just diseases; they are treating a person who has a disease. That is, physicians must also treat a patient's *illness* – their thoughts and feelings related to the impact of a disease on them. To do this, physicians need to pay attention to and try to understand patients' thoughts and feelings. Viewing medical problems from this perspective places physician–patient communication in a prominent role in modern medical practice. That is, racial treatment disparities not only include disparities in the medications prescribed and the surgical procedures performed, but they also involve disparities in how non-Black physicians and Black patients communicate with and react to one another. The quality of communication can have significant ramifications for the health of Black patients.

Medical Interactions: The Importance of Good Communication

Even in the age of "tele-health," in which physicians and patients may have virtual interactions (i.e., by telephone or computer-mediated communication), a major part of treating an illness involves conversations between a physician (or other healthcare professionals) and a patient. The nature of the communication that occurs during these conversations can directly affect patients' medical outcomes because both physicians and patients possess information that is valuable to the other person and must be exchanged clearly and accurately. Each patient's illness has unique aspects, and patients are the primary source of information when it comes to the symptoms they are experiencing and the circumstances under which these

---

[4] A full comparison of the traditional and modern Hippocratic Oaths can be found at www.medicinenet.com/hippocratic_oath/definition.htm

symptoms are better or worse. Patients also possess valuable background information, such as their health-related habits (e.g., diet and exercise) and other aspects of their health history. Therefore, it is as important that physicians understand what patients have to say as it is for patients to understand what physicians are telling them. The quality of this information exchange may be especially important for Black patients because, as we noted in Chapter 5, many Black patients may interact with a physician they have never met before and who may not have access to their medical records.

Good, clear communication is a challenge in virtually all medical interactions. But, problems in communication appear to be substantially greater when the interaction is between a Black patient and a non-Black physician – and such interactions comprise more than 80 percent of Black patients' medical interactions [52]. Dr. Megan Shen, professor of psychology in medicine at Weil Cornell Medical College, and her colleagues conducted a comprehensive review of the research on racial disparities in various aspects of communication between physicians and patients across a wide variety of medical settings. The studies they reviewed used physician and patient self-reports of their communication and the ratings of trained observers who watched interactions between them. Dr. Shen and her colleagues found that, on average, "Black patients consistently experienced poorer communication quality, information giving [from physicians], patient participation, and less participatory decision making than [did] White patients" [53]. In addition, medical interactions involving Black patients were usually shorter than those with White patients and more likely to be verbally dominated by the physician. Other studies have also shown that there is less rapport between patients and physicians and less expression of positive feelings in these "racially discordant" (i.e., non-Black physician and Black patient) medical interactions than in racially concordant ones [54].

Patient-Centered Communication

Racial disparities can also be found in "patient-centered communication," a specific component of effective communication in medical interactions that is considered an important part of overall patient-centered care. According to the National Institutes of Health, patient-centered communication has three distinct components involving the physician: "(1) eliciting and understanding patient perspectives (concerns, ideas, expectations, needs, feelings, and functioning), (2) understanding the patient within his or her unique psychosocial and cultural contexts, and (3) reaching a shared understanding of patient problems and the treatments that are concordant with patient values" [55]. Even though physicians enter medical interactions with their own agenda for treating an illness, good patient-centered communication requires that they reconcile their agenda with the patient's desire to get understandable information about their illness and to be a partner in the decisions made about their treatment [51]. Notably, patients generally prefer higher levels of patient-centered communication. For example, when one patient with a long history of chronic illnesses was asked specifically what he believed would improve his care, he responded, "Please tell me what you are going to do before you do it to me; . . . and please ask me what I think" [56].

Patient-centered communication is associated with better outcomes for patients. For example, a year-long study of patients seen by different physicians in several different types of clinics found that higher levels of patient-centered communication were associated with better medical outcomes, such as significantly fewer subsequent visits for specialty care, less frequent hospitalizations, fewer laboratory and diagnostic tests, and significantly lower medical costs [57]. Greater patient-centered communication between physicians and patients is also directly associated with a higher level of patient adherence to physicians' recommended treatment protocols (e.g., taking certain medications, following certain dietary restrictions) [58–60]. There are also often less tangible but equally important benefits for patients who feel that they have received patient-centered care: In studies of patients with hypertension and at risk for heart failure, those who reported higher levels of patient-centered care reported that there were improvements in their general health status, reductions in uncertainties regarding their illness, increases in their emotional well-being, and stronger feelings of control over their medical problem [61, 62].

The 2021 report from the federal government's National Agency for Healthcare and Quality (AHRQ) showed some evidence of racial disparities in patient-centered care [63]. In studies that measured the quality of patient-centered care, White patients were twice as likely to receive better patient-centered care than Black patients. At the same time, it is encouraging that racial disparities in patient-centered care were found in less than half the studies surveyed. However, a separate analysis of over 3,000 medical interactions found that Black male patients reported significantly fewer experiences of patient-centered communication than did White male patients [64].

Cultural Competence Training: A Way to Reduce Treatment Disparities?

Within the medical community, there has been considerable investment in training healthcare providers to be more "culturally competent" as a way to improve communication in medical interactions with patients from ethnic or racial minority groups. According to Dr. Laurence Kirmayer, professor of psychiatry at McGill University, "The clinical encounter is shaped by differences between patient and clinician in social position and power, which are associated with differences in cultural knowledge and identity, language, religion and other aspects of cultural identity" [65]. From this perspective, healthcare professionals who are more culturally competent would be expected to be more effective in their communication with patients and thus more successful in producing positive medical outcomes. While efforts to improve cross-cultural competence are clearly well-intended, the impact of these investments is not clear-cut. A review of the effects of cultural competence training produces mixed findings. While cultural competence leads healthcare providers to feel more confident and believe that they are more effective in working with diverse patients, the limited evidence that exists does not consistently show that cultural competence training improves patient trust, satisfaction, or utilization of services [66].

One reason for the limited evidence of increased effectiveness in care is that the models used have overemphasized the discrete, specific character-istics of a limited number of cultures (e.g., African American, Asian American and Pacific Islanders, Latinx, Native American and Alaska Native, and White) with insufficient recognition of the dynamics of culture and cultural change. As a consequence, scholars have proposed a shift in the paradigm from cultural competence to "cultural safety," "cultural humility," and "cultural responsiveness." Although there may be some benefits in healthcare from these various approaches, more work needs to be done to fully realize these benefits in practice.

Race-Related Thoughts and Feelings and Racial Disparities in Healthcare

What explains racial disparities in the quality of communication in medical interactions? Some of the communication issues between non-Black phy-sicians and Black patients may have their origins in the general social and economic disparities produced by systemic racism. For example, limited educational opportunities and other social disadvantages created by systemic racism are likely causes of the fact that health literacy – the ability to understand medical information well enough to make informed treatment decisions and understand treatment instructions – is often much lower among Black patients than among White patients [67]. Lower health literacy may, in turn, affect the quality of Black patients' communication with their physicians and how physicians react to them.

This is, however, at best only a partial explanation of why interactions between Black patients and non-Black physicians (i.e., racially discordant interactions) are so much less productive and effective than are same-race interactions for White patients. A major reason is that racially discordant medical interactions are affected by both physicians' and patients' race-related thoughts and feelings. These are the product of their personal experiences, the ways in which the media portray Black people and White people, and the nature of race relations in the United States. One of the major conclusions in the 2003 IOM report on healthcare disparities is that the thoughts and feelings held by both physicians and their patients play a critical role in racial and ethnic healthcare disparities. We examine the impact of these thoughts and feelings among non-Black physicians and other healthcare providers first because they have attracted the most research attention.[5] Later we discuss the impact of the thoughts and feelings of Black patients on medical interactions and outcomes.

The Effects of Racial Bias among Healthcare Providers:
The Elephant in the Room

As we have noted in several places in this book, most White Americans are reluctant to discuss race relations or to acknowledge that they may be racially prejudiced. Because of the especially strong professional norms in medicine against the expression of racial prejudice, this is particularly true among healthcare providers. One way people avoid any suggestion that they could harbor racial bias is to deny that they see a person's race: They assert they are color blind. Their reasoning is that if they do not see a person's race, they cannot be racially biased. One of the co-authors of this book (LAP) spent almost 18 years as a faculty member in a medical school as part of a research group that studied racial disparities in healthcare. When members of the research group would present their findings on racial

---

[5] We are often asked about racial bias among Black physicians and its effects on medical interactions with either Black patients or White patients. Because of the great dearth of Black physicians, relatively little is known about their race-related attitudes or their impact on medical interactions.

healthcare disparities to an audience of physicians, afterward, they would frequently be approached by a physician who had attended the talk. The physician would typically first clearly state that racial disparities in health-care are deplorable. However, more often than not, these physicians would then say something like, "When I have a patient, I don't see their race."

"Color blindness" is a widely expressed sentiment among non-Black physicians. However, if they did not actually see a patient's race, these physicians would be very different from the vast majority of people in the United States. As discussed in Chapter 1, people often automatically place new acquaintances into social categories. In the United States, an individ-ual's perceived race is an incredibly powerful determinant of how the person will be categorized by others. It is one of the most common forms of automatic social categorization, and it will, in turn, spontaneously activate race-related thoughts and feelings. However, because of social norms and many people's aversion to thinking of themselves as being racist, these reactions may not be openly expressed – and they are often even strongly denied (e.g., "I don't have a racist bone in my body"). Nevertheless, the activation of race-related thoughts and feelings among non-Black physicians is almost inevitable when they interact with Black patients. Many of these thoughts and feelings involve racial bias.

As also discussed at length in Chapter 1, humans have evolved to use two parallel and largely independent systems to process information from the world around them. Daniel Kahneman, professor of psychology and public affairs at Princeton University, described them as the "slow-think-ing" and "fast-thinking" systems [68]. The "slow-thinking" system is activated when people have the time and motivation to reflect on their decisions and potential actions. The slow-thinking system is associated with race-related thoughts and feelings that people are aware of, con-sciously endorse, and can largely control whether or not they express them in their actions. The impact of the slow-thinking system on racial dispar-ities in healthcare primarily involves consciously held negative racial stereotypes about and negative feelings toward Black people among health-care providers. This is known as explicit racial bias.

By contrast, the "fast-thinking" system uses information that a person has already learned extremely well over the course of their life and can access very quickly to guide their thoughts and feelings about different social groups. It operates so rapidly and automatically that a person may not even be aware that these reactions have been activated. The fast-thinking system is associated with implicit racial bias, that is, thoughts and feelings about social groups that are automatically activated and frequently nonconscious. They exist largely outside a person's conscious awareness. As a result, their expression may be difficult to control. The impact of the fast-thinking system on racial disparities in healthcare primarily involves implicit racial stereotypes about and negative feelings toward Black people among healthcare providers. Explicit and implicit racial bias operate somewhat differently to produce racial disparities in healthcare.

Large numbers of Americans honestly believe they are egalitarian and strongly desire to be unbiased. Thus, any evidence that suggests they are racially biased is psychologically threatening to them. Racial stereotypes often provide a convenient self-rationalization or justification for discriminatory actions. That is, a person may think, "I am not acting in this way toward a Black person because I dislike Black people; rather, there is some objectively true characteristic of that person that justifies my action." The problem, however, is that these supposedly "true characteristics" are very often inaccurate beliefs that have their origins in racist myths.

Explicit Racial Bias among Healthcare Providers

Studies of the impact of physicians' racial bias on healthcare disparities have typically used samples primarily composed of White physicians. However, these studies also sometimes include a small number of physicians who would not identify themselves as White (or Black). As noted at the beginning of this book and this chapter, when we discuss this body of research in the pages that follow, we describe the physicians studied as "non-Black." Prior research findings do not inform us about any possible effects of racial/ethnic diversity among the non-Black physicians studied.

Racial Stereotyping and Medical Judgments

Non-Black physicians are not immune from harboring potentially damaging stereotypes. In fact, evidence of their impact on treatment recommendations comes both from experiments that simulate real-life treatment recommendations and from studies of what actually transpires between Black patients and their non-Black physicians. These stereotypes are explicit expressions of racial bias. However, a physician may sometimes express such biases in the absence of any malevolent intentions; these stereotypes simply reflect what a physician believes. Yet, these beliefs can do substantial harm to Black patients.

In simulation studies, hypothetical scenarios involving patients with some medical problems are created. The patients in these scenarios vary by race but are identical in all other respects. Physicians are then asked to make recommendations about the most appropriate treatments for different patients (i.e., either Black patients or White patients). Simulation studies avoid the ethical problems of conducting real-life experiments with actual medical treatments that might affect the quality of care a patient receives. Further, these studies allow researchers to draw much stronger causal inferences about whether any treatment disparities identified were solely because of a patient's race.

Simulation studies conducted with medical professionals quite clearly show that a patient's race alone can substantially affect hypothetical treatment decisions in a variety of contexts. One example is decisions about beginning treatments for socially stigmatized diseases such as HIV. Dr. Sarah Calabrese, professor of psychological and brain sciences at George Washington University, and her colleagues asked medical students (97 percent of whom identified as non-Black) whether they would give hypothetical male patients a medication that would protect them from contracting the HIV virus if they had sex with an HIV-positive partner. Other than race, the characteristics of the two men in each scenario were identical. This study found that the medical students believed that if the Black man had access to the medication, he would be more likely than the White man to engage in unprotected sex [69]. Additionally, the medical students who more strongly held this belief were also less likely to prescribe the medication to the Black patient. Dr. Calabrese and her colleagues believed that these medical students' assumptions about how the Black man in the scenario might act has its roots in a very old and pervasive racist stereotype dating back to the time of slavery – namely, that Black men are more inherently sexually promiscuous and uninhibited in their sexual behaviors than White men. Other simulation studies with large numbers of practicing physicians have yielded the same kinds of results. For example, one study of about 500 physicians found that they believed a hypothetical Black man with HIV would be less likely than a White man with HIV to adhere to their treatment regimens, and because of this stereotype, the physicians would be less likely to prescribe any HIV medications to the Black man [70].

Simulation studies provide clear conclusions about the effects of patient race on hypothetical treatment decisions, but skeptics often question whether similar kinds of results would be found in real medical interactions, in which healthcare providers' decisions would actually make a difference. Nevertheless, studies conducted in actual medical settings also provide evidence that racial stereotypes held by non-Black physicians can affect the quality of the care received by their Black patients. One important study of the impact of racial stereotypes on actual treatment recommendations was conducted by Dr. Michelle van Ryn and her colleagues while she was a professor in the Department of Family Medicine and Community Health and Division of Epidemiology at the University of Minnesota. The researchers recruited about 600 patients who were all considered viable candidates for coronary bypass surgery, as well as their primary physicians [71]. The focus of this study was on the physicians' recommendations regarding whether their patients should receive bypass surgery. Their recommendations would become part of the patients' medical records and, presumably, would later be used by the patients' heart surgeons to help determine whether they would perform coronary bypass surgery.

Coronary bypass surgery entails a number of potential risks for a patient, and the physicians in the study were very cautious in their recommendations – they recommended only a minority of all the patients for the surgery. However, there were significant racial disparities among the male patients: 40 percent of the White patients were recommended for bypass surgery, compared to only 21 percent of the Black patients. While many studies would stop there and simply document this racial treatment disparity, Dr. van Ryn and her colleagues went one important step further and tried to determine *why* this disparity existed. Shortly after each physician had met with their patient, the researchers asked them to complete a questionnaire about their perceptions of the patient's personal characteristics and health-related behaviors.

Analyses of their responses disclosed a number of important differences in how the physicians saw their Black male and White male patients. For example, the physicians saw their Black patients as less educated and more likely than their White patients to abuse drugs. They also saw them as less likely to follow medical advice, complete cardiac rehabilitation, or be physically active. Importantly, the physicians had not received any objective information about their patients' characteristics, including their level of education. But they did have negative racial stereotypes. The major reasons why physicians were less likely to recommend their Black patients for bypass surgery was that they believed the Black men had less education and were less physically active than their White counterparts. Indeed, the physicians' estimate of their Black male patients' level of education was just as important in their recommendations as were the actual characteristics of the patient's heart disease. In other words, the direct cause of the racial disparity in recommending patients for coronary bypass surgery was the physicians' beliefs in specific racial stereotypes.

Another kind of racial stereotype held by many physicians is that Black patients are sometimes not honest or cannot be trusted. Black patients seem to pick up on this. They often report that their physicians seem to doubt their honesty or accuracy when they talk about their symptoms and, as a result, do not take what they say seriously. One Black patient interviewed about this kind of racial bias in healthcare put it this way: "If there was ever a book on medical racism, it should probably just be called, 'They Don't Believe Us'" [72]. Or as another Black patient quoted in the same article put it, "Nine times out of 10, I was completely brushed off."

Derogation of Black Patients in Health Records

Research that has examined the case notes physicians make about their patients suggests that there is good reason for Black patients to have these kinds of concerns. For example, researchers at the Johns Hopkins University School of Medicine found substantial evidence of racial stereotyping in an analysis of physicians' case notes at an outpatient clinic with a predominantly (80 percent) Black patient population [73, 74]. Immediately after seeing a patient, physicians create case notes about the patient's symptoms; these often also contain their more subjective impressions of the patient. These notes facilitate continuity of care across patient visits: Anyone with authorized access to a patient's electronic health records can look at these notes. Notably, they are almost never shared with patients.

In this study, it was necessary to ensure the anonymity of the physicians who wrote these notes; thus, no information about their race (or gender) was collected. However, given that about 95 percent of all physicians in the United States identify as non-Black, it is very likely that the vast majority of these physicians were also non-Black. A linguistic analysis of the case notes disclosed that the physicians seemed much more skeptical of what their Black patients told them about their symptoms than they were of what their White patients told them. For example, when White patients said they had some symptom (e.g., a sharp pain), the physicians would usually just simply write, "patient started to have sharp pain yesterday." By contrast, when Black patients said they had the same symptom, the physicians tended to write that "the patient *reports that* s/he started to have sharp pain yesterday."

The physicians also expressed their lack of trust in the Black patients in other ways. One physician reported in the case notes that they tested a Black patient's credibility by asking them if they took several medications that did not actually exist. There are no comparable examples of any physician doing this kind of "test" with a White patient. Further, physicians' case notes often communicated greater skepticism about what Black patients versus White patients told them about their symptoms. Specifically, physicians were more likely to put quotation marks around Black patients' reported symptoms than when these same symptoms were reported by White patients. Using quotes in this way conveys doubts about whether a patient's self-report was reliable. Finally, in their notes, the physicians often portrayed Black patients as difficult or belligerent.

A separate analysis of electronic health records of over 18,000 patients at a different major urban medical center provided even more direct evidence of physicians' negative thoughts about their Black patients. The researchers first identified the most common negative descriptions of patients that appeared in physicians' case notes. These included words such as non-adherent, aggressive, uncooperative, defensive, and unpleasant. Then the researchers compared the frequency with which these words appeared in the health records of Black patients and White patients. After controlling for things like age, gender, type of insurance, comorbidities, and whether a patient was admitted before or after the COVID-19 pandemic began, the researchers still found that a patient's race was a significant predictor of how they were described by their physicians. The odds that a Black patient would have one or more of these negative descriptors in their health records were 2.5 times greater than for a White patient [75].

It is important to remember that these kinds of seemingly gratuitous entries in a patient's case notes become a permanent part of their medical records. They would be seen by other physicians within the same facility, and because these records are digitized, they could rather easily be accessed at any other facility a patient might visit. Thus, these entries will likely trail that patient whenever they seek healthcare. This kind of information would almost certainly influence subsequent physicians' initial perceptions of their Black patients in a way that could produce poorer medical care from the other providers. That is, an individual physician's racial bias can become part of systemic racism within and across medical facilities.[6]

---

[6] A study published as this book was in production provided another example of physicians' racial stereotypes. The patients in this study were about 4,000 Black and White pregnant women with no history of substance (e.g., cannabis, opioids) use. Despite this, the Black women were significantly more likely to be tested for substance use than were the White women. The tests showed that there no racial differences in substance use. In sum, in the absence of any real evidence of substance use the physicians' racial stereotypes about Black people's substance use made them more likely to believe that the Black women had used substances that would endanger the health of their newborn children. This led them to perform more largely unnecessary tests on these women. This study appeared in the JAMA Health Forum April 7, 2023. https://jamanetwork.com/journals/jama-health-forum/fullarticle/2803729/

It is not surprising that non-Black physicians have explicit racial stereotypes about Black patients that are similar to the kinds of racial stereotypes held by lay people. Certainly, as previously suggested, there seems to be widespread awareness of this among Black patients. But because this kind of bias is consciously held and people can reflect on it, it is possible that physicians may also recognize their own racial biases, be concerned about them, and try to exert some degree of control over the behaviors associated with them. Thus, physicians may often make treatment recommendations for a Black patient that are not dependent on the physicians' racial stereotypes. However, it is much harder to recognize and control the expression of nonconscious, or implicit, thoughts and feelings, and thus they may play a greater role in racial disparities in healthcare.

Implicit Racial Bias among Healthcare Providers

When the 2003 IOM report on healthcare disparities was published, the conclusion that individual racial and ethnic bias among physicians can adversely affect the quality of the healthcare that minority patients receive was contrary to what most Americans and healthcare professionals believed (and many still believe). Indeed, among the general public today, 74 percent of White Americans believe that Black Americans and White Americans are treated equally when they seek medical care [76]. One study of White physicians found that 88 percent of them reported that they gave their Black patients *higher* quality of care than their White patients; the other 12 percent said there was no difference in their care based on their patients' race [77]. It is possible that the physicians surveyed honestly believed this – at least consciously.

The IOM report argued, however, that treatment disparities did not necessarily involve physicians' consciously held feelings or behaviors intended to harm Black patients. Rather, a substantial part of the problem is that physicians could have implicit and often nonconscious thoughts and feelings toward Black people (and other ethnic/racial minorities) that are automatically activated. Physicians may therefore be unaware of the impact of these on their behaviors. It is these kinds of biases that can cause spontaneous behaviors that disadvantage Black patients. Social and cognitive psychologists who studied the fast-thinking system were quite aware that implicit processes were involved in racial bias. But at the time the IOM report was published, most physicians were not familiar with the psychological research on this subtle but important social phenomenon, and some even directly challenged the IOM report on this conclusion. For example, one prominent critic of the IOM report wrote, "It is doubtful that hidden forms of discrimination are prevalent in a profession whose professional norms are set so strongly against it" [78]. Time and a great deal of research has proven this critic quite wrong.

The Project Implicit website at Harvard University has provided data that clearly reveal subtle kinds of racial bias among healthcare providers. As previously discussed in Chapters 1 and 3, this website invites people to anonymously complete measures that access their thoughts and feelings about a range of groups and topics, including race. One race-related measure on this website assesses people's explicit racial attitudes; another measure (the Implicit Association Test, or "IAT") assesses people's implicit racial bias.[7] In the past 10 years alone, nearly 3.75 million individuals across almost 150 countries have completed the measures of racial bias available on the Project Implicit website.

The data collected in Project Implicit have shown that, on average, non-Black Americans have only moderately more favorable explicit attitudes toward White people than they do toward Black people [79]. However, they have substantially more favorable implicit attitudes toward White people than they do toward Black people. This pattern occurs across all socioeconomic classes and geographic regions of the United States and among members of all non-Black racial and ethnic groups. Implicit racial bias is an important part of individual anti-Black racism that can exist outside of people's conscious awareness (Figure 6.1).

The Project Implicit website also includes information on the racial attitudes of about 13,500 people who identified themselves as non-Black physicians [80]. Their attitudes are, overall, not much different from the general public. That is, non-Black physicians, on average, display low-to-moderate levels of explicit racial bias, but rather high levels of implicit racial bias. A similar pattern is found among medical students about to enter the profession. They show a somewhat lower level of explicit racial bias than do physicians but a comparably high level of implicit racial bias [81, 82]. Similar differences in levels of explicit and implicit racial bias have been found among nurses, genetic counselors, mental health professionals, and dentists [77, 79–81].

Psychologists who study racial prejudice do not find it surprising that the level of implicit racial bias among non-Black healthcare professionals is

---

[7] As discussed in Chapter 1, the IAT measures how quickly people automatically associate Black people versus White people with positive and negative feelings. The greater the difference, the greater is their implicit racial bias.

"That's the racist bone in your body you claimed you didn't have."

Figure 6.1   A physician makes a startling discovery.
Source Cartoonstock

similar to that in the general public. Over the course of their lives, physicians and other healthcare professionals are exposed to the same kinds of systemic and individual racism that every other American is. Such experiences create implicit racial bias. Thus, when we talk to professional audiences about the fact that many non-Black physicians have high levels of implicit racial bias, we almost always say that this does not make them villains; it makes them human. But are these feelings important when physicians actually interact with Black patients? Maybe what our clinical colleagues are really saying when they claim their "color blindness" is that while they do, of course, see a patient's race, it does not affect how they deal with them. Unfortunately, this also does not seem to be true.

Implicit Racial Bias and Physician "Tells"
Professional poker players are often worried about displaying a "tell": some seemingly innocuous verbal or nonverbal cue that signals what cards they

have in their hands or that they are bluffing. This is why they often say very little and many of them wear sunglasses or even hoodies. When physicians with high levels of implicit bias interact with Black patients, they also have "tells" – which are readily picked up on by Black patients.

We discovered this about seven years after the IOM report on health-care disparities was published. The story of our discovery begins with a serendipitous research decision. We were preparing a study on ways to improve the quality of interactions between non-Black physicians at a primary care clinic and their Black patients. We were, of course, familiar with basic laboratory research about the negative effects of implicit racial bias in racially discordant social interactions. However, we did not think that we would necessarily find these effects in the quality of racially discordant *medical* interactions. This assumption stemmed from the fact that racially discordant primary care medical interactions are quite different than the racially discordant *social* interactions that had been previously studied by experimental social psychologists.

Whereas social interactions are usually unstructured and quite informal, most medical interactions rely on an underlying "script" that physicians typically follow in order to obtain information about the patient's illness. In highly structured interactions such as medical ones, the characteristics of the situation are typically much more important determinants of what people say or do than are their personal attitudes. In addition, we were aware that even if physicians' implicit racial bias subtly affected their behavior, this would have to be detected by a good percentage of the Black patients *and* influence their feelings about their physician. Moreover, if these feelings were negative, the patients would need to be willing to report this when they filled out questionnaires after the interactions were over. However, patients are usually reluctant to say negative things about their physicians.

Nevertheless, we thought, "Why not measure the physicians' implicit racial bias?" After all, it would be quite easy to do, we could not locate any published studies that had done this, and we were curious as to what we would find. So, a few weeks before they interacted with Black patients at the primary care clinic, we asked the non-Black physicians to complete a measure of their implicit racial bias and a measure of their explicit racial bias.[8] What

---

[8] The IAT – the same measure used in Project Implicit – was used to measure the physicians' implicit racial bias. Their explicit racial bias was determined by using a scale that assessed "modern racism." Modern racism involves negative feelings about the things that might benefit Black Americans and/ or questioning whether racial discrimination remains a serious problem. This was done to deal with White people's common reluctance to openly express negative feelings toward Black people. The modern racism scale is a more subtle measure of explicit racial bias.

we found provided the impetus for much of our research over the
next decade.

*Implicit Racial Bias in Racially Discordant Medical Interactions: Something Is
Not Right Here*
Even within the brief, highly structured interactions that took place in the
clinic, the Black patients saw something in the behaviors of physicians with
higher levels of implicit bias and reacted rather negatively to what they saw.
The physicians who were significantly higher in implicit racial bias were
rated by their Black patients as less warm and friendly, not on their "team,"
and not working with them to treat their medical problem [86]. The same
pattern of patient reactions to high implicit bias physicians has subsequently been independently reported in publications by several other
researchers and has been found among other kinds of healthcare providers,
such as genetic counselors [83–85, 87–89].

Because we had also information about the physicians' level of explicit
racial bias, we could analyze how patients reacted to an even more subtle
kind of racial bias, known as "aversive racism." As we discussed in
Chapter 1, aversive racism is the term used to describe individuals who
at an explicit level report not being biased toward Black people but who
simultaneously harbor high levels of bias at an implicit level. This could be
because such people are not being honest about their explicit feelings.
However, because the two thinking systems operate more or less independently, it is also quite possible for people to genuinely have explicit feelings
that greatly differ from their implicit ones.

When we looked at interactions involving physicians who fit the aversive
racist profile, we found some more intriguing results. One of these involved
differences between how Black patients reacted to the aversive racist
physicians versus the other physicians they encountered. Basic social psychological research has shown that Black people often have particularly
negative reactions when they interact with aversive racists [90]. One reason
why aversive racists may evoke such negative responses from Black people
with whom they interact is that they give off mixed messages. The positive
things they say, which conform to an aversive racist's explicitly positive
feelings, are belied by their nonverbal behaviors, which are rooted in their
implicit bias and indicate discomfort with or dislike of the Black person
with whom they are speaking. This engenders suspicion and mistrust
among Black people who interact with aversive racists because as one of
us has said, "the words and the music don't match." The Black patients
whom we studied also showed an analogous pattern. They reacted much

more negatively to the physicians who displayed the aversive racism profile (i.e., low explicit racial bias, high implicit racial bias) than any other physicians – even those who were high in both explicit and implicit racial bias. Black patients who were treated by physicians with the aversive racism profile were least satisfied with their physicians, saw them as least warm and friendly, felt least like they were on the same team with the physicians, and when contacted a week after the interaction, they reported that they trusted them less than did patients with any other of the physicians.

But what were the physicians' behaviors that led to the patients' negative reactions? We explored this question in other studies. We discovered that, compared to other physicians, those who were higher in implicit racial bias were more likely to dominate their conversations with their Black patients and to use more first-person plural pronouns (e.g., we, us, our). Such pronouns are used by speakers who believe they are of higher social status than the people they are speaking with – in this case it would be their Black patients [91].

We also found that the aversive racist physicians behaved differently than the other physicians – but primarily under certain circumstances. They had more negative reactions than did the other physicians when they interacted with Black patients who had previously reported (unbeknownst to the physicians) that they had experienced racial discrimination in their daily lives. Relative to these other physicians, the aversive racist physicians displayed significantly lower levels of positive emotions, higher levels of negative emotions, and less engagement when interacting with these Black patients [92].

This last finding illustrates two important things about non-Black physicians in racially discordant medical interactions. First, as we discussed earlier, they do attend to what their patients say and do: Black patients play an important role in the outcomes of racially discordant medical interactions. Second, physicians' racial bias influences how they react to what patients say and do, but usually in ways that may serve to mask their racial bias. As discussed in Chapter 1, aversive racists typically seize upon some rationalization that is ostensibly unrelated to the person's race and justify responding negatively to a Black person. In this instance, that justification may have been how aversive racist physicians chose to interpret a particular aspect of a Black patient's behavior. Black patients who report high levels of past discrimination talk significantly more during medical interactions than do Black patients who report low levels of discrimination [93]. Given that high levels of verbal activity are not the norm for Black patients, the Black patients who had experienced more personal discrimination may have been seen as more "difficult" and "uncooperative" than the other patients. If so, this would have provided the aversive racist physicians with a non-racist explanation for how they interacted with and responded to these patients. That is, these physicians might claim they acted as they did not because their patients were Black, but rather because these patients were just more difficult to deal with. It is important to recognize that this non-racist explanation might seem to provide an "out" for the aversive racist physicians. However, this explanation is seriously undercut by the fact that they were the only physicians who responded in this way to Black patients who had previously experienced discrimination in their lives.

In science, replication is important because it confirms both the reliability and validity of a finding. Therefore, we conducted another study of the effects of physicians' implicit racial bias in medical interactions with Black patients. This time, however, the patients were primarily Black women with breast cancer; the physicians were non-Black medical oncologists. We again measured physicians' implicit and explicit racial bias. The measure of explicit racial bias that we used was, however, more obvious than the one we used in our earlier studies – it directly asked the physicians about their feelings toward Black people. Perhaps as a consequence, none of the physicians in this study gave responses that would identify them as being explicitly racially biased. As we noted earlier, there are strong professional norms in medicine against openly expressing racial bias. It is also possible that because these physicians had chosen to work at a hospital where a large percentage of the patients were Black, they were, in fact, quite low in explicit racial bias. But whatever the reasons, the fact that the physicians uniformly scored low on explicit bias meant that we could only test the impact of implicit racial bias on these oncological interactions.

Compared to the primary care setting, finding effects of physician implicit racial bias in oncology interactions presented a much tougher challenge for us. There are several aspects of oncology interactions that could suppress any effects of physician implicit racial bias on their Black patients' reactions to them. Perhaps the most important of these was that in most of these oncological interactions, patients were either first learning they had cancer or being informed that their cancer would require additional treatments. Under such circumstances, patients might be much more likely to focus on the very bad news they have just received than on any subtle behaviors of the oncologists while they gave their patients this information.

However, once again, physicians' implicit racial bias affected the Black patients' responses to them. Physicians who had higher levels of implicit bias were described by patients as less patient-centered and supportive.

Observers who watched video recordings of the interactions also rated the high implicit bias physicians as less supportive of their Black patients. Further, the Black patients reported that it was more difficult to remember the content of their conversations with higher implicit bias oncologists. Finally, in follow-up interviews conducted a week or so after the interactions, patients who interacted with oncologists higher in implicit bias tended to report less trust in them. These latter feelings may have been due to the fact that physicians who were relatively high in implicit bias (and at least reported no explicit bias) were less supportive and patient-oriented and spent less time with their patients [94].[9]

Notably, physician implicit racial bias also indirectly affected the Black patients' feelings about the cancer treatments recommended to them. Black patients who met with oncologists who were relatively high in implicit bias had less confidence that the recommended treatment would work, and they expected more difficulties completing it. This last set of findings about how the physicians' implicit racial bias affected the patients' feelings about their chemotherapy is medically significant because of the particular challenges associated with extended chemotherapy treatments. The drugs used to treat breast cancer often have very negative side effects and are quite costly, and the treatment regimens require rather strict adherence. As a result, the nonadherence rate among all women receiving chemotherapy for breast cancer can be as high as 50 percent, and it is usually even higher among Black women [95, 96]. It seems quite probable that the patients who had lower levels of confidence in their treatment and/or expected more difficulty completing it even before treatment began would be less likely to adhere to their chemotherapy regimen.

Some critics of our own and other researchers' work on the impact of racial bias on medical interactions accept that implicit physician racial bias can affect how physicians act and Black patients feel about them. However, they point out there is a dearth of research showing that implicit bias can actually affect the decisions physicians make about their patients' treatments. In the articles we have written about implicit racial bias, we have acknowledged this. Nevertheless, it is hard to believe that the kinds of physician behaviors and strong patient feelings that we have found to be associated with implicit racial bias would play no role in the medical

---

[9] For various reasons, we were not able to include White patients in either of these studies. However, other studies have included White patients. They have found that White patients often react *more* favorably to higher implicit bias physicians than lower implicit bias physicians. High implicit bias physicians only engender negative reactions in Black patients.

outcomes of racially discordant medical interactions, including subsequent patient adherence.

Further, there is now some direct evidence that physicians' implicit feelings can affect treatment decisions involving Black patients. Dr. Kevin Fiscella, professor of family medicine at the University of Rochester Medical Center, and his colleagues examined how non-Black physicians' implicit racial attitudes affected their decisions to prescribe opioid-based pain medications to Black patients and White patients [97]. The researchers used a modified version of the IAT to assess implicit racial bias in physicians' feelings when they saw a Black person in pain and a White person in pain. Then, sometime later, the physicians encountered Black "patients" or White "patients" who were actually actors carefully trained to play the role of a person with severe pain from lung cancer. These simulated "patients" told the physicians they had recently moved to the area where the physicians practiced and did not yet have regular medical care but needed a new prescription for pain medication.[10]

The researchers compared willingness to provide that prescription among physicians who were low in implicit racial bias to those who were high in implicit racial bias. Among the physicians relatively low in implicit bias, there were no disparities in the likelihood they would prescribe the needed pain medication to Black patients and White patients. By contrast, among the physicians relatively high in implicit bias, there was a significant difference in their willingness to prescribe the pain medication to Black patients and White patients. The likelihood that the physicians relatively high in implicit racial bias would prescribe an opioid medication to a Black patient was a fraction of what it was for the White patients. These physicians' implicit racial feelings were associated with differences in a treatment decision. In sum, this rather large body of research on the impact of implicit racial bias provides rather strong confirmation of its role in racial healthcare disparities. This fact has come to be widely accepted by individual physicians and the professional organizations that represent them.

Race-Related Thoughts and Feelings of Black Patients and Healthcare Disparities

As we mentioned earlier, the 2003 IOM report on healthcare inequities gave relatively more attention to how healthcare professionals' race-related

---

[10] The physicians had previously agreed to be in this study and knew that at some point in the next year they would have a patient who was really an actor and that the interaction would be recorded. The study was approved by Institutional Review Boards at several different universities.

thoughts and feelings might affect the healthcare received by minority patients than to the potential effects of the thoughts and feelings of those patients. But medical interactions represent interpersonal interactions between both physicians and their patients. The medical outcomes of these interactions, like all interpersonal interactions, are thus jointly determined by both participants in them. Further, it is patients who ultimately decide what they will do about their health. Thus, in order to more fully understand individual-level causes of racial disparities in healthcare, it is important to study Black patients' thoughts, feelings, experiences, and behavior in racially discordant medical interactions.

Black Patients in Medical Interactions: Being on the Lookout

Research on racially discordant medical interactions suggests that one consequence of the lived experiences of Black patients is that they are vigilant for signs of racial bias in physicians with whom they interact. Black patients in our own and other studies have displayed an incredibly accurate "radar" that can detect underlying implicit racial bias in their physicians. This ability is not peculiar to medical interactions. One study found that a 20-second glimpse of a White person interacting with a Black person was enough for Black observers to accurately identify White people with higher levels of racial prejudice [98]. Thus, even if providers are not aware of the "tells" they are emitting, their Black patients are very much aware of them.

One likely explanation of why Black people are so good at detecting cues of bias is that daily exposure to racial discrimination and the subordinate social positions that society has historically forced on Black Americans have made them especially attuned to the nonverbal behaviors of the non-Black people with whom they interact [99]. Evidence of this kind of focus was found among Black patients who were asked to watch video recordings of interactions they had just had with their non-Black physicians and stop the recordings when they thought they saw their physicians display either positive or negative behaviors [100]. The clear majority of behaviors that caught patients' attention were subtle nonverbal and verbal physician behaviors, which included eye contact, blinking, smiling, hand-shaking, tone of voice, and even clearing of throats. One patient talked quite specifically about apparent contradiction in the physician's facial expressions. The patient explained, "She's got a lot of facial expressions... I don't see her looking at me. It's like she's... her face is this way, but her eyes are like she's thinking about something else... She's just um ... physically there but mentally she's probably making a grocery list or something." This patient not only picked up on some very subtle behaviors, she also used these to make inferences about the physician's true underlying feelings. We do not know the actual accuracy of these particular inferences, but this does show how vigilant Black patients are for signs of possible racial bias in the physicians they see.

Black Patients' Impact on Racially Discordant Medical Interactions

Like non-Black physicians, Black patients bring their own race-related thoughts and feelings to racially discordant medical interactions. Data from the Project Implicit website shows that Black Americans differ somewhat from other Americans in the pattern of their explicit and implicit race-related feelings. The Black people who completed the assessments exhibited a strong explicit preference for Black people over White people, but a small implicit preference for White people [80]. This latter finding most likely reflects the fact that over the course of their lives many Black Americans have been exposed to many of the same race-related thoughts and feelings as have other Americans.

Prior Experiences with Discrimination

The explicit attitudes of Black patients may explain partially why they typically communicate more easily with physicians who are also Black. However, other things besides the race of a physician play important roles in the outcomes of medical interactions involving Black patients. One of these is Black patients' experiences with past racial discrimination in general; another is their feelings about how they have been treated by medical professionals [101]. Thus, in our research on racially discordant medical interactions we obtained patient reports of how frequently they had experienced various kinds of racial discrimination (e.g., employment, education, law enforcement) and measured their mistrust of medical providers as a group, as well as suspicions about how the healthcare system generally treats Black patients.

Higher levels of past discrimination were associated with Black patients being less satisfied with the physicians they saw, feeling less like they and the physician were on the same team, having more negative views of the treatments recommended to them (e.g., expecting them to be more difficult to complete), and subsequently adhering less to physician recommendations [102]. Also, mistrust of physicians and suspicion of the healthcare system in general are both associated with more negative patient feelings about the treatments physicians recommend to them [93, 102].

In addition, as noted earlier, greater past discrimination is associated with Black patients talking more and their physicians talking less. Interracial interactions are often stressful and challenging to Black people, in part, because of anticipated racial discrimination. Thus, talking more during racially discordant medical interactions may be a way for Black patients to establish a greater sense of control in these interactions and protect themselves from the anticipated mistreatment [103]. Higher levels of Black patients' mistrust in physicians are also associated with the patients using fewer words that express positive emotions, even though they talk more overall. They are also assciated with lower evaluations of the physicians' supportiveness and less trust of physicians after their visit. In sum, while relatively less attention has been given to what Black patients say and do in racially discordant medical interactions, Black patients' prior experiences and their thoughts and feelings related to how they have been treated by the medical establishment play critical roles in the dynamics of these interactions and their outcomes.

Thus far we have, for organizational purposes, separately discussed the effects of the race-related thoughts and feelings of non-Black physicians and Black patients. However, these thoughts and feelings are expressed in an interpersonal interaction, and it is axiomatic that the outcomes of such interactions are *jointly* determined. We have found that the two parties mutually influence one another and their feelings about their interactions. For example, in the oncology interactions physicians rated their Black patients who had higher levels of mistrust in physicians as less likely to adhere to a chemotherapy regimen than other patients. We could not unambiguously identify the specific patient behaviors that produced these perceptions, but a statistical analysis suggests it was likely due to the higher-mistrust patients expressing fewer positive emotions during the interactions.

In another analysis of the oncology interactions, we investigated the joint effects of patient explicit and physician implicit race-related feelings. We found that when Black patients with higher levels of mistrust of physicians interacted with non-Black physicians with higher levels of implicit racial bias, these interactions produced the lowest physician estimates of how well the Black patients would tolerate their chemotherapy. Also, the interactions between patients high in suspicion and physicians high in implicit racial bias resulted in the highest patient estimates of the difficulty in tolerating the recommended treatments [104]. Thus, it seems that this combination of patients' and physicians' race-related thoughts and feelings created an almost "perfect storm" of negative expectations about the success of the recommended treatments for the patients suffering from cancer. This very likely affected whether patients successfully completed the treatments recommended by their physicians.

Broad-Based Mistrust of Healthcare

Our own work has largely focused on the impact of two specific kinds of mistrust-related feelings - mistrust of physicians and suspicions about healthcare - on Black patients' thoughts and behavior within racially discordant medical interactions. Other researchers have investigated how more general kinds of mistrust can affect a wide range of health-related behaviors among Black people. These researchers measure "medical mistrust," which more broadly encompasses mistrust of individual healthcare providers, the healthcare system in general, medical treatments, and the government as a provider of public health [105, 106].

As a group, Black Americans have much higher levels of medical mistrust than do White Americans. A 2020 national poll gathered information on Black Americans' and White Americans' views of the US healthcare system. Seventy percent of the Black respondents felt that the healthcare system treats people unfairly because of their race or ethnicity – almost double the percentage of the White respondents who believed this to be true. Black respondents were over twice as likely as White respondents to believe that Black patients receive a substandard quality of care (54 percent versus 26 percent). Additionally, while 78 percent of White respondents said they trusted their physicians, 59 percent of Black respondents felt this way [107].

Medical mistrust among Black Americans has many interrelated causes. The most immediate of these are the kinds of negative experiences Black patients very often have in the medical encounters we have described throughout this book. Of course, anyone can have a bad interaction with a healthcare professional, but the disturbing similarity among Black patients' accounts of physicians either apparently failing to hear them or simply ignoring their requests for certain medications and treatments may be placed in a broader context. Black patients often quite reasonably see their own and acquaintances' negative encounters as part of the systemic and individual racism that permeates American society, in general, and healthcare, in particular.

There is also the impact of Black patients knowing about the shameful legacy of racism in medicine, including the kinds of unethical medical studies, which used Black people as unwilling subjects (see Chapter 4). For example, a number of years after the Tuskegee Syphilis Study ended, learning about it engendered substantial medical mistrust and less use of medical services among Black men who closely identified with the study's Black victims [108].

Further, social media provide other "data" to support feelings of medical mistrust. The YouTube video of Dr. Susan Moore, which we described at the beginning of this chapter, is one example. Another one is tennis star Serena Williams' story of how she was treated after the birth of her daughter. It was widely circulated in various media outlets. Shortly before Ms. Williams underwent emergency surgery for a Cesarean delivery, she felt short of breath and then found herself gasping for air soon after the birth of her daughter. Believing she might have blood clots in her lungs (she had them before), she immediately requested a CT scan of her lungs and a blood thinner. But initially the medical staff refused to do this because they thought that pain medication had made her confused. When she finally received the scan, it was disclosed that she did indeed have several small blood clots in her lungs. In a widely read CNN article about the consequences of the inadequate treatment she received, Ms. Williams wrote that "[t]his [mistreatment] sparked a slew of health complications that I am lucky to have survived. First my C-section wound popped open due to the intense coughing I endured as a result of the embolism. I returned to surgery, where the doctors found a large hematoma, a swelling of clotted blood, in my abdomen. And then I returned to the operating room for a procedure that prevents clots from traveling to my lungs. When I finally made it home to my family, I had to spend the first six weeks of motherhood in bed" [109].[11]

One of the negative health outcomes stemming from medical mistrust is that it often leads Black Americans to be less likely to engage in behaviors that would prevent certain illnesses or facilitate their resolution. Dr. Laura Bogart of the RAND Corporation succinctly states this problem: "Mistrust becomes problematic when it stops [Black] people from engaging in healthy behaviors or when it leads to avoidance of the healthcare system" [111].

National and regional surveys have found, for example, that Black Americans had much less trust in COVID-19 vaccines than did White Americans. One Black respondent in these surveys explained their reluctance to get the vaccine by saying, "I don't trust the medical community

---

[11] Ms. Williams' experiences were not unique. The maternal mortality rate among Black women is 2.5 times as great as the rate for White women (37 per 100,000 pregnancies versus 15 per 100,000) [110].

because of mistakes in the past" [112]. This mistrust of vaccines among Black Americans is so pervasive that it has even made it to the long-running TV show, *Saturday Night Live*. In a December 2020 show, comedian Michael Che, one of the anchors on the news parody "Weekend Update," used Black people's deeply held mistrust of vaccines to make a joke about the CDC starting to recommend that all people receive COVID-19 vaccines. Alluding to the fact that the Black men in the Tuskegee Study were falsely led to believe they were receiving treatment for their syphilis, Che remarked, "I got mixed feelings on this vaccine. On one hand, I'm Black. [So] naturally, I don't really trust it. But on the other hand, I'm on a White TV show. So, I might actually get the real one" [113].

Black patients with higher levels of medical mistrust are also less likely to get preventive screenings for various cancers, such as breast cancer, cervical cancer, and prostate cancer [114–116]. Across a variety of illnesses, medical mistrust is a major reason why Black patients are significantly less likely than White patients to adhere to treatment recommendations. For example, Black men with HIV who have higher levels of medical mistrust are less likely to adhere to antiretroviral medications [117]. A review of 58 studies that included several thousands of patients with hypertension and high cholesterol found that Black patients were significantly less likely to take their prescribed medications than White patients. After analyzing all the factors that could explain this disparity (e.g., cost of medications, ease of filling prescriptions, socioeconomic factors), the authors concluded that the primary cause of these adherence disparities was "medical mistrust" [118].

Before concluding this discussion of medical mistrust among Black patients, it is important to underscore the point that this mistrust is not some sort of paranoid fantasy. The material on racial disparities in health-care that we presented in Chapters 4 and 5 and in this chapter provides more than ample reasons for Black patients to be mistrustful of the system providing their healthcare. Further, systemic and individual anti-Black racism in the healthcare system creates a vicious circle that represents yet another path to racial disparities in Americans' health. Anti-Black racism creates medical mistrust, which makes it less likely that Black people will engage in behaviors that will benefit their health.

Putting It All Together

Although race is a social construct and does not represent any actual medical or biological characteristic, it significantly affects the quality of the medical treatments Black patients receive. This is largely because of the enormous significance of a person's socially assigned race in almost all social interactions, including medical ones. One result of this is the difficulties in communication that occur when Black patients and non-Black physicians interact. The race-related thoughts and feelings of healthcare providers produce racial healthcare disparities, as well. Among providers, both explicit and implicit kinds of racial bias can result in Black patients receiving a lower quality of care. For example, racial stereotyping can produce racial disparities in medical treatments. Also, in racially discordant medical interactions, racial bias produces physician behaviors that can directly and indirectly create racial disparities in the outcomes of these interactions.

Additionally, the race-related experiences, thoughts, and feelings of Black patients also affect their healthcare. In racially discordant medical interactions, the experience of past discrimination and general mistrust of healthcare providers can negatively influence Black patients' perceptions of specific physicians and the treatments they recommend. Moreover, the race-related thoughts, feelings, and behaviors of non-Black physicians and Black patients can mutually influence one another and exacerbate racial disparities in healthcare. General mistrust of the US healthcare system can further promote racial health disparities by making Black people less likely to engage in behaviors that would prevent or control certain illnesses.

In sum, racism at the individual level presents as great a barrier to racial equity in health and healthcare as does systemic racism. It joins the other specific causes we have discussed in previous chapters in causing a morally unjustifiable public health crisis in the United States. The final chapter offers possible ways to effectively address this crisis.

REFERENCES

1. Galarneau, C. (2018). Getting King's words right. *Journal of Health Care for the Poor and Underserved, 29*(1), 5–8. https://muse.jhu.edu/article/686948/pdf

2. Democracy Now. (2020, December 30). *"This is how black people get killed": Dr. Susan Moore dies of COVID after decrying racist care* [Video].YouTube. https://www.youtube.com/watch?v=7v1Oyp_bBGk

3. Edwards, R. R., Doleys, D. M., Fillingim, R. B., & Lowery, D. (2001). Ethnic differences in pain tolerance: Clinical implications in a chronic pain population. *Psychosomatic Medicine, 63*(2), 316–323. https://doi.org/10.1097/00006842-200103000-00018

4. Campbell, C. M., & Edwards, R. R. (2012). Ethnic differences in pain and pain management. *Pain Management*, *2*(3), 219–230. https://doi.org/10 .2217/pmt.12.7

5. Joynt, M., Train, M. K., Robbins, B. W., Halterman, J. S., Caiola, E., & Fortuna, R. J. (2013). The impact of neighborhood socioeconomic status and race on the prescribing of opioids in emergency departments throughout the United States. *Journal of General Internal Medicine*, *28*(12), 1604–1610. https://pubmed.ncbi.nlm.nih.gov/23797920/

6. Lee, H. H., Lewis, C. W., & McKinney, C. M. (2016). Disparities in emergency department pain treatment for toothache. *JDR Clinical & Translational Research*, *1*(3), 226–233. https://doi.org/10.1177/2380084416655745

7. Berger, A. J., Wang, Y., Rowe, C., Chung, B., Chang, S., & Haleblian, G. (2021). Racial disparities in analgesic use amongst patients presenting to the emergency department for kidney stones in the United States. *The American Journal of Emergency Medicine*, *39*(1), 71–74. https://doi.org/10.1016/j.ajem .2020.01.017

8. Islam, J. Y., Deveaux, A., Previs, R. A., & Akinyemiju, T. (2021). Racial and ethnic disparities in palliative care utilization among gynecological cancer patients. *Gynecologic Oncology*, *160*(2), 469–476. https://doi.org/10.1016/j .ygyno.2020.11.031

9. Mukhopadhyay, A., D'Angelo, R., Senser, E., Whelan, K., Wee, C. C., & Mukamal, K. J. (2020). Racial and insurance disparities among patients presenting with chest pain in the US: 2009–2015. *The American Journal of Emergency Medicine*, *38*(7), 1373–1376. https://doi.org/10.1016/j.ajem.2019 .11.018

10. Meghani, S. H., Kang, Y., Chittams, J., McMenamin, E., Mao, J. J., & Fudin, J. (2014). African Americans with cancer pain are more likely to receive an analgesic with toxic metabolite despite clinical risks: A mediation analysis study. *Journal of Clinical Oncology*, *32*(25), 2773–2779. https://doi .org/10.1200/jco.2013.54.7992

11. Schuler, M. S., Schell, T. L., & Wong, E. C. (2021). Racial/ethnic differences in prescription opioid misuse and heroin use among a national sample, 1999–2018. *Drug and Alcohol Dependence*, *221*, 108588. https://www.ncbi .nlm.nih.gov/pmc/articles/PMC8026521/

12. Subramaniam, A. V., Patlolla, S. H., Cheungpasitporn, W., Sundaragiri, P. R., Miller, P. E., Barsness, G. W., Bell, M. R., Holmes, D. R., Jr., & Vallabhajosyula, S. (2021). Racial and ethnic disparities in management and outcomes of cardiac arrest complicating acute myocardial infarction. *Journal of American Heart Association*, *10*(11), e019907. https://doi.org/10 .1161/jaha.120.019907

13. Simon, S., & Ho, P. M. (2020). Ethnic and racial disparities in acute myocardial infarction. *Current Cardiology Reports*, *22*(9), 88. https:// pubmed.ncbi.nlm.nih.gov/32648143/

14. Alkhouli, M., Alqahtani, F., Holmes, D. R., & Berzingi, C. (2019). Racial disparities in the utilization and outcomes of structural heart disease

interventions in the United States. *Journal of American Heart Association, 8* (15), e012125. https://doi.org/10.1161/jaha.119.012125

15. Bach, P. B., Schrag, D., Brawley, O. W., Galaznik, A., Yakren, S., & Begg, C. B. (2002). Survival of Blacks and Whites after a cancer diagnosis. *Journal of the American Medical Association (JAMA), 287*(16), 2106–2113. https://doi .org/10.1001/jama.287.16.2106

16. Griggs, J. J., Sorbero, M. E., Stark, A. T., Heininger, S. E., & Dick, A. W. (2003). Racial disparity in the dose and dose intensity of breast cancer adjuvant chemotherapy. *Breast Cancer Research and Treatment, 81*(1), 21–31. https://doi.org/10.1023/a:1025481505537

17. Riggio, A. I., Varley, K. E., & Welm, A. L. (2021). The lingering mysteries of metastatic recurrence in breast cancer. *British Journal of Cancer, 124*(1), 13–26. https://www.nature.com/articles/s41416-020-01161-4

18. Memorial Sloan Kettering Cancer Center. (2021). Adjuvant therapy for breast cancer: What it is, how to manage side effects, and answers to common questions. https://www.mskcc.org/cancer-care/patient-education/adjuvant-therapy-breast

19. Snead, F., Slade, A. N., Oppong, B. A., Sutton, A. L., & Sheppard, V. B. (2020). Narrowing racial gaps in breast cancer: Factors affecting probability of adjuvant radiation therapy. *Advances in Radiation Oncology, 5*(1), 17–26. https://doi.org/10.1016/j.adro.2019.07.014

20. Kheirandish, P., & Chinegwundoh, F. (2011). Ethnic differences in prostate cancer. *British Journal of Cancer, 105*(4), 481–485. https://doi.org/10.1038/ bjc.2011.273

21. Hayn, M. H., Orom, H., Shavers, V. L., Sanda, M. G., Glasgow, M., Mohler, J. L., & Underwood, W., III (2011). Racial/ethnic differences in receipt of pelvic lymph node dissection among men with localized/regional prostate cancer. *Cancer, 117*(20), 4651–4658. https://doi.org/10.1002/cncr.26103

22. Rude, T., Walter, D., Ciprut, S., Kelly, M. D., Wang, C., Fagerlin, A., Langford, A. T., Lepor, H., Becker, D. J., Li, H., Loeb, S., Ravenell, J., Leppert, J. T., & Makarov, D. V. (2021). Interaction between race and prostate cancer treatment benefit in the Veterans Health Administration. *Cancer, 127*(21), 3985–3990. https://doi.org/10.1002/cncr.33643

23. Schwartz, K., Powell, I. J., Underwood, W., George, J., Yee, C., & Banerjee, M. (2009). Interplay of race, socioeconomic status, and treatment on survival of patients with prostate cancer. *Urology, 74*(6), 1296–1302. https://doi.org/ 10.1016/j.urology.2009.02.058

24. Bliton, J. N., Parides, M., Muscarella, P., Papalezova, K. T., & In, H. (2021). Understanding racial disparities in gastrointestinal cancer outcomes: Lack of surgery contributes to lower survival in African American patients. *Cancer Epidemiology Biomarkers and Prevention, 30*(3), 529–538. https://doi .org/10.1158/1055-9965.Epi-20-0950

25. Shavers, V. L., & Brown, M. L. (2002). Racial and ethnic disparities in the receipt of cancer treatment. *JNCI: Journal of the National Cancer Institute, 94* (5), 334–357. https://doi.org/10.1093/jnci/94.5.334

26. National Institute on Aging. (n. d.). *End of life: What are palliative care and hospice care?* National Institutes of Health. https://www.nia.nih.gov/health/what-are-palliative-care-and-hospice-care

27. National Cancer Institute. (2023, January 18). Planning the transition to end-of-life care in advanced cancer (PDQ®)–Health Professional Version. National Institutes of Health. https://pubmed.ncbi.nlm.nih.gov/26389513/

28. Mullins, M. A., Ruterbusch, J. J., Clarke, P., Uppal, S., Wallner, L. P., & Cote, M. L. (2021). Trends and racial disparities in aggressive end-of-life care for a national sample of women with ovarian cancer. *Cancer, 127*(13), 2229–2237. https://doi.org/10.1002/cncr.33488

29. Perry, L. M., Walsh, L. E., Horswell, R., Miele, L., Chu, S., Melancon, B., Lefante, J., Blais, C. M., Rogers, J. L., & Hoerger, M. (2021). Racial disparities in end-of-life care between Black and White adults with metastatic cancer. *Journal of Pain and Symptom Management, 61*(2), 342–349.e1. https://pubmed.ncbi.nlm.nih.gov/32947018

30. Karanth, S., Rajan, S. S., Revere, F. L., & Sharma, G. (2019). Factors affecting racial disparities in end-of-life care costs among lung cancer patients: A SEER-Medicare-based Study. *American Journal of Clinical Oncology, 42*(2), 143–153. https://doi.org/10.1097/coc.0000000000000485

31. Mar, J. (2018, November 16). *Racial disparities in end-of-life care – How mistrust keeps many African Americans away from hospice.* Center for Health Journalism. https://centerforhealthjournalism.org/fellowships/projects/racial-disparities-end-life-care-how-mistrust-keeps-many-african-americans-away

32. Mack, J. W., Paulk, M. E., Viswanath, K., & Prigerson, H. G. (2010). Racial disparities in the outcomes of communication on medical care received near death. *Archives of Internal Medicine, 170*(17), 1533–1540. https://doi.org/10.1001/archinternmed.2010.322

33. Goyal, M. K., Kuppermann, N., Cleary, S. D., Teach, S. J., & Chamberlain, J. M. (2015). Racial disparities in pain management of children with appendicitis in emergency departments. *JAMA Pediatrics, 169*(11), 996–1002. https://doi.org/10.1001/jamapediatrics.2015.1915

34. Gerber, J. S., Prasad, P. A., Localio, A. R., Fiks, A. G., Grundmeier, R. W., Bell, L. M., Wasserman, R. C., Rubin, D. M., Keren, R., & Zaoutis, T. E. (2013). Racial differences in antibiotic prescribing by primary care pediatricians. *Pediatrics, 131*(4), 677–684. https://doi.org/10.1542/peds.2012-2500

35. Lipman, T. H., Smith, J. A., Patil, O., Willi, S. M., & Hawkes, C. P. (2021). Racial disparities in treatment and outcomes of children with type 1 diabetes. *Pediatric Diabetes, 22*(2), 241–248. https://doi.org/10.1111/pedi.13139

36. Bitterman, D. S., Bona, K., Laurie, F., Kao, P.-C., Terezakis, S. A., London, W. B., & Haas-Kogan, D. A. (2020). Race disparities in proton radiotherapy use for cancer treatment in patients enrolled in Children's Oncology Group trials. *JAMA Oncology, 6*(9), 1465–1468. https://doi.org/10.1001/jamaoncol.2020.2259

37. Jacobs, A. J., Lindholm, E. B., Levy, C. F., Fish, J. D., & Glick, R. D. (2017). Racial and ethnic disparities in treatment and survival of pediatric

sarcoma. *Journal of Surgical Research, 219*, 43–49. https://pubmed.ncbi.nlm
.nih.gov/29078908/
38. Gallegos, A., Dudovitz, R., Biely, C., Chung, P. J., Coker, T. R., Barnert, E.,
Guerrero, A. D., Szilagyi, P. G., & Nelson, B. B. (2021). Racial disparities in
developmental delay diagnosis and services received in early childhood.
Academic Pediatrics, 21(7), 1230–1238. https://pubmed.ncbi.nlm.nih.gov/
34020100/
39. Morgan, P., Staff, J., Hillemeier, M. M., Farkas, G., & Maczuga, S. (2013).
Racial and ethnic disparities in ADHD diagnosis from kindergarten to eighth
grade. *Pediatrics, 132*(1) 85–93. https://pubmed.ncbi.nlm.nih.gov/23796743/
40. Arnold, M., Hsu, L., Pipkin, S., McFarland, W., & Rutherford, G. W.
(2009). Race, place and AIDS: The role of socioeconomic context on racial
disparities in treatment and survival in San Francisco. *Social Science &
Medicine, 69*(1), 121–128. https://doi.org/10.1016/j.socscimed.2009.04.019
41. Oloyede, E. O. (2017). A review of hypertension treatment disparities.
Journal of Cardiology and Cardiovascular Therapy, 7(1), 24–28. https://
EconPapers.repec.org/RePEc:adp:ojocct:v:7:y:2017:i:1:p:24-28
42. Balla, S., Gomez, S. E., & Rodriguez, F. (2020). Disparities in cardiovascular
care and outcomes for women from racial/ethnic minority backgrounds.
Current Treatment Options in Cardiovascular Medicine, 22(12), 75. https://
pubmed.ncbi.nlm.nih.gov/33223802/
43. Curtis, J. R., McClure, L. A., Delzell, E., Howard, V. J., Orwoll, E., Saag, K.
G., Safford, M., & Howard, G. (2009). Population-based fracture risk
assessment and osteoporosis treatment disparities by race and gender.
Journal of General Internal Medicine, 24(8), 956–962. https://www.ncbi
.nlm.nih.gov/pmc/articles/PMC2710475/
44. Branson, C. O., Ferree, A., Hohler, A. D., & Saint-Hilaire, M.-H. (2016).
Racial disparities in Parkinson disease: A systematic review of the literature.
Advances in Parkinson's Disease, 5(4), 87. https://www.ncbi.nlm.nih.gov/
pmc/articles/PMC7458499/
45. Akinhanmi, M. O., Biernacka, J. M., Strakowski, S. M., McElroy, S. L.,
Balls Berry, J. E., Merikangas, K. R., Assari, S., McInnis, M. G., Schulze, T.
G., LeBoyer, M., Tamminga, C., Patten, C., & Frye, M. A. (2018). Racial
disparities in bipolar disorder treatment and research: A call to action. *Bipolar
Disorders, 20*(6), 506–514. https://doi.org/10.1111/bdi.12638
46. Wiltz, J. L., Feehan, A. K., Molinari, N. M., Ladva, C. N., Truman, B. I.,
Hall, J., Block, J. P., Reasmussen, S. A., Denson, J. L., Trick, W. E., Weiner, M.
G., Koumans, W., Gundlapalli, A., Carton, T. W., & Boehmer, T. K. (2022).
Racial and ethnic disparities in receipt of medications for treatment of COVID-
19 – United States, March 2020–August 2021. *Morbidity and Mortality Weekly
Report, 71*(3), 96–102. https://www.asahp.org/asahp-newswire/2022/1/18/racial-
and-ethnic-disparities-in-receipt-of-treatment-medications
47. Gangopadhyaya, A. (2021, July). *Do Black and White patients experience
similar rates of adverse safety events at the same hospital?* Robert Wood
Johnson Foundation. https://www.rwjf.org/en/insights/our-research/2021/

07/do-black-and-white-patients-experience-similar-rates-of-adverse-safety-events-at-the-same-hospital.html

48. Saha, S., Freeman, M., Toure, J., Tippens, K. M., Weeks, C., & Ibrahim, S. (2008). Racial and ethnic disparities in the VA health care system: A systematic review. *Journal of Internal Medicine, 23*(5), 651–671. https://pubmed.ncbi.nlm.nih.gov/18301951/

49. Kanwal, F., Kramer, J., El-Serag, H., Frayne, S., Clark, J., Cao, Y., Taylor, T., Smith, D., White, D., & Asch, S. M. (2006). Race and gender differences in the use of direct acting antiviral agents for hepatitis c virus. *Clinical Infectious Diseases, 63*(3), 291–299. https://academic.oup.com/cid/article/63/3/291/2595031

50. Yong, C., Azarabal, F., Abnousi, F., Heidenreich, P., Schmitt, S., Fan, J., Than, C., Ullal, A., Yang, F., Phibbs, C., Frayne, S., Ho, M., Shore, S., Mahaffey, K., & Turakhia, M. (2016). Racial differences in quality of anticoagulation therapy for atrial fibrillation (from the TREAT-AF Study) *The American Journal of Cardiology, 117*(1), 61–63. https://pubmed.ncbi.nlm.nih.gov/26552504/

51. Tehranifar, P., Neugut, A. I., Phelan, J. C., Link, B. G., Liao, Y., Desai, M., & Terry, M. B. (2009). Medical advances and racial/ethnic disparities in cancer survival. *Cancer Epidemiology, Biomarkers, and Prevention, 18*(10), 2701–2708. https://doi.org/10.1158/1055-9965.Epi-09-0305

52. Takeshita, J., Wang, S., Loren, A. W., Mitra, N., Shults, J., Shin, D. B., & Sawinski, D. L. (2020). Association of racial/ethnic and gender concordance between patients and physicians with patient experience ratings. *JAMA Network Open, 3*(11), e2024583–e2024583. https://doi.org/10.1001/jamanetworkopen.2020.24583

53. Shen, M. J., Peterson, E. B., Costas-Muñiz, R., Hernandez, M. H., Jewell, S. T., Matsoukas, K., & Bylund, C. L. (2018). The effects of race and racial concordance on patient-physician communication: A systematic review of the literature. *Journal of Racial and Ethnic Health Disparities, 5*(1), 117–140. https://pubmed.ncbi.nlm.nih.gov/28275996/

54. Hagiwara, N., Dovidio, J. F., Stone, J., & Penner, L. A. (2020). Applied racial/ethnic healthcare research using implicit measures. *Social Cognition, 38* (suppl) s68–s97. https://guilfordjournals.com/doi/pdf/10.1521/soco.2020.38.supp.s68

55. Epstein, R. M., & Street, R. L. Jr. (2007). *Patient-centered communication in cancer care: Promoting healing and reducing suffering.* National Cancer Institute, NIH Publication No. 07-6225, Bethesda. https://scirp.org/reference/referencespapers.aspx?referenceid=1678055

56. King, A., & Hoppe, R. B. (2013). "Best practice" for patient-centered communication: A narrative review. *Journal of Graduate Medical Education, 5*(3), 385–393. https://doi.org/10.4300/jgme-d-13-00072.1

57. Berwick, D. M. (2009, July 9). Berwick on patient-centered care: Comments and responses. *Health Affairs.* https://www.healthaffairs.org/do/10.1377/forefront.20090709.001521

58. Bertakis, K. D., & Azari, R. (2011). Patient-centered care is associated with decreased health care utilization. *Journal of American Board of Family Medicine, 24*(3), 229–239. https://doi.org/10.3122/jabfm.2011.03.100170

59. Zolnierek, K. B., & Dimatteo, M. R. (2009). Physician communication and patient adherence to treatment: A meta-analysis. *Medical Care, 47*(8), 826–834. https://doi.org/10.1097/MLR.0b013e31819a5acc

60. Sany, S. B. T., Behzhad, F., Ferns, G., & Peyman, N. (2020). Communication skills training for physicians improves health literacy and medical outcomes among patients with hypertension: A randomized controlled trial. *BMC Health Services Research, 20*(1), "Article number" 60. https://pubmed.ncbi.nlm.nih.gov/31973765/

61. Schoenthaler, A., Knafl, G. J., Fiscella, K., & Ogedegbe, G. (2017). Addressing the social needs of hypertensive patients: The role of patient-provider communication as a predictor of medication adherence. *Circulation: Cardiovascular Quality and Outcomes, 10*(9), e003659. https://doi.org/10.1161/circoutcomes.117.003659

62. Ulin, K., Malm, D., & Nygårdh, A. (2015). What is known about the benefits of patient-centered care in patients with heart failure. *Current Heart Failure Reports, 12*(6), 350–359. https://pubmed.ncbi.nlm.nih.gov/26497193/

63. Agency for Healthcare Research and Quality. (2021). *National healthcare quality and disparities reports: Disparities by race/ethnicity, income, insurance coverage, and metropolitan status by priority areas.* https://www.ncbi.nlm.nih.gov/books/NBK587186/

64. Mitchell, J. A., & Perry, R. (2020). Disparities in patient-centered communication for Black and Latino men in the U.S.: Cross-sectional results from the 2010 health and retirement study. *PLoS ONE, 15*(9), e0238356. https://doi.org/10.1371/journal.pone.0238356

65. Kirmayer, L. (2012). Rethinking cultural competence. *Transcultural Psychiatry, 49*(2) 149–164. https://journals.sagepub.com/doi/pdf/10.1177/1363461512444673

66. Devine, P. G., & Ash, T. L. (2022). Diversity training goals, limitations, and promise: A review of the multidisciplinary literature. *Annual Review of Psychology, 73*, 403–429. https://pubmed.ncbi.nlm.nih.gov/34280325/

67. Muvuka, B., Combs, R. M., Ayangeakaa, S. D., Ali, N. M., Wendel, M. L., & Jackson, T. (2020). Health literacy in African-American communities: Barriers and strategies. *Health Literacy Research and Practice, 4*(3), e138–e143. https://www.ncbi.nlm.nih.gov/pmc/articles/PMC7365659/

68. Kahneman, D. (2011). *Thinking, fast and slow.* Farrar, Strauss, and Giroux.

69. Calabrese, S. K., Earnshaw, V. A., Underhill, K., Hansen, N. B., & Dovidio, J. F. (2014). The impact of patient race on clinical decisions related to prescribing HIV pre-exposure prophylaxis (PrEP): Assumptions about sexual risk compensation and implications for access. *AIDS and Behavior, 18*(2), 226–240. https://pubmed.ncbi.nlm.nih.gov/24366572/

70. Bogart, L. M., Catz, S. L., Kelly, J. A., & Benotsch, E. G. (2001). Factors influencing physicians' judgments of adherence and treatment decisions for

patients with HIV disease. *Medical Decision Making*, *21*(1), 28–36. https://doi.org/10.1177/0272989x0102100104

71. van Ryn, M., Burgess, D., Malat, J., & Griffin, J. (2006). Physicians' perceptions of patients' social and behavioral characteristics and race disparities in treatment recommendations for men with coronary artery disease. *American Journal of Public Health*, *96*(2), 351–357. https://doi.org/10.2105/ajph.2004.041806

72. Schenker, L. (2020, August 13). 'Nine times out of 10, I was completely brushed off': Black Chicagoans confront bias in health care, hope for change. *Chicago Tribune*. https://www.chicagotribune.com/news/breaking/ct-chicago-health-care-racism-george-floyd-implicit-bias–20200813-nxrujltiyvg37pks2hyf6iwb7m-story.html

73. Beach, M. C., Saha, S., Park, J., Taylor, J., Drew, P., Plank, E., Cooper, L. A., & Chee, B. (2021). Testimonial injustice: Linguistic bias in the medical records of black patients and women. *Journal of General Internal Medicine, 36* (6), 1708–1714. https://pubmed.ncbi.nlm.nih.gov/33754318/

74. Park, J., Saha, S., Chee, B., Taylor, J., & Beach, M. C. (2021). Physician use of stigmatizing language in patient medical records. *JAMA Network Open, 4* (7), e2117052–e2117052. https://doi.org/10.1001/jamanetworkopen.2021.17052

75. Sun, M., Oliwa, T., Peek, M. E., & Tung, E. L. (2022). Negative patient descriptors: Documenting racial bias in the electronic health record. *Health Affairs, 41*(2). https://doi.org/10.1377/hlthaff.2021.01423

76. Horowitz, J. M., Brown, A., & Cox, K. (2019, April 9). *Race in America 2019*. Pew Research Center. www.pewresearch.org/social-trends/2019/04/09/race-in-america-2019/

77. Sabin, J., Nosek, B. A., Greenwald, A., & Rivara, F. P. (2009). Physicians' implicit and explicit attitudes about race by MD race, ethnicity, and gender. *Journal of Health Care for the Poor and Underserved*, *20*(3), 896–913. https://doi.org/10.1353/hpu.0.0185

78. Epstein, R. A. (2005). Disparities and discrimination in health care coverage: A critique of the Institute of Medicine study. *Perspectives in Biological Medicine*, *48*(1 Suppl), S26–S41. https://pubmed.ncbi.nlm.nih.gov/15842085/

79. Greenwald, A. G., Dasgupta, N., Dovidio, J. F., Kang, J., Moss-Racusin, C. A., & Teachman, B. A. (2022). Implicit bias remedies: Treating discriminatory bias as a public health problem. *Psychological Science in the Public Interest*, *23*(1), 7–40. https://pubmed.ncbi.nlm.nih.gov/35587951/

80. Gran-Ruaz, S., Feliciano, J., Bartlett, A., & Williams, M. (2002). Implicit racial bias across ethnoracial groups in Canada and the United States and Black mental health. *Canadian Psychology/Psychogie Cannadienne*, *63*(4), 608–622. https://psycnet.apa.org/doi/10.1037/cap0000323

81. Haider, A. H., Sexton, J., Sriram, N., Cooper, L. A., Efron, D. T., Swoboda, S., Villegas, C. V., Haut, E. R., Bonds, M., Pronovost, P. J., Lipsett, P. A., Freischlag, J. A., & Cornwell, E. E., III (2011). Association of unconscious

race and social class bias with vignette-based clinical assessments by medical students. *Journal of the American Medical Association (JAMA)*, *306*(9), 942–951. https://doi.org/10.1001/jama.2011.1248

82. van Ryn, M., Hardeman, R., Phelan, S. M., Burgess, D. J., Dovidio, J. F., Herrin, J., Burke, S. E., Nelson, D. B., Perry, S., Yeazel, M., & Przedworski, J. M. (2015). Medical school experiences associated with change in implicit racial bias among 3547 students: A Medical Student CHANGES Study Report. *Journal of General Internal Medicine*, *30*(12), 1748–1756. https://pubmed.ncbi.nlm.nih.gov/26129779/

83. Schaa, K. L., Roter, D. L., Biesecker, B. B., Cooper, L. A., & Erby, L. H. (2015). Genetic counselors' implicit racial attitudes and their relationship to communication. *Health Psychology*, *34*(2), 111–119. https://doi.org/10.1037/hea0000155

84. Ivers, N. N., Johnson, D. A., & Rogers, J. L. (2021). The association between implicit racial bias and mindfulness in mental health practitioners. *Journal of Counselling & Development*, *99*(1), 11–23. https://onlinelibrary.wiley.com/doi/abs/10.1002/jcad.12350

85. Patel, N., Patel, S., Cotti, E., Bardini, G., & Mannocci, F. (2019). Unconscious racial bias may affect dentists' clinical decisions on tooth restorability: A randomized clinical trial. *JDR Clinical Translational Research*, *4*(1), 19–28. https://pubmed.ncbi.nlm.nih.gov/30931761/

86. Penner, L. A., Dovidio, J. F., West, T., Gaertner, S., Albrecht, T., Dailey, R., & Markova, T. (2010). Aversive racism and medical interactions with Black patients: A field study. *Journal of Experimental Social Psychology*, *48*(2), 436–440. https://www.ncbi.nlm.nih.gov/pmc/articles/PMC2835170/

87. Blair, I. V., Steiner, J. F., Fairclough, D. L., Hanratty, R., Price, D. W., Hirsh, H. K., Wright, L. A., Bronsert, M., Karimkhani, E., Magid, D. J., & Havranek, E. P. (2013). Clinicians' implicit ethnic/racial bias and perceptions of care among Black and Latino patients. *Annals of Family Medicine*, *11*(1), 43–52. https://doi.org/10.1370/afm.1442

88. Cooper, L. A., Roter, D. L., Carson, K. A., Beach, M. C., Sabin, J. A., Greenwald, A. G., & Inui, T. S. (2012). The associations of clinicians' implicit attitudes about race with medical visit communication and patient ratings of interpersonal care. *American Journal of Public Health*, *102*(5), 979–987. https://doi.org/10.2105/ajph.2011.300558

89. Lowe, C., Beach, M., & Roter, D. (2020). Genetic counselor implicit bias and its effects on cognitive and affective exchanges in racially discordant simulations. *Journal of Genetic Counseling*, *29*(3), 332–341. https://onlinelibrary.wiley.com/doi/abs/10.1002/jgc4.1243

90. Dovidio, J. F., Gaertner, S. E., Kawakami, K., & Hodson, G. (2002). Why can't we just get along? Interpersonal biases and interracial distrust. *Cultural Diversity & Ethnic Minority Psychology*, *8*(2), 88–102. https://doi.org/10.1037/1099-9809.8.2.88

91. Hagiwara, N., Slatcher, R. B., Eggly, S., & Penner, L. A. (2017). Physician racial bias and word us during racially discordant medical interactions. *Health*

Communication, 32(4), 40–48. https://www.ncbi.nlm.nih.gov/pmc/articles/PMC5161737/

92. Hagiwara, N., Dovidio, J. F., Eggly, S., Penner, L. A. (2016). The effects of racial attitudes on affect and engagement in racially discordant medical interactions between non-Black physicians and Black patients. *Group Processes and Intergroup Relations, 19*(4), 509–527. https://pubmed.ncbi.nlm.nih.gov/27642254/

93. Penner, L. A., Harper, F. W. K., Dovidio, J. F., Albrecht, T. L., Hamel, L. M., Senft, N., & Eggly, S. (2017). The impact of Black cancer patients' race-related beliefs and attitudes on racially-discordant oncology interactions: A field study. *Social Science and Medicine, 191*(10), 99–108. https://doi.org/10.1016/j.socscimed.2017.08.034

94. Penner, L. A., Dovidio, J. F., Gonzalez, R., Albrecht, T., Chapman, R., Foster, T., Harper, F., Hagiwara, N., Hamel, L., Gadgeel, S., Simon, M., & Eggly, S. (2016). The effects of oncologist implicit racial bias in racially discordant oncology interactions. *Journal of Clinical Oncology, 34*(24), 2874–2880. https://pubmed.ncbi.nlm.nih.gov/27325865/

95. Moon, Z., Moss-Morris, R., Hunter, M. S., Norton, S., & Hughes, L. D. (2019). Nonadherence to tamoxifen in breast cancer survivors: A 12 month longitudinal analysis. *Health Psychology, 38*(10), 888–899. https://doi.org/10.1037/hea0000785

96. Camacho, F. T., Tan, X., Alcalá, H. E., Shah, S., Anderson, R. T., & Balkrishnan, R. (2017). Impact of patient race and geographical factors on initiation and adherence to adjuvant endocrine therapy in medicare breast cancer survivors. *Medicine, 96*(24), e7147. https://doi.org/10.1097/md.0000000000007147

97. Fiscella, K., Epstein, R. M., Griggs, J. J., Marshall, M. M., & Shields, C. G. (2021). Is physician implicit bias associated with differences in care by patient race for metastatic cancer-related pain? *PLoS ONE, 16*(10), e0257794. https://doi.org/10.1371/journal.pone.0257794

98. Richeson, J. A., & Shelton, J. N. (2005). Thin slices of racial bias. *Journal of Nonverbal Behavior, 29*(1), 75–86. https://link.springer.com/article/10.1007/s10919-004-0890-2

99. Dovidio, J. F., & LaFrance, M. (2013). Race, ethnicity, and nonverbal behavior. In J. A. K. Hall, M. (Ed.), *Nonverbal communication* (pp. 671–696). DeGruyter-Mouton.

100. Hagiwara, N., Mezuk, B., Elston Lafata, J., Vrana, S. R., & Fetters, M. D. (2018). Study protocol for investigating physician communication behaviours that link physician implicit racial bias and patient outcomes in Black patients with type 2 diabetes using an exploratory sequential mixed methods design. *BMJ Open, 8*(10), e022623. https://doi.org/10.1136/bmjopen-2018-022623

101. Johnson, J. D., & Lecci, L. (2003). Assessing anti-White attitudes and predicting perceived racism: The Johnson-Lecci scale. *Personality and*

Social Psychology Bulletin, *29*(3), 299–312. https://doi.org/10.1177/0146167202250041

102. Hagiwara, N., Penner, L. A., Gonzalez, R., Eggly, S., Dovidio, J. F., Gaertner, S. L., West, T., & Albrecht, T. L. (2013). Racial attitudes, physician-patient talk time ratio, and adherence in racially discordant medical interactions. *Social Science and Medicine*, *87*, 123–131. https://pubmed.ncbi.nlm.nih.gov/23631787/

103. Trawalter, S., Richeson, J. A., & Shelton, J. N. (2009). Predicting behavior during interracial interactions: A stress and coping approach. *Personality and Social Psychology Review*, *13*(4), 243–268. https://doi.org/10.1177/1088868309345850

104. Penner, L. A., Albrecht., T. L., & Dovidio, J. F. (2018, June). Stigmatized patients with cancer: The impact of providers and patient's attitudes on clinical interactions. Annual Meeting of International Conference in Communication in Healthcare, Porto, Portugal.

105. Jaiswal, J., & Halkitis, P. N. (2019). Towards a more inclusive and dynamic understanding of medical mistrust informed by science. *Behavioral Medicine*, *45*(2), 79–85. https://doi.org/10.1080/08964289.2019.1619511

106. Benkert, R., Cuevas, A., Thompson, H. S., Dove-Meadows, E., & Knuckles, D. (2019). Ubiquitous yet unclear: A systematic review of medical mistrust. *Behavioral Medicine*, *45*(2), 86–101. https://doi.org/10.1080/08964289.2019.1588220

107. Hamel, L., Lopes, L., Munana, C., Artiga, S., & Brodie, M. (2020, October 13). *KFF/The undefeated survey on race and health*. Kaiser Family Foundation. www.kff.org/report-section/kff-the-undefeated-survey-on-race-and-health-main-findings/

108. Alsan, M., & Wanamaker, M. (2017). Tuskegee and the health of Black men. *The Quarterly Journal of Economics*, *133*(1), 407–455. https://doi.org/10.1093/qje/qjx029

109. Williams, S. (2018, February 20). *Serena Williams: What my life-threatening experience taught me about giving birth*. CNN. www.cnn.com/2018/02/20/opinions/protect-mother-pregnancy-williams-opinion/index.html

110. Declercq, E., & Zephyrin, L. (2020). *Maternal mortality in the United States: A primer*. Commonwealth Fund. https://www.commonwealthfund.org/publications/issue-brief-report/2020/dec/maternal-mortality-united-states-primer

111. Hostetter, M., & Klein, S. (2021, January 14). *Understanding and ameliorating medical mistrust among Black Americans*. The Commonwealth Fund. www.commonwealthfund.org/publications/newsletter-article/2021/jan/medical-mistrust-among-black-americans

112. Thompson, H. S., Manning, M., Mitchell, J., Kim, S., Harper, F. W. K., Cresswell, S., Johns, K., Pal, S., Dowe, B., Tariq, M., Sayed, N., Saigh, L. M., Rutledge, L., Lipscomb, C., Lilly, J. Y., Gustine, H., Sanders, A., Landry, M., & Marks, B. (2021). Factors associated with racial/ethnic group-based medical mistrust and perspectives on COVID-19 vaccine trial

participation and vaccine uptake in the US. *JAMA Network Open*, 4(5), e2111629. https://doi.org/10.1001/jamanetworkopen.2021.11629

113. Bennett, A. (2020, December 6). 'SNL': Michael Che expresses concerns about COVID-19 Vaccine. *Urban Hollywood*. https://urbanhollywood411.com/2020/12/06/snl-michael-che-has-doubts-about-covid-vaccine/

114. Hall, M. B., Vos, P., Bess, J. J., Reburn, K. L., Locklear, G. D., McAlister, J., & Bell, R. A. (2018). Cervical cancer screening behaviors and perceptions of medical mistrust among rural Black and White women. *Journal of Healthcare for the Poor and Underserved*, 29(4), 1368–1385. https://doi.org/10.1353/hpu.2018.0101

115. Thompson, H. S., Valdimarsdottir, H. B., Winkel, G., Jandorf, L., & Redd, W. (2004). The Group-Based Medical Mistrust Scale: Psychometric properties and association with breast cancer screening. *Preventive Medicine*, 38(2), 209–218. https://doi.org/10.1016/j.ypmed.2003.09.041

116. Shelton, R. C., Winkel, G., Davis, S. N., Roberts, N., Valdimarsdottir, H., Hall, S. J., & Thompson, H. S. (2010). Validation of the Group-Based Medical Mistrust Scale among urban Black men. *Journal of General Internal Medicine*, 25(6), 549–555. https://www.ncbi.nlm.nih.gov/pmc/articles/PMC2869405/

117. Galvan, F. H., Bogart, L. M., Klein, D. J., Wagner, G. J., & Chen, Y. T. (2017). Medical mistrust as a key mediator in the association between perceived discrimination and adherence to antiretroviral therapy among HIV-positive Latino men. *Journal of Behavioral Medicine*, 40(5), 784–793. https://www.ncbi.nlm.nih.gov/pmc/articles/PMC5610598/

118. Hall, G. L., & Heath, M. (2021). Poor medication adherence in African Americans is a matter of trust. *Journal of Racial and Ethnic Health Disparities*, 8(4), 927–942. https://pubmed.ncbi.nlm.nih.gov/33215358/

CHAPTER 7

Paths to a Solution
Ensuring a Basic Human Right

Health is not a consumer good, but rather a universal human right.
Pope Francis (May 9, 2016) [1]

Healthcare is a right. It is not a privilege reserved for a wealthy few.
US Representative John Lewis (January 11, 2017) [2]

Across the previous chapters, we documented the numerous ways in which anti-Black racism endangers the health of Black Americans and creates significant health and healthcare disparities between Black Americans and White Americans. The information we presented is troubling not only because of the profound impact it has on the lives of Black people but also because of the broad social injustices it reveals. This material thus challenges many people's assumptions that justice and fairness, supposedly core principles of the United States, actually apply to all its citizens. Moreover, these racial disparities in health and healthcare are of sufficient magnitude to constitute a serious threat to the health of all Americans.

Long after more formal kinds of racism were prohibited by federal, state, and local laws, and blatant acts of racial bigotry became both strongly socially sanctioned and illegal, pervasive anti-Black racism still operates at multiple levels. It is woven into the fabric of contemporary American society. Anti-Black racism produces and perpetuates a host of interrelated racial inequities. This, of course, includes the large and pervasive racial disparities in health and healthcare that are the focus of this book. Anti-Black racism threatens the basic human right of Black Americans to have good health and to live long and productive lives. In this final chapter, we turn our focus to actionable steps that can improve the health of Black Americans.

The potential benefits of reducing health and healthcare disparities are not limited to Black Americans or members of other socially or economically disadvantaged groups. Every person in the United States who interacts with the healthcare system (i.e., all Americans) would also share in

297

these benefits in some way. Improving the health of a substantial portion of people in the United States would reduce the overall demands on an already over-burdened healthcare system and thus improve the quality of healthcare for all Americans.

Everyone in the United States pays some portion of the enormous costs of treating illnesses that are not caused by some biological or genetic anomaly but rather are the direct or indirect result of anti-Black racism. These costs are manifested in governmental insurance programs needing to either reduce their benefits or raise patient costs, hospitals raising their fees to defray the costs of treating uninsured patients, and private health insurance companies dealing with the rising costs of healthcare by increasing their rates in order to remain in business. In other words, reducing the disparities in health and healthcare for Black Americans does not represent a zero-sum game in which one group's gain necessarily means another group's loss. Improving the health of and healthcare for Black Americans does *not* mean there would be a corresponding reduction in the health and healthcare of White Americans, or any other group of Americans. To the contrary, if major racial health disparities were reduced or eliminated, almost all Americans would experience better and less expensive healthcare for themselves and their families.

We are not naïve about the scope of these disparities or about the enormous political and social obstacles to reducing them. Doing this will not be easy. The forces that have produced racial disparities in health and healthcare have been part of the US history even before it became an independent country. Even today, their legacy makes the lives of Black people in the United States less healthy and shorter than those of White people. Racial disparities in health and healthcare are a national problem with life-or-death consequences. It is essential that we, as a society and as individuals, be part of effective solutions to these disparities.

When we first began writing this book, some of us thought it would mostly be about racial disparities in *healthcare* – inequities in the quality of care received by Black patients relative to White patients. Indeed, we have given special emphasis to racial disparities in healthcare throughout the book. However, as documented in Chapters 2 and 3, there are other quite significant causes of racial health disparities – the physiological impact of exposure to racial discrimination and the health threats that exist in segregated and under-resourced neighborhoods. Thus, even if all of the racial disadvantages embedded within the American healthcare system were somehow miraculously eliminated tomorrow, Black Americans would still suffer poorer health than White Americans. But both health and healthcare disparities share common causes. Our core thesis has been these common causes involve anti-Black racism. There is a strong consensus among public health experts in both the public and private sectors that the broad-based racial disparities in health and healthcare that exist in the United States are the results of the social, economic, and political inequities caused by anti-Black racism [3]. Thus, the solutions proposed in this chapter must address substantially more than just inequities in the American healthcare system.[1]

It is unrealistic to expect that racial disparities in health and healthcare can be totally eliminated in the near future. However, meaningful actions now can significantly reduce the magnitude of these problems. In fact, there has already been some movement in this direction. In the past 60 or 70 years, many of the more blatant forms of racism in the American healthcare system (e.g., legally segregated healthcare) have been eliminated. Further, although they may disagree on specific issues, most Americans believe that good health and healthcare is a fundamental right of all its citizens. Thus, the potential to reduce health-related inequities is there, but it will require dedicated efforts to achieve this goal.

Summarizing the Threats to Racial Equity in Health and Healthcare

The ways in which anti-Black racism leads to racial disparities in health and in healthcare are complex and multifaceted, but they broadly fall into two categories. There are those that have their origins in certain aspects of many Black people's daily lives, and there are those that involve the way healthcare is provided to many Black people. Here, we identify eight major threats to the health and longevity of Black people living in America that reflect the combined effects of these sources. The threats are presented separately, but they are intertwined in both their causes and consequences. While the list is far from exhaustive, it highlights particular threats that are among those most directly caused by anti-Black racism and it serves as a reminder of the scope of the problems confronting the United States.

---

[1] As we noted in the Introduction chapter, health and healthcare inequities are not only experienced by Black Americans. Members of other racial/ethnic minorities and socially stigmatized groups experience them as well. Although there are often differences in specific proximal causes of these disparities, social and economic inequities and some form of prejudice and discrimination are almost always among the causes. Thus, some of the proposals we offer may benefit members of these other groups.

- **Socioeconomic Disparities between Black Americans and White Americans**

    Substantial economic and social disparities, which are largely due to systemic and individual anti-Black racism, are major reasons why Black Americans are more likely than White Americans to encounter daily challenges to their health, live in less healthy environments, and receive poorer healthcare (see Introduction chapter). Because of these disparities, Black Americans are more likely than White Americans to become ill, die from their illness, and live shorter lives.

- **Direct and Indirect Encounters with Racial Discrimination**

    One major consequence of pervasive anti-Black racism in the United States, described in Chapter 2, is that Black Americans frequently experience some form of racial discrimination as they go about their daily lives. There is no single source of racial discrimination; it is a pervasive phenomenon that cuts across business, professional, and social interactions. Anti-Black racism, thus, almost inevitability impinges on the daily lives of Black Americans. Persistent exposure to racial discrimination creates chronic stress, which begins a cascade of physiological and psychological stress responses. In turn, these stress responses cause many of the diseases and disorders that afflict large numbers of Black people and lead to substantially higher premature mortality rates than among White Americans.

- **Under-Resourced and Racially Segregated Neighborhoods**

    For well over 100 years after the Civil War ended, federal, state, and local governments and private institutions enacted laws and engaged in practices that deliberately created segregated neighborhoods and vigorously maintained racial segregation in American housing. Many of the under-resourced, segregated, Black neighborhoods are the legacy of the intentional separation of where White Americans and Black Americans live (see Chapter 3). These neighborhoods perpetuate poverty by restricting residents' access to educational and financial resources and limiting social mobility. Poverty, in turn, directly and indirectly harms people's health. The neighborhoods also expose Black Americans to multiple hazards to their health, including poor water and air quality, a dearth of healthy foods, an excess of unhealthy food options, substandard and dangerous housing, and limited availability of adequate medical care.

- **Less Access to Medical Care**

  The healthcare system in the United States is essentially a patchwork of primarily private healthcare providers whose fees are paid either by private or public health insurance, and the patient who receives the care (or their family) is responsible for the balance. Thus, access to high-quality healthcare in America depends greatly on the type of insurance a person has and the individual's ability to pay the costs not covered by their insurance. Even with significant improvements in the availability of publicly financed health insurance since the 1960s, Black Americans are still, on average, substantially less able than White Americans to pay for needed medical care. As discussed in Chapter 5, this economic disparity means that getting good medical care may be beyond the financial reach of many Black Americans. This, in turn, seriously jeopardizes their health and longevity.

- **Lower Quality of Medical Care**

  Even when Black patients can access medical care, the quality of the care they receive is, on average, significantly poorer than that received by White patients (see Chapter 6). This disparity is, in part, another legacy of past racism in American medicine in the form of segregated and unequal access to medical care on the basis of a patient's race. It continues to date due to the impact of contemporary systemic racism on the institutions that provide medical treatment. Medical facilities serving a disproportionate number of Black patients provide an overall lower quality of care than do medical facilities that predominantly serve White patients (see Chapter 5). This occurs primarily because these facilities typically receive fewer resources to support the medical care they are supposed to provide. Yet, they often treat patients with the most serious medical problems. In addition, even when Black patients and White patients are treated within the same healthcare institutions, Black patients often receive a lower quality of care.

- **A Dearth of Black Physicians**

  Although there is evidence that Black patients derive some substantial benefits from seeing Black physicians, it is relatively unlikely they will be treated by one. There is a significant dearth of Black physicians in the United States. The limited number of Black health professionals is in part a result of the historical exclusion of Black people from the profession (see Chapter 4), as well as the reality of systemic bias in medical training that persists even today (see Chapter 5). Thus, many Black patients may not have the same freedom of choice in selecting a physician that is enjoyed by White patients. This large imbalance between the proportion of Black healthcare professionals available to Black patients and the proportion of White healthcare professionals available to White patients has existed for a long time in America, enforced by racist laws and social customs. However, today this imbalance is perpetuated by the different kinds of barriers encountered by Black people interested in a career in healthcare. These include educational obstacles before and during undergraduate education, the high costs of postgraduate education in medicine, the difficult social climate at most medical schools, and the systemic and individual racism encountered by Black professionals in healthcare settings.

- **Inappropriate Use of Patient Race in Medical Diagnoses and Treatments**

  Among healthcare professionals there is widespread misunderstanding regarding the importance of a patient's race in diagnoses and treatment decisions. Race, which is a social construct, is often treated as a biological characteristic or a strong determinant of how an individual Black person thinks and acts (see Introduction chapter). As shown in Chapter 5, treating race as a biological characteristic in diagnoses often has its roots in racist myths and can result in treatment decisions that endanger the health of Black patients.

- **Race-Related Thoughts and Feelings That Create Disparities in Healthcare**

  A patient's perceived race and the resultant racial stereotypes can unduly affect how healthcare professionals see Black patients' personal characteristics and their medical problems, which can also influence providers' treatment decisions (see Chapters 5 and 6). In addition, physicians and other healthcare professionals typically have some degree of both explicit and implicit racial bias (see Chapter 1). These biases can result in behaviors that create significant racial healthcare disparities (see Chapter 6). Also, Black patients have their own thoughts and feelings that affect their medical care. Because of direct and indirect encounters with racism both outside of and within the healthcare system, Black patients may often have a higher level of medical mistrust than

White patients. Medical mistrust can contribute to racial disparities in health and healthcare because of the negative impact it has on Black patients' interactions with their non-Black healthcare providers and on Black people's willingness to engage in health-promoting behaviors.

Reducing Racial Disparities in American Health and Healthcare: Some Immodest Proposals

Bold actions are needed to reverse the historical and contemporary forces that unnecessarily and unfairly endanger the lives of Black Americans. Because these forces involve both systemic and individual-level racial biases, their solutions require changes in (1) public policies at both national and local levels, (2) the way treatment is provided at the level of healthcare facilities, and (3) peoples' thoughts, feelings, and behaviors at the level of individual healthcare professionals and patients. In the remainder of this chapter, we consider a range of ways to address the major causes of the racial health disparities we have identified. Some of them are new, but many of them are already in place and have achieved some degree of success. Their success suggests that part of the solution to racial health and healthcare disparities is to expand programs like these and provide them with greater support.

In the interest of clarity, we present the interventions separately, organized around the threats to racial equity in health and healthcare that we have identified. However, many of the solutions we propose cut across the individual threats and address more than one of them. We adopt this approach because the broad-based racial disparities in health and healthcare that exist in the United States are the result of the intertwined effects of the social, economic, and political racial inequities, as well as of the systemic and individual racism that are part of contemporary American society. Thus, to be truly effective at addressing the forces that currently shape racial health and healthcare disparities, intervention strategies need to be multifaceted, multilevel, and, where possible, implemented in concert with one another.

Reducing Racial Disparities in Socioeconomic Status

Socioeconomic status is one of the most powerful determinants of people's health and the healthcare they receive. One of the core causes of racial disparities in health is the significant disparity in the overall socioeconomic status of Black Americans and White Americans. There are many ways in which socioeconomic racial disparities might be reduced, and no single intervention is likely to have a sufficient impact. However, because of the substantial influence that education has on socioeconomic status, the massive disparities in the quality of education that Black children and White children receive should be one major focus of attention [4].

Creating Equity in Educational Opportunities
Poorer educational opportunities play a critical role in the racial disparities in socioeconomic status that exist in the United States, which, in turn, directly affect Black Americans' health and the healthcare they receive (see Introduction chapter and Chapter 5). Seventy years after the US Supreme Court ruled that the racial segregation of schools was unconstitutional, systemic and individual racism in a variety of forms have continued to keep American public schools highly segregated. For example, currently 70 percent of Black children attend schools that are highly segregated by race and ethnicity, and an equal percentage attend schools in which the majority of students come from families that live in poverty [5]. The long-term harm done by segregated and unequal education was quite eloquently described in President Lyndon B. Johnson's 1965 commencement address at Howard University: "Men and women of all races are born with the same range of abilities. But ability is not just the product of birth. Ability is stretched or stunted by the family that you live with, and the neighborhood you live in – by the school you go to and the poverty or the richness of your surroundings. It is the product of a hundred unseen forces playing upon the little infant, the child, and finally the [adult]" [6]. There is a moral and ethical wrong in perpetuating the de facto segregation of students because of their race or family's income level, which limits their intellectual and economic achievements.

One significant component of the broad, complex problem of continued racial segregation in American public education is the differential support that schools receive to educate their students. In general, schools with predominately poor Black children as students are dramatically under-resourced relative to integrated schools or those in which the students are predominately White. Although some state and local programs specifically allocate extra funds to schools that primarily teach Black and economically disadvantaged students, these efforts are not enough. Nationally, school districts serving predominantly minority students receive $23 billion less in financial support than do majority-White school districts, despite serving the same number of children [7]. Overall, the per student financial support for Black students in poor neighborhoods is $1,500 less than for White students in poor neighborhoods. As a result, the schools with majority-Black student bodies may have fewer dollars for teacher salaries, which often means they will have fewer experienced teachers and fewer teachers credentialed in the subjects they teach. These schools are also more likely to have outdated textbooks and less likely to have access to educational resources such as Advanced Placement courses. Schools that primarily teach Black students, compared to those that primarily teach White students, are more often in physical disrepair and contain environmental hazards to the students' health (e.g., unsafe temperatures, high levels of lead, mold, and various vermin) [8]. Limited resources and difficult environments, in turn, greatly reduce the overall quality of the education provided to Black students and thus limits these students' subsequent educational opportunities.

Part of the problem is that state and local governments are the primary sources of funding for public schools, contributing over 90 cents of every dollar spent on education from sources like property taxes [9]. But, many majority-Black school districts have a suppressed local tax base due to the high concentration of poverty that too often accompanies de facto residential segregation. These districts thus often face serious financial barriers to adequately resourcing schools. Further, as school districts become more segregated, these financial disparities increase [10]. Efforts to equalize school funding across the nation's richest and poorest school districts have been in place for several decades, but they need to be intensified.

Increasing funding for the schools that teach children from poor families has clear, positive effects. A study that followed reforms in school funding over time found that a 10 percent increase in per-pupil spending each year for all 12 years of public school led to a significantly higher likelihood of students pursuing higher education. This increased funding also affected students after graduation. Students at the schools that received this funding earned about 7 percent higher wages as adults, and the incidence of adult poverty was reduced by over 3 percent. These effects were much more pronounced for children from lower-income families [11].

For years, the federal government has provided additional resources to high-poverty schools through Title I of the original Elementary and Secondary Schools Act. However, these dollars actually cover only about 5 percent of the cost of educating poor and disadvantaged children. And because of some administrative quirks in Title I, low-poverty schools actually receive *more* per student funding than high-poverty schools [12].

The federal government should increase its funding for the nation's poorest schools and concentrate these resources where they are needed most. In addition, state and local governments, as the primary sources of school funding, can better target where their money is spent. For example, the Education Trust, a nonprofit educational research and policy organization, recommends that states provide two to three times more resources for students from low-income than high-income families, supply more resources to school districts in areas with low property wealth (resulting in lower property taxes to support education), and share clear and transparent data about the amount of funding that schools actually receive from the state [13]. We strongly endorse these kinds of recommendations.

Supplementing state and federal support with an infusion of funds from private foundations can also have dramatic effects when they are specifically directed toward assisting under-resourced schools. For example, in 2009 the Bill and Melinda Gates Foundation gave $90 million to the public school system in Memphis, Tennessee [14]. One of the schools that particularly benefited from this infusion of funds was Manassas High School, whose student body was almost entirely Black. Among other things, the funds were used for new technology to aid in instruction and to support bonuses for teachers who raised student achievement. The effects were significant. In the year before the funding (and the changes) began, only a fraction of graduating seniors applied to college and only a handful were accepted. In the following year, 111 of the 131 seniors who applied for college were accepted [15].

Other governmental and private programs of this type have similarly demonstrated how extremely effective supplemental funds can be. Promise Neighborhoods, for example, is a federal grant program that provides a range of services to children and families living in under-resourced and marginalized neighborhoods, with the goal of improving academic and family outcomes [16]. The program focuses on family, school, and community factors that shape educational outcomes in communities facing systemic barriers to educational opportunity. Services include school readiness programs for children who might otherwise face early disadvantages related to family or neighborhood circumstances, academic support from early childhood through college, and community-level interventions to support healthy child development. While evaluations of the Promise Neighborhoods program itself are ongoing, a program on which it is based, Harlem Children's Zone (HCZ, a private nonprofit organization) is already showing some impressive results: Almost 100 percent of the students who graduate from the HCZ's Promise Academy earn admission to college. If these kinds of goals are realized on a broader scale, it would have enormous economic and social benefits for children at schools that are currently under-resourced. Given the strong role of personal income in health and healthcare disparities, increasing the economic and social mobility of students who graduate from predominantly Black schools would almost certainly have health benefits for them and likely the communities in which they reside.

Addressing Economic Racial Disparities

Improving the educational opportunities for Black children will not, alone, solve the enormous economic disparities between Black Americans and White Americans, which play such an important role in Black Americans' health challenges. Attaining a postsecondary education does not necessarily yield the same economic benefits for Black college graduates as for White college graduates. Black students are more likely than their White counterparts to have a high student loan burden. In addition, after college, Black graduates are more likely than White graduates to financially support their parents, reducing their own wealth, while White college students are more likely to continue to receive financial assistance from their parents. Thus, graduating from college does not reduce the large disparity in wealth between Black college graduates and their White counterparts. In fact, currently, households headed by Black people with a college education have 33 percent less wealth than households headed by White people who did not complete high school [17].

In large part, this economic disparity is due to two and a half centuries of American slavery and another century of legalized racial discrimination that left many Black Americans in perilous economic positions. As we discussed in Chapter 3, both governmental and private sector policies systematically deprived Black Americans of opportunities to accumulate wealth by either denying them home ownership (the principal source of family wealth in the United States) or restricting (sometimes violently) economic growth in Black communities, such as was the case in Tulsa, Oklahoma, and Wilmington, North Carolina, in the early years of the twentieth century. Even today racial bias in real estate and bank loan policies contributes to the stark disparities in wealth between Black Americans and White Americans.

Professor of economics at The New School for Social Research, Darrick Hamilton, and professor of African and African American Studies at Duke University, William Darity Jr., believe that this large racial disparity in family wealth needs to be addressed. They do not believe, however, that governmental programs that directly attempt to remediate racial disparities in wealth (e.g., reparations for Black descendants of enslaved people) will ever gain broad public acceptance or legal approval. Thus, they have proposed a progressive strategy to indirectly address broad economic racial disparities by using family wealth as a standard for helping ensure a brighter economic future for babies when they become young adults. Their Baby Bonds proposal would provide a trust for newborns, starting with all babies born into families below the national median for wealth; the trust would be greatest for children in the lowest wealth quartile [18]. These funds, guaranteed to grow in federally managed accounts, would be accessible when the child turns 18 years to provide needed capital to pay for education, a home, or invest in a business. Because Black families are far less likely than White families to transfer wealth from parents to their children (the results of systemic economic racism), Baby Bonds would disproportionately benefit Black babies, and by extension, their families. As Hamilton and Darity write, "Rather than a race-neutral America, the ideal should be a race-fair America ... Public provision of a substantial trust fund for newborns from families that are wealth-poor would go a long way toward achieving [that] ideal." This reduction in racial wealth disparities might, in turn, attenuate many of the race-related disparities in health and healthcare.

Reducing Racial Discrimination

As we have repeatedly said throughout this book, a sweeping reduction of racial discrimination in the United States, no matter how desirable, is not a realistic goal at this time. However, there are specific forms of racial discrimination that can be reduced. We discuss two of them here.

Reducing the Impact of Implicit Racial Bias

Throughout this book we have talked about racial discrimination and its deleterious effects on the health and well-being of Black people. In addition to the dangerous physiological effects of racial discrimination (see Chapter 2), there is racial discrimination in employment decisions (see the Introduction chapter), opportunities to accrue wealth (see Chapter 3), and in the way Black people are treated in medical settings (see Chapters 5 and 6). One significant source of this discrimination is implicit racial bias – frequently nonconscious and automatic negative feelings toward Black people (see Chapter 1).

Dr. Anthony Greenwald, professor of psychology at the University of Washington, has spent most of his career documenting the existence of implicit racial bias and examining its impact on decisions that affect people of color. Dr. Greenwald and several colleagues (including one of the authors of this book – JFD) have proposed that implicit racial bias should be treated in a manner akin to some threat to the public's health and safety [19]. While there is no consistent evidence that it is possible to reduce people's level of implicit racial bias in an enduring way, it is possible to prevent implicit bias from being translated into discriminatory actions or policies. If individuals, as well as public and private entities, are aware of how implicit biases produce inequities, they can take proactive steps to prevent its discriminatory effects. For example, cities can limit public gatherings because of the potential threat of some airborne infection or build levees because of the threat of flooding. These researchers proposed that the leaders of governmental and private institutions can take similar proactive steps, based on psychological science, to reduce the threat of racial discrimination.

One area in which they make suggestions is the reduction of racial discrimination in individual employment decisions. Dr. Greenwald and his collaborators suggest that both public and private organizations can enact policies to reduce the impact of an applicant's demographic characteristics on employment decisions. These include not informing decision makers about the demographic characteristics of job applicants, requiring that employment decisions be based on clearly specified and relevant job qualifications, and implementing highly structured employment interviews to limit the impact of biased subtle verbal and nonverbal behaviors that can affect the course of the interview.

Dr. Greenwald and his colleagues also recommend that organizations implement policies that make finding and addressing discrimination a standard practice. This would include regular internal audits that identify specific areas of racial discrimination. (We discuss the implementation of such practices in hospitals later in this chapter.) Further, organizations should view racial discrimination in a manner akin to the safety practices they might put in place to prevent certain dangers to their employees (e.g., exposure to toxic chemicals). That is, these researchers recommend that organizations establish procedures that prevent the problem of racial discrimination before it occurs. Part of this would be to make a diversity officer an integral part of the institution's organizational structure. People who occupy these positions should have the staff necessary to carry out their job and the authority to recommend or initiate changes in an organization's current practices.

We strongly endorse the approaches recommended by Dr. Greenwald and his colleagues. Their recommendations are based on scientific findings about what is and is not possible in the reduction of racial discrimination. These recommendations represent some practical ways to reduce certain kinds of racial discrimination.

Reducing Racial Discrimination in Law Enforcement
As discussed in Chapter 3, being regularly exposed to racial discrimination creates high levels of chronic stress, which is a direct threat to the health of many Black people. Here we focus on one major source of stress for Black Americans: the actions of law enforcement agencies. More than 80 percent of Black Americans believe that they are treated less fairly by police officers than are White Americans [20]. Racial discrimination in policing is thus a source of extreme stress in the lives of Black Americans. Racist law enforcement practices do not just affect specific Black individuals stopped by the police; they have a cascading impact on Black communities more generally. A young Black man asked about his greatest fears succinctly captured the feelings of many Black Americans when they encounter police officers: "That's my number one fear in life," he replied. "It's the police" [21].

Policing is often more aggressive in majority-Black communities than in majority-White communities. As we discussed in the Introduction chapter, "stop-and-frisk" policies that allow police officers to detain and search civilians based solely on officers' suspicions of illegal activity disproportionately target Black (and Latino) men. Police officers also treat Black men more aggressively than White men, and often speak to Black people in a way that contributes to their fear and mistrust of police officers [22]. A national survey of Black Americans found that their level of fear about being the target of police violence is five times as great as the level among White Americans [23]. In addition, specific well-publicized events such as murders of unarmed Black people by police officers (and individual White citizens) have dramatically increased anxiety and depression among Black Americans [24]. Such feelings can elicit stress responses and add to the already high allostatic load that usually exists among Black people. (See the stress models of disease presented in Chapter 2 for extensive documentation regarding the health consequences stemming from chronically high levels of allostatic load.)

Thus, ways to improve the treatment of Black Americans by law enforcement agencies need to be considered. Of course, this is not a new proposal. However, there has been substantial recent attention given to the actions and policies of police departments, including excessive violence against Black people by police officers. This may make now an opportune time to propose interventions that concern the way Black people are often treated by police officers.

Training is needed to address some of the racial stereotypes harbored by some police officers. For example, tall Black men (but not tall White men) are at increased risk of being arrested because they are seen by police as more threatening [25]. Another serious problem that should be the target of strategic interventions involves the ongoing efforts of White supremacy groups to affiliate themselves with police officers. These efforts have met with some degree of success. There are many police officers across the United States who are now affiliated with White supremacy groups.

Moreover, even among those officers without a formal affiliation with such groups a, views are often expressed that are compatible with a White supremacist perspective [26]. For example, an analysis of texts sent between Berkeley, California, police officers in 2019 and 2020 found that these officers "engage in vile dehumanization of (Black people) and express views that are openly racist" [27]. Moreover, as we discussed in the Introduction chapter, until recently Los Angeles police officers commonly used the abbreviation "NHI" when they encountered a homicide involving a Black victim. NHI stood for "No humans involved" [28].

Dr. Philip Atiba Goff, professor of African American Studies and Psychology at Yale University, co-founded the Center for Policing Equity and has worked with police departments around the country on the problem of White supremacy in their departments. The Center has created a document titled "White Supremacy in Policing: How Law Enforcement Agencies Can Respond." It is available to the public and contains a number of recommendations concerned with the problem of White supremacist ideology within departments and among individual officers [25]. The recommendations include not allowing police officers to be members of White supremacy groups; prohibiting the use of racist language, jokes, and statements; banning the display of patches or other similar items associated with known hate groups (whether an officer is on duty or off); and adopting social media policies that explicitly prohibit the posting of memes, retweets, or other statements that "advocate racism, violence, misogyny, homophobia, or other kinds of hate or discrimination."

Another very comprehensive plan for reducing racial bias in law enforcement has been produced by "The Justice Collaboratory" at Yale Law School. The Justice Collaboratory's report contains a number of practical recommendations that could be implemented by individual police departments [29]. The report is also publicly available on the Justice Collaboratory's website.[2] The underlying goal of these recommendations is to encourage police departments to institute policies that create *procedural justice* – that is, to have them operate in a manner that is fair to all the citizens in their jurisdiction – and to do so in a way that increases confidence in the departments among the community members they serve. The report recommends that departments review, revise, and monitor their operating procedures to ensure procedural justice, while actively seeking input about these activities from members of the communities in which they are located. It also recommends that departments clearly communicate the rationale behind policy decisions and make relevant information about their old and new policies easily available to the community. These general principles are accompanied by more specific recommendations for implementation, such as the appropriate use of body cameras, teaching police officers best practices in ways to conduct stops for suspicious activities and/or traffic violations, and instruction in ways to de-escalate encounters with members of the public.

Implementing interventions of this sort is a necessary step for alleviating the physical and psychological threats associated with racial bias in policing, but monitoring the interventions' specific impact is a key component of creating sustainable changes. To assess the effects of such interventions, the federal government should therefore collect and publish data on racial inequities in policing, arrests, arraignment outcomes, and sentencing. During the Obama administration, the Justice Department used data of this type in legal actions against specific police departments (e.g., the Seattle, Washington police department in 2012) and in decisions about the allocation of federal funds. This led to several significant reforms in the ways the Seattle police department dealt with members of minority groups. Unfortunately, federal oversight of police departments was largely abandoned by the Trump administration. With its efficacy clearly demonstrated in the preceding years, this kind of oversight needs to be restored [30].

We acknowledge that there are many obstacles to the implementation of these kinds of new policies and practices. In many US cities, powerful police unions vigorously oppose any changes to how their members carry out their duties. However, this challenge needs to be overcome. Constructive negotiations could start with creating a *fact-based* understanding among police officers, political leaders, and community members that the changes envisioned within policing will not be used as a tool of

---

[2] The report can be found at www.justicehappenshere.yale.edu

oppression. Instead, the new policies and practices will be implemented fairly in a way that will benefit both the community and law enforcement. Indeed, they could serve to make policing more effective and less dangerous because they may engender greater cooperation between the police and the community. In the context of racial health inequities, reforms in policing may serve to reduce at least some of the chronic stress experienced by Black Americans.

Reducing the Health Effects of Residential Racial Segregation

The widespread residential segregation that exists in the United States also constitutes a major threat to the health of Black Americans. Living in under-resourced and racially segregated neighborhoods creates many direct threats to their residents' health (see Chapter 3). Today, many of the health problems in segregated neighborhoods are related to poor families being "cost burdened" by their housing. That is, they have to spend too much of their monthly income on rent and do not have enough money left for other life necessities [31]. About half of the Black people who rent in the United States have this burden [32].

Providing Rent Vouchers to Neighborhood Residents

One way to approach the inequitable cost burden on low-income renters is by providing them with vouchers that cover part of their rent. Currently, the Housing Choice Voucher Program Section 8, sponsored by the US Department of Housing and Urban Development, offers such support [33]. However, both the Center on Budget and Policy Priorities and the Brookings Institute (large nonprofit private research and public policy organizations) have proposed that the availability of government-issued rent vouchers be substantially increased. These groups believe that an increase would have profound benefits for children's mental and physical health, as well as their educational success [34]. These organizations argue, for example, that if a family were able to spend less on rent, they could spend more on healthy food and healthcare for their children. Increasing the support provided by rent vouchers would also reduce housing instability (i.e., having to move frequently), which is a serious chronic stressor. The health and educational costs of housing instability are estimated at about $11 billion per year, and the social and emotional costs to the families who experience it are incalculable [35].

Notably, increasing the availability and value of rent vouchers would also increase the ability of Black families to move if and when they *want* to.

As the Moving-to-Opportunity study (discussed in Chapter 3) shows, there may be potential health benefits associated with such increased mobility. The intervention in the Moving-to-Opportunity study was providing rent vouchers that enabled families to move from high-poverty to low-poverty neighborhoods. The result was much better health among the families that actually moved. However, increasing residential mobility also requires that de facto segregation in housing be addressed. As discussed earlier, in 2015, the Obama administration established a new initiative, "Affirmatively Furthering Fair Housing," that incentivized jurisdictions around the country to work with community and civic leaders to assess patterns of segregation in their community and to develop and implement plans to make them less common [36]. Although this rule was suspended by the Trump administration, the Biden administration restored this program in July 2021.

Improving Housing Quality
There is also a great need to improve the quality of the residences in many segregated and under-resourced neighborhoods. As discussed in Chapter 3, these residences often contain environmental hazards (e.g., lead and mold) and structural defects that endanger their residents' physical and mental health [37]. One federal effort concerned with this problem is the Healthy Homes Program that began in 1999. This program provides support to remediate the health risks present in many of the homes in predominantly Black and poor neighborhoods. For instance, it funds programs to reduce environmental toxins such as mold, lead, various allergens, pesticides, and radon [38]. The Department of Housing and Urban Development also offers other grants to improve housing quality in economically disadvantaged neighborhoods. However, these programs and grants provide only a small fraction of the money that is needed. Additional funds could be provided by executive orders from the President; we believe such orders are needed now.

The Build Back Better Bill proposed in 2021 by the Biden administration included $65 billion dollars for initiatives to rebuild and improve public housing [39]. The bill also contained several provisions to improve access to affordable housing. It allocated about $25 billion dollars for rent vouchers, which, according to the Biden administration, would benefit about 300,000 low-income families. Like many of the interventions proposed in this chapter, the ones involving rent vouchers and housing improvements would benefit all low-income families. However, because Black families are disproportionately represented among Americans who live in substandard housing and/or suffer from housing instability, it would have had a special impact on the racial disparities they disproportionately experience in the United States. Unfortunately, this part of the Build Back Better Bill was not passed by the US Congress in 2022. It and other significant social safety-net proposals were not included in the final version of the bill that Congress approved.[3] The political realities as this book is being written make it unlikely that the federal government will enact this part of the original bill in the near future. Nevertheless, local governments could expand smaller programs that address the quality of housing in segregated and under-resourced neighborhoods. Such investments would very likely pay returns in terms of lower expenditures on the health of their residents who live in substandard housing.

Increasing the Availability of Healthy Food
Another health threat in segregated and under-resourced neighborhoods, which we discussed in Chapter 3, is the kinds of food available to their residents. There is often a dearth of healthy foods and a spate of unhealthy ones. There are, however, already programs in place to address this health risk. To improve access to healthy food, in 2010 the Obama administration launched the Fresh Food Financing Initiative. It provided financing to developers and grocers to attract grocery stores that provide healthy foods (e.g., fresh fruits and vegetables) to neighborhoods that are currently food deserts [40]. There are also other state and private Fresh Food Financing Initiatives (usually supported by large private corporations) with the same goals. The governmental programs typically offer tax advantages and ease land-use restrictions, but they and the private initiatives also offer direct grants for food-related businesses that are located in under-served communities and increase access to healthy foods. Such programs provide a "win-win-win" outcome: consumers in these neighborhoods have more access to better nutritional options, residents benefit from the jobs the stores create, and grocers can enter new markets and earn additional profits. These programs already exist in several urban centers.

Another way to increase the availability of fresh fruits and vegetables is to actually grow them within under-resourced communities. As an example of how to do this, the Renewal Project (financed by Allstate, a large private insurance company) has successfully underwritten the creation of urban gardens in poor neighborhoods in many cities, including Detroit,

---

[3] The initial version of the Build Back Better Bill also proposed tripling the funding for the nation's poorest school districts. Unfortunately, this was also left out of the final bill.

Michigan, and Lincoln, Nebraska [41]. Sometimes the gardens are publicly owned, and sometimes they are private businesses run by community residents. The gardens provide affordable fresh fruits and vegetables to community residents and are sometimes associated with small parks, which provide more green spaces for outdoor recreation [42]. This model of private financing of local projects for the public good seems to be a very viable way to improve the health of the residents of segregated inner-city communities and should be adopted by other large private businesses.

Investing in Under-Resourced Neighborhoods

Yet another threat to the health of people living in poor Black neighborhoods is, quite simply, poverty due to a lack of available jobs. As we have repeatedly noted, the strongest single predictor of a person's health is their socioeconomic status. One reason for the limited availability of jobs is the lack of investment in these communities. Unfortunately, the solutions tried thus far have not have solved this problem.

One program that was supposed to increase investment in these neighborhoods was the establishment of Opportunity Zones in economically distressed areas. A small version of this program was enacted during the Obama administration. In 2018, the Trump administration initiated a new and larger version of Opportunity Zones. It offered tax incentives to businesses that invested capital in economically disadvantaged neighborhoods. The goal was to create more jobs and new businesses in these areas [43]. However, according to the Urban Institute (a nonprofit research organization focused on social and economic policies) and other critics, the program seems to be primarily benefiting investors rather than the community members themselves [44].

The Urban Institute recommends at least four actions to improve this program: (1) redesigning the incentives to better support direct investments in small businesses rather than in real estate; (2) prioritizing projects that have the most immediate economic impact on the community (such as job creation) over those that generate the most profit for the investors; (3) broadening who can invest by offering tax credits rather than tax reductions, which would benefit investors with fewer financial resources; and (4) directing more of the funds to community development financial institutions, which are private institutions that are dedicated to providing affordable lending to help low-income and socially disadvantaged people and communities improve their economic standing [44]. These recommendations provide a sound basis for any program designed to infuse communities with jobs and investments – economic improvements that will, in turn, have significant health benefits. However, in addition to bringing capital into poor and under-resourced Black neighborhoods, these investments must also ameliorate the social ills that are at the core of their problems. Advocates of so-called placemaking argue that unless outside investments are directed at the *causes* of a neighborhood's problems, they will not create any sustainable change [45].

These kinds of programs that attempt to change the scope and impact of racial segregation would have tangible benefits for the health of Black people living in low-income communities. This certainly does not, however, exhaust the list of needed interventions. There is also, for example, a need to reduce the physical and social isolation of these neighborhoods by substantially improving public transportation systems and developing programs that increase the economic mobility of residents of these neighborhoods. As with the other areas we have discussed, multiple interlocking solutions are needed.

Increasing Access to Healthcare

The racial inequities that exist regarding access to high-quality healthcare represent a major threat to the health of Black Americans. Addressing them requires fundamental structural changes that will enable the US healthcare system to serve the needs of all Americans much more equitably (see Chapters 5 and 6). While pervasive systemic and individual racism both continue to exist in the United States today, many of the enduring racial disparities in the American healthcare system are more a result of structural inequities than they are of conscious malevolent intentions at the individual level. It may have taken a while for medical professionals and the organizations that represent them to "get on board," but today they speak with one voice about the need to provide high-quality healthcare to all patients irrespective of their income, race, or ethnicity.

Establishing a "Single-Payer" System

One structural barrier standing in the way of meeting this shared goal is the fact that healthcare in the United States is primarily a privatized system. This means that good healthcare is largely dependent on the financial resources of the people seeking medical care. As we discussed at the beginning of Chapter 5, even with subsidized health insurance programs, such as Medicare, Medicaid, and the Affordable Care Act, paying for healthcare still depends primarily on the financial resources of the individual patient. Because of the large economic racial disparities that exist in the United States, Black people are on average, less able than White people to afford access to high-quality medical care. Thus, the best way to reduce racial inequities in healthcare access would be to change the way healthcare is financed.

If the priority is to achieve some degree of racial and economic equity in healthcare for all people in the United States, the most direct – and likely the only – way is to create a national, universal health insurance system (e.g., single-payer proposals, such as Medicare-for-All). Such a national health insurance plan would reduce the role of individual wealth in obtaining high-quality healthcare and the disproportionate concentration of resources in the healthcare facilities that serve the most privileged Americans but leave the most disadvantaged people medically underserved. A fully inclusive, single-payer health insurance coverage system could also be viewed as partial recognition of the critical, and sometimes coerced, contributions of Black Americans to building a US economy that often excludes them from its benefits [46].

Such a major change in how healthcare is financed in the United States need not compromise the quality of healthcare that is available to many (but certainly not all) Americans today. Indeed, it might improve it. In 2021, the United States was not even among the top 10 countries in terms of the quality of its healthcare. Worldwide, it ranked 18th.[4] The primary characteristic that differentiated the United States from the top 10 countries is that it does not have some sort of publicly financed healthcare system [47]. This deviation does not stem from differences in economic systems. In fact, there are single-payer health plans in almost all highly industrialized countries with free-market economies. All, that is, except the United States.

To some, a national, single-payer healthcare system may sound like a radical new idea, bordering on "socialism." However, this kind of idea has a long history in mainstream American politics and has been proposed by several US presidents. For example, in 1947, President Harry S. Truman introduced legislation to Congress that would have provided healthcare for all Americans through a payroll tax. In his prescient message supporting the legislation, President Truman said, "The principal reason why people do not receive the care they need is that they cannot afford to pay for it on an individual basis at the time they need it. This is true not only for needy persons. It is also true for a large proportion of normally self-supporting

---

[4] This ranking will vary a bit across different ranking systems, but none of them have the US healthcare system ranked higher than 18th.

persons" [48]. Unfortunately, President Truman's proposal was rejected by Congress, as was a similar plan proposed by President Bill Clinton in 1992.

The current approach to healthcare in the United States assumes that market forces will result in the highest quality healthcare for most people. This is simply not true. While private markets may work well for most consumer goods and services, healthcare is different from automobile maintenance and sirloin steaks. As the civil rights icon US Representative John Lewis said in the quote that begins this chapter, "Healthcare is a right. It is not a privilege reserved for a wealthy few." The government must protect this right, particularly for its most vulnerable citizens, and this requires a different approach to financing healthcare in the United States.

We recognize, of course, that a national health insurance plan is not, by itself, a panacea that would eliminate all health and healthcare disparities. The United States has a free-market economy, and one's socioeconomic status will continue to affect health and healthcare even with a national health insurance plan. Indeed, countries that already have national health insurance still have some significant racial and ethnic health disparities [49]. Nevertheless, implementing a program such as Medicare-for-All, which addresses the foundational economic and social issues that contribute to healthcare disparities, would represent a significant step toward closing the racial health and healthcare gaps in the United States.

Notably, despite the strong partisan divide in Congress about national healthcare programs like Medicare-for-All, national polling indicates that a majority of Americans support at least the concept of the government ensuring that all Americans get healthcare coverage. For example, a 2020 poll conducted by Pew Research Center found that 62 percent of all Americans believed that it is "the federal government's responsibility to make sure all Americans have health care coverage" [50]. In another poll, 52 percent of Americans said that they supported Medicare-for-All. Even among Republicans, a party that has historically opposed this kind of government safety net, there was a substantial minority (35 percent) who supported the program. Still, the person who directed this poll offered an important caveat: "[H]ealth-care questions like this are [often answered] before there has been a public debate on the costs and the effect of a single source for plans and we have often seen support disappear after that kind of debate" [51]. It is unfortunate that people's support often fades when they learn about the costs of such plans, as it is "penny-wise and pound-foolish."

Underwriting the Cost of Private Health Insurance
Even if a Medicare-for-All program cannot be implemented in the near future, there are other options that may help reduce racial and ethnic disparities in healthcare, albeit likely not to the same degree. The Commonwealth Fund, a large private foundation with the goal of developing a high-performing and equitable healthcare system in the United States, offers several specific proposals that might change the current levels of racial healthcare inequities. The recommendations include making permanent the provision in the 2021 American Rescue Plan Act (ARPA) that temporarily underwrote the costs of "marketplace" (i.e., private) insurance and reduced the size of the deductibles and out-of-pocket costs associated with these plans [52]. The Commonwealth Fund further recommends offering financial subsidies to people whose employer-provided health plans do not fully cover their healthcare costs, as well as aggressive outreach programs that try to enroll groups of people who are eligible for Medicaid or subsidized private insurance but are not currently enrolled. We fully support these proposals.

Significantly, the Commonwealth Fund has also proposed that more attention be paid to reducing the administrative burdens associated with obtaining healthcare (e.g., the complicated application process to apply for state Medicaid programs). The challenges of navigating complex bureaucratic procedures may disproportionately affect poor and socially disadvantaged applicants and present another barrier to their accessing healthcare. Furthermore, consistent with the findings reported in this book, a 2021 report from the Commonwealth Fund identified socioeconomic factors as a major source of racial disparities in healthcare and recommends that government agencies provide much more economic and social support to lower-income families. This support should include things such as better "unemployment compensation, Earned Income Tax Credit and child tax credit programs, as well as [support for] childcare, food security, and targeted wealth-building programs" [52].

While the broad range of specific recommendations included here reflects the scope of structural interventions necessary to ensure equitable healthcare for all, it also demonstrates that there are practical and effective changes that can be made today to meet this broadly shared goal. But without major federal intervention to significantly reduce the number of people in the United States without adequate healthcare insurance coverage, the legacy of past racism and the impact of current systemic and individual anti-Black racism on racial and ethnic disparities in healthcare cannot be overcome.

Making American Healthcare More Equitable

Black Americans not only have less access to medical care than do White Americans because of differences in health insurance coverage, when they do obtain medical care, on average, it is of substantially lower quality than that provided to White patients. The significant gap between the quality of the medical care provided by healthcare facilities that predominantly serve Black Americans and those that predominantly serve White Americans is yet another major structural threat to the health of Black people in the United States. This is a problem that has its roots in the long history of segregated medical care in America and is perpetuated by the systemic racism in American healthcare that still exists today (see Chapters 4 and 5). The obvious solution to this disparity would be to close the gap by improving the quality of care that Black Americans receive while not reducing the quality of the healthcare that other patients receive. Addressing this threat to the health of Black Americans requires several key interventions.

Changing the Ways Hospitals Serve Their Communities

One of these interventions is to significantly change the operations of medical facilities located in areas whose residents are economically and socially disadvantaged. It is critical that these facilities become more responsive to the needs of the communities in which they are located, and they do so in ways that go beyond the medical care they provide. These facilities should promote equitable economic growth and consider the broader systemic inequities that are often at the root of health inequities. For example, the Democracy Collaborative (a research center at Marquette University) proposes that healthcare facilities need to become "anchor institutions," which the Democracy Collaborative describes as "nonprofit or public place-based entities such as universities and hospitals that are rooted in their local community by mission, invested capital, or relationships to customers, employees, residents, and vendors" [53]. Because hospitals are often among the largest employers in their communities and have enormous purchasing power, their decisions regarding hiring, procurement, contracting, and other investments can have enormous implications for economically marginalized communities.

Another promising initiative is "upstream healthcare," which is based on ideas proposed by physicians and public health experts such as Dr. Rishi Manchanda, who is the founder of the organization HealthBegins [54]. The underlying philosophy of upstream healthcare is grounded in one simple question, "What would it take for this [health] problem to never happen again?" [55]. More specifically, this approach to healthcare is premised on an idea that we have presented in several previous chapters – namely, that social, economic, and environmental factors are major determinants of people's health. Thus, this perspective on healthcare proposes that medical institutions in poor neighborhoods need to focus more on such causes of poor health and direct their attention "upstream" of the illnesses they treat. Proponents of this approach to healthcare argue that medical institutions need to proactively address factors such as the neighborhood characteristics that cause illnesses and pose dangers to residents' health. Reducing community-level food insecurity is one example of the kinds of preventive actions that the upstream healthcare movement says the community healthcare facilities need to include in their activities.

In addition, the upstream movement encourages greater integration of health and social services to confront the interrelated challenges that people face. The organizations that provide upstream healthcare are gaining acceptance in both the public and private sectors. Integrating health and social services may well lead to better health outcomes at medical facilities. Facilities that offer these kinds of preventative care should have better patient outcomes. If so, they would be rewarded by the federal government's "value-based care" programs, which financially reward hospitals and health systems for improvements in their treatment outcomes. Thus, the integration of healthcare and community-focused preventive actions promises to provide a significant financial boost for institutions because they would receive funds in addition to those based only on the volume of the clinical services they provide [56]. But, more importantly, upstream healthcare should improve the health of people in high health risk, medically underserved communities.

Documenting Racial Disparities in Medical Services
In order to reduce racial healthcare disparities, it is also critical to document them accurately and thoroughly. As William Thomson (also known as Lord Kelvin), the famous nineteenth-century British mathematician, once (purportedly) observed, "If you cannot measure it, you cannot improve it" [57]. In one example of doing this, the state of Minnesota has developed an exemplary approach to the collection and reporting of healthcare access, quality, and outcomes by race and other factors in an attempt to improve medical care. Minnesota Community Measurement is a statewide resource for information on healthcare costs and quality that works with physicians, hospitals, clinics, insurance companies, purchasers,

and state agencies to design, collect, analyze, and share data on healthcare quality and cost [58]. Its annual healthcare disparities report provides information on disparities by race, ethnicity, language, and country of origin. The information is not only being used as a means to remediate many of these disparities, it is also being used to facilitate research designed to determine what interventions work best to eliminate them. This program provides a model of accountability in healthcare that should be widely replicated. Making healthcare facilities report these kinds of data would create a powerful impetus toward reducing racial disparities in the healthcare they provide.

The recent massive consolidation of private hospitals into large private healthcare systems in the United States can also help provide a path toward better documentation and more effective approaches to the reduction of racial disparities in the quality of healthcare patients receive. Large healthcare systems typically have a single administrative structure that manages multiple hospitals and clinics. The extensive data that these systems collect on treatments (e.g., changes in medication and number of return visits) and outcomes can readily be aggregated and analyzed by patient race and other variables related to racial disparities in the healthcare they provide (e.g., low socioeconomic status). Analyses would move racial treatment disparities from an abstraction that occurs "elsewhere" to an immediate administrative problem within a particular organization. More specifically, this information could stimulate plans for action among these facilities' leaders, who are likely already publicly committed to racially equitable medical care. Moreover, the impact of the resulting initiatives could lead to higher revenues based on the kinds of value-based-care reimbursement models mentioned earlier. Thus, there may be a strong financial incentive for these systems to reduce racial disparities in treatment outcomes.

Standardizing Medical Treatment Protocols
Another possible intervention for reducing racial disparities in treatment quality is based on an (admittedly controversial) idea first proposed by the noted surgeon and writer Dr. Atul Gawande in an article titled "Big Med" [59]. Dr. Gawande proposed that healthcare facilities should better standardize and control the care they provide for the same illnesses across physicians within the same facilities. He used a large restaurant chain, The Cheesecake Factory, as the model for his proposal. He noted that no matter where one goes in the world, the food that people eat at a Cheesecake Factory is exactly the same. This is because the people who prepare the food are required to follow the same set of precise instructions

to create the meals. By contrast, physicians have considerable discretion in the ways they treat patients. To be sure, there are broad standard-of-care guidelines, but within them individual physicians are relatively free to choose the treatment they think is best. Dr. Gawande contends that this individual latitude produces uneven care, even within the same medical facilities. His proposal is that standardizing care across patients to a reasonable degree would greatly reduce medical errors and improve the overall quality of care offered in hospitals and clinics. From our own perspective, more quality control and standardized treatments – when criteria for such decisions are clear and formalized – would reduce racial disparities in healthcare because racial biases would be less likely to affect treatment decisions. While Dr. Gawande's proposal has many critics, we believe its potential benefits far outweigh the drawbacks [60, 61].

Increasing Diversity in Healthcare Professions

Given the great racial disparities in educational and economic opportunities that exist in the United States today, there needs to be proactive efforts to increase the number of Black students attending colleges and universities, which provide gateways to healthcare-training institutions. However, on June 29, 2023 the United States Supreme Court issued a decision in suits brought by "Students for Fair Admissions" against Harvard and the University of North Carolina. The court ruled that affirmative action in college admission decisions was unconstitutional. Up until this decision, affirmative action for admission to a university involved consideration of an applicant's race, ethnicity, and a limited number of other personal characteristics (e.g., physical disabilities and past military service) along with other kinds of information (e.g., grade-point average). A main objective of affirmative action was to provide a partial solution to the substantial race-based social and economic inequities in the United States because of racism and other kinds of discrimination.

Whether universities should have affirmative action admission policies has long been a source of contentious debate. One significant legal case occurred in 2003 when the University of Michigan's use of race in admission decisions was challenged by individuals and organizations opposed to affirmative action. In an Amicus Brief to the US Supreme Court – which two of the authors of this book (JFD and LAP) helped to write – the American Psychological Association argued strongly in favor of the university's admission policies not only because they created opportunities for racial/ethnic minority applicants, disadvantaged by systemic and individual racism, but also because they benefitted White students. Indeed, being educated in a diverse environment better prepares White students for more productive interactions with people from racial or ethnic minority groups. This would almost certainly make healthcare more equitable [63]. For example, one of the most potent predictors of practicing physicians having lower levels of both explicit and implicit racial bias is that they more frequently engaged in interracial interactions while in medical school [64]. In response to subsequent challenges to affirmative action, the Supreme Court further ruled that affirmative action programs were legal only if they were "narrowly-tailored" – that is, if there were no race-neutral alternatives that would work "about as well" [65].

There is currently a great deal of uncertainty in higher education about the implications of the 2023 Supreme Court decision. Both undergraduate institutions and institutions that train healthcare professionals will have to review and likely modify their admission procedures. They will need to find new and creative ways to increase the representation of students from racial and ethnic minority groups that conform to the new legal restrictions. Specifically, universities and healthcare-training institutions should consider broader, more inclusive ways of assessing the qualifications of applicants. For example, they could place more emphasis on community service, work experiences, and other "non-scholastic" attributes.

Importantly, this new Supreme Court ruling does not prohibit applicants from including in their personal statements how they have overcome adversity encountered because of their race, ethnicity, or other aspects of their background. It appears that the court's decision allows colleges and universities to consider this personal information as one of multiple factors in admissions decisions. This part of the ruling is particularly important because research shows that people become supportive of compensatory actions if they perceive it as an effective means to reduce discriminatory outcomes [66]. This is particularly true when people – especially those who strongly believe in the importance of merit – become aware of the unjust effects of systemic or individual biases that unfairly prevent individuals from achieving success in a particular domain. Alternative initiatives, such as providing much better support to Black students before they enter professional schools, should also be pursued. However, we anticipate efforts to increase diversity at universities will remain the subject of ongoing legal actions.

Helping Students from Traditionally Disadvantaged Groups Have Greater Academic Success

There is a great need to enroll, retain, and graduate Black students and members of other socially disadvantaged groups at large, predominantly White universities, and especially the public ones. The Michael and Susan Dell Foundation is a large charitable foundation (founded by Michael Dell of Dell computers) that supports programs intended to further educational achievement among minority and low-income students. This charitable foundation has identified certain areas where support for these students should be provided [67]. Some of the foundation's programs focus on high schools that do not have college preparatory programs. The foundation does things such as providing resources to specifically train teachers at these schools in ways to prepare their students for college. These programs begin well before students' senior year and serve to make it more likely that socially and economically disadvantaged high school students will apply to and be accepted by colleges and universities.

The Foundation's OneGoal and Braven programs involve coordinated efforts to support current college students who may be the first generation from their family to attend college, come from low-income backgrounds, and/or are people of color, who often would especially benefit from support while in college. These college-based programs include elements such as small grants to projects that help these students graduate, proactive early alerts to academic advisors for academic problems, and individual mentoring that improves the connections between the students' academic studies and jobs when they graduate. In the 2019–2020 school year, 95 percent of the students enrolled in the Braven program "persisted or graduated from college" [68], and about 70 percent of them either were employed in jobs commensurate with their education or went on for advanced degrees.

Finally, the Foundation underwrites the University Alliance Program, which promotes public university consortia, whose members jointly develop innovative programs that increase graduation rates for at-risk poor and minority students. This program has been in place at 11 universities since 2014. As of 2021, the program had helped increase the number of students of color graduating from these universities by 73 percent [69]. Substantially improving college-level acceptance, retention, and graduation rates among socially and economically disadvantaged minority students is quite possible if the investments are made.

These programs are not specifically intended for students who want to pursue careers in healthcare but, given the kinds of barriers to such careers (see Chapter 5), they would almost certainly increase the success rates of premed and related majors at large public universities, which should increase the number of healthcare professionals in the United States. As the COVID-19 pandemic amply demonstrated, expanding the healthcare workforce would have significant benefits for all Americans. Most large public universities have the resources and expertise to create programs like the ones we have described on their own. They should substantially expand the ones already in place and initiate new programs.[5]

Better Preparing Black Students for Medical Careers

Before students can enter a healthcare profession, they must successfully complete a rigorous undergraduate curriculum that qualifies them for medical training. There is also a great need for programs that are specifically aimed at addressing the lack of diversity in this part of the pipeline to healthcare professions. In 2004, a blue-ribbon panel assembled by the former Institute of Medicine (IOM; now the National Academy of Medicine) published a document, *In the Nation's Compelling Interest*, for which one of our co-authors, BDS, was the primary editor [70]. The report considered what institutions like medical, nursing, and dental schools can do to ensure greater representation of ethnic and racial minorities among their students and faculty and offered a number of recommendations, which provide a framework for our own suggestions to increase diversity among healthcare professionals.

Increasing "STEM(M)" Enrollment

One path to increasing diversity among healthcare professionals is to increase the percentage of Black students enrolled in universities' "STEM" (Science, Technology, Engineering, and Mathematics) and Medically related ("M") programs. Participating in such programs makes it more likely that students will pursue careers in science and medicine. Currently, Black college students are greatly underrepresented in STEMM programs. According to the Pew Research Center, Black students account for only 7 percent of the graduates of bachelor's level science, technology, engineering, and mathematics programs [71]. And, as we discussed in

---

[5] In the time since this was originally written several states have passed laws that specifically prohibit universities from having programs that would benefit economically and socially disadvantaged students, who are often members of racial or ethnic minority groups. If this trend continues, it will certainly inhibit universities' ability to create the kind of programs we have discussed and increase the challenges that Black college students will face in pursuing their educational goals.

Chapter 5, Black students are vastly underrepresented among premedical graduates and in medical schools.

There is no shortage of university programs that attempt to increase STEMM training among Black students. However, it may be necessary to address interest in STEMM subjects much earlier in Black students' lives. One example of an intervention that does this is the STEM Steps 8.0 Program offered by the African American Regional Educational Alliances. It differs from many other such programs in that it identifies students well before they reach college. That is, it attempts to increase awareness of the practical value of STEMM subjects among children in middle school by providing "culturally relevant outreach efforts and ... seminars, activities and services for (students and their) parents/guardians" [72]. The logic of this program is that waiting until Black students enter college may be too late to get them interested in a STEMM program. Instead, students must be made aware of such opportunities much earlier in their lives and in a manner that takes into account the importance of the students' culture when trying to interest them in STEMM topics. We could not find any data on this particular program's success, but based on our own experiences at universities attempting to increase representation in STEMM majors, implementing such interventions before college, and the kinds of educational reforms discussed earlier in this chapter may be a particularly effective way to achieve this goal.

Increasing the Number of Black Premed Majors

In addition to increasing the number of Black students majoring in STEMM subjects, interventions may focus more narrowly on premed programs. Many historically Black colleges and universities (HBCUs) have already developed programs to increase the number of Black students who successfully complete a premed major. As we explained in Chapter 5, their model is to provide students with additional academic and personal support to enable them to complete this major rather than attempting to cull out potentially weaker students. As a result, HBCUs produce about 50 percent of all the Black physicians in the United States. Their educational models for premed programs need to be adopted by much larger universities. Also, the HBCUs that already offer such successful programs merit increased support from both governmental agencies and private foundations.

Beyond initiatives that foster effective educational practices at every level of medical training, there needs to be programs that remove financial barriers that often confront qualified but economically disadvantaged students who desire a career in the medical field. One program that attempts to do this is funded by the National Institutes of Health. It offers up to $50,000 per year to reduce existing "educational debt" for people who have obtained a degree in medicine or other healthcare professions [73]. However, this program is concerned with accumulated debt but not the "upfront" costs of paying tuition and related expenses, which may discourage many economically disadvantaged Black students from even applying to a medical school. Sallie Mae, the private corporation that underwrites many student loans, says that grants and interest-free loans for tuition are available, but they are almost as rare as "unicorns" [74]. The availability of such programs needs to be greatly expanded.

Institutions that train healthcare professionals also need to develop and publicly disseminate clear mission statements that recognize the value of diversity. They should assess and improve the institutional climate for minority students because numerical diversity alone is not enough. In too many instances professional schools can produce inequitable outcomes for minority students, because the climate for these students is difficult and unwelcoming. Unhealthy racial climates at these schools adversely affect the experiences and performance of Black and other racial and ethnic minority students in healthcare training. In addition, these climates increase the levels of racial bias among White students, with downstream consequences for racial inequities in healthcare [75].

Making Student Diversity an Accreditation Criterion
Another way to support diversity in medical education is through the accreditation process. Professional accreditation of an educational institution or program is a sine qua non for their operation. The 2004 IOM-sponsored blue-ribbon panel on increasing diversity in healthcare proposed that professional bodies should create and then enforce accreditation criteria that would include diversity and develop explicit policies that articulate the value and importance of culturally competent healthcare and the role of racial and ethnic diversity among students and faculty for achieving this shared goal [70]. The panel recommended systematic evaluation of how schools measured up to these criteria. Many professional accrediting bodies now specifically consider these things in their accreditation decisions. However, the review should be broadened to also include the kinds of mentoring offered to minority professional staff and the extent to which members of racial and ethnic minority groups are in leadership positions.

As the broad range of interventions proposed here demonstrate, producing a well-trained healthcare workforce that reflects the diverse racial and ethnic character of the US population requires rethinking access and support structures at every phase of the educational pipeline. To accomplish this, a comprehensive agenda is needed that focuses on ensuring unobstructed pathways for talented students of color to enter health professions training, as well as expanding the skills and improving the cultural competence of nonminority students when they enter medical professions.

Reducing the Inappropriate Influence of Patient Race in Medical Diagnoses and Treatments

Another threat to equitable healthcare is the way a patient's race is often used in medical practice. When making diagnoses and treatment plans, physicians usually consider a patient's racial or ethnic identification along with their personal and medical history. This is often done with good intentions: In some instances, it may represent good medical practice, as there are differences among racial/ethnic groups in the incidence of certain illnesses. However, the way in which race is often used in Black patients' diagnoses and treatment recommendations can be quite problematic. Making assumptions about a patient's propensity toward certain illnesses and the nature of their genome solely on the basis of the racial group to which the patient *appears* to belong is truly bad science and even worse medical practice. It can do untold damage. Like many of the other healthcare inequities we have discussed, the inappropriate use of a patient's race is also partially the legacy of past racist dogma among healthcare professionals and systemic racism in the contemporary healthcare system (see Chapters 4 and 5).

Challenging the Validity of Race-Based Diagnostic Algorithms
Currently there are still a number of instances where the tests used to determine the presence of an illness or the risks associated with some procedures contain a "race correction." A race correction uses a patient's (perceived) race to adjust the value produced by a diagnostic algorithm. Often these adjustments are based on old racist myths (see Chapter 5). There is a great need for medical organizations to examine their predictive equations and make sure they are yielding accurate diagnoses or predictions.

Fortunately, it appears that such actions are beginning to be taken by number of different professional organizations, including the National

Institutes of Health. There appears to be substantial momentum toward eliminating fallacious race corrections. Indeed, a recent article that appeared in the most-cited medical journal in the world, the *Lancet*, concluded that race is a "poor proxy for human variation" and that race corrections are typically unnecessary and can contribute to healthcare disparities among the exact populations they are intended to help [76]. With this level of increased awareness, it seems likely that race corrections for illnesses such as chronic kidney disease will become substantially less common in medical practice in the coming years. Nevertheless, the medical community needs to do more than just internal reforms. They need to aggressively provide information about these race-based diagnostic errors to the individual practitioners and nonmedical organizations that use these tests in ways that adversely affect Black people. For example, as discussed in Chapter 6, as late as the fall of 2022, the Federal Bureau of Prisons was still using an invalid race correction to evaluate the kidney functions of their prisoners.

Reducing Racial Stereotyping among Healthcare Professionals
Racial disparities in healthcare often arise when individual Black patients are viewed by their physicians primarily in terms of stereotypical beliefs about the racial group they appear to belong to (see Chapter 6). Therefore, physicians need to be able to "individuate" their Black patients – that is, to see them as unique individuals with their own personal histories and life circumstances, who happen to belong to a certain socially defined racial group. Individuation can prevent the activation of the erroneous racial stereotypes about Black patients' personal characteristics that can negatively affect a physician's treatment recommendations, and it is recognized as a highly effective way to reduce the effects of racial bias among healthcare providers [77]. The kinds of information physicians gather about race as part of the diagnostic process should not be ignored, but they should be secondary to knowing and understanding the patient's individual characteristics as they relate to the patient's illness.

One way to increase individuation of Black patients is to teach physicians particular communication skills and strategies, such as patient-centered communication. As discussed in Chapter 6, patient-centered communication involves establishing rapport with a patient, paying attention to and responding to the emotions they express, providing clear information, and making sure the patient understands it. It also includes actively involving patients and their families in decisions about how to deal with patients' illnesses. This communication-focused approach to medical care encourages physicians to fully consider a patient's perspectives about their own illnesses, which has been shown to reduce the impact of stereotyping on the ways individuals think about and evaluate Black people [78]. Notably, physicians who engage in effective patient-centered interaction do not attempt to ignore a patient's race; in fact, doing so would likely have a negative effect on Black patients because it denies a valued aspect of their personal identity. Rather, a positive consequence of patient-centered communication is that it puts a patient's race in the proper context in order to provide the best care possible. In the last 20 years or so, there has been a dramatic increase in the professional popularity of patient-centered communication. However, much of the training occurs in medical schools and is not necessarily reinforced in professional practice. There are established ways to teach better communication techniques (e.g., Training to Advance Physicians' Communication Skills, provided by the federal Agency for Healthcare Research and Quality), and these should be part of the continuing medical education that is required of all practicing healthcare professionals.

Reducing the Impact of Race-Related Attitudes on the Quality of Black Patients' Healthcare

The final threat to Black people's health that we have examined in this book is the impact of race-related attitudes on the quality of healthcare received by Black patients. As documented in Chapter 6, healthcare for Black patients continues to be influenced by racial bias among healthcare professionals. This fact is recognized by almost every major professional medical association and is a topic that has received great attention from the American Association of Medical Colleges [79]. Attempts to reduce racial bias among physicians and other healthcare providers have steadily grown since the 2003 publication of the IOM-sponsored report, *Unequal Treatment*. Racial bias and related topics, such as cultural competence, are now a part of courses taught in medical schools and are covered either in stand-alone courses or as elements integrated into various courses across the curriculum. Anti-bias training sessions for healthcare professionals have also become quite common as part of continuing medical education at healthcare facilities around the country. Much of this training promises to reduce not only explicit racial bias but also automatically activated and often nonconscious implicit racial bias.

Implementing Effective Anti-bias Training
Anti-bias training at large private and public institutions, especially medical facilities, is now a booming business that earns billions of dollars
annually. However, the effectiveness of the current training is debatable
[80, 81]. Determining whether anti-bias training is effective depends upon
the criteria applied. Both explicit and implicit racial biases are deeply
entrenched, often supported – intentionally and sometimes unintention-
ally – by images in the media and interconnected within a web of social
and political orientations and socialization experiences. As a likely consequence, there is no reliable evidence that any kind of anti-bias training can
actually reduce people's implicit or explicit racial biases in a long-lasting
way [82]. For example, a study that followed over 3,000 non-Black
medical students from their first year in medical school through their
second year in medical residency found that the number of hours they
had spent on topics of bias or diversity in medical school was unrelated to
their explicit or implicit racial attitudes two years later as practicing
physicians [64]. The reality is that the impact that anti-bias training or
education has on racial attitudes is fleeting [83].

Nonetheless, there are other potential benefits of anti-bias training and
education. Anti-bias training does increase people's knowledge about
concepts like implicit bias and topics that include cultural diversity issues.
This increased knowledge and awareness expands participants' understanding of diversity, as well as its challenges and benefits. For example, anti-bias
training has been shown to increase nurses' perceptions of their cultural
competence in terms of their interest in diversity, knowledge, and feelings
of preparation for treating diverse patients. While there is no consistent
evidence that they change attitudes or behavior in a direct way, the impact
of anti-bias training and education for developing an understanding of
diversity-related issues appears to be durable and self-sustaining. Notably,
it often piques people's interest to increase their knowledge about healthcare disparities and ways to reduce them.

Another potential benefit of anti-bias training is what it communicates
about the values and normative expectations of an organization. Norms are
informal standards of behavior describing how one should behave in a
given context. With respect to intergroup attitudes, beliefs, and behaviors,
norms critically shape whether and how intergroup biases are expressed,
often in ways that become internalized. For example, medical students
who reported hearing attending physicians or residents make negative
comments about Black patients showed a significant increase in their
explicit and implicit racial bias compared to students in medical

environments where they were not exposed to such disparaging comments [84]. Even occasional acts of bias in medical contexts can have a cascading negative impact on the attitudes and beliefs of generations of medical professionals. While anti-bias training establishes normative expectations that may reduce the expression of individual bias, there is more that should be done. The often outdated and insensitive ways in which race is presented in medical school curricula (see Chapter 5) also need to be carefully reexamined and, within the bounds of respect for academic freedom, substantially changed.

It is important to recognize, however, that while anti-bias training and education can be inspiring (and thereby positively motivating), it can also create backlash. For example, if material is presented in a way that makes White people feel defensive or frames diversity as a zero-sum game around access and resources – thus threatening White people's sense of their own well-being – they may react quite negatively. Similarly, making people more aware of their personal implicit biases can increase people's motivation to engage in activities to reduce bias, or depending on how it is framed, it can lead them to avoid intergroup contact that they believe may further identify them as being racially biased. For instance, with respect to healthcare, White medical students who were more aware of their potential for behaving in a racially biased way – particularly those higher in racial bias – displayed greater anxiety about interacting with Black people. Consequently, they showed less interest in serving minority patients after medical school [85].

Notably, medical school training and educational interventions that emphasize more strongly that human attributes are dynamic and change over time tend to activate more concern about discrimination being a societal problem rather than a personal problem. This can arouse greater motivation among students and practicing physicians alike to engage in personal and societal change more intensely [86]. Such training and education programs can be even more effective if they increase students' awareness of the impact of systemic racism, in general, and within medicine, in particular, on racial disparities in health and healthcare.

Increasing Black Patients' Medical Trust

The quality of medical care Black patients receive is also determined by their own race-related thoughts and feelings. Thus, interventions to reduce racial disparities in healthcare need to consider the factors that influence Black patients' thoughts, feelings, and resultant behaviors when they interact with healthcare professionals. These efforts should primarily address medical mistrust among Black patients. These interventions must, however, respect the fact that much of this mistrust is based on the realities of past and present mistreatment of Black patients (see Chapters 4–6).

One intervention that we developed was designed to reduce the negative consequences of medical mistrust among Black patients rather than challenge beliefs about the basis for this mistrust. It was based on an idea originally proposed by Dr. Samuel Gaertner, professor in the Department of Psychological and Brain Sciences at the University of Delaware, and one of this book's co-authors (JFD) about a way to reduce intergroup conflict and increase cooperation and trust [87]. The idea is that one can change the perspective of people in different racial groups from an "us versus them" attitude to a sense of "we-ness" by creating a common in-group identity. This shared identity can be induced when members of different groups focus on common interests or goals. In general, when people share a sense of common identity with a different social group, they become more trusting of members of that group.

We tested the effects of an intervention based on this idea at a primary care clinic. We created a common in-group identity between Black patients and their non-Black physicians by using techniques that repeatedly stressed the team nature of the interaction. For example, right before the interactions, patients received buttons and pens that contained a team-themed logo, along with a written message emphasizing that they should think of themselves and their physician as a team working to improve their health. Compared to patients in a standard-of-care control condition, patients who received this intervention trusted their physicians more and adhered more to the physicians' recommendations four months later [88].

In the final analysis, however, the thing most critically needed to reduce medical mistrust among Black patients is for medical facilities to engage in *actions* that serve to earn greater trust among their Black patients. We have already presented some of the actions medical systems might take. For example, healthcare facilities in Black communities might adapt some of the ideas that have been proposed for increasing trust in police departments among members of the communities that they serve. As with Black people's mistrust of law enforcement agencies, medical mistrust among Black patients is a realistic reaction to the racism that has permeated healthcare for centuries, and this reality needs to be directly acknowledged and addressed in ways that will produce practical, actionable solutions.

Beyond the issue of medical mistrust, steps need to be taken to change what often transpires in racially discordant medical interactions. Black patients in such interactions may sometimes experience a phenomenon called "stereotype threat" [89]. Stereotype threat involves members of a stigmatized group fearing they will be judged with a negative group-based stereotype and that any misstep they make will serve to confirm its validity. In medical visits, for example, a Black patient might be concerned about confirming racial negative stereotypes, such as Black people are generally not as intelligent as White people or have poorer health habits. Patients experiencing stereotype threat may therefore be reluctant to volunteer certain kinds of information about their medical problems because they fear they might say something wrong or confirm racial stereotypes. This may, however, lead to physicians seeing them as uninterested in their medical problem and/or not able to understand it. That is, paradoxically, the patient's relative lack of communication due to stereotype threat might actually reinforce negative racial stereotypes in the physician, and the physician's behavior might reflect this. When stereotype threat operates like this, patient–physician communication is less effective and productive, and it yields poorer medical outcomes.

One way to reduce stereotype threat and strengthen a person's self-integrity is by using interventions that help patients affirm important personal values. For example, one intervention commonly used to ame-liorate the negative impact of stereotype threat is a values affirmation task in which people are asked to identify values that best characterize them. They are then asked to write a paragraph about why these values are important. In one study, Black patients with hypertension were asked to complete either a values affirmation exercise or a control exercise just prior to a regularly scheduled primary care visit [90]. The patients who com-pleted the exercise requested and provided more information about their medical conditions and had interactions that were more positive in emo-tional tone. Preliminary evidence suggests that values affirmation can also increase patient adherence, although the effectiveness of the technique may be limited by practical constraints, such as the cost of medications [91].

Increasing Patient Participation in Medical Interactions
There are also other, more direct, ways to help Black patients become more active and involved when they interact with physicians. For a variety of reasons (including stereotype threat), Black patients typically ask fewer questions and talk less than do White patients [92, 93]. This makes it less likely that they and their physician will communicate effectively about the medical problem at hand and come to jointly agreed-upon solutions to it. Lack of involvement by a Black patient may also make it less likely that

physicians will be able to individuate them, and thus physicians may be more influenced by racial stereotypes.

One intervention that focuses on this problem of low patient participation in medical interactions is providing them with a Question Prompt List (QPL). A QPL is a list of questions that patients can ask their physician to obtain the most useful kinds of information about a specific kind of illness. The list is created by an iterative process involving both patients and physicians. It produces question lists that usually concern things like diagnosis, prognosis, and possible treatment options. When patients receive this list of questions, they are told why they are receiving the QPL, encouraged to discuss it with friends and family, and asked to use the list in their meeting with the physician [94]. Dr. Susan Eggly, professor of oncology at Wayne State University, and her colleagues have used the QPL technique with Black patients with cancer and found that it significantly increased their level of participation during their interactions with their oncologists [95, 96]. Furthermore, helping patients become more involved in the decisions made about their treatment has been reliably shown to increase adherence to treatment recommendations [97]. Although the ability to use QPLs to specifically reduce racial healthcare disparities has yet to be fully tested, increasing Black patients' active participation is highly likely to improve the outcomes of their medical interactions.

However, it is crucial to note that the patient-focused approaches we have recommended here do not suggest or assume that it is somehow the fault of Black patients that such communication problems exist. The higher level of medical mistrust that exists among Black patients than among White patients is, as we noted earlier, well-grounded in the historical and current mistreatment of Black Americans within the healthcare system and any patient-focused approach must acknowledge this reality. Interventions that deny the realities of racism and racial healthcare disparities are disingenuous and may generate very strong negative reactions among Black patients. Thus, they almost always fail.

Putting It All Together

The eight factors we have identified as the major sources of the racial disparities that negatively affect the health and healthcare of Black Americans and White Americans in the United States are, of course, only a subset of myriad interrelated dynamics operating in concert to seriously endanger the health of Black Americans. Thus, the individual programs we have identified and changes we have proposed are neither exhaustive nor independent from one another. Implemented in concert, they should have synergistic effects on healthcare disparities. Furthermore, because the root causes of racial health disparities are historical as well as contemporary and operate through both systemic and individual-level anti-Black racism, the steps to solving them will need to involve both broad and specific actions. Solutions must also take place within society generally and within healthcare specifically.

As we said earlier, we are not naïve about the political and social realities of living in the United States in the twenty-first century. Racial disparities in health and healthcare have great inertia, and there is often substantial and direct resistance to the actions needed to reduce them. However, this massive public health problem is not going away on its own. Moreover, unlike many problems confronting the United States, this one does not stem from some natural or external threat. Racial disparities in health and healthcare were created by Americans and are sustained by Americans. US government agencies, large public and private institutions, nonprofit organizations, and individual citizens therefore need to actively confront the causes we have identified in the preceding seven chapters. Only Americans will be able to solve them.

The enormous personal, social, and fiscal costs associated with racial health disparities will only grow, perhaps even at an exponential rate. Even beyond the immorality of this kind of inequity taking place in the wealthiest country in the world, this is a massive public health problem with devastating and wide-ranging effects. While the consequences of racial health disparities most directly affect Black Americans, they will continue to impact all people living in the United States. Beyond the immorality of large health and healthcare racial inequities, they also very directly affect public health in the United States and the quality of the healthcare all Americans receive. Taking action is thus a personal necessity as well as an ethical imperative. It is in everyone's best interest to find ways to make health and healthcare fairer and more equitable for all.

REFERENCES

1. Britannica ProCon.org. (2017, February 23). *Pro & con quotes: Should all Americans have the right (be entitled) to health care?* https://healthcare.procon .org/should-all-americans-have-the-right-be-entitled-to-health-care-pro-con-quotes/

2. Quinlan, C. (2017, March 24). *Rep. John Lewis: 'Health care is a right. It is not a privilege.'* ThinkProgress. https://archive.thinkprogress.org/rep-lewis-health-care-is-a-right-22452ad7e9a4/

3. Walensky, R. (2021, July 4). *Media statement from CDC Director Rochelle P. Walensky, MD, MPH, on Racism and health.* CDC. www.cdc.gov/media/releases/2021/s0408-racism-health.html

4. Torpey, E. (2019, April). *Measuring the value of education.* U.S. Bureau of Labor Statistics. https://www.bls.gov/careeroutlook/2018/data-on-display/education-pays.htm

5. Garcia, E. (2020, February 12). *Schools are still segregated, and black children are paying a price.* Economic Policy Institute. www.epi.org/publication/schools-are-still-segregated-and-black-children-are-paying-a-price/

6. Johnson, L. B. (1965, June 4). *Commencement address at Howard University: "To fulfill these rights."* www.presidency.ucsb.edu/documents/commencement-address-howard-university-fulfill-these-rights

7. Lombardo, C. (2019, February 26). *Why white school districts have so much more money.* NPR. www.npr.org/2019/02/26/696794821/why-white-school-districts-have-so-much-more-money

8. Labi, H., & Haberle, M. (2021, August 5). Students deserve better than to be left out of the infrastructure spending package. *The Hill.* https://thehill.com/opinion/education/566220-students-deserve-better-than-to-be-left-out-of-the-infrastructure-spending

9 Peter G. Peterson Foundation. (2021, July 14). *How is K-12 education funded?* www.pgpf.org/budget-basics/how-is-k-12-education-funded

10. Sosina, V. E., & Weathers, E. S. (2019, September 4). Pathways to inequality: Between-district segregation and racial disparities in school district expenditures. *AERA Open, 5*(3). https://doi.org/10.1177/2332858419872445

11. Jackson, C. K., Johnson, R. C., & Persico, C. (2015). The effects of school spending on educational and economic outcomes: Evidence from school finance reforms. *The Quarterly Journal of Economics, 131*(1), 157–218. https://doi.org/10.1093/qje/qjv036

12. Dynarski, M. K., & Kainz, K. (2015, November 20). *Why federal spending on disadvantaged students (Title I) doesn't work.* Brookings. www.brookings.edu/research/why-federal-spending-on-disadvantaged-students-title-i-doesnt-work/

13. The Education Trust. (2019, December 8). *5 Things to advance equity in state funding systems.* https://edtrust.org/resource/5-things-to-advance-equity-in-state-funding-systems/

14. Sheffield, M. (2010, November 3). Bill and Melinda Gates visit Memphis city schools to oversee foundation progress. *Memphis Business Journal.* www.bizjournals.com/memphis/news/2010/11/03/bill-and-melinda-gates-visit-memphis.html

15. Garland, S. (2012, February 13). In Memphis classrooms, the ghost of segregation lingers on. *The Atlantic.* www.theatlantic.com/national/archive/2012/02/in-memphis-classrooms-the-ghost-of-segregation-lingers-on/252992/

16. U.S. Department of Education. (2018, March 5). *Promise Neighborhoods.* www..ed.gov/programs/promiseneighborhoods/index.html

17. Mescheda, T., Taylor, J., Mann, A., & Shapiro, T. (2017). Family achievements?: How a college degree accumulates wealth for Whites and not for Blacks. *Federal Reserve Bank of St. Louis Review, 99*(1), 121–137. https://files.stlouisfed.org/files/htdocs/publications/review/2017-02-15/family-achievements-how-a-college-degree-accumulates-wealth-for-whites-and-not-for-blacks.pdf

18. Hamilton, D., & Darity, W. Jr. (2010). Can 'Baby Bonds' eliminate the racial wealth gap in putative post-racial America? *Review of Black Politics and Economics, 37*, 207–216 https://DOI10.1007/s12114–010-9063-1

19. Greenwald, A. G., Dasgupta, N., Dovidio, J. F., Kang, J., Moss-Racusin, C. A., & Teachman, B. A. (2022). Implicit-bias remedies: Treating discriminatory bias as a public-health problem. *Psychological Science in the Public Interest, 23*(1), 7–40. https://pubmed.ncbi.nlm.nih.gov/35587951/.

20. Desilver, D., Lipka, M., & Fahmy, D. (2020, June 3). *10 things we know about race and policing in the U.S.* Pew Research Center. www.pewresearch.org/fact-tank/2020/06/03/10-things-we-know-about-race-and-policing-in-the-u-s/

21. Smith Lee, J. R., & Robinson, M. A. (2019). "That's my number one fear in life. It's the police": Examining young Black men's exposures to trauma and loss resulting from police violence and police killings. *Journal of Black Psychology, 45*(3), 143–184. https://doi.org/10.1177/0095798419865152

22. Camp, N. P., Voigt, R., Jurafsky, D., & Eberhardt, J. L. (2021). The thin blue waveform: Racial disparities in officer prosody undermine institutional trust in the police. *Journal of Personality and Social Psychology, 121*(6), 1157–1171. https://doi.org/10.1037/pspa0000270

23. Graham, A., Haner, M., Sloan, M. M., Cullen, F. T., Kulig, T. C., & Jonson, C. L. (2020). Race and worrying about police brutality: The hidden injuries of minority status in America. *Victims & Offenders, 15*(5), 549–573. https://doi.org/10.1080/15564886.2020.1767252

24. Eichstaedt, J. C., Sherman, G. T., Giorgi, S., Roberts, S. O., Reynolds, M. E., Ungar, L. H., & Guntuku, S. C. (2021). The emotional and mental health impact of the murder of George Floyd on the US population. *Proceedings of the National Academy of Sciences, 118*(39), e2109139118. https://doi.org/10.1073/pnas.2109139118

25. Hester, N., & Gray, K. (2018). For Black men, being tall increases threat stereotyping and police stops. *Proceedings of the National Academy of Sciences, 115*(11), 2711. https://doi.org/10.1073/pnas.1714454115

26. Buchanan, K. S., Rao, H., Mulligan, K., Keesee, T., & Goff, P. A. (2021, January 6). *White supremacy in policing: How law enforcement agencies can respond.* Center for Policing Equity. https://policingequity.org/images/pdfs-doc/CPE-WhiteSupremacy.pdf

27. Savidge, N., Markovich, A., & Yelimeli, S. (2022, November, 14). Leaked texts show Berkeley police union leader made derogatory comments about homeless

residents, people of color, ex-officer says. *Berkeleyside*. www.berkeleyside.org/2022/11/14/berkeley-police-text-messages-darren-kacalek-bpa

28. Wynter, S. (1994, Fall). No humans involved: An open letter to my colleagues. *Forum NHI Knowledge for the 21st Century 1.1.* https://people.ucsc.edu/~nmitchel/sylvia.wynter_-_no.humans.allowed.pdf

29. Quattlebaum, M., Meares, T. L., & Tyler, T. (2018). *Principles of procedurally just policing.* SSRN 3179519. https://law.yale.edu/sites/default/files/area/center/justice/principles_of_procedurally_just_policing_report.pdf

30. Faturechi, R. (2020, September 29). The Obama justice department had a plan to hold police accountable for abuses. The Trump DOJ has undermined it. *ProPublica.* www.propublica.org/article/the-obama-justice-department-had-a-plan-to-hold-police-accountable-for-abuses-the-trump-doj-has-undermined-it

31. Schuetz, J. (2019, October 15). *How can government make housing more affordable?* Brookings. www.brookings.edu/policy2020/votervital/how-can-government-make-housing-more-affordable/

32. Joint Center for Housing Studies of Harvard University. (2017). *Renter Cost Burden By Race and Ethnicity.* https://www.jchs.harvard.edu/ARH_2017_cost_burdens_by_race

33. U.S. Department of Housing and Urban Development. (2022). *Housing choice vouchers fact sheet.* www.hud.gov/topics/housing_choice_voucher_program_section_8

34. Acosta, S. (2021, November 16). *Investing in housing vouchers critical to protecting children from hardship, building more equitable future.* Center on Budget and Policy Priorities. www.cbpp.org/research/housing/investing-in-housing-vouchers-critical-to-protecting-children-from-hardship

35. Children's Health Watch. (n. d.). *Stable homes make healthy families.* https://childrenshealthwatch.org/stablehomeshealthyfamilies/

36. U.S. Department of Housing and Urban Development. (n. d.). *Affirmatively Furthering Fair Housing (AFFH).* www.hud.gov/program_offices/fair_housing_equal_opp/affh

37. Wolverton, S. (2019, May 29). *Low-Income housing: The negative effects on both physical and mental health.* National Community Reinvestment Center. https://ncrc.org/low-income-housing-the-negative-effects-on-both-physical-and-mental-health/

38. U.S. Department of Housing and Urban Development. (n. d.). *The Healthy Homes Program.* https://www.hud.gov/program_offices/healthy_homes/hhi

39. Locke, T. (2021, November 24). Build Back Better includes $170 billion for affordable housing–here's where it would go. *CNBC.* www.cnbc.com/2021/11/24/build-back-better-includes-170-billion-for-housing.html

40. U.S. Department of Agriculture. Rural Development. (n. d.). *Healthy Food Financing Initiative.* www.rd.usda.gov/about-rd/initiatives/healthy-food-financing-initiative

41. The Renewal Project. (n. d.). About the Renewal Project. www.therenewalproject.com/about/

42. Cartier, K. M. S. (2021, May 21). *Growing equity in city green space.* EOS. https://eos.org/features/growing-equity-in-city-green-space

43. Urban Institute. (n. d.). Project Opportunity Zones. www.urban.org/policy-centers/metropolitan-housing-and-communities-policy-center/projects/opportunity-zones

44. Theodus, B., Gonzalez-Hermoso, J., & Meixell, B. (2020, July 17). *The opportunity zone incentive isn't living up to its equitable development goals. here are four ways to improve it.* Urban Institute. www.urban.org/urban-wire/opportunity-zone-incentive-isnt-living-its-equitable-development-goals-here-are-four-ways-improve-it

45. Adebowale-Schwarte, M. (2017). *The place-making factor: A catalyst for disrupting environment and social grant making.* Living Space Project.

46. Hochschild, A. (2021, November 15). A landmark reckoning with America's past and present. *New York Times.* www.nytimes.com/2021/11/15/books/review/the-1619-project-nikole-hannah-jones-caitlin-roper-ilena-silverman-jake-silverstein.html

47. World Population Review. (2023). *Best healthcare in the world 2023.* https://worldpopulationreview.com/country-rankings/best-healthcare-in-the-world

48. Markel, H. (2014, November 19). 69 years ago, a president pitches his idea for national health care. *PBS.* www.pbs.org/newshour/health/november-19-1945-harry-truman-calls-national-health-insurance-program

49. Penner, L. A., Hagiwara, N., Eggly, S., Gaertner, S. L., Albrecht, T. L., & Dovidio, J. F. (2013). Racial healthcare disparities: A social psychological analysis. *European Review of Social Psychology,* 24(1), 70–122. https://doi.org/10.1080/10463283.2013.840973

50. Jones, B. (2020, September 29). *Increasing share of Americans favor a single government program to provide health care coverage.* Pew Research Center. www.pewresearch.org/fact-tank/2020/09/29/increasing-share-of-americans-favor-a-single-government-program-to-provide-health-care-coverage/

51. Easley, J. (2017, September 22). Poll: Majority supports single-payer health care. *The Hill.* https://thehill.com/policy/healthcare/351928-poll-majority-supports-single-payer-healthcare

52. Radley, D. C., Baumgartner, J. C., Collins, S. R., Zephyrin, L., & Schneider, E. C. (2021, November 18). *Achieving racial and ethnic equity in U.S. health care.* The Commonwealth Fund. www.commonwealthfund.org/publications/scorecard/2021/nov/achieving-racial-ethnic-equity-us-health-care-state-performance

53. Porter, J., Fisher-Bruns, D., & Ha Pham, B. (2019). Anchor collaboratives: Building bridges with place-based partnerships and anchor institutions. *E-Publications@Marquette.* https://epublications.marquette.edu/commen gage_admin/3/

54. HealthBegins. (n. d.). *Health begins upstream.* https://healthbegins.org/

55. James, T. (2020, April 21). *What is upstream healthcare?* HealthCity. https://healthcity.bmc.org/population-health/upstream-healthcare-sdoh-root-causes

56. Center for Medicare & Medicaid Services. (2021). *What are the value-based programs?* www.cms.gov/Medicare/Quality-Initiatives-Patient-Assessment-Instruments/Value-Based-Programs/Value-Based-Programs

57. Skeptics. (n. d.). *Did Lord Kelvin say "If you can not measure it, you can not improve it"?* https://skeptics.stackexchange.com/questions/42436/did-lord-kelvin-say-if-you-can-not-measure-it-you-can-not-improve-it

58. MN Community Measurement. (2022). *MNCM annual reports.* https://mncm.org/reports/#annual-reports

59. Gawande, A. (2012). Big med. *The New Yorker.* www.newyorker.com/magazine/2012/08/13/big-med

60. Denning, S. (2012, August 13). How not to fix US health care: Copy the Cheesecake Factory. *Forbes.* https://www.forbes.com/sites/stevedenning/2012/08/13/how-not-to-fix-us-health-care-copy-the-cheesecake-factory/?sh=118e0c2e2bd2

61. Trygstad, T. (2018, July 1). I am living proof that Atul Gawande's Cheesecake Factory missed the mark when it comes to patient-centered care. *Pharmacy Times.* www.pharmacytimes.com/view/i-am-living-proof-that-atul-gawandes-cheesecake-factory-missed-the-mark-when-it-comes-to-patientcentered-care

62. Takeshita, J., Wang, S., Loren, A. W., Mitra, N., Shults, J., Shin, D. B., & Sawinski, D. L. (2020). Association of racial/ethnic and gender concordance between patients and physicians with patient experience ratings. *JAMA Network Open, 3*(11), e2024583–e2024583. https://doi.org/10.1001/jamanetworkopen.2020.24583

63. Brief Amicus Curiae of the American Psychological Association in Support of Respondents Grutter v. Bollinger, 539 U.S. 306, and Gratz v. Bollinger, 539 U.S. 244 (2003). https://www.apa.org/about/offices/ogc/amicus/grutter.pdf

64. Onyeador, I. N., Wittlin, N. M., Burke, S. E., Dovidio, J. F., Perry, S. P., Hardeman, R. R., Dyrbye, L. N., Herrin, J., Phelan, S. M., & van Ryn, M. (2019). The value of interracial contact for reducing anti-black bias among non-black physicians: A Cognitive Habits and Growth Evaluation (CHANGE) Study Report. *Psychological Science, 31*(1), 18–30. https://doi.org/10.1177/0956797619879139

65. Fisher v. University of Texas. At Austin, 133 S. Ct. 2411, 2415–16. (2013). https://tarlton.law.utexas.edu/fisher-ut

66. Son Hing, L. S., Bobocel, D. R., & Zanna, M. P. (2002). Meritocracy and opposition to affirmative action: Making concessions in the face of discrimination. *Journal of Personality and Social Psychology, 83*(3), 493–509. https://doi:10.1037/0022-3514.83.3.493

67. Michael & Susan Dell Foundation. (n. d.). www.dell.org/

68. Michael & Susan Dell Foundation. (n. d.). *Braven prepares underrepresented young adults for career success.* www.dell.org/story/braven-career-readiness-college-students/

69. Michael & Susan Dell Foundation. (n. d.). *University Innovation Alliance improves higher ed graduation rates.* www.dell.org/story/improve-graduation-rates-higher-ed-university-innovation-alliance/

70. Smedley, B., Butler, A., & Bristow, L. (2004). *In the nation's compelling interest: Ensuring diversity in the health care workforce.* Institute of Medicine.

71. Fry, R., Kennedy, B., & Funk, C. (2021, April 1). *STEM jobs see uneven progress in increasing gender, racial and ethnic diversity.* Pew Research Center. www.pewresearch.org/science/2021/04/01/stem-jobs-see-uneven-progress-in-increasing-gender-racial-and-ethnic-diversity/

72. STEM Steps 8.0 Scholarship Program. (n. d.). www.theaarea.org/stem-steps-8/

73. National Institutes of Health. (n. d.). *Eligibility & programs.* www.lrp.nih.gov/eligibility-programs

74. Thompson, K. (2019, February 20). *Interest free student loans: Do they exist?* Sallie Mae. www.salliemae.com/blog/do-interest-free-loans-exist/

75. van Ryn, M., Hardeman, R., Phelan, S. M., Burgess, D. J., Dovidio, J. F., Herrin, J., Burke, S. E., Nelson, D. B., Perry, S., Yeazel, M., & Przedworski, J. M. (2015). Medical school experiences associated with change in implicit racial bias among 3547 students: A medical student CHANGES study report. *Journal of General Internal Medicine, 30*(12), 1748–1756. https://doi.org/10.1007/s11606-015-3447-7

76. Cerdeña, J. P., Plaisime, M. V., & Tsai, J. (2020). From race-based to race-conscious medicine: How anti-racist uprisings call us to act. *Lancet, 396* (10257), 1125–1128. https://doi.org/10.1016/s0140-6736(20)32076-6

77. Burgess, D., van Ryn, M., Dovidio, J. F., & Saha, S. (2007). Reducing racial bias among health care providers: Lessons from social-cognitive psychology. *Journal of General Internal Medicine, 22*(6), 882–887. https://doi.org/10.1007/s11606-007-0160-1

78. Todd, A. R., & Galinsky, A. D. (2014, July 2). Perspective taking undermines stereotype maintenance processes: Evidence from social memory, behavior explanation, and information solicitation. *Social and Personality Psychology Compass, 8*(7), 374–387. https://doi.org/10.1111/spc3.12116

79. American Association of Medical Colleges. (n. d.). *Equity, diversity, & inclusion.* www.aamc.org/what-we-do/equity-diversity-inclusion

80. Newkirk, P. (2019, October 10). Diversity has become a booming business. So where are the results? *Time.* https://time.com/5696943/diversity-business/

81. Kalev, A., Dobbin, F., & Kelly, E. (2006). Best practices or best guesses? Assessing the efficacy of corporate affirmative action and diversity policies. *American Sociological Review, 71*(4), 589–617. https://doi.org/10.1177/000312240607100404

82. Paluck, E. L., Porat, R., Clark, C. S., & Green, D. P. (2021). Prejudice reduction: Progress and challenges. *Annual Review of Psychology, 72*(1), 533–560. https://doi.org/10.1146/annurev-psych-071620-030619

83. Bezrukova, K., Spell, C. S., Perry, J. L., & Jehn, K. A. (2016). A meta-analytical integration of over 40 years of research on diversity training evaluation. *Psychological Bulletin, 142*(11), 1227–1274. https://doi.org/10.1037/bul0000067

84. Burke, S. E., Dovidio, J. F., Perry, S. P., Burgess, D. J., Hardeman, R. R., Phelan, S. M., Cunningham, B. A., Yeazel, M. W., Przedworski, J. M., & van Ryn, M. (2016). Informal training experiences and explicit bias against African Americans among medical students. *Social Psychology Quarterly, 80* (1), 65–84. https://doi.org/10.1177/0190272516668166

85. Burgess, D. J., Burke, S. E., Cunningham, B. A., Dovidio, J. F., Hardeman, R. R., Hou, Y., Nelson, D. B., Perry, S. P., Phelan, S. M., Yeazel, M. W., & van Ryn, M. (2016). Medical students' learning orientation regarding interracial interactions affects preparedness to care for minority patients: A report from Medical Student CHANGES. *BMC Medical Education, 16*(1), 254. https://bmcmededuc.biomedcentral.com/articles/10.1186/s12909-016-0769-z

86. Perry, S. P., Dovidio, J. F., Murphy, M. C., & van Ryn, M. (2015). The joint effect of bias awareness and self-reported prejudice on intergroup anxiety and intentions for intergroup contact. *Cultural Diversity and Ethnic Minority Psychology, 21*(1), 89–96. https://www.ncbi.nlm.nih.gov/pmc/articles/PMC4411950/

87. Gaertner, S. L., Dovidio, J. F., Guerra, R., Hehman, E., & Saguy, T. (2016). A common ingroup identity: Categorization, identity, and intergroup relations. In T. Nelson (Ed.), *Handbook of prejudice, stereotyping, and discrimination* (2nd ed., pp. 433–454). Psychology Press.

88. Penner, L. A., Gaertner, S. L., Dovidio, J. F., Hagiwara, N., Porcerelli, J., Markova, T., & Albrecht, T.L. (2013). A Social psychological approach to improving the outcomes of racially discordant medical interactions. *Journal of General Internal Medicine, 28*(9), 1143–1149. doi: 10.1007/s11606-013-2339-y

89. Aronson, J., Burgess, D., Phelan, S. M., & Juarez, L. (2013). Unhealthy interactions: The role of stereotype threat in health disparities. *American Journal of Public Health, 103*(1), 50–56. www.ncbi.nlm.nih.gov/pmc/articles/PMC3518353/pdf/AJPH.2012.300828.pdf

90. Havranek, E. P., Hanratty, R., Tate, C., Dickinson, L. M., Steiner, J. F., Cohen, G., & Blair, I. A. (2012). The effect of values affirmation on race-discordant patient-provider communication. *Archives of Internal Medicine, 172*(21), 1662–1667. https://doi.org/10.1001/2013.jamainternmed.258

91. Daugherty, S. L., Helmkamp, L., Vupputuri, S., Hanratty, R., Steiner, J. F., Blair, I. V., Dickinson, L. M., Maertens, J. A., & Havranek, E. P. (2021). Effect of values affirmation on reducing racial differences in adherence to hypertension medication: The HYVALUE Randomized Clinical Trial. *JAMA Network Open, 4*(12), e2139533–e2139533. https://doi.org/10.1001/jamanetworkopen.2021.39533

92. Eggly, S., Harper, F. W. K., Penner, L. A., Gleason, M. J., Foster, T., & Albrecht, T. L. (2011). Variation in question asking during cancer clinical interactions: A potential source of disparities in access to information. *Patient Education and Counseling, 82*(1), 63–68. https://doi.org/https://doi.org/10.1016/j.pec.2010.04.008

93. Beach, M. C., Saha, S., Korthuis, P. T., Sharp, V., Cohn, J., Wilson, I. B., Eggly, S., Cooper, L. A., Roter, D., Sankar, A., & Moore, R. (2011).

Patient–provider communication differs for black compared to white HIV-infected patients. *Aids and Behavior*, *15*(4), 805–811. https://doi.org/10.1007/s10461–009-9664-5

94. Rodenbach, R. A., Brandes, K., Fiscella, K., Kravitz, R. L., Butow, P. N., Walczak, A., Duberstein, P. R., Sullivan, P., Hoh, B., Xing, G., Plumb, S., & Epstein, R. M. (2017). Promoting end-of-life discussions in advanced cancer: Effects of patient coaching and question prompt lists. *Journal of Clinical Oncology: Official Journal of the American Society of Clinical Oncology*, *35*(8), 842–851. https://doi.org/10.1200/JCO.2016.68.5651

95. Eggly, S., Hamel, L. M., Foster, T. S., Albrecht, T. L., Chapman, R., Harper, F. W. K., Thompson, H., Griggs, J. J., Gonzalez, R., Berry-Bobovski, L., Tkatch, R., Simon, M., Shields, A., Gadgeel, S., Loutfi, R., Ali, H., Wollner, I., & Penner, L. A. (2017). Randomized trial of a question prompt list to increase patient active participation during interactions with black patients and their oncologists. *Patient Education and Counselling*, *100*(5), 818–826. https://doi.org/https://doi.org/10.1016/j.pec.2016.12.026

96. Barton, E., Moore, T. F., Hamel, L., Penner, L. A., Albrecht, T. L., & Eggly, S. (2020). The influence of a question prompt list on patient-oncologist information exchange in an African-American population. *Patient Education and Counselling*, *103*(3), 505–513. https://doi.org/10.1016/j.pec.2019.09.020

97. Okoli, C., Brough, G., Allan, B., Castellanos, E., Young, B., Eremin, A., Corbelli, G. M., Mc Britton, M., Muchenje, M., Van de Velde, N., & de los Rios, P. (2021). Shared decision making between patients and healthcare providers and its association with favorable health outcomes among people living with HIV. *AIDS and Behavior*, *25*(5), 1384–1395. https://doi.org/10.1007/s10461-020-02973-4

Index